Managerial Accounting Principles
An Introductory Managerial Accounting Course

AME | Learning

Instructions to access the AME online course

1. Go to www.amelearning.com
2. Click on CREATE A NEW ACCOUNT
3. Follow the steps to create a new account

UNIQUE PIN NUMBER

AKVZLSQKKP

ONE TIME USE

4. Your enrollment key will be provided to you by your instructor
5. Click on Create My New Account

For assistance, call 1.888.401.3881 x 2 or email support@amelearning.com

© 2007 AME Learning Inc. All rights reserved.

Username   Password
User Login

Neville Joffe

Anthony A. Atkinson

AME | Learning

Textbook ISBN: 978-1-926751-46-7

Workbook ISBN: 978-1-926751-47-4

Managerial Accounting Principles
Author: Neville Joffe
       Anthony A. Atkinson
Publisher: AME Learning
Project Manager: Linda Zhang
Developmental Editor: Graeme Gomes
Production Editor: Miresh Puradchithasan
Assistant Editors: Helen Y. He, Afroze Shaheen
Content Contributor: Trevor Monteiro
Content Reviewer: Kaki Hor
Typesetter: Paragon Prepress Inc.
Cover Design: AME Multimedia Team
Online Course Design & Production: AME Multimedia Team

This book is written to provide accurate information on the covered topics.
It is not meant to take the place of professional advice.

For more information contact:

AME Learning Inc.
410-1220 Sheppard Avenue East
Toronto, ON, Canada M2K 2S5
Phone: 416.848.4399
Toll-free: 1.888.401.3881
E-mail: info@amelearning.com
Visit our website at: www.amelearning.com

Content Reviewers

A special thank you to the following reviewers:

John G. Ahmad, Northern Virginia Community College

Richard Andrews, Sinclair Community College

Charles K. Boxell, Owens State Community College

Amy Browning, Ivy Tech Community College

Heather Cornish, NAIT JR Shaw School of Business

Louann Hofheins Cummings, The University of Findlay

John Harris, Centennial College

Merrily Joy Hoffman, San Jacinto College Central

Christopher Kelly, College of Southern Nevada

Shirly A. Kleiner, Johnson County Community College

DeAnna Lehmann, Golden West College

Patricia Lopez, Valencia Community College

Gina Lord, Santa Rosa Junior College

Earl Mitchell, Santa Ana College

Reed Peoples, Austin Community College

John Ribezzo, Community College of Rhode Island

Linda Hayden Tarrago, Hillsborough Community College

About the Author - Neville Joffe

Neville Joffe is the founder and CEO of AME Learning Inc. Prior to AME Learning, Neville spent over 20 years as owner, President, and manager of small and large international manufacturing companies. Neville is a member of the Worldwide Presidents Organization and former member of the Young Presidents Organization. He holds a patent related to the unique methodology he developed to teach accounting concepts. Neville is the author of four leading college textbooks. He has been featured in newspapers and magazines, and is a frequent speaker at national conferences where he presents as a thought leader in introductory accounting curriculum. The AME system has been used to train tens of thousands of employees at leading Fortune 1000 firms and students at premier colleges and universities across North America. Students have commented that they find the course remarkably easy to follow by using the numerous interactive tools that supplement the textbook and workbook. Students using AME materials consistently achieve higher grades compared to those who use traditional materials, and student engagement and retention rates have improved significantly. Professors have described the AME methodology as "refreshing", "intriguing", "amazing", "never thought it could be this simple", "inspiring to see that someone has changed the rules of teaching accounting" and "you have broken the mold of the way this subject has been taught".

About the Author - Anthony A. Atkinson

Dr. Anthony (Tony) Atkinson is the Associate Director-Faculty, Doctoral Program Director, and Management Accounting Area Head in the School of Accounting and Finance at the University of Waterloo. Tony has held previous university positions in the Schools of Business at Queen's University, the University of British Columbia, Carleton University, Dalhousie University, and Mount Allison University. He received a Bachelor of Commerce and a Master of Business Administration from the School of Business at Queen's University and a Master of Science and a Doctorate in Industrial Administration from the Graduate School of Industrial Administration at Carnegie-Mellon University. Tony is a Certified Management Accountant and a Fellow of the Society of Management Accountants of Ontario (SMAO).

Tony's research and consulting focus on issues in costing, strategic performance measurement and governance. He has published more than 50 articles in both academic and professional journals and has served as an editor, and on the editorial boards, of both academic and professional management accounting journals. In 1989 he received the Canadian Academic Accounting Association's Haim Falk award for outstanding contributions to accounting thought. He has also received five awards from the International Federation of Accountants (IFAC) for articles he coauthored deemed to be of "outstanding merit" and the Alan G. Ross award for an article appearing in the Financial Management Institute journal.

Tony is the coauthor (with Robert S. Kaplan) of an advanced management accounting text and a coauthor (with Robert S. Kaplan, Ella Mae Matsumura and Mark Young) of an introductory management accounting text. Tony is the author or coauthor of five monographs exploring issues in costing and strategic performance measurement. He is the author of the SMAO's management accounting guidelines, the Society of Management Accountants of Canada's (SMAC) management accounting standards, and the author of the Government of Canada's contract costing standards.

In the course of research and consulting Tony has visited more than 200 companies in all sectors of the Canadian economy and has delivered more than a hundred seminars to financial managers and consultants on emerging topics in cost accounting and financial management.

Preface by Neville Joffe

Twelve years ago, I founded AME Learning with a mission to change the perception of accounting from dry and boring to intuitive, engaging and an essential life skill. Today, the AME system is used by some of the most prestigious corporations and academic institutions in the world with outstanding results. The company has been recognized with top training and education awards including the 2009 CODiE Finalist for the Best Postsecondary Instructional Solution.

The AME System was initially conceived after I experienced the power of financial education as part of a turnaround I managed at a mid-sized manufacturing company. As part of the turnaround process I adopted an assortment of initiatives including Just-In-Time Inventory (JIT), Lean Manufacturing, The Theory Of Constraints (TOC) and Total Quality Management (TQM). The most powerful enabler of the turnaround was the creation of an open book environment and profit-sharing program with 400 unionized workers. The initiative required non-finance employees to understand and interpret financial statements and the financial implications of their actions.

I began educating the employees about income statements and balance sheets using traditional materials, including some content from college accounting curriculum. The materials over-complicated simple concepts and ineffectively connected the lessons to the practical implications of personal and business financial management. I then tried a very non-traditional approach to teaching these concepts. I cashed $2,000 in small bills and crumpled them into a plastic garbage bag. I assembled all the staff in a room and then poured the crumpled bills onto a table. "This is called revenue," I said. I placed a handful of cash in a bucket and labelled it "wages". I continued the exercise with different buckets labelled "material", "rent", "maintenance", "insurance" and then started tearing up $20 bills and throwing them into a bucket called "waste". The employees were silently shocked when I tore up the bills. "Why are you so surprised?" I asked. "You do this every day but just don't see it."

At the end of the demonstration, some cash remained on the table and I said, "What is left and lying on the table is called profit." I shifted some of the remaining cash toward the crowd and said, "This is for all of you for your special hard work performed this year. The remainder is for the owners in return for all the financial risk they take to support this business." The group was stunned, and they finally understood the message I was trying to deliver. As a result of successfully implementing this initiative, key financial metrics dramatically improved, inventory levels decreased, accounts receivable were collected faster, low margin products were eliminated and unprofitable customers were turned away.

So why did the crumpled-money exercise have such a profound impact on the company? It was not the employees' fault they didn't understand the traditional materials, it was the fault of the materials that taught the concepts from the teacher's point of view.

Elizabeth Newton summed it up:

In 1990, Elizabeth Newton earned a Ph.D. in psychology at Stanford by studying a simple game in which she assigned people to one of two roles: "tappers" or "listeners." Tappers received a list of twenty-five well-known songs, such as "Happy Birthday to You" and "The Star Spangled Banner." Each tapper was asked to pick a song and tap out the rhythm to a listener (by knocking on a table). The listener's job was to guess the song, based on the rhythm being tapped.

The listener's job in this game is quite difficult. Over the course of Newton's experiment, 120 songs were tapped out. Listeners guessed only 2.5 percent of the songs: 3 out of 120. But here's what made the result worthy of a dissertation in psychology. Before the listeners guessed the name of the song, Newton asked the tappers to predict the odds that the listeners would guess correctly. They predicted that the odds were 50 percent. The tappers got their message across 1 time in 40, but they thought they were getting their message across 1 time in 2. Why?

When a tapper taps, she is hearing the song in her head and it's impossible to avoid hearing the tune in your head. Meanwhile, the listeners can't hear that tune — all they can hear is a bunch of disconnected taps, like a kind of bizarre Morse Code.

It's hard to be a tapper. The problem is that tappers (teachers) have been given knowledge (the song title) that makes it impossible for them to imagine what it's like to lack that knowledge. When they're tapping, they can't imagine what it's like for the listeners (the student) to hear isolated taps rather than a song. This has been referred to as the Curse of Knowledge. Once we know something, we find it hard to imagine what it was like not to know it. And it becomes difficult for us to share our knowledge with others, because we can't readily re-create our listeners' state of mind.

After successfully turning the company around and selling my ownership, I founded AME Learning and spent years refining a teaching tool that would help teach financial accounting principles to non-financial people. The AME system has been used to train over 30,000 people ranging from front line employees to directors of publicly traded companies. I am still surprised at the lack of financial literacy of managers and executives. Why is it then, that so many adults in the business world lack basic financial acumen when they have studied one or more accounting courses at college or university? It would appear that many people underestimate the importance and usefulness of basic accounting skills and learn by rote memory rather than practical lessons that have long-term retention and applicability. Perhaps our economic world would be better off if more people were financially literate.

Over the years I have learned to appreciate the concept of "tappers and listeners" every time I deliver a management training program or when writing textbooks for college and university students. My years of research and experiments both on the factory floor and in the boardroom was the start of the development of AME, which has become an award-winning patented system of teaching accounting as it is used today.

I strongly believe in "getting the basics right and the rest will follow". I believe that basic financial literacy is a crucial life skill that is required of everyone, not only accountants. I have written this material from the students' point of view while still meeting curriculum requirements. You will notice that I have eliminated unnecessary jargon wherever possible.

I have a wonderful, dedicated team that produces world class material with one thought in mind: to educate the student so they can transfer basic accounting skills either to their professional lives or be better prepared for a higher level of accounting. Like all good sciences, AME provides a solid base that prepares students for either an accounting or business career.

I am a true advocate of student-centric teaching and believe that I have successfully offered the opportunity to bring together the minds of both the "tappers" and the "listeners".

So my message to you the student is this: whether you choose to continue your accounting studies or not, take this subject seriously since it will stand you in good stead when you enter your professional life regardless of the career you choose.

Neville Joffe
Author

Brief Table of Contents

Detailed Table of Contents

Chapter 3: Job-Order Costing

Chapter 5: Activity-Based Costing

Chapter 6: Cost-Volume-Profit Analysis

Chapter 7: Costing and Pricing Strategies

Chapter 10: Variance Analysis and Standard Costing

Chapter 11: Relevant Cost and Decision Making

Chapter 12: Capital Budgeting

Chapter 13: Balanced Scorecard

A Message to Students

There are three distinct types of accounting students in college: those who wish to study accounting as a career, those who have to complete the course as part of their program, and those who simply wish to have more business knowledge.

Regardless of your choice, when you enter the business world, you will have responsibilities that will impact the financial health of the business either directly or indirectly. Whether you start your own business, buy a franchise or work for a large organization, you will need to understand the financial implications of your actions in all departments. Here are some examples:

- If you run a company that manufactures and sells goods, you will need to know how many items you need to sell before you start making a profit.
- If you are managing the entire business or just a branch, you may be required to create a forecast (budget) relating to various aspects of the business. In addition, you would have to be competent in communicating these matters with your accounting department.
- If you are a project manager you will need to compare actual performance against budgeted performance and be able to account for the differences.

The number of examples is endless but one principle remains constant for all: a clear understanding of how your responsibilities link to the bigger corporate picture is essential for your professional success. To that end, this managerial accounting course will provide you with an excellent foundation to manage your own specific responsibilities, a business department or an entire business.

Managerial accounting utilizes two clearly defined skill sets. The first is the ability to understand the managerial principles (or business principles) and the second is the numerical skills required to apply those principles. This course focuses primarily on the instruction of managerial principles rather than numerical skills. Therefore, wherever possible, we have separated managerial principles from numeracy. However, we do encourage students to brush up on their mathematical skills as it will not only help them to get the most out of this course, but will prove to be useful in their professional and personal life as well.

In this course, you will find many examples relating to the manufacturing industry. However, the application of these concepts is not limited to only the world of manufacturing. As a result, to enhance your learning experience, we have included examples of various principles in different industries where appropriate.

It is important to mention that the discipline of management accounting is different from financial accounting. Since managerial accounting is primarily for internal use, it does not have to comply with Generally Accepted Accounting Principles (GAAP) or International Financial Reporting Standards (IFRS). Therefore, it is less formal in the manner in which many of the concepts are used. You are encouraged to stretch your imagination wherever possible, because it will significantly enhance your learning experience.

The AME Method of Learning Accounting

AME utilizes a unique and patented method that has simplified accounting principles, using step-by-step logic to ensure that the subject is extremely easy to understand. Accounting concepts are communicated using straightforward language and AME Accounting Maps™ that make potentially complex transactions simpler and easier to follow.

This textbook is part of a larger and blended program that is being used to teach the course. The steps of the program are as follows:

1. A highly interactive online section must be completed before attending each class.

2. A quiz will be given to test your knowledge and comprehension of the online section.

3. Building on the online segment and the quiz, the class will then reinforce and improve your understanding of the concepts that have already been introduced and studied.

4. Once the basic learning is done, it will be time to take the next step and apply the lessons learned by completing the exercises provided in the textbook.

Navigating the Accounting Map™

Given that accounting is somewhat abstract for most accounting students, financial statements are represented by Accounting Maps™ which are used as a multi-sensory communication tool. The manner in which the Maps are used in conjunction with simulated money tokens and journals will be explained when you log onto the online course. A description of each of the accounts can be found after the Map.

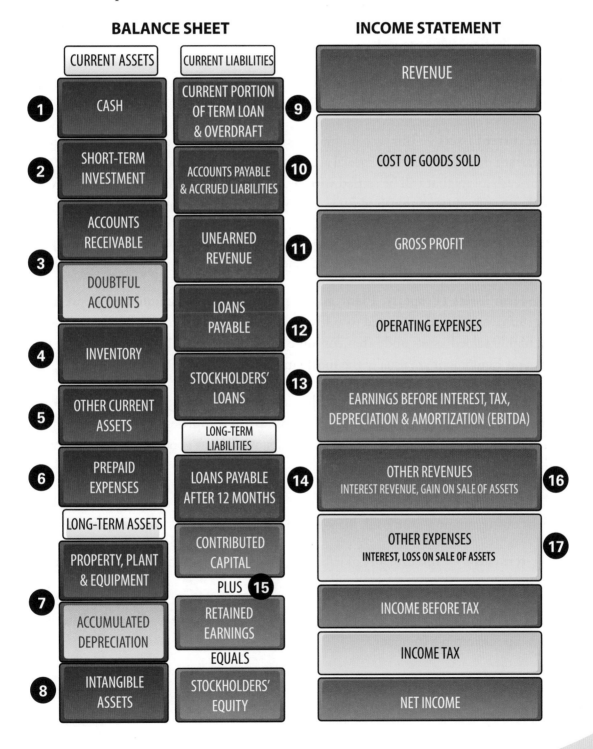

BALANCE SHEET

INCOME STATEMENT

CURRENT ASSETS

CURRENT LIABILITIES

1 CASH

9 CURRENT PORTION OF TERM LOAN & OVERDRAFT

2 SHORT-TERM INVESTMENT

10 ACCOUNTS PAYABLE & ACCRUED LIABILITIES

3 ACCOUNTS RECEIVABLE

DOUBTFUL ACCOUNTS

11 UNEARNED REVENUE

12 LOANS PAYABLE

4 INVENTORY

13 STOCKHOLDERS' LOANS

5 OTHER CURRENT ASSETS

LONG-TERM LIABILITIES

6 PREPAID EXPENSES

14 LOANS PAYABLE AFTER 12 MONTHS

LONG-TERM ASSETS

CONTRIBUTED CAPITAL

PLUS **15**

7 PROPERTY, PLANT & EQUIPMENT

ACCUMULATED DEPRECIATION

RETAINED EARNINGS

EQUALS

8 INTANGIBLE ASSETS

STOCKHOLDERS' EQUITY

REVENUE

COST OF GOODS SOLD

GROSS PROFIT

OPERATING EXPENSES

EARNINGS BEFORE INTEREST, TAX, DEPRECIATION & AMORTIZATION (EBITDA)

16 OTHER REVENUES
INTEREST REVENUE, GAIN ON SALE OF ASSETS

17 OTHER EXPENSES
INTEREST, LOSS ON SALE OF ASSETS

INCOME BEFORE TAX

INCOME TAX

NET INCOME

1. **Cash** — This account includes the balances of the company's checking and savings accounts and petty cash.

2. **Investments** — Organizations often invest surplus cash in investments outside the company. These investments can include short-term and long-term debt and equity.

3. **Accounts receivable and doubtful accounts** — One of a company's most important assets is its accounts receivable, which constitutes debt owed by customers who have bought goods or services on account, subject to payment terms. Doubtful accounts (also known as allowance for doubtful accounts) reduces total accounts receivable by the sum of all account balances for which collection is uncertain.

4. **Inventory** — Represents the value of products that are either in the manufacturing process or are finished goods ready for sale.

5. **Other current assets** — This account includes items that are not used on a regular basis and do not warrant the assignment of a special account code. Other current assets is usually comprised of non-cash assets that will be settled within one year. Some examples of other current assets include tax refund receivable, interest receivable and employee loans receivable.

6. **Prepaid expenses** — This asset is made up of prepayments that are not considered expenses on the income statement at the time they are paid.

7. **Long-term assets (Property, Plant and Equipment) and accumulated depreciation** — Long-term assets are also referred to as fixed assets. They usually consist of the company's most vital, highly valued assets and often consume most of the available cash resources. Property, Plant and Equipment are usually the most vital assets in a manufacturing company.

8. **Intangible assets** — The word intangible literally describes something that cannot be touched or felt. It is therefore understood that intangible assets comprise things that are not physical in nature but, nevertheless, is owned by the company (such as goodwill, copyright, trademarks and patents).

9.–13. **Debt** — Items 9 to 13 on our Accounting Map™ represent the company's current liabilities, or debt owing, ranging from bank loans to stockholder loans.

14. **Long-term debt** — This category of liabilities represents amounts owing that are due after 12 months.

15. **Equity** — Equity represents a company's net worth (total assets minus total liabilities) or ownership interest in a company.

Some additional segments

This textbook was designed to make your learning experience productive and engaging. To that end, we have added some segments to each chapter that highlight learning objectives. They include:

A CLOSER LK

The *Closer Look* segments in each chapter are meant to more closely examine a part of the chapter that might need to be expanded in order to broaden your understanding of an underlying concept or principle. Or they might include an example that applies the concepts being learned, in a way that is easy to understand and follow.

WORTH REPEATING...

The *Worth Repeating* segments in each chapter are meant to remind students of concepts in accounting already learned, and to highlight current concepts being taught that are "worth repeating."

IN THE REAL WORLD

The *In The Real World* segments in each chapter are meant to provide applied examples of elements being learned in a particular chapter. They are meant to put some of the concepts being learned in context and to drive home the point that, eventually, accounting has to be done outside the classroom. We hope that these segments give you a sense of what "the real world" can be like for the accountant or business professional.

Notes

Chapter 1

AN INTRODUCTION TO THE PRINCIPLES OF MANAGERIAL ACCOUNTING

LEARNING OUTCOMES:

❶ Define managerial accounting and how it differs from financial accounting

❷ Describe the importance of managerial accounting

❸ Define the three types of business models

❹ Understand the importance of analyzing cost behavior

❺ Identify the three ways to classify costs

❻ Compare contribution margin statement with formal income statement format

❼ Understand the concept of break-even

❽ Explain the concept of cost behavior and relevant range

❾ Understand the significance of balanced scorecard

❿ Use reasonable standards to make ethical judgments

Managerial Accounting: An Introduction

Imagine embarking on a mountain climb without mapping out the route, forecasting the weather, or planning the equipment required for summiting the mountain. The climb would not only be dangerous but might also end in tragedy and hardship. Business success is no different. Using historical data, careful planning and good judgment is crucial for business success.

Financial accounting is the branch of accounting concerned with formal financial statement preparation, including classifying, measuring and recording the transactions of a business. The formal financial statements governed by the *Generally Accepted Accounting Principles* include: the balance sheet, the income statement and the cash flow statement. The information extracted from these financial statements is used by both internal stakeholders (e.g. owners and managers) and external stakeholders (e.g. investors and creditors).

Managerial accounting relies on financial information to help managers and employees make informed business decisions. Reports prepared using managerial accounting principles are used by internal stakeholders and are not usually supplied to external stakeholders.

Cost accounting is an integral part of managerial accounting which tracks the costs incurred to produce goods or provide services. Imagine quoting a price for a product or service to a customer without even knowing how much it costs to make the product or provide the service. You would take the risk of significant losses because you might under-price your goods or services (sell for less than the costs incurred). Your ability to set an appropriate selling price would depend largely on historical cost information which is extracted from the financial reporting system. In short, cost accounting assists management in answering the question, "What does it cost us to produce and sell our products and services?"

Other differences between financial and managerial accounting is provided in figure 1.1:

Financial Accounting	Managerial Accounting
Financial accountants follow Generally Accepted Accounting Principles (GAAP) or International Financial Reporting Standards (IFRS) set by professional bodies.	Managerial accountants make use of procedures and processes that are not regulated by standard-setting bodies.
For public companies, financial statements must, by law, be prepared at the end of a fiscal year.	Managerial accounting statements and reports are not a legal requirement.
Financial accounting is concerned with collecting data of historical nature. The table below shows the important components of a company's income statement. All figures presented here are historical in nature.	Managerial accounting is largely based on forecasting future sales and cash flows, calculating costs and preparing budgets. Below is a simplified budgeted income statement for a company. It is forward-looking in nature as opposed to the formal income statement presented to the left, which is based on historical data.

Excerpt of Income Statement For the Year Ended December 31, 2009	
Sales	$1,000,000
Cost of Goods Sold	144,500
Gross Profit	855,500
Operating Expenses	600,000
Operating Income	$400,000

Excerpt of Budgeted Income Statement For the Year Ending December 31, 2011	
Budgeted Sales	$2,000,000
Budgeted Cost of Goods Sold	200,000
Budgeted Gross Profit	1,800,000
Budgeted Operating Expenses	500,000
Budgeted Operating Income	$1,300,000

Financial Accounting	Managerial Accounting
Financial statements and reports are primarily prepared for external users such as creditors and stockholders so that they can make sound financial or investment decisions.	Managerial reports are primarily prepared for internal use, which will help management make sound operation decisions.
Statements of publicly traded companies must be audited.	Managerial reports do not require independent examination.
Financial reports can be less detailed. Figures are often rounded for reports to stockholders.	Reports are very detailed and provide a wealth of information.

FIGURE 1.1

One of the main differences of financial accounting and managerial accounting is regarding the focus and time dimension of the prepared reports and statements. In financial accounting, the focus is on being reliable and objective about past performance. For example, 2009's actual performance will be prepared in the year of 2010. In managerial accounting, the focus is on the future and providing relevant financial information to management. For example, the 2011 budget may be prepared in 2010. Management may then use the 2011 budget to monitor the company's performance at various intervals in 2011. For instance, if the company has reached the budgeted cost of goods sold for all of 2011 by the third quarter, then it will come to management's attention that too much is being spent to produce the goods. Costs will have to be reduced significantly.

In addition, regardless of your profession, it is important to understand managerial accounting and cost management. Let us illustrate this principle with a few selected occupations.

Sales Professionals

To sell effectively, it is important to have a solid grasp of the cost of a product or service. For example, if you know that it will cost more than average to service a potential client, you may adjust your sales strategy and sale price to compensate for the increased costs.

Project Managers

If a contractor has no clue about the costs involved in constructing a building, the company may over or under-bill the home buyers. Professional project managers, engineers or job supervisors are often responsible for estimating, budgeting and controlling costs to ensure that the job is completed on time, effectively and efficiently.

Entrepreneurs

If an entrepreneur consistently suffers losses or does not manage the cash flow responsibly, there is a possibility that his or her business will fail. Many businesses fail not because the operator is technically incompetent, but because the operator does not understand costing principles and the importance of budgeting.

It is also beneficial to understand costs and budgets in your personal life, as it will help you manage your economic life more effectively. It goes without saying that the principles covered in this textbook will be useful regardless of which profession you choose.

Three Types of Organizations

Organizations fall into three main categories:

- **Manufacturing:**
  Manufacturing businesses purchase raw materials and convert them into finished goods. Examples include automotive, computer and textile manufacturers.

- **Merchandising:**

   Merchandising businesses purchase and re-sell tangible goods to consumers. Examples are retail stores (department stores and boutiques), distributors and wholesalers.

- **Service:**

   Service businesses provide a service to consumers. Examples of service businesses include law firms, advertising agencies and tutoring companies.

While most organizations are concerned with making a profit, there also exists not-for-profit organizations. A **not-for-profit organization (NPO)** is an organization that exists for the purpose of striving for a public benefit rather than for profit. NPOs may be manufacturers, merchandisers or service organizations. Examples of NPOs include charities, academic institutions, museums and religious organizations.

In this chapter, we will discuss managerial accounting principles primarily in the context of manufacturing businesses. However, it is important to understand that the same principles can be applied to all types of businesses including not-for-profit organizations..

Need for Management Accounting

Managers of a company must constantly make decisions that affect the future direction and financial performance of the business. The decisions made encompass two rather broad stages: planning and controlling. The planning stage involves creating objectives and developing strategies to achieve those objectives. The controlling stage involves implementing the objective, reviewing the results and applying corrective action. Figure 1.2 illustrates how the planning and controlling stages are closely connected. Business will move seamlessly from one stage to the next. Decision making is involved in all aspects of planning and control, so both stages are included with decision making process.

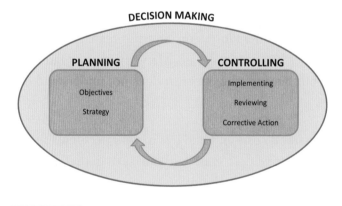

DECISION MAKING

PLANNING

Objectives

Strategy

CONTROLLING

Implementing

Reviewing

Corrective Action

FIGURE 1.2

Setting Objectives

Setting objectives requires looking into the future to desired outcomes and determining how these outcomes can be achieved. An objective is a target that must be measurable in time and value. For example, if you want to run a race, the objective will not be clear if were to set yourself a target to run a race by the end of May. The date (time) may be clear but the distance is

undefined. Conversely, if you were to set a target to run a marathon of 26 miles "sometime in the future", you will be still not have made your target objective clear. You know the distance but are unclear by when you intend to achieve this target. To set a clearly defined objective you will need to state the distance you wish to run and by what date you want to achieve the objective.

Business is no different. Every objective must be measurable in time and value. Examples could include:

- Assemble 20 computers per day to meet customer demand
- Increase sales by 5% in the next year
- Achieve a 30% market share in a new state by year end
- Sign contracts with three new large clients in the next three months
- Improve customer satisfaction to 85% by the end of July

Formulating Strategy

Once an objective is set, a strategy must be created to reach that objective. If you have set an objective to run a 26 mile marathon by the end of May, you will need to decide how you will accomplish it. Your strategy would likely include vigorous training every day and a diet to provide you with the energy required to make a long run.

Suppose a business assembles computers from components that are purchased from various sources. If the business set an objective to assemble 20 computers per day to meet customer demand, the strategy must answer how the objective will be met. Managers may hire enough employees so 20 computers can be assembled per day, investigate automated systems to assemble computers, or try any other creative ideas that may come to mind.

Implementing Strategies

Controlling work initially begins with implementing the strategies that were created. Once you have identified the training regime and diet required to be able to run a marathon, you must implement those strategies.

For the business wanting to assemble 20 computers per day, managers may have made the decision that hiring enough employees is the ideal strategy. If the assumption is made that each employee can assemble two computers per day, management must hire 10 employees.

Reviewing and Monitoring Results

As you begin training for the marathon and switch to the proper diet, you will want to ensure that positive changes are happening. You will measure how long you are able to run and how quickly you can run each distance. You will gradually work your way to running the full 26 miles in preparation for the marathon. If you are not progressing as you should, examine why. Perhaps you are not eating properly or getting enough rest, or you may be expecting too much improvement too soon.

In a business, reviewing and monitoring results will require the manager to read over many reports, including accounting information. The accounting reports provided would be very detailed; more so than what would normally be reported on the financial statements prepared for the stockholders of the business. These reports would inform on the changes in productivity and profit compared to the costs incurred to make the changes. The reports may also compare the actual financial results with the projected results that were created in the setting objectives stage.

Now that the computer business has hired 10 employees to assemble computers, the business expects 20 computers to be assembled each day. If only 18 computers are assembled per day, the business should investigate why it did not achieve its objective. The reasons could be numerous. Here are a few examples:

- The business may have underestimated how long it takes to assemble a computer.
- Customers are requesting more components than originally anticipated.
- After some research on the assembly floor, it was found that the employees were not working efficiently. As a result, additional training and adjusting production methods may be required.
- Production may improve by reorganizing the assembly floor because the business discovered that workers are spending too much time walking back and forth to pick up components.
- The business may decide employing another supervisor to watch over the workers will help. However the cost of the supervisor may exceed the increase in production in which case it would make no economic sense to hire that person.

Applying Corrective Action

Applying corrective action may be required based on the results of reviewing and monitoring results. If your training for the marathon is not progressing as it should, perhaps some adjustments are needed. The date of the marathon may be too close for you to properly prepare, so your objective may have to be revised. A shorter distance (half a marathon) or a long time period (September instead of May) may make the objective more attainable.

The computer business may decide to reorganize the assembly floor to make it more efficient. If the employees are able to build 20 computers per day after the reorganization, then the problem is solved. If the reorganization is not getting the results hoped for, management will have to take other action to solve the problem. This may involve more analysis of the problem and perhaps even setting new objectives that work with the new information that is available.

Managerial accounting provides the necessary financial information which, in conjunction with sound people management principles, can lead managers to make the best decisions for the business. Many companies have set objectives to increase their productivity and managerial accounting can be used to identify potential opportunities and areas for improvements. The planning and controlling principles apply to any industry such as manufacturing, merchandising, services, not-for-profit and government.

The management activities can lead to a variety of tools to help with the decision-making process. One such tool is known as cost-volume-profit analysis (CVP). This tool examines the relationship among the costs of the product or service, the volume sold and the resulting profit. Another valuable tool is called the balanced scorecard, which is a strategic performance management framework. It helps analyze the cause-and-effect relationships of business decisions from four different perspectives, including a financial perspective.

The Importance of Analysing Cost Behavior

For most businesses, the key objective is to make a profit. Therefore, it is important for managers to ensure that enough revenue is generated to cover all costs of the business. The relationship among costs, volume and profit will be discussed in detail in chapter 6. The process of evaluating these relationships is known as cost-volume-profit analysis.

All costs incurred by a company, including the costs of manufacturing products or providing services, can be broken down to three components: variable, fixed and mixed. When managers classify costs based on how they change at different activity levels (i.e. classify them as variable, fixed or mixed), they are describing their **cost behavior**. Costs that vary with the amount of products manufactured or services provided are called **variable costs**. On the other hand, **fixed costs** are costs that remain the same for any given level of activity. A mixed cost is one that has both a variable cost portion and a fixed cost portion. For example, a taxi driver's gas expense is a variable cost because it varies with the total distance driven. The annual taxi registration, monthly insurance and lease payments for the car are fixed because it does not depend on any other factor such as total distance driven or number of customers picked up. The repair and maintenance on the taxi may be considered mixed because maintenance must be done, but will likely increase as more distance is driven. It is important to understand that there is a delicate balance between how much a product or service costs to produce, the value for which they are sold, and the resulting profit. To highlight this point, examine the business case below.

Cost Behavior: StickIt Manufacturing Inc.

StickIt Manufacturing Inc. is a mid-sized company that makes wooden hockey sticks for minor league hockey players. They produce one standard type of hockey stick which is painted in different colors. The contracts that they have secured with several house league programs require them to deliver 10,000 sticks each month.

During May 2010, the company sold 10,000 hockey sticks at a sale price of $20 per stick, resulting in total sales of $200,000.

The following are financial data relating to StickIt Manufacturing's operations for May 2010:

List of Financial Information for May 2010	
Sales	$200,000
Manufacturing Costs	
Wood	$80,000
Paint	27,000
Labor	30,000
Rent	15,000
Total Manufacturing Costs	$152,000

FIGURE 1.3

The wood and paint refer to the materials used to manufacture the hockey sticks and labor refers to the workers required to physically carve and assemble the hockey sticks. For simplicity, assume that the hockey sticks are hand-made for the most part (i.e. piecework) and each worker is paid based on the number of hockey sticks produced. From these descriptions, it can be concluded that if StickIt Manufacturing has to produce and sell more hockey sticks, then more wood, paint and labor will be needed. Similarly, if fewer hockey sticks are to be produced, then less wood, paint and labor will be needed. As a result, StickIt Manufacturing will refer these items as variable costs since they vary with the amount of products manufactured.

All these manufacturing activities are housed in a small facility for which the company pays a monthly rent. The amount of rent paid every month will be the same regardless of how many hockey sticks are manufactured. The rent expense is considered a fixed cost because it remains the same regardless of the quantity of hockey sticks produced. Other examples of fixed costs can include depreciation, insurance, administration, leases etc.

Up to this point in your financial accounting studies, only the formal income statement has been discussed as a means of presenting a business' financial operations for a specific accounting period. The income statement is

WORTH REPEATING...

The matching principle requires expenses to be reported in the same period as the revenues that were earned as a result of the expenses incurred.

prepared using financial reporting standards such as GAAP or IFRS (International Financial Reporting Standards). As a result, costs related to the manufacturing of a product are initially capitalized in inventory and, based on the matching principle, the expense is only recognized (i.e. cost of goods sold) when the corresponding revenue has been earned. See figure 1.4 below for an illustration of the flow of costs related to manufacturing.

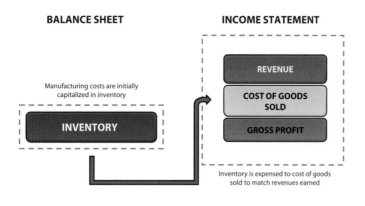

BALANCE SHEET   INCOME STATEMENT

FIGURE 1.4

In figure 1.5, the income statement of StickIt Manufacturing is presented for the month of May 2010. The cost of goods sold includes the costs of wood, paint, and a portion of the rent expense (the process of allocating rent expense to the production of the goods will be discussed in upcoming chapters). The income statement also shows the company's gross profit, which identifies what portion of earnings contributes to covering operating expenses.

While a formal income statement provides useful information to external users, it may not provide detailed and timely information required by the managers and other internal users. Therefore, to assess operational issues, managerial accountants prepare financial information in the form of a **contribution margin statement**, which is a detailed report that separates variable costs from fixed costs (see figure 1.6). This report contains the same information as a traditional income statement, but reconfigures the details into a different format. Managers use the contribution margin statement as a tool to analyze current operations and to plan future operations.

StickIt Manufacturing Income Statement For the month ending on May 31, 2010	
Sales	$200,000
Less: Cost of Goods Sold	144,500
Gross Profit	55,500
Less: Operating Expenses	
Rent	7,500
Net Income	$48,000

FIGURE 1.5

StickIt Manufacturing Contribution Margin Statement For the month ending on May 31, 2010		
Sales		$200,000
Less Variable Costs:		
Wood	$80,000	
Paint	27,000	
Labor	30,000	137,000
Contribution Margin		63,000
Less: Fixed Costs:		
Rent		15,000
Operating Income		$48,000

FIGURE 1.6

Figure 1.6 represents the current situation of StickIt Manufacturing. They produce and sell exactly 10,000 hockey sticks each month and use a total of $137,000 worth of materials and labor to build the hockey sticks. Monthly rent expenses amount to $15,000 per month. For the purpose of this simple example, the only fixed cost we have considered is the rent expense. However, in reality, businesses have other fixed costs such as salaries paid to administrative staff, telephone and internet connections, etc.

After taking into account all the fixed and variable costs, StickIt Manufacturing makes an operating income of $48,000 per month.

The following scenarios will provide a brief example of the relationship between costs, volume produced and profits.

1. Suppose Barry, the manager of StickIt Manufacturing, was able to negotiate a discount on the wood. With all other facts remaining the same, this would reduce the costs relating to wood by the total discount and ultimately increase operating income.
2. Alternatively, Barry may decide to reduce the selling price of the hockey sticks to close a deal with a particular house league. This action would reduce total revenue while all costs remain the same as before, and therefore operating income would decrease.
3. Lastly, suppose Barry decides to only increase the volume of the number of hockey sticks produced. Assume that StickIt Manufacturing is able to sell all of the hockey sticks it produces in the month. This operational decision would not only increase total sales for the month, but it would also increase the total variable costs since materials and labor costs are directly related to the number of hockey sticks produced. The fixed cost would not change, and if we assume the variable costs remain proportionate to sales, operating income would increase.

The above scenarios briefly outline the relationship between the costs of running the business and producing the product, the volume produced, and the resulting profits. A detailed analysis of these various scenarios will be discussed in chapter 6.

The Importance of Break-Even Analysis

Being able to determine the break-even point is a critical step in analyzing business operations. The **break-even point** is defined as the level of sales at which the company's operating profit is zero (i.e. total sales equal total expenses). For example, if a company determined that total sales equalled total expenses in a period when 10,000 units were sold, then the break-even point for that period was precisely 10,000 units. If more than 10,000 units were sold, the company would have been *above* the break-even point. Conversely, the company would have been *below* the break-even point for a level of sales less than 10,000 units. Break-even analysis can help answer significant questions posed by management such as, "How far can sales drop before the company starts to lose money?" In chapter 6, we will focus on how to determine the break-even point for a cost-volume-profit relationship using both the graphical method and the equation method which requires a mathematical formula.

Break-even is largely about the concept of the relationship between the cost of the product, the volume produced and sold, and the profits generated as a result thereof. By studying the relationships between costs, volume and profit, management could better cope with many planning decisions. For example:

1. How much sales volume is required to break even?
2. How much sales volume is required to earn a desired (target) profit?
3. How much profit can be expected for a given sales volume?
4. How would changes in the selling price, variable costs, fixed costs, and volume produced affect profits?

The Concept of Cost Behavior and Relevant Range

One of the assumptions made in the StickIt Manufacturing case is that the volume of production has been within the relevant range. The **relevant range** refers to the range where certain cost behavior remains the same. It can relate to fixed costs which will only change if sales activity is outside a minimum or maximum parameter of the current fixed cost structure. We have assumed that rental costs will remain the same regardless of the quantity of hockey sticks produced. However, in reality, the current manufacturing facility is only capable of manufacturing a maximum of 20,000 hockey sticks per month. If StickIt Manufacturing needed to produce more than 20,000 hockey sticks per month, it would be required to rent additional space and thus incur higher rent costs. Therefore, for our earlier cost-volume-profit analysis on StickIt Manufacturing, the relevant range with respect to the production volume of hockey sticks would be up to 20,000 hockey sticks per month.

Relevant Range: A Service Business Example

Frank Smith operates a web hosting business and employs four people to maintain the IT system and to service customers. His business is housed in a 600 square foot facility with five telephone lines.

Frank currently has 300 customers and calculates that he is able to take on another 100 customers with the same four IT support staff. He also knows that if his customer base drops to 200, he will still need to employ all four support staff. However, if the customer base drops below 200, he will require less support staff. In other words, he has identified the relevant range of sales activity (200 - 400 customers) using the same overhead structure. If Frank secures another 150 customers on top of the original 300 customers, the customer base of 450 would be outside the relevant range. Therefore, Frank will have to employ more staff to serve the 450 customers. He may even have to increase his rental space to accommodate another desk. Notice that he stepped up his overhead because the amount of increased sales activity requires him to

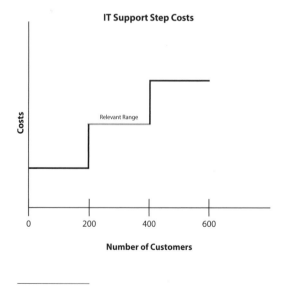

FIGURE 1.7

move out of the current relevant range of fixed overhead. In this textbook, the costs that increase in steps due to increase in business activity will be referred to as **step costs.**

The Significance of Balanced Scorecards

If you felt ill and went to your doctor, he may take your temperature or measure your blood pressure. If you were running a fever or your blood pressure was too high, your doctor may not know the cause before further examination. However, the results will determine whether a further investigation is required. The doctor may then create a strategy to provide you with a cure. Businesses also use the equivalent of a thermometer and blood pressure gauge before implementing a strategy to control or solve a problem. There are various forms of measurements that managers use which include financial ratios and performance metrics. These measurements can be found in the company's **balanced scorecard (BSC)**, which is a strategic performance management framework to help implement the company's strategy.

A typical BSC is made up of an integrated set of performance measures that should support the company's strategy by breaking down high-level objectives into specific performance metrics and measures called **key performance indicators (KPI)**. BSC often involves a chain of cause-and-effect relationships, which will allow management to gain a strong understanding of what particular measures affect the company's strategy. For instance, hotels often adopt a strategy to increase sales by consistently attracting more and more occupants. A KPI from the customer perspective, for example, can be the customer satisfaction rating for those that have stayed at the hotel. A good satisfaction rating will increase the chances customers will return, which ultimately would contribute to increasing the number of occupants over time. Conversely if the quality of the hotels' service decreases, there would be less satisfied customers resulting in less hotel occupancy. In other words the <u>cause</u> of the problem is that the service was not good and the <u>effect</u> is less room occupancy. Measuring customer satisfaction in this instance is therefore a crucial measurement for business success.

A CLOSER LOOK

Although its origins are unclear, there is documented use in the late 19th century of managers using the cost-volume-profit analysis described in this chapter. Because cost-volume-profit analysis at that time was carried out using pencil and paper, its practicality required the assumption that all costs were either fixed or variable. Today's financial modeling, which has its roots in cost-volume-profit analysis, is undertaken using computer spreadsheets like Microsoft Excel or OpenOffice Calc. The simplifying assumptions underlying basic cost-volume-profit analysis are no longer required since spreadsheets can accommodate any type of cost or revenue behavior. However, the concepts mentioned in this chapter are essential in understanding more complex analyses.

Managerial Accounting and Ethics

Internal and external stakeholders place significant trust in the accuracy of financial records to enable them to make informed decisions about a business. Management accounts are primarily responsible for internal stakeholders and must prepare accounting information legally and ethically.

All management accountants must conform to a code of ethics, similar to the one shown below (in figure 1.8) from the Institute of Management Accountants (IMA). IMA is a worldwide association for accounts and financial professionals. It awards the Certified Management Accountant (CMA) designation. Part of IMA's objective is to ensure that professionals are properly qualified and ethically sound to work in businesses. Members must maintain a high level of competence, keep all private information about their clients confidential, maintain integrity by avoiding conflicts of interest and report information objectively. Failure to abide by the code of ethics can result in disciplinary measures taken by the association.

In addition to the association's code of ethics, the business that a management accountant works for will likely have their own code of ethics. The business code of ethics will apply to everyone in the business, from a front line employee to all levels of management (including the CEO). If an accountant is ever uncertain of an action to take in an ethical dilemma, they should seek advice from a supervisor, an appropriate committee or a lawyer.

IN THE REAL WORLD

The Institute of Management Accountants (IMA) has over 60,000 members. Their mission is to:

"provide a forum for research, practice development, education, knowledge sharing, and the advocacy of the highest ethical and best business practices in management accounting and finance."

To help meet their mission statement, the IMA constantly provided updated information and materials to its members to keep them current on changing accounting concepts. The organization is active in contributing to key legislative issues globally and contributing to the International Accounting Standards Board (IASB) and Financial Accounting Standards Board (FASB). Both the IASB and the FASB create reporting standards such as GAAP and IFRS.

The IMA also provides the Certified Management Accountant (CMA) certification which is recognized as a valuable certification by employers. Having a CMA certificate indicates that the individual is recognized as a professional in the accounting or finance fields and will behave professionally in all their dealings.

The CMA certification is different from the Certified Public Accountant (CPA) certification. CPA certification is required for professional public practice and audits. The CMA certification is focused on internal finance and management. Both certifications, however, require their members to uphold a strict code of ethics.

IMA Statement of Ethical Professional Practice

Principles

IMA's overarching ethical principles include: Honesty, Fairness, Objectivity, and Responsibility. Members shall act in accordance with these principles and shall encourage others within their organizations to adhere to them.

Standards

A member's failure to comply with the following standards may result in disciplinary action.

I. Competence

Each member has a responsibility to:

1. Maintain an appropriate level of professional expertise by continually developing knowledge and skills.
2. Perform professional duties in accordance with relevant laws, regulations, and technical standards.
3. Provide decision support information and recommendations that are accurate, clear, concise, and timely.
4. Recognize and communicate professional limitations or other constraints that would preclude responsible judgment or successful performance of an activity.

II. Confidentiality

Each member has a responsibility to:

1. Keep information confidential except when disclosure is authorized or legally required.
2. Inform all relevant parties regarding appropriate use of confidential information. Monitor subordinates' activities to ensure compliance.
3. Refrain from using confidential information for unethical or illegal advantage.

III. Integrity

Each member has a responsibility to:

1. Mitigate actual conflicts of interest, regularly communicate with business associates to avoid apparent conflicts of interest. Advise all parties of any potential conflicts.
2. Refrain from engaging in any conduct that would prejudice carrying out duties ethically.
3. Abstain from engaging in or supporting any activity that might discredit the profession.

IV. Credibility

Each member has a responsibility to:

1. Communicate information fairly and objectively.
2. Disclose all relevant information that could reasonably be expected to influence an intended user's understanding of the reports, analyses, or recommendations.
3. Disclose delays or deficiencies in information, timeliness, processing, or internal controls in conformance with organization policy and/or applicable law.

Institute of Management Accountants (accessed November 8, 2010)

FIGURE 1.8

In Summary

- **Managerial accounting** relies on financial information to help managers and employees make informed decisions.

- Managerial accounting differs from financial accounting in a number of ways. For example, the primary users of management accounting reports are internal stakeholders (e.g. management) while the primary users of the statements using financial accounting principles and processes are the external stakeholders (such as stockholders).

- **Cost accounting** is an integral part of managerial accounting that analyzes the costs incurred in producing goods and/or providing a service.

- Regardless of the profession or occupation one is in, a strong grasp of management accounting principles is essential for success.

- The three main categories of for-profit businesses are: manufacturing, merchandising and service.

- A **not-for-profit organization (NPO)** is an organization that exists to strive for a public benefit rather than provide a financial return to its board members and contributors.

- Making decisions require two broad stages: planning and controlling.

- The **planning** stage involves creating objectives and developing strategies to achieve those objectives.

- The **controlling** stage involves implementing the objective, reviewing the results and applying corrective action

- **Cost behavior** is referred as classifying costs based on how they change at different activity levels.

- **Variable costs** vary with the amount of products manufactured or services provided.

- **Fixed costs** remain relatively the same regardless of the volume produced within the relevant range.

- The **contribution margin statement** is, primarily, a managerial accounting report which outlines operational data for a specific time period. It separates variable from fixed costs and determines the contribution margin for the period.

- The **break-even point** is the level of sales at which the company's operating profit is zero.

- The **relevant range** refers to the range where certain cost behavior remains the same.

- **Step costs** are costs that increase in steps depending on the level of business activity.

- **Balanced scorecard (BSC)** is a strategic performance management framework to help implement the company's strategy.

- **Key performance indicators (KPI)** are measures that determine a company's ability to meet certain objectives.

- All management accountants must conform to a code of ethics.

- According to the Institute of Management Accountants (IMA), members must maintain a high level of competence, keep all private information about their client confidential, maintain integrity by avoiding conflicts of interest, and report information objectively.

Notes

Chapter 2
AN OVERVIEW OF COSTING METHODS

LEARNING OUTCOMES:

❶ Understand the importance of the value chain

❷ Explain the difference between product costs and period costs

❸ Identify direct, indirect and overhead costs

❹ Explain raw material, work-in-process and finished goods

❺ Calculate cost of goods manufactured

❻ Prepare an income statement that includes cost of goods manufactured

❼ Understand perpetual vs. periodic inventory systems

❽ Describe the concept of job-order costing

❾ Explain the process of allocating costs in the job-costing system

❿ Describe the concept of process costing

⓫ Understand FIFO vs. weighted-average cost inventory valuation methods

Job-Order Costing and Process Costing: An Introduction

It is crucial to understand what goes into determining the cost of a product or service so that managers can properly anticipate and control costs. Managers can also use the cost information to appropriately price the product to make a profit. For most merchandising companies, the cost of a product is simply the price it paid to the supplier in order to purchase and physically receive the tangible good. For a manufacturing or service business, determining the cost of a product can be a more complex process. For example, a production manager in a manufacturing company would need to know how much material, labor and other costs are consumed by each product during the production process. In this chapter, we will discuss how managers use different costing systems to determine the costs of producing each unit of product or service. The two different costing systems are: **job-order costing** (also called job costing) and **process costing**.

For example, consider the auditing services that a public accounting firm offers to its clients. The size and financial situation of each client can be very different. The partners of the firm would likely want to know how much it costs to perform an audit for a particular client. The firm would have to track how much time each employee spends on the job. The firm would also have to allocate office rent and administrative salaries to that job. This is an example of a job-order costing system. In managerial accounting, a **cost object** is anything for which separate cost data is desired. In the accounting firm example, a specific auditing job is a cost object. In a manufacturing firm, a component of a product can be a cost object because the cost of the item needs to be calculated. A **cost driver** is any activity that incurs cost. In this case, the time an auditor spent on the job is the cost driver for the salaries incurred. In addition, these salary costs incurred will be part of the job costs. In a manufacturing situation, a cost driver could be labor or machine hours.

Now consider a manufacturing company such as a cookie factory. The plant manager would like to know how much it costs to produce a box of cookies. The manager might also want to know the amount of inventory on hand at any given point in time. It will be nearly impossible for him to assign costs to each box of cookies directly and separately. Instead, he would have to allocate costs to a large quantity (e.g. a month worth of cookie production) then assign average costs to each box. This is almost the exact opposite of the accounting firm example in which the auditors trace the cost to each individual auditing job. Chartered Institute of Management Accountants (CIMA) defines process costing as *"The costing method applicable where goods or services result from a sequence of continuous or repetitive operations or processes. Costs are averaged over the units produced during the period."* The cookie factory is an example of process costing.

Job costing and process costing systems are designed to help managers determine the costs of their products. The choice of which costing system to use largely depends on a company's products and the nature of its production process. It is important to note that both systems will not be able to measure the exact cost of a specific product. In the case of an accounting firm, while the labor hour and billing rate are easy to trace, the rent and administrative salaries related to each job are hard to determine accurately. Therefore, the firm will have to take the average cost of rent and administrative salaries in order to allocate them to different jobs. Similarly, process costing system average total costs and allocates them to the products.

The Value Chain

Pine Furniture Manufacturer is a small company that makes pine chairs. They produce one type of chair which is painted in different colors. They recently secured sales contracts with the school boards in its surrounding area. Let us use Pine Furniture Manufacturer to illustrate the concept of a **value chain**. An organization's value chain outlines the steps required to bring their products or services to the market. As a product or service passes each phase, more value is added.

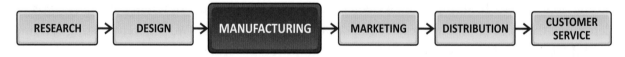

FIGURE 2.1

Generally, a manufacturing organization's value chain includes six phases. They are **research**, **design**, **manufacturing**, **marketing**, **distribution** and **customer service**. Let us use the Pine Furniture Manufacturer to explain these phases.

- **Research**: the research phase is the process of generating ideas related to new products, services or processes. Pine Furniture Manufacturer might want to research on different materials that will increase the comfort of its chairs.
- **Design**: the design phase may involve developing new processes and design work-flows to build and assemble the products. For instance, if Pine Furniture Manufacturer were to design arms for its chairs, the cost incurred during the process would be classified as design cost.
- **Manufacturing**: the manufacturing phase includes all the activities required to produce the chairs. To create the chairs, Pine Furniture Manufacturer will need to cut the wood, assemble the pieces and paint the surface.
- **Marketing**: the marketing phase involves promoting the product or service. Pine Furniture Manufacturer may advertise its products in a magazine to increase brand awareness.
- **Distribution**: the distribution phase includes activities necessary to ensure products are accessible to clients. Pine Manufacturer can send its products to retailers or directly to customers.
- **Customer Service**: the customer service phase occurs after the sale has been made and involves providing customer support. For example, Pine Furniture Manufacturer can address any customer concerns through a support phone line.

In summary, the value chain includes all costs incurred to bring a product or service to the market. These costs start with the cost of research all the way through to the costs of selling the product or service to a customer. This chapter will focus on analyzing costs related to the manufacturing phase.

Product Costs and Period Costs

The costs related to the manufacturing phase of a product are called **product costs**. All other costs are called **period costs**. This method of classifying costs is in accordance with *Generally Accepted Accounting Principles (GAAP)*. Usually, these product costs are regarded as *inventory (an asset)* on the balance sheet when incurred. Once products are sold, the cost of inventory are expensed through income statement in the form of cost of goods sold. However, the period costs (e.g. costs related to marketing) are usually expensed in the accounting period in which they are incurred without going through the inventory account. In other words, product costs are the cost of manufacturing the product. Period costs are all those costs that are not regarded to be part of the manufacturing process of the product, and are recorded directly in the income statement when they are incurred. The concept of product cost and period cost in context to the value chain is illustrated in figure 2.2 below.

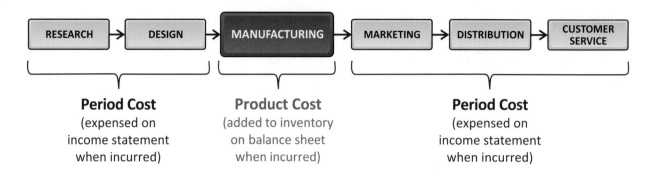

FIGURE 2.2

Product Costs: Direct and Indirect

Product costs include **direct costs** and **indirect costs**. Direct costs are costs that can be directly traced to the product or service provided. For example, the amount of wood that Pine Furniture Manufacturer used in the production of chairs can be easily traced directly to each chair. Therefore, the cost of wood would be considered as a *direct cost*. Indirect costs are costs that cannot be tied directly to the product or service in a practical or economical way. For example, it can be very time consuming to trace the proportionate amount of electricity to the production of each chair. Therefore, electricity costs would be considered an *indirect cost*.

The three categories of product cost that an organization will incur during the manufacturing phase are:

1. **Direct Materials**: Materials that are purchased to make a product. Direct materials are easily traceable as part of the finished goods. In the Pine Furniture Manufacturer example, direct materials for producing chairs include items such as wood, screws and paint.

2. **Direct Labor**: Includes the wages paid to employees who directly work on converting materials into the final products. In the Pine Furniture Manufacturer example, direct labor includes carpenters and chair assembly line workers.

3. **Manufacturing Overhead**: Includes all indirect manufacturing costs such as **indirect materials**, salaries paid to **indirect labor**, rental fees for the plant, and depreciation of machinery. Indirect materials refer to materials which cannot be easily traced to a product. In the Pine Furniture Manufacturer example, the sandpaper used to smooth the wood would be considered as an indirect material. Indirect labor includes wages paid to employees who do not directly work on the products. An example of indirect labor could be the salary paid to the plant manager.

All product costs can also be classified as variable or fixed. Some items, such as indirect materials, are considered variable overhead costs because their value changes based on the volume of production. Other items, such as the salary paid to the plant manager, are considered fixed overhead costs because the cost is incurred regardless of the volume of production.

Figure 2.3 shows a list of costs in a recent month of operations for StickIt Manufacturing, the hockey stick manufacturer introduced in chapter 1.

Costs:	Amount	Type of Cost
Supplies Used (office only)	$ 1,000	Period cost
Plant Manager's Salary	5,000	Manufacturing overhead
Stick Cutters' Salaries	12,000	Direct labor
Assembly Line Workers' Salaries	11,000	Direct labor
Wood	15,000	Direct material
Factory insurance	2,000	Manufacturing overhead
Factory utilities	3,000	Manufacturing overhead
Advertising	850	Period cost
Paint	4,550	Direct material
Sandpaper	700	Manufacturing overhead
	$ 55,100	

FIGURE 2.3

Period costs are made up of costs of advertising and office supplies because they are not related to the manufacturing process. This amounts to $1,850 and will be expensed in the month they occurred without being charged to inventory.

The rest of the costs are used to produce the product (i.e. product costs) and they total $53,250. Within the product costs, we can identify direct materials, direct labor and manufacturing overhead.

- Direct materials for producing hockey sticks are comprised of wood and paint since they can easily be traced as components of the finished hockey sticks. Therefore, total cost of direct materials is $19,550.
- Direct labor costs include the stick cutters' and assembly line workers' salaries since these workers directly worked on converting materials into the finished products. Total cost for direct labor is $23,000.
- Manufacturing overhead is comprised of all other indirect manufacturing costs with a total cost of $10,700. These costs can be broken down into the following sections:
  1. Indirect materials: We can assume that sandpaper can be reused several times to smooth the wood.
  2. Indirect labor: The plant manager did not directly work on the product.

3. Other indirect manufacturing costs: It is not practical or economical to tie the cost of the factory insurance and utilities directly to the product. Therefore, these costs are also part of manufacturing overhead.

Classifying manufacturing costs as direct materials, direct labor and manufacturing overhead is required when tracing and allocating costs to inventory. The following is a description of the cost flow at Pine Furniture Manufacturer.

When materials (e.g. wood, screws and paint) are first purchased, they are considered **raw materials**. When the raw materials are entered into production, the costs are transferred out of the raw materials account and classified as **work-in-process (WIP)**. WIP refers to inventory that is partially built. Finally, when the products are completed and ready for sale, they are considered **finished goods**.

Cost accounting principles allow us to trace and calculate the costs of direct materials, direct labor and manufacturing overhead for each product. The raw materials account in the financial reporting system includes the costs of direct and indirect materials. When these raw materials are moved into production, the corresponding costs in the raw materials account are transferred to the work-in-process (WIP) account. Other product costs such as direct labor and manufacturing overhead are also added to the WIP account as the product is being worked on. Once the product is completed and ready to be sold, the related costs are transferred out of the WIP account and into the finished goods account. Note that the costs associated with each of these three stages of production are considered *an asset* (inventory) on the balance sheet until they are finally sold. The flow of the material and cost is illustrated in figure 2.4.

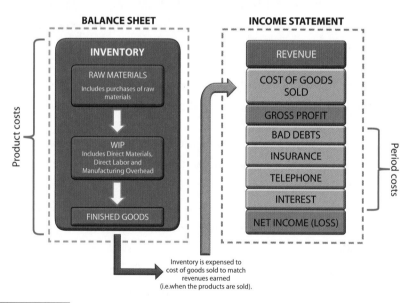

FIGURE 2.4

For a service company, these basic principles of the cost flow from inventory to cost of goods sold still hold. However, a service company would use a term such as "cost of sales" or "cost of services" in place of "cost of goods sold" on the income statement. This is because it does not sell a tangible product. Also, a service business does not have any physical inventory. However, it may have a work in process "inventory" of partial services rendered if the service spans a long time period. For instance, consider a typical law firm. Assume that a particular client is only billed after a verdict for the case has been reached. The total bill amount will depend on the number of hours worked on the case by each lawyer to assigned to the case. Before a client is billed, the firm may periodically accumulate a portion of these lawyers' salaries in a WIP "inventory" account for unbilled partial services provided. It will be recognized as cost of sales when the revenue is recognized (i.e. when the case proceedings have ended and the client has been billed).

Inventory Systems and Cost of Goods Manufactured

You have learned in financial accounting that a company may choose to use either a perpetual inventory system or a periodic inventory system. In a periodic inventory system, inventory is only updated periodically when a physical count of inventory takes place. This physical count allows the company to properly calculate the value of inventory and the cost of goods sold.

All businesses, whether they are in the service industry or the manufacturing industry, must know how much it costs them to produce their services or goods. The cost can determine what the selling price must be in order to cover the costs and generate a profit. Imagine what would happen to an accounting firm if they charged their clients $80 per hour for a particular service but paid their accountants $100 per hour to provide that service. Very quickly, the accounting firm would be out of business if the selling price of their service remains below their cost.

Similarly, a manufacturing company must carefully calculate how much it costs to manufacture the goods they sell in order to properly set a selling price. This is done by calculating the cost of new completed products prepared for sale that is added to the inventory of finished goods during the period. This cost is termed as the **cost of goods manufactured**. If the cost of goods manufactured is incorrectly calculated too low, then the selling price may not be set high enough to cover costs and generate a profit.

Schedule of Cost of Goods Manufactured

The cost of goods manufactured includes manufacturing costs associated with goods that were finished during the period. For example, a student club may decide to make sandwiches and sell them to raise money for a charity. Assume the activity starts at the beginning of May and lasts for a month. If 600 sandwiches were made in May and each sandwich costs $5 to make, the cost of goods manufactured is $3,000.

Recall that for a merchandising company, cost of goods sold is calculated as follows:

Cost of Goods Sold = Beginning Inventory + Purchases – Ending Inventory

As shown above, a merchandising company calculates cost of goods sold by adding purchases to beginning inventory and then subtracting ending inventory. The dollar amount of purchases for the period is easily determined as the total inventory purchased from suppliers for resale. Now consider the calculation of cost of goods sold for a manufacturing company as shown below:

Cost of Goods Sold = Beginning Inventory + Cost of Goods Manufactured – Ending Inventory

You may notice that the composition of the cost of goods sold formulas for both merchandising and manufacturing companies are similar. The difference is that "Purchases" is substituted with "Cost of Goods Manufactured". Since a manufacturing company produces its own products internally instead of purchasing completed goods, it is not nearly as straightforward to determine cost of goods manufactured. We will now take a look at the steps required to calculate cost of goods manufactured.

When there is no beginning and ending work in process inventory, cost of goods manufactured is equal to the total manufacturing costs (or product costs). Total **manufacturing costs** is equal to the sum of direct materials used in production, direct labor, and manufacturing overhead.

Manufacturing Costs = Direct Materials Used in Production + Direct Labor + Manufacturing Overhead

However, for a given period, manufacturing companies usually have some beginning and ending inventory with respect to partially completed goods (i.e. beginning and ending WIP inventory). The beginning WIP inventory must be added to total manufacturing costs, and the ending WIP inventory must be deducted to finally arrive at cost of goods manufactured. In summary, the formula for cost of goods manufactured is as follows:

Cost of Goods Manufactured = Direct Materials Used in Production + Direct Labor
                         + Manufacturing Overhead + Beginning WIP inventory
                         – Ending WIP inventory

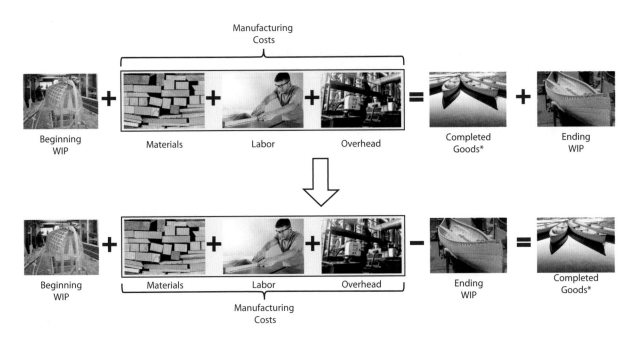

Cost of goods manufactured is equal to the completed goods in the period.

FIGURE 2.5

You will notice that only the direct materials *used in production* is included in the calculation of cost of goods manufactured. Any raw materials that the company already had in inventory or had purchased during the period that were not used are simply left over in ending materials inventory. They will be used in a future period. Direct materials used in production is calculated using the following formula:

Direct Materials Used in Production = Beginning Materials Inventory + Materials Purchases – Ending Materials Inventory

The **schedule of cost of goods manufactured** is used to determine the total cost of goods that were completed during the period. Essentially, it turns the cost of goods manufactured formula into a clear and easy-to-follow schedule. There will be separate sections for each of the direct materials, direct labor and manufacturing overhead. Making adjustments for WIP implies that any costs related to direct materials, direct labor or manufacturing overhead that belong to goods not completed in this period will show up on a later period's schedule. Specifically, these costs will appear in the schedule for the period that the goods are completed.

Below is an example of a schedule of cost of goods manufactured for Delta Company, followed by the explanation of each section.

Delta Company
Schedule of Cost of Goods Manufactured
For the Year Ended October 31, 2010

Direct materials:		
Beginning materials inventory	$ 100,000	
Add: Materials purchases	450,000	
Materials available for use	550,000	
Deduct: Ending materials inventory	40,000	
Materials used in production		$ 510,000
Direct labor		80,000
Manufacturing overhead:		
Indirect materials	11,000	
Indirect labor	60,000	
Utilities, factory	70,000	
Insurance, factory	12,000	
Depreciation	50,000	
Property taxes	9,000	
Total overhead costs		212,000
Total manufacturing costs		802,000
Add: Beginning work in process inventory		90,000
		892,000
Deduct: Ending work in process inventory		20,000
Cost of goods manufactured		$ 872,000

FIGURE 2.6

(a) Direct materials cost is the cost of materials used in production for the period, not merely what was purchased. By adding purchases to the beginning materials inventory and then subtracting the ending materials inventory, an accurate count of materials used is achieved.

(b) Direct labor is the cost of all work performed by workers who actually work on the product.

(c) Manufacturing overhead represents all the indirect costs that are associated with production during the current period.

(d) Total manufacturing costs is the total of direct materials, direct labor and manufacturing overhead. This represents the costs of manufacturing related to any goods that were worked on during the period (regardless of whether the goods were completed in the period or not).

(e) As mentioned earlier, adjustments need to be made for partially completed goods to properly calculate the cost of goods manufactured. The cost of goods manufactured figure should only consider the costs related to goods that were completed at some point in the period. Therefore, the beginning work in process inventory is added to the manufacturing costs, and ending work in process inventory is deducted to arrive at cost of goods manufactured for the period.

The Income Statement

Under a periodic inventory system, the cost of goods sold for a manufacturing company can be calculated once the cost of goods manufactured is calculated. Both line items will then be included in a detailed income statement. A sample income statement for Delta Company is provided as shown below.

Delta Company Income Statement For the Year Ended October 31, 2010		
Sales		$1,600,000
Cost of Goods Sold:		
Beginning Finished Goods Inventory	$200,000	
Add: Cost of Goods Manufactured*	872,000	
Goods Available for Sale	1,072,000	
Deduct: Ending Finished Goods inventory	150,000	922,000
Gross Profit		678,000
Less: Operating Expenses		185,000
Operating Income		$493,000
* From schedule of Cost of Goods Manufactured (Figure 2.6)		

FIGURE 2.7

In a perpetual inventory system, the inventory account is updated whenever a purchase or sale takes place (i.e. continuously). For the rest of this text, all scenarios will be based on a perpetual inventory system since it is most widely used by all businesses.

Job-Order Costing Overview

Job-order costing is commonly used in organizations that provide custom-made services or products. For example, consider Derek's Tailoring Services. Derek, the owner, tailors suits for his clients based on their specific requirements. The clients provide the suits and any other raw materials required to perform the job. Since each of his clients has to have a suit that meets their individual needs, Derek has decided to use a job-order costing system to cost his service. In a job-order costing system, costs related to a specific job are accumulated on a **job card**. Derek starts a new job card every time he receives a new order from a client. The format of the job card is shown in figure 2.8.

Derek's job card includes the following information: the job number, client's name and address, job description, amount of direct material, direct labor and overhead related to the job, and cost summary. In this case, the direct materials section will be empty because Derek's clients provide all the materials required for tailoring. If Derek was required to purchase the direct materials (e.g. cloth) himself, then he would have to include the cost of materials on the job card.

As a job is started, Derek tracks how much time was spent taking measurements, stitching and making alterations. Derek considers these activities as direct labor because they can be tied directly to the production of each specific suit. The total time spent is then summed and multiplied by Derek's hourly labor rate to determine the total direct labor cost for the job.

The job card is also used to record the amount of overhead allocated for each tailored suit. Some examples of typical overheads are rent of the store and depreciation of the working equipment. Recall that since overheads are indirect costs, they cannot be directly traced to the products or services provided. In this case, Derek would find it nearly impossible to tie the rent and depreciation expenses proportionately and directly to each suit. Therefore, Derek would make an estimate and allocate a reasonable amount of overhead to a particular job. To determine the reasonable amount, Derek would likely base his assumption on accurately measurable units, such as direct labor hours. The logic would be that the more time a job takes, the more overhead costs the job would incur. In industry practice, it is common for businesses to allocate overhead expenses based on a traceable factor. The details of overhead allocation will be discussed in the next chapter.

Job Card		
Derek's Tailoring Services		
Job No.:		
Client Name and Address:		
Job Description:		
Direct Materials		
Date	Material Requisition Numbers	Amount
	Total Direct Materials:	
Direct Labor		
Date	Time Card Numbers	Amount
	Total Direct Labor:	
Overhead		
Date	Rate	Amount
	Total Overhead:	
Summary of Job Costs		
	Total Direct Materials:	
	Total Direct Labor:	
	Total Overhead:	
	Total Job Cost:	

FIGURE 2.8

Job-order costing can also be used in a manufacturing setting based on the same principle. Assume Derek manufactures costumes instead of providing tailoring services. He would need to purchase raw materials such as different types of fabric, leather, thread and buttons. Suppose he receives an order from a customer who would like to order a Queen Victoria stage costume. Derek gets started right away, cutting fabric and sewing buttons. The raw materials are transferred to work-in-process and recorded on the job card. As the costume is being worked on, direct labor and allocated manufacturing overhead are also transferred to work-in-process and recorded on the job card. After the costume is completed, all costs on the job card would be totaled and transferred to the finished goods account. This information allows Derek to calculate the cost of the costume and also price it appropriately to earn a profit. When the finished costume is sold, the cost of the costume is transferred from finished goods (a balance sheet item) to cost of goods sold (an income statement item).

A more detailed example of job-order costing in a manufacturing environment is shown below.

Job Costing: Baldwin's Boat Building Company

Consider Baldwin's Boat Building Company, which is located in a fishing village on the east coast. The company has been commissioned to build a 15-foot wooden boat with an out-board motor, a

steering wheel to control the rudder and four seats. After Baldwin, the owner of the company, has quoted a price to the client, he draws up plans for the boat and hands it off to his team for production.

Since this is a unique boat tailored to the client's specific requirements, Baldwin would use job-order costing to properly track costs related to its construction.

Step 1 – Track Direct Materials

Assume the raw materials for building the boat have been purchased. The first step involves transferring raw materials from the storage room into the production area. Raw materials consist of items like wood and fiber glass. The raw materials that can be directly traced to the boat are considered *direct materials*. The costs of the direct materials should be included in the cost of the boat.

Step 2 – Track Direct Labor

In the workshop, the laborers are now working on the boat using the materials that came from the storage room. Since Baldwin pays wages to the laborers, the wages have to be included into the cost of the boat. The company keeps detailed records of how long each laborer spends working on each job. Therefore, once the job is completed, the company can determine how much in wages to assign to each boat. Since these wages can be traced directly to each job, the amount of hours laborers spent on each job is referred to as *direct labor hours*.

Step 3 – Estimate Overhead Costs

The boat is now complete. Up to this point, the company has only tracked direct material costs and direct labor costs related to the boat. However, to properly cost the boat, Baldwin must include manufacturing overhead costs into the cost of the boat. These costs include factory rent, factory insurance premiums, factory utilities, indirect materials and indirect labor. These costs are considered indirect because it is difficult to trace them directly to each particular boat built throughout the year.

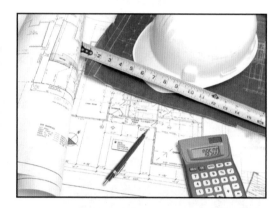

For example, consider the electrical devices you have in your home (e.g. washing machine, dryer, blender, dishwasher, central heating). When you receive your electricity bill, it would be very difficult for you to trace the exact electricity costs related to each appliance. Unless there was an electricity meter attached specifically to each appliance, it is almost impossible to trace exactly how many watts of electricity each appliance consumed throughout the year.

The same is true for businesses. In Baldwin's case, the electricity expenses cannot be directly tied to each boat that was completed throughout the year. In addition, he paid factory insurance premiums that cannot be assigned to each boat in an economical fashion. Therefore, he can only estimate overhead costs for a particular boat.

As mentioned earlier, overhead costs are estimated and allocated to specific jobs by using a cost driver. A cost driver can be anything that drives costs. For example, the amount of direct labor hours can be a cost driver since the more labor hours worked, the more of the company's resources will be consumed by the job. Recall that direct labor hours refer to the number of hours a laborer worked on jobs. Since Baldwin can accurately determine how many labor hours were consumed by a particular job, the company uses direct labor hours as a cost driver to allocate overhead costs.

For example, from past experience, the company expects to incur $500,000 in overhead costs for the year. This includes factory rent, factory utility expenses, indirect materials and indirect labor. Baldwin also knows that the company will have approximately 10,000 hours of direct labor. To calculate an overhead rate, they can divide total overhead costs by total direct labor hours: $500,000 ÷ 10,000 = $50/direct labor hour. Therefore, for every direct labor hour consumed for a job, Baldwin will use this rate to estimate and apply $50 worth of overhead costs to that job. If a job consumes 3,000 direct labor hours (it took workers 3,000 hours to build a boat), then the company will multiply 3,000 direct labor hours by the rate of $50/direct labor hour to estimate $150,000 of overhead costs and assign it to the particular job.

Step 4 – Transfer Costs to Finished Goods

Up to this point, Baldwin has included all manufacturing costs into the costs of the boat. He has included the costs of direct materials, direct labor and estimated overhead. The boat is now complete and ready for sale. It can now be moved into finished goods inventory.

Summary

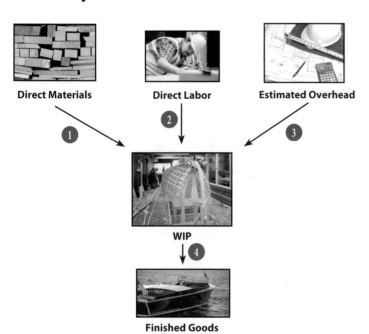

Figure 2.9 outlines the steps involved in tracking costs related to the building of the boat.

Step 1 – Track Direct Materials

Step 2 – Track Direct Labor

Step 3 – Estimate Overhead Costs

Step 4 – Transfer Costs to Finished Goods

FIGURE 2.9

Actual Overhead vs. Estimated Overhead

At the end of the year, the company finds that they actually spent more on overhead costs than estimated. They actually spent $506,667 on overhead in contrast to the $500,000 they estimated earlier. Actual overhead costs may be higher than estimated costs for a number of reasons. For example, the electricity rates may have increased from last year or insurance premiums may have risen as a result of government regulations. This will result in actual overhead costs being greater than estimated overhead costs. There are multiple ways of dealing with the difference between actual and estimated overhead costs. These will be discussed later in this book.

Process Costing Overview

Recall that job-order costing is typically used in businesses where the final product or service is provided to meet different customers' individual needs. However, there are other businesses which produce similar final products regardless of who the customer is. Examples include cookies, cell phones and cars. These similar products typically go through the same production steps. Since the goods are mass-produced in a number of identical processes, it is more beneficial and more efficient to use process costing to cost each unit of product.

Let us return to the Pine Furniture Manufacturer example and take a closer look at the manufacturing process. Remember that the company produces a line of identical chairs for a local school board.

For all chairs that Pine Furniture Manufacturer produces, there are three processes to be completed as shown below:

- Cutting wood to form appropriate shapes
- Assembling
- Painting

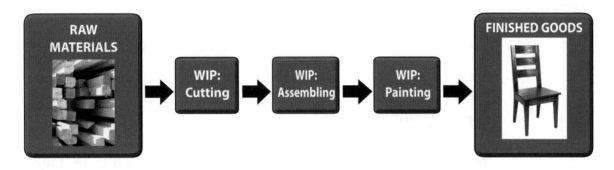

FIGURE 2.10

Process costing can be used to cost the chairs because each chair goes through the exact same processes. Process costing differs from job-order costing in that the costs of each chair are not tracked separately. Instead, costs are accumulated for each process in the production flow. Note that the concept of costs flowing from raw materials to work-in-process to finished goods still exists in process costing. However, because of the multiple processes involved, products go from one process to another before finally reaching the finished goods inventory.

Process Costing: CarPainter Inc. & Tanya's Canoe Company

In the previous section, an example of Baldwin's Boat Building Company was used to show how they tracked costs related to the customized boat they built. However, in businesses that produce similar final products or services, process costing is commonly used instead. Note that process

costing differs from job-order costing in that the costs of each individual product are not tracked separately. Process costing is used to determine an average cost for a group of products manufactured or services provided.

It is common for process costing to be used in a manufacturing setting where the goods produced are indistinguishable from each other. Examples of such products include cookies, cell phones and generic cars. Since each mass-produced cookie, cell phone or car goes through the same production steps, it is beneficial to use process costing to cost each unit of product.

Consider a cookie company that manufactures 10,000 boxes of cookies a year. Imagine using job-order costing to track the production of each box of cookies. The company would have 10,000 job-order cards in their system. In addition, the company would have to track the amount of flour, butter and sugar for each box. Since each box of cookies goes through the same production steps, it is more cost and time efficient to determine how much it costs to make 1,000 boxes at a time. The managers can then divide this cost by 1,000 to determine an average cost per box of cookies.

Process costing can also be used in the service industry. Consider the public service department that issues marriage licenses. Since the paperwork and activities needed to issue marriage licenses are essentially the same for each license, managers at the department can use process costing to track costs in order to determine the cost to issue a single marriage license.

We will now work through a straight-forward scenario to highlight important concepts in process costing.

A Simple Example of Process Costing

A car manufacturer has found that they can save costs if they outsource the painting of their cars to CarPainter Inc. Every month, CarPainter receives standard cars from the automaker that only need to be painted before being shipped back to the automaker. The steps are shown in figure 2.11. Since paint is applied the same way to each car, it is more efficient to use process costing to determine the cost of painting a single car.

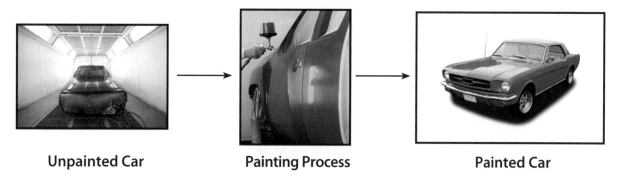

| Unpainted Car | Painting Process | Painted Car |

FIGURE 2.11

Suppose that at the beginning of the month, CarPainter received 100 cars to be painted. Similar to job-order costing, process costing also uses the costs related to direct materials, direct labor and manufacturing overhead to cost the product or service. At the end of the month, the workers had completed painting all 100 cars. The managers at CarPainter accumulated the following costs, as illustrated in figure 2.12:

- Direct Materials: $14,000
- Direct Labor: $8,000
- Manufacturing Overhead: $8,000

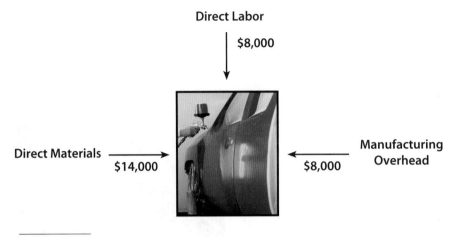

FIGURE 2.12

Total costs for the month are $30,000 ($14,000 + $8,000 + $8,000). Since 100 cars were painted, the cost to paint one car is calculated by dividing the total cost by the number of cars painted ($30,000 ÷ 100 = $300 per car). In this example, process costing is really just average costing. This happens when there is only one process involved and all goods are completed during the period. This example offers a clear comparison between job costing and process costing. *Job costing accumulates specific costs per job while process costing accumulates costs for a process and then averages it out to each product.*

Process costing is also commonly used for production involving multiple processes. In the next section, the application of process costing will be discussed in more complex situations.

Process Costing for Multiple Processes

Tanya's Canoe Company produces standard canoes that are purchased by resorts and campsites throughout the country. Each canoe that Tanya produces has to go through three processes to be completed:

- Cutting: Laborers obtain wood from raw materials inventory and carefully cut out strips of wood for the canoe. Each time a set of wood has been cut and is ready for assembly, the cutting department transfers over the wood to the assembling department.
- Assembling: The strips of wood from the cutting department are put together and the stern seat and bow seat are inserted into the canoe. Once the canoe is assembled, it is transferred to the painting department.
- Painting: Once the canoe is received from the assembling department, the painting department applies paint and other finishing touches to the canoe. Once the canoe is painted, it is completed and transferred into finished goods inventory.

Each of the above processes occurs in a separate department (cutting department, assembling department and painting department). Once these three processes are completed, the canoe is ready to be sold.

Tanya can use process costing to cost her canoes because each canoe goes through the exact same process and it would be impractical to accumulate the cost for each one of them separately. Figure 2.13 outlines the different processes in building a canoe.

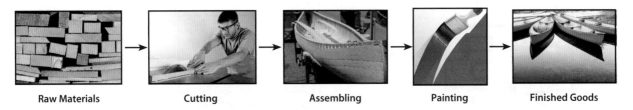

| Raw Materials | Cutting | Assembling | Painting | Finished Goods |

FIGURE 2.13

Similar to job costing, direct materials, direct labor and manufacturing overhead need to be assigned. Unlike job-order costing where there is one work-in-process (WIP) account for each job, in process costing each process (or department) has its own WIP account.

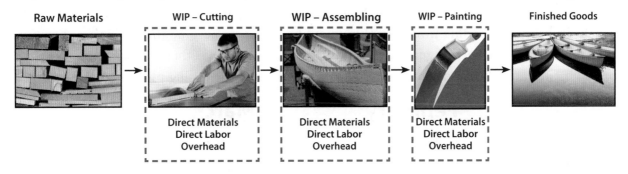

FIGURE 2.14

Notice in figure 2.14 that each department has its own WIP account (WIP-Cutting, WIP-Assembling, WIP-Painting). The figure shows how costs flow from one WIP to the next and eventually go to finished goods. It also shows some examples of the type of costs that would be involved in each WIP. It is important to note that only amounts in the last WIP will flow through to finished goods.

Flow of Material and Inventory Valuation

Consider Tanya's Canoe Company and suppose that during February, the cutting department received 200 canoes worth of raw materials from storage that were ready to be cut. During the month, the workers in the cutting department worked diligently to finish the 200 canoes but by the end of the month, they were only able to complete the cutting for 180 canoes. These 180 canoes were transferred to the assembling department at the end of February. Therefore, at the end of February, the cutting department still had 20 canoes worth of raw materials which they had started but did not finish cutting. Since the cutting department has partially completed cutting 20 canoes at the end of the month, the cutting department has *ending inventory* at the end of February. This is illustrated in figure 2.15.

February

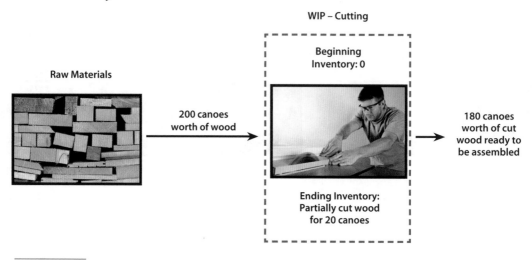

FIGURE 2.15

Now, consider the next month (March). Since the cutting department had 20 partially completed canoes in February's ending inventory, this amount would now become the beginning inventory for March. This is shown in figure 2.16. It is important to know whether a process has beginning or ending inventory because it affects the calculation of costs when using process costing.

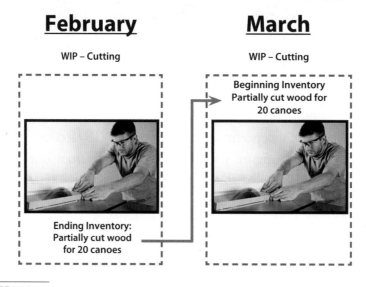

FIGURE 2.16

It is important to understand that having ending inventory in a *process* has nothing to do with having ending inventory in *finished goods,* since each department's WIP account can have its own beginning and ending inventory.

For example, ending inventory for the assembling department can refer to canoes that are partially assembled. They cannot be transferred to the painting department yet because they are not complete;

therefore, these partially assembled canoes would still be part of the WIP account in the assembling department. In a WIP account, **ending inventory** refers to units that are only partially complete by the end of the accounting period. **Beginning inventory** in a WIP is a result of having ending inventory at the end of the prior period.

Importance of Inventory Valuation

Remember that one of the objectives of process costing is to determine the costs of the inventory transferred out to the next department and to determine the costs of the remaining ending inventory. When there is beginning inventory present for a specific process, the value of the ending inventory may vary depending on the valuation method the department chooses to use. In order to properly determine the cost of inventory, each department must also calculate **equivalent units of production**. The equivalent units of production estimates the number of whole units completed based on the number of partially completed units and their percentage of completion. Calculating equivalent units of production will be covered in detail in chapter 4.

Recall from your financial accounting course that there are various inventory valuation methods. The ones commonly used in process costing are First-In, First-Out (FIFO) and weighted-average cost (WAC). At the end of a period, a company will value its inventory using one of the methods. Each method produces a different value for ending inventory and cost of goods sold. For example, if a company chooses to use FIFO, the inventory received first is assumed to be the first inventory to leave. On the other hand, if a company chooses to use WAC, the cost of inventory would be averaged out throughout the entire period.

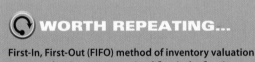

WORTH REPEATING...

First-In, First-Out (FIFO) method of inventory valuation assumes that inventory received first is the first inventory to be consumed.

Weighted-average cost (WAC) method of inventory valuation averages the cost of inventory throughout the entire period.

The same principle applies to a WIP department. Since the costs in beginning inventory are carried over from the previous period, the method used to value inventory will have an effect on the inventory balance. Since the choice of inventory valuation method affects the inventory balance, the cost of goods sold is also affected, which in turn will have an effect on gross profit.

For an example, at the beginning of February, the painting department started off with 30 partially painted canoes in beginning inventory. Note that these partially painted canoes were ending inventory from January. During the month of February, the painting department received 40 unpainted canoes from the assembling department. By the end of the period, they were able to finish painting 50 canoes. This left them with an ending inventory of 20 canoes which were only partially painted. Under the FIFO method as shown in figure 2.17, the cost of inventory transferred to the next department first includes the costs of the beginning inventory and then the costs of inventory added during the current period. Whatever costs are left over are considered part of ending inventory (the 20 canoes remaining).

First-In-First-Out (FIFO)

WIP - Painting

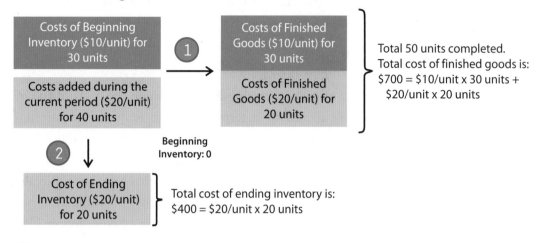

FIGURE 2.17

Under the WAC method as shown in figure 2.18, it does not matter which period the costs were incurred. Total costs of painting canoes from both the previous period and the current period are combined and divided by the equivalent units of canoes. For simplicity, assume that in this case, the number of canoes in beginning inventory is equal to the number of canoes added during the period.

Weighted-Average Cost (WAC)

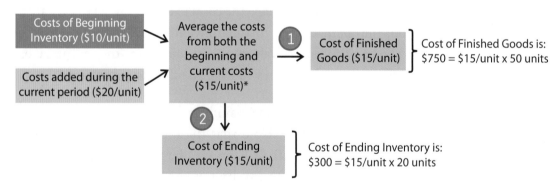

* Average cost per unit is: [$10/unit + $20/unit] / 2 = $15/unit

FIGURE 2.18

Thus if a department has beginning inventory for a given period, the company should select a valuation method and use it consistently. This will affect the cost of inventory reported on the financial statements. In chapter 4, process costing will be further discussed and a comprehensive examination of this application will be performed.

Ethical Considerations

Ethical dilemmas can occur at any level of business management. Consider the following hypothetical situation. A company currently discharges a lot of pollutants into the environment, damaging wildlife, ecosystems and creating health concerns for nearby citizens. The government has required a new technology be used to reduce the amount of pollutants being discharged, and it must be implemented by the end of the year.

The new technology is very expensive and if the company buys it now, the company will experience a large decrease in profitability and major cash flow issues. This will not please the stockholders. The company estimates that they can implement the new technology in three years, but will face fines from the government for each year they do not implement the change. In the meantime, pollutants will continue to be discharged and cause damage. Should the company do what is right for the stockholders, or do what is right for the environment?

There isn't always a clear right or wrong solution for all issues in a business. In hopes of making the "right" decision, managers should:

- evaluate the decision by considering all the possible alternatives
- identify all groups or individuals that are affected by any decision made
- determine which alternative will cause the least amount of harm

While the above considerations aid in ethical decision making, the first step in resolving an ethical conflict is to identify unethical behavior. In the rest of this text, we will address various ethical topics specific to the subject matter presented in each chapter.

In Summary

⇨ A **cost object** is anything for which a separate cost measurement is desired.

⇨ A **cost driver** is any activity in an organization that incurs cost.

⇨ An organization's **value chain** outlines all the steps that need to be completed in order to bring their products or services to market.

⇨ **Product costs** are costs incurred during the manufacturing phase of the product.

⇨ **Period costs** are costs which do not relate to the manufacturing phase of the product.

⇨ **Direct costs** are costs that can be directly traced to the cost of the product or service provided.

⇨ **Indirect costs** are costs that cannot easily be tied directly to the product or service.

⇨ **Direct materials** are materials which are purchased for making a product. Direct materials should be easily traceable as part of the finished goods.

⇨ **Direct labor** includes the wages paid to employees who directly work on converting materials to a company's products.

⇨ **Manufacturing overhead** includes all other indirect manufacturing expenses such as indirect materials, indirect labor, rent and depreciation.

⇨ **Raw materials** are materials that are used as building material to create a product.

⇨ **Work-in-process** includes unfinished items or services which are still in the production process.

⇨ **Finished goods** include products which have been completed but have not been sold or delivered.

⇨ The **cost of goods manufactured** for a period is the cost of new completed products that is added to finished goods inventory during the period.

⇨ In a **perpetual inventory system**, the inventory account is updated whenever a purchase or sale is made.

⇨ In a **periodic inventory system**, inventory is only updated periodically when a physical count takes place.

⇨ **Job-order costing** involves calculating costs for a specific job. It is commonly used in organizations that provide custom delivered services or products.

⇨ **Process costing** is the costing method applicable where goods or services result from a sequence of continuous or repetitive operations or processes. Costs are averaged over the units produced during the period.

⇨ **Ending inventory** in WIP refers to units that are only partially complete by the end of the accounting period.

⇨ **Beginning inventory** in WIP is a result of ending inventory carrying over from the end of the period.

⇨ **Equivalent units of production** is the number of completed units that approximately equal the number of partially completed units based on their percentage of completion.

⇨ The **first-in-first-out (FIFO)** method of inventory valuation assumes that inventory received first is the first inventory to be consumed.

⇨ The **weighted-average cost (WAC)** method of inventory valuation averages the cost of inventory throughout the entire period.

Review Exercise

Grecian Inc. manufactures decorative urns. Specialized machines form the basic model of the urn out of ceramic. The urns are hand painted in different designs before being fired to harden the ceramic and seal the paint. The company is able to trace the exact amount of ceramic used to make each urn, but cannot easily trace the amount of paint used on each urn.

Grecian needs to create a schedule of cost of goods manufactured and an income statement for the year ended July 31, 2011 and has compiled a list of all the costs incurred during the year.

Advertising	$6,000
Ceramic material purchased	300,000
Depreciation on machines	8,000
Factory utilities	14,000
Office supplies used	3,500
Paint	40,000
Paint brushes	4,000
Paint solvent	3,000
Painter's salaries	240,000
Plant supervisor's salary	50,000

In addition to the costs, Grecian also has the following information available.

Beginning finished goods inventory	$200,000
Beginning materials inventory	20,000
Beginning work in process inventory	55,000
Ending finished goods inventory	180,000
Ending materials inventory	25,000
Ending work in process inventory	65,000
Sales	700,000

Required:

1. Should Grecian Inc. use job-order costing or process costing to properly track costs of their products? Explain your answer.

2. Using the information provided, create a schedule of cost of goods manufactured and an income statement for the year ended July 31, 2011.

Review Exercise – Answer

Part 1

Grecian Inc. should use process costing to properly track the cost of the urns. The company uses the same steps to make the urns regardless of who the customer is. The processes indicated are forming, painting and firing.

Part 2

Paint, paint brushes and paint solvent are viewed as indirect costs because they cannot easily trace to each product (as stated in question).

Grecian Inc. Schedule of Cost of Goods Manufactured For the Year Ended July 31, 2011		
Direct Materials:		
Beginning materials inventory	$20,000	
Add: Materials purchased	300,000	
Materials available for use	320,000	
Deduct: Ending materials Inventory	25,000	
Materials used in production		$295,000
Direct Labor		240,000
Manufacturing Overhead:		
Depreciation on machines	8,000	
Factory utilities	14,000	
Indirect materials (paint)	40,000	
Indirect materials (paint brushes)	4,000	
Indirect materials (paint solvent)	3,000	
Indirect labor (plant supervisor's salary)	50,000	
Total overhead costs		119,000
Total manufacturing costs		654,000
Add: Beginning work in process inventory		55,000
		709,000
Deduct: Ending work in process inventory		65,000
Cost of Goods Manufactured		$644,000

Grecian Inc. Income Statement For the Year Ended July 31, 2011		
Sales		$700,000
Cost of Goods Sold		
Beginning Finished Goods Inventory	200,000	
Add: Cost of Goods Manufactured	644,000*	
Goods Available for Sale	844,000	
Deduct: Ending Finished Goods Inventory	180,000	664,000
Gross Profit		36,000
Operating Expenses		
Advertising Expense	6,000	
Office Supplies Expense	3,500	
Total Operating Expense		9,500
Operating Income		$26,500

*From Schedule of Cost of Goods Manufactured (above)

Chapter 3
JOB-ORDER COSTING

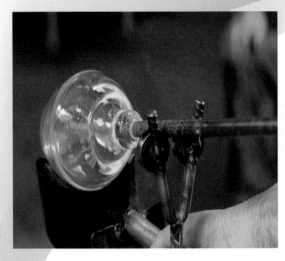

LEARNING OUTCOMES:

❶ Describe the concept of job-order costing

❷ Understand the use of subsidiary ledgers

❸ Account for direct materials

❹ Account for direct labor

❺ Account for manufacturing overhead using the manufacturing overhead account

❻ Account for under-allocated or over-allocated overhead using the cost of goods sold method

Appendix

❼ Account for manufacturing overhead using manufacturing overhead allocated and manufacturing overhead control accounts

❽ Account for under-allocated or over-allocated overhead using the proration method

An Introduction to New Accounts and Recordkeeping

In chapter 2, two main methods of product costing were discussed: job-order and process costing. Both costing systems are part of cost accounting. They provide information on the organization's purchases and consumption of resources during the production process, in order to allocate costs to a product or service. Job-order costing is often used when a company produces a product or provides a service that is tailored to meet the needs of a particular client (e.g. custom made costumes). Process costing is usually used when a manufacturer produces large volumes of products that are indistinguishable from each other (i.e. cookies, chips, canoes, etc). Job-order costing accumulates costs pertaining to specific jobs while process costing accumulates costs for each process.

In this chapter, job-order costing will be discussed in depth and the calculations and journal entries required to cost a job will be illustrated.

Recall from chapter 2 that product costs are made up of direct materials, direct labor and manufacturing overhead. Direct materials are materials whose costs can be directly traced to the product. Direct labor includes all the wages paid to manufacturing employees who work directly on the product. Manufacturing overhead includes all other indirect manufacturing costs such as indirect materials, indirect labor and other indirect factory costs. Overhead (indirect) costs refer to costs that cannot be easily traced to the product or service being produced. Examples of overhead costs can include factory rent, electricity expense, depreciation of equipment, indirect materials and indirect labor. These costs are considered indirect because it is not possible to trace them to each product in an economical manner.

As the product is being built, it is relatively easy to record costs related to direct materials and direct labor in the accounting system. However, recording manufacturing overhead costs is more complex because the amount of overhead costs, may not be known while the product is being produced. For example, indirect electricity costs for products built at the beginning of the month may not be known until the electricity bill is received, which may be at the end of the month. Therefore, for most businesses, it is difficult to allocate actual overhead costs to the product as the product is being made. Instead, many companies *estimate* manufacturing overhead costs. These estimated manufacturing overhead costs are recorded in the financial accounting system in what is known as the **manufacturing overhead account**. Note that during the month or accounting period, the company will receive overhead bills which will provide details about the *actual* overhead costs. These actual overhead costs are also recorded in the manufacturing overhead account. At the end of the accounting period, a company may find that they have actually incurred more or less on overhead costs than they had initially estimated. Later on in the chapter, different methods of treating the difference between actual and estimated overhead costs will be discussed.

We will now describe the manufacturing overhead account and how it is used to track manufacturing overhead costs.

The Manufacturing Overhead Account

The manufacturing overhead account is a temporary account used to allocate estimated manufacturing overhead costs to inventory and to accumulate actual overhead costs incurred by the factory. This temporary account tracks costs during the period. It will eventually be closed and have a zero balance at the end of the period. *Allocated* overhead costs are recorded on the right (credit) side of the account while *actual* overhead costs are recorded on the left (debit) side of the account. The manufacturing overhead account represents an accurate tracking of actual overhead costs versus allocated overhead costs.

MANUFACTURING OVERHEAD	
Record *Actual* Overhead Costs	Record *Allocated* Overhead Costs

At the end of an accounting period, the manufacturing overhead account may have a debit or a credit balance. For example, if a company incurs more actual overhead than they had estimated, the manufacturing overhead account would have a debit balance. On the other hand, if a company incurs less actual overhead than they had estimated, the manufacturing overhead account would have a credit balance. Either way, the balance will have to be cleared and the account will not appear on any of the financial statements. Note that the difference between actual manufacturing overhead and allocated manufacturing overhead must be eliminated. By the end of the fiscal period, the financial statements must report actual costs

WORTH REPEATING...

The income summary account is a clearing account that closes all the revenues and expenses. The balance in the income summary account is then closed to equity.

amounts (and not estimated figures). A balance remaining in the manufacturing overhead account at the end of a period would mean the financial statements are reporting incorrect cost amounts. In general, a company has two options of dealing with the overhead difference. They can either:

1. Write-off this amount to cost of goods sold
2. Write-off this amount to a combination of inventory accounts and cost of goods sold

Notice that the manufacturing overhead account is in both blue and yellow. This is to indicate that at the end of the year, the difference between actual and allocated costs will be associated with either an asset (blue), an expense (yellow) or both. The details behind how *actual* costs are recorded and how the overhead account is cleared will be covered later in this chapter.

The Use of Subsidiary Ledgers

Recall that the cost of inventory includes direct materials, direct labor and manufacturing overhead costs. These costs are capitalized into inventory (an asset) and are only expensed through COGS once the inventory is sold to a customer.

Since job-order costing involves accumulating the cost of raw materials, it is important to understand how raw materials are controlled in a business. Financial accounting looks at the flow of accounting information in a business. Accounting information systems use source documents, journals and ledgers to prepare the trial balance and then the financial statements. Source documents provide evidence that a business transaction has occurred. Examples of source documents include purchase orders, sales invoices, cash receipts and contracts. These documents are used to prepare journal entries to record business transactions. The amounts are then transferred to the general ledger, which contains the balances for each account in the accounting system.

In an accounting system, for information to be readily available for management, it has to be thoroughly organized. For example, if all types of raw materials that a company purchases were to be posted into a single general ledger account, it would be very difficult to maintain proper inventory quantities for different types of material.

The details regarding the different types of raw materials a company purchases should be clearly organized. To maintain these types of details in the accounting records, **subsidiary ledgers (or sub-ledgers)** are used in addition to the general ledger accounts. For example, an organization's accounting records could contain a sub-ledger for each type of raw material. Whenever raw materials are purchased or moved into production, the appropriate sub-ledger would be increased or decreased. This would make it easier to track the flow of different types of raw materials.

Sub-ledgers are used to group information in the general ledger. They also contain the details to support the general ledger. Therefore, to determine the dollar amount of a specific general ledger, one must take the sum of all its sub-ledgers.

Examples of typical sub-ledgers include:

- Accounts Receivable Sub-Ledger
- Accounts Payable Sub-Ledger
- Raw Materials Sub-Ledger

Recording information into sub-ledgers can be a time-consuming process. However, with the incorporation of computerized accounting systems, it has become possible to store detailed information in the sub-ledgers in a time-effective manner. For example, it is now possible to scan the bar codes of materials entered in inventory directly into the appropriate sub-ledger. This information is automatically organized and readily available to be viewed by the accounting staff.

Assume a company purchased the following raw materials: $4,600 worth of wood, $500 worth of paint and $300 worth of nails. Each raw material would be recorded in its own respective sub-ledger, and the total amount of $5,400 would be recorded in the raw materials general ledger account. The relationship between the sub-ledger and the general ledger account is illustrated in figure 3.1.

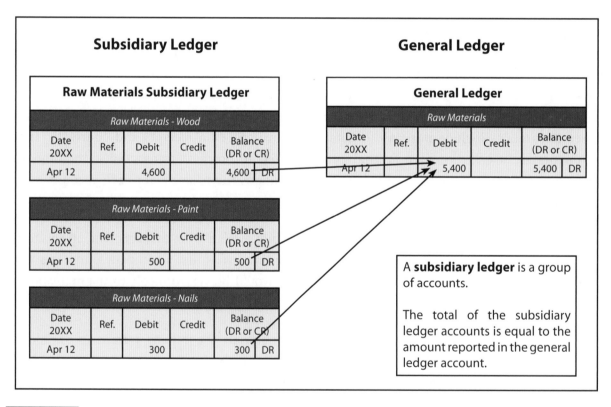

FIGURE 3.1

Job-Order Costing in Pine Furniture Manufacturer Inc.

Let us return to the Pine Furniture Manufacturer example, introduced in chapter 2. Suppose that Pine Furniture Manufacturer received a special request from a new customer, aLogic Inc., on March 1, 2010. The client would like Pine Furniture Manufacturer to build a set of customized furniture for their office. Since Pine Furniture Manufacturer is specifically building the furniture to meet this customer's request, it would be appropriate to use job-order costing to calculate the cost of the furniture. Let us now go through the individual transactions involved in using job-order costing for this special order. A summary of the transactions can be found near the end of this chapter.

Raw Materials

First, Pine Furniture Manufacturer has to purchase raw materials from its suppliers. Examples of raw materials needed for this job include wood, metal casters and upholstery. On March 3, Pine Furniture Manufacturer purchased $2,000 worth of raw materials on account. For the purposes of this chapter, all raw materials will be recorded in one raw materials account. The journal entry to record this transaction is shown in figure 3.2.

Transaction 1

GENERAL JOURNAL			
DATE	**DESCRIPTION**	**DR**	**CR**
Mar 3	Raw Materials	2,000	
	Accounts Payable		2,000
	To record purchase of raw materials on account		

Purchasing raw material on account increases raw material inventory (asset) and increases accounts payable (liability) by the same amount.

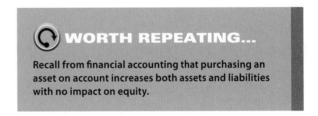

WORTH REPEATING...

Recall from financial accounting that purchasing an asset on account increases both assets and liabilities with no impact on equity.

FIGURE 3.2

Before starting the work for aLogic Inc., Pine Furniture Manufacturer sets up a job card to accumulate all the costs related to the special order in one document. As per their system records, this particular job has been assigned Job ID #312. Up to this point, the job card includes the job ID number, the client's name and a brief description of the job as shown in figure 3.3.

To start the job, the production department will need to transfer raw materials from the storage room to the factory. A **materials requisition form** is issued to request raw materials from the storage room, which are then released to the factory. Assume that the production department requested $1,000 worth of raw materials and that the materials requisition form number is 456. A sample materials requisition form is provided as shown in figure 3.4.

Job Card
Pine Furniture Manufacturer Inc.
Job ID: 312
Client Name: aLogic Inc.
Job Description: Build customized furniture

Direct Materials

Date	Material Requisition Numbers	Amount
	Total Direct Materials:	

Direct Labor

Date	Time Card Numbers	Amount
	Total Direct Labor:	

Manufacturing Overhead

Date	Rate	Amount
	Total Manufacturing Overhead:	

Summary of Job Costs

Total Direct Materials:	
Total Direct Labor:	
Total Manufacturing Overhead:	
Total Job Cost:	

FIGURE 3.3

Material Requisition Form
Pine Furniture Manufacturer Inc.
Form #: 456
Job ID: 312

Direct Materials

Type	Description	Amount
1-A, 2-C, 4-D	wood, metal casters, upholstery	$1,000
	Total Direct Materials:	$1,000

FIGURE 3.4

The above form shows that $1,000 worth of raw materials were drawn from the storage room to be used for Job ID #312. The information from the material requisition form would then be transferred to the job card for Job ID #312 under the direct materials section.

Work-in-Process: Accounting for Direct and Indirect Materials Costs

After the materials requisition form has been processed, Pine Furniture Manufacturer starts production on Job ID #312. Recall that raw materials include both direct and indirect materials. Direct materials are those items that can be traced to a specific job. In the case of Pine Furniture Manufacturer, these are wood, metal casters and upholstery. Direct material costs of $1,000 will be recorded into the WIP account (as shown in figure 3.5).

Recall that indirect materials include raw materials which cannot be traced directly to the product. For example, it is costly, time consuming and impractical for Pine Furniture Manufacturer to tie the costs of glue to each individual piece of furniture because it is difficult to determine how much glue is being used in each order. Therefore, the cost of the glue is treated as an indirect cost. Note that actual indirect materials costs are not entered directly into the WIP account. Instead, they are accumulated in the manufacturing overhead account (on the debit side). Assume that Pine

Furniture Manufacturer takes $500 worth of indirect materials from raw materials inventory for use on this job and future jobs.

On March 13, Pine Furniture Manufacturer records the transfer of raw materials to work-in-process and manufacturing overhead. Pine Furniture Manufacturer credits raw materials for $1,500, debits WIP for $1,000 (direct materials) and debits manufacturing overhead for $500 (indirect materials). Notice that the raw materials and WIP accounts appear on the asset side of the balance sheet and are a part of inventory. The journal entry to record this transaction on March 13 is shown in figure 3.5.

Note: Manufacturing overhead account is not part of the regular accounting map, because the balance will eventually be cleared and transferred to either inventory or cost of goods sold.

Transaction 2

GENERAL JOURNAL

DATE	DESCRIPTION	DR	CR
Mar 13	WIP	1,000	
	Manufacturing Overhead	500	
	Raw Materials		1,500
	To enter direct and indirect materials into production		

FIGURE 3.5

Accounting for the flow of raw materials may be a manual or an automated process. In a computerized information system, the requisition form and accompanying accounting transactions are electronically prepared.

Work-in-Process: Accounting for Direct and Indirect Labor Costs

Now that the materials are in production, the factory workers will work on the raw materials to build the furniture. Similar to raw materials, labor costs also include both direct and indirect costs. Direct labor costs in a factory are measured using the labor time cards. A labor time card is prepared for each factory worker. Information on the time cards include the worker's hourly wage rate and the amount of time they spent on each specific job in the plant. The direct labor costs relating to

Job ID #312 will then be added to WIP. These costs can be determined by reviewing the labor time cards and counting all the direct labor hours spent on Job ID #312.

Assume that Pine Furniture Manufacturer incurred $1,400 of wages and salaries liabilities for all employees during the month of March. It is important to remember that the $1,400 of salaries include all salaries incurred in the factory. This includes both direct labor and indirect labor. Indirect labor amounted to $800 for the month.

WORTH REPEATING...

Accrual accounting is a method of accounting in which revenues and expenses are recognized in the time period in which they occur, regardless of when the payment is received or made.

To determine the exact amount of direct labor cost for the job, the time cards of the employees who worked on Job ID #312 were selected. Two employees, William Adama and Kara Thrace, worked on the job. Both William and Kara earn an hourly wage rate of $15. Time card #75 lists William's activities. It shows that he spent a total of 18 hours on Job ID #312, costing $270. Time card #76 shows that Kara spent 22 hours on the job, costing $330. In total, the direct labor cost for Job ID #312 equals $600 ($270 + $330). The time cards are illustrated in figure 3.6.

Labor Time Card				
Pine Furniture Manufacturer Inc.				
Card #: 75		Week Start:	Mar 15, 2010	
		Week End:	Mar 19, 2010	
William Adama				
Date	Description	Hours	Rate	Total
Mar 15	Job ID # 312	6	$15	$90
Mar 16	Job ID # 312	6	$15	$90
Mar 18	Job ID # 312	6	$15	$90
	Total	18		$270
	Total Direct Labor:			$270

Labor Time Card				
Pine Furniture Manufacturer Inc.				
Card #: 76		Week Start:	Mar 15, 2010	
		Week End:	Mar 19, 2010	
Kara Thrace				
Date	Description	Hours	Rate	Total
Mar 15	Job ID # 312	7	$15	$105
Mar 17	Job ID # 312	7	$15	$105
Mar 19	Job ID # 312	8	$15	$105
	Total	22		$330
	Total Direct Labor:			$330

FIGURE 3.6

Pine Furniture Manufacturer also incurred indirect labor costs (labor costs related to the entire production facility that cannot be traced directly to a particular job). These are accumulated in the manufacturing overhead account. An example of indirect labor includes the wages paid to the maintenance staff. Since the maintenance staff work on machines that are used for many different jobs throughout the day, it is difficult and costly to keep a log of their time for each job. Therefore, their wages are considered to be indirect labor costs. Similar to indirect materials, indirect labor costs are not applied directly to the WIP account, but are included in the manufacturing overhead account.

Direct labor costs are considered product costs. Therefore, they have to be capitalized into the cost of inventory. These costs will only be expensed through cost of goods sold once the inventory is sold.

The transaction to transfer labor costs to WIP and manufacturing overhead is shown in figure 3.7.

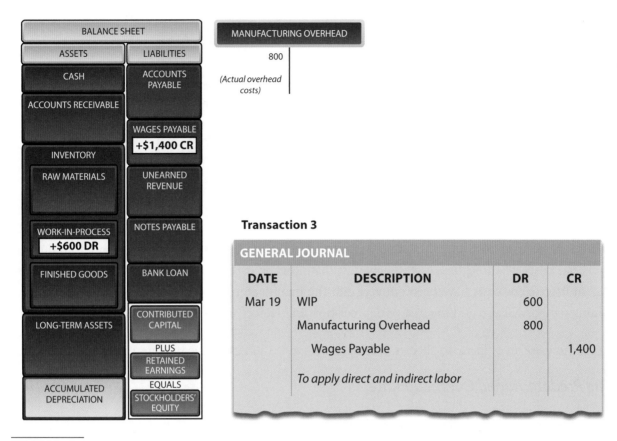

FIGURE 3.7

Work-In-Process: Allocation of Manufacturing Overhead

So far, Pine Furniture Manufacturer has recorded the direct material and direct labor costs for Job ID #312. Recall from chapter 2 that manufacturing overhead, such as indirect materials, must also be accounted for. These costs also need to be included in WIP. In the case of Pine Furniture Manufacturer, assume the manufacturing overhead costs include:

- Indirect materials
- Indirect labor (e.g. supervisor/ manager salaries)
- Depreciation on factory equipment
- Factory electricity expenses

If the actual manufacturing overhead costs are known *as soon as* the job is completed, Pine Furniture Manufacturer would include the exact costs into the cost of the job. However, recall that it is unlikely for actual overhead costs to be known at the time the job is completed. For example, Pine Furniture Manufacturer may complete a job

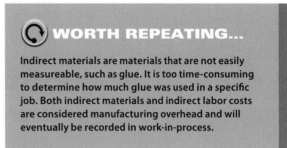

WORTH REPEATING...

Indirect materials are materials that are not easily measureable, such as glue. It is too time-consuming to determine how much glue was used in a specific job. Both indirect materials and indirect labor costs are considered manufacturing overhead and will eventually be recorded in work-in-process.

at the beginning of the month but will not receive the electricity bill until the end of the month. In this case, it would be impossible to know the exact amount of overhead at the beginning of the month. In fact, some manufacturing costs may not be exactly known until the end of the year.

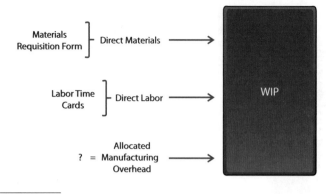

FIGURE 3.8

Managers need to cost jobs in a timely manner. If it is impossible to obtain the exact amount of overhead costs when needed, a reasonable estimate can be used. As shown earlier, indirect material and indirect labor costs have been entered into the manufacturing overhead account. Pine Furniture Manufacturer will also add the cost of depreciation and factory electricity expenses into this account.

Let us now use an estimate to allocate overhead costs to the job using the predetermined overhead rate.

The Predetermined Overhead Rate

An intuitive measure of how much estimated manufacturing overhead costs to allocate to a particular job is the time the factory workers spent on the job. For example, it should make sense that the more time workers spend on Job ID #312, the more manufacturing overhead costs should be allocated to it. Since all the overhead costs cannot be directly traced to each job, Pine Furniture Manufacturer will allocate the manufacturing overhead cost based on direct labor hours. More overhead cost will be allocated to the jobs which consume a greater number of direct labor hours. Similarly, less overhead cost will be allocated to the jobs which consume fewer direct labor hours.

Note that when Pine Furniture Manufacturer uses estimated direct labor hours to allocate manufacturing overhead, it is using direct labor hours as a **cost allocation base**. A cost allocation base is used to allocate overhead costs to products or services. In this case, direct labor hours is chosen as the allocation base because the company utilizes a considerable amount of direct labor throughout the year, and because direct labor hours can be measured with reasonable accuracy. As a result, the amount of direct labor hours consumed by a job is a good indicator of how much overhead cost was consumed by that particular job.

To allocate manufacturing overhead costs to Job ID #312 using a cost allocation base, a managerial accounting tool called the **predetermined overhead rate** is used.

The formula for Pine Furniture Manufacturer's predetermined overhead rate is:

$$\text{Predetermined Overhead Rate} = \frac{\text{Total Estimated Manufacturing Overhead Costs for the Period}}{\text{Total Estimated Direct Labor Hours for the Period}}$$

Pine Furniture Manufacturer prepare its reports on a monthly basis. Assume that during the month of March, Pine Furniture Manufacturer worked only on Job ID #312. At the beginning of the month, Pine Furniture Manufacturer's managerial accountants estimated the total overhead costs for the upcoming month based on their past experience. Total overhead costs include indirect material costs, indirect labor costs, depreciation and electricity expenses. Pine Furniture Manufacturer then estimated the total direct labor hours that will be consumed, based on the operations' forecasts.

Suppose that at the beginning of March, Pine Furniture Manufacturer estimated that total manufacturing overhead costs for the month would amount to $5,000. Pine Furniture Manufacturer also estimated that total direct labor hours would amount to 50 hours. Therefore, Pine Furniture Manufacturer's predetermined overhead rate for the month will be:

$$\text{Predetermined Overhead Rate (POHR)} = \frac{\$5,000}{50 \text{ Direct Labor Hours}}$$

$$= \$100/ \text{ Direct Labor Hour (\$100/DLH)}$$

The POHR is calculated using *estimated* labor hours, but manufacturing overhead is allocated based on the *actual* direct labor hours incurred. The above rate tells Pine Furniture Manufacturer managers that they should allocate $100 of overhead for each hour of direct labor a job uses. Recall that the time cards include information on how much direct labor time was spent on the job (see figure 3.6). Since 40 direct labor hours (18 hours for William and 22 hours for Kara) were spent on Job ID #312, the allocated manufacturing overhead for this job is calculated as shown below:

$$\text{Amount of Overhead Allocated} = \text{Actual Direct Labor Hours} \times \text{Predetermined Overhead Rate}$$

$$= 40 \text{ Direct Labor Hours} \times \$100/\text{Direct Labor Hour}$$

$$= \$4,000$$

Therefore, $4,000 of overhead costs will be allocated to Job ID #312.

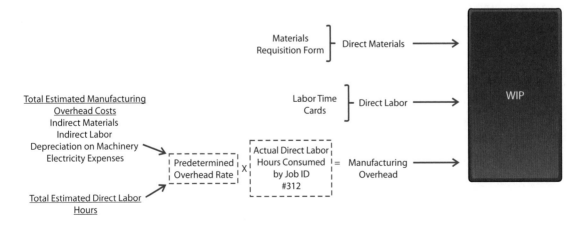

FIGURE 3.9

Figure 3.9 provides a quick summary of how costs are accumulated for Job ID #312.

Since the manufacturing environment in Pine Furniture Manufacturer is labor-intensive, using direct labor hours as a cost allocation base provides the company with a good approximation of the actual overhead cost consumed by the job. However, companies are not limited to using only direct labor hours as a cost allocation base. For example, a company that utilizes a lot of machinery during production may prefer to use machine hours as a cost allocation base. Machine hours refer to how many hours a particular machine was used in factory production activities. Similar to the labor time cards, each machine in the factory has a log which includes information on how long it worked on a particular product/job. In a factory where machines are heavily relied upon, it would be appropriate to use machine hours as a cost allocation base. As a result, the more machine hours it takes to complete a job, the more manufacturing overhead costs will be allocated to it. The less machine hours used by a job, the less manufacturing overhead will be allocated to it.

In such a case, the predetermined overhead rate formula would be:

$$\text{Predetermined Overhead Rate} = \frac{\text{Total Estimated Manufacturing Costs for the Period}}{\text{Total Estimated Machine Hours for the Period}}$$

If a company had estimated total manufacturing costs for the year to be \$5,000,000 and the total machine hours for the year to be 250,000, then the predetermined overhead rate would be:

$$\text{Predetermined Overhead Rate} = \frac{\$5,000,000}{250,000 \text{ Machine Hours}}$$

$$= \$20/\text{Machine Hour}$$

The above amount indicates that \$20 of overhead should be allocated for each machine hour used. To determine the amount of overhead to allocate to a specific job, the company would multiply the number of machine hours by the predetermined overhead rate. For example, if a job consumed 27 machine hours, the amount of overhead allocated to the job would be:

$$\text{Amount of Overhead Allocated} = \text{Number of Machine Hours} \times \text{Predetermined Overhead Rate}$$

$$= 27 \text{ Machine Hours} \times \$20/\text{Machine Hour}$$

$$= \$540$$

Therefore, \$540 of overhead costs should be allocated to the job.

Let us return to Pine Furniture Manufacturer and the allocation of $4,000 of manufacturing overhead costs to Job ID #312. The journal entry to record the allocation of manufacturing overhead costs to Job ID #312 on March 21 is shown in figure 3.10.

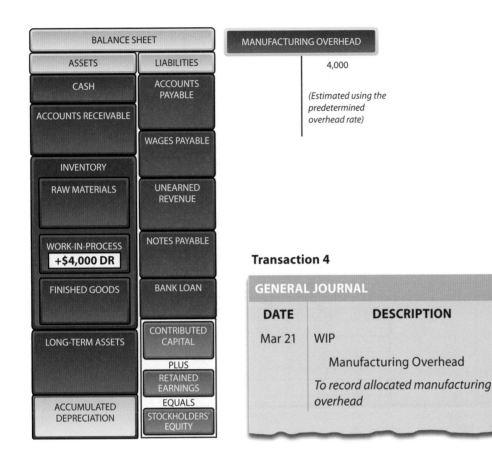

Transaction 4

GENERAL JOURNAL

DATE	DESCRIPTION	DR	CR
Mar 21	WIP	4,000	
	Manufacturing Overhead		4,000
	To record allocated manufacturing overhead		

FIGURE 3.10

A CLOSER LOOK

Many organizations will accumulate manufacturing overhead costs in departmental cost pools. In those organizations, each department will allocate its overhead costs to jobs using a departmental rate rather than using a plant-wide rate for the entire factory. Organizations use departmental rather than plant-wide rates when they believe the result will provide more accurate product costing. Departmental rates are particularly useful when different jobs place different demands on different departments.

Pine Furniture Manufacturer has completed building the customized furniture and has tracked direct materials, direct labor and manufacturing overhead costs related to the job. A summary of the costs for Job ID #312 is provided in figure 3.11.

Job Card		
Pine Furniture Manufacturer Inc.		

Job ID: 312

Client Name: aLogic Inc.

Job Description: Build customized furniture

Direct Materials		
Date	Material Requisition Numbers	Amount
	#456	$1,000
		Total Direct Materials: $1,000

Direct Labor		
Date	Time Card Numbers	Amount
	#75, #76 ($15/hr x 40 hours)	$600
		Total Direct Labor: $600

Manufacturing Overhead		
Date	Rate	Amount
	$100/DLH x 40 direct labor hours	$4,000
		Total Manufacturing Overhead: $4,000

Summary of Job Costs	
Total Direct Materials:	$1,000
Total Direct Labor:	$600
Total Manufacturing Overhead:	$4,000
Total Job Cost:	**$5,600**

FIGURE 3.11

The total cost for Job ID #312 amounts to $5,600. Refer back to figure 3.5 for the $1,000 of direct materials calculations, figure 3.7 for the $600 of direct labor calculations and figure 3.10 for the $4,000 of manufacturing overhead calculations.

Now that the job has been completed, Pine Furniture Manufacturer will move it from WIP to finished goods inventory. The journal entry to move the WIP costs to finished goods inventory on March 26 is illustrated in figure 3.12.

INVENTORY

RAW MATERIALS

WORK-IN-PROCESS
−$5,600 CR

FINISHED GOODS
+$5,600 DR

Transaction 5

GENERAL JOURNAL			
DATE	**DESCRIPTION**	**DR**	**CR**
Mar 26	Finished Goods	5,600	
	WIP		5,600
	To transfer WIP to FG		

FIGURE 3.12

On March 27, Pine Furniture Manufacturer delivers the furniture to aLogic Inc. and records the sale of $20,000 on account. Sales increase (credit) and accounts receiveable also increase (debit). Since inventory is sold, the cost of inventory is expensed through an increase (debit) in COGS and a decrease (credit) in inventory. The journal entry is shown in figure 3.13.

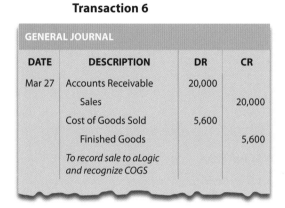

Transaction 6

DATE	DESCRIPTION	DR	CR
Mar 27	Accounts Receivable	20,000	
	Sales		20,000
	Cost of Goods Sold	5,600	
	Finished Goods		5,600
	To record sale to aLogic and recognize COGS		

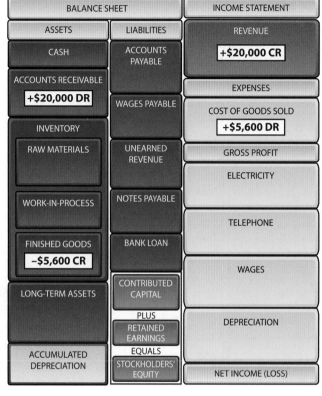

WORTH REPEATING...

In order to comply with the matching principle, COGS must be debited when a sale is made.

FIGURE 3.13

Actual Manufacturing Overhead Costs

During the year, Pine Furniture Manufacturer records the *actual* manufacturing overhead costs into its financial reporting system. In the transactions above, actual manufacturing overhead costs were recorded on the debit side of the manufacturing overhead account. Then, the manufacturing overhead account was credited to allocate some overhead into work-in-process. Note that the process of recording *actual* manufacturing overhead costs (on the debit side of the manufacturing overhead account) is entirely different from the process of recording *allocated* manufacturing overhead costs to the WIP account.

MANUFACTURING OVERHEAD

Record *Actual* Overhead Costs | Record *Allocated* Overhead Costs

During the month, other manufacturing overhead costs were also incurred. These include depreciation of the factory equipment and electricity expense. The entries to record these transactions can be found in figure 3.14. Notice that the journal entries to record these overhead expenses are slightly different from the journal entries for a service company. At the end of the month, depreciation is recorded by increasing (debiting) manufacting overhead and increasing (crediting) accumulated depreciation. This represents the capitalization of depreciation manufacturing overhead.

Similarly, to record electricity expenses paid on account, Pine Furniture Manufacturer will increase (debit) manufacturing overhead and increase (credit) accounts payable by the amount owing for electricity expenses. This capitalizes electricity expenses into the overhead account.

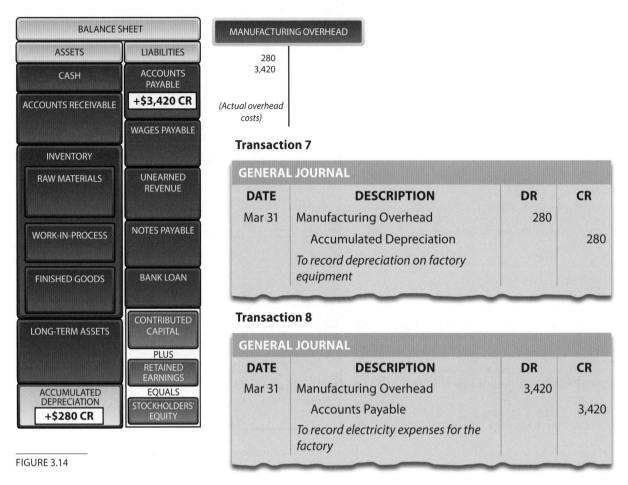

FIGURE 3.14

Recall that the credit side of the manufacturing overhead account includes *estimated* costs that have been allocated to inventory using a predetermined overhead rate; and the debit side of the manufacturing overhead account contains *actual* costs experienced by Pine Furniture Manufacturer during the course of the month. It includes costs of indirect materials, indirect labor and other indirect costs related to production, such as depreciation and electricity expenses. Also note that actual manufacturing overhead costs are not charged to the individual jobs, which means these costs will not appear in the job cards or the work-in-process account. Only the allocated manufacturing overhead costs, based on the predetermined overhead rate, will be included in the job cards and work-in-process account.

At this point, let us take a step back and review what has been accomplished so far. Pine Furniture Manufacturer has:

- Purchased raw materials (Transaction #1)
- Applied direct and indirect material costs to Job ID #312 (Transaction #2)
- Applied direct and indirect labor costs to Job ID #312 (Transaction #3)
- Allocated manufacturing overhead costs to Job ID #312 (Transaction #4)

- Transferred the furniture from WIP to Finished Goods (Transaction #5)
- Sold the furniture to aLogic Inc. and expensed the inventory through COGS (Transaction #6)
- Included the actual costs of depreciation and electricity expenses in the manufacturing overhead account (Transactions #7, #8)

Summary of Job-Order Costing Transactions

Following is a summary of transactions 1 to 8.

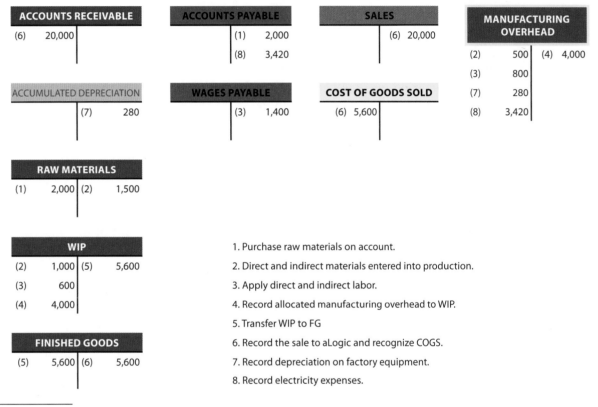

FIGURE 3.15

The raw materials account includes amounts related to the purchase of raw materials (transaction 1) and the subsequent removal of these materials into the WIP account for production (transaction 2). The WIP account includes costs related to direct labor (transaction 3) and an estimate of the amount of manufacturing overhead consumed by Job ID #312 (transaction 4). The finished goods account includes the total cost of producing Job ID #312 (transaction 5). Once the furniture made for aLogic Inc. is sold, revenue is recognized and the cost of the job is removed from finished goods inventory (transaction 6) and expensed through cost of goods sold on the income statement. Actual depreciation and electricity expenses are recorded into the manufacturing overhead account (transactions 7 and 8)

A quick summary of the manufacturing overhead account balance is provided in figure 3.16.

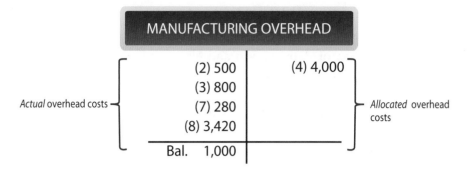

The bracketed numbers in the above figure indicate which transaction (from figure 3.15) the amount relates to.

FIGURE 3.16

The *allocated* manufacturing overhead cost is on the right (credit) side of the manufacturing overhead account. The *actual* manufacturing overhead costs are on the left (debit) side of the manufacturing overhead account. The actual costs ($500 + $800 + $280 + $3,420 = $5,000) are $1,000 more than the allocated amount ($4,000). As shown in figure 3.16, this results in a debit balance of $1,000 in the manufacturing overhead account.

Recall that since the process of recording *actual* manufacturing overhead costs is entirely different from the process of allocating *estimated* manufacturing overhead costs, it is very likely that at the end of the period there will be a difference between the *actual* and *allocated* amount of manufacturing overhead costs.

The estimated allocated manufacturing overhead costs were calculated based on the predetermined overhead rate. The predetermined overhead rate was calculated based on the estimated total manufacturing overhead costs and the estimated total direct labor hours. If these estimates are different from the actual manufacturing overhead costs or the actual direct labor hours, a difference between actual manufacturing overhead costs and allocated manufacturing overhead costs occurs. For simplicity, only the costs involved with working on one job (Job ID #312) are considered. In reality, a company will work on multiple projects during an accounting period.

For example, assume Pine Furniture Manufacturer has received another special order. This time it is from Argon Limited. Since this request is unique and different from Job ID #312, Pine Furniture Manufacturer decided to assign this project as Job ID #410. Just like aLogic's project, Job ID#410 will have its own job card.

All the direct materials and direct labor costs incurred in producing Job ID#410 will be shown in the job card. Pine Furniture Manufacturer indicated that Job ID #410 required 20 labor hours. The estimated manufacturing overhead costs will be allocated based on the predetermined overhead rate. Using the predetermined overhead of $100/DLH (which was calculated previously), Job ID #410 will have $2,000 of allocated manufacturing overhead. Note that the manufacturing overhead account will now include both Job ID #312 and Job ID #410's allocated manufacturing overhead. By the end of the period, a total of $6,000 ($4,000 for Job ID #312 + $2,000 for Job ID #410) will be transferred from the manufacturing overhead account to the WIP account. The following diagram shows how the manufacturing overhead account will transfer the allocated manufacturing overhead costs to the WIP account.

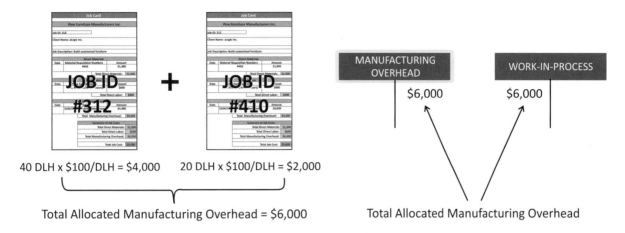

40 DLH x $100/DLH = $4,000   20 DLH x $100/DLH = $2,000

Total Allocated Manufacturing Overhead = $6,000

Total Allocated Manufacturing Overhead

Under-Allocated and Over-Allocated Manufacturing Overhead

How is the difference between actual and estimated overhead treated?

Let us return to the scenario where Pine Furniture Manufacturer only has one job (i.e. Job ID #312). In this case, the company has incurred more overhead costs ($5,000) than they had allocated ($4,000). This means that Pine Furniture Manufacturer did not allocate enough overhead costs to the WIP account. Pine Furniture Manufacturer has **under-allocated** overhead, and there is a difference between the costs actually incurred and the costs allocated to inventory.

If they had estimated more overhead costs than they had actually incurred, then they would have **over-allocated** overhead costs.

Since the manufacturing overhead account is a temporary account, the difference between the allocated and actual costs needs to be cleared at the end of every accounting period. Recall that a difference between actual and allocated overhead costs implies that inventory costs on the income statement are either over or under-stated.

Two methods can be used to resolve this difference: the **cost of goods sold method** and the **proration method**. The cost of goods sold method writes-off the difference between actual and estimated overhead costs to the cost of goods sold account. On the other hand, the proration method applies proportionate amounts of the difference to WIP, finished goods and cost of goods sold.

In most cases, the results of the two methods are not significantly different from each other. In fact, the cost of goods sold method is commonly used unless the amount to be adjusted is material. The cost of goods sold method will be demonstrated in this chapter, and the proration method will be analyzed in the appendix.

Cost of Goods Sold Method

In the cost of goods sold method, the under- or over-allocated overhead costs are simply expensed through the cost of goods sold account. Since Pine Furniture Manufacturer had under-allocated their manufacturing overhead costs, they would have to increase (debit) cost of goods sold and decrease (credit) manufacturing overhead in order to clear the balance. This would transfer the under-allocated amount to cost of goods sold. This allows the company to properly measure its gross profit for the reporting period. The journal entry is shown in figure 3.17.

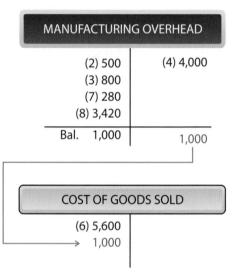

GENERAL JOURNAL			
DATE	**DESCRIPTION**	**DR**	**CR**
Mar 31	Cost of Goods Sold	1,000	
	Manufacturing Overhead		1,000
	To close under-allocated manufacturing overhead		

FIGURE 3.17

MANUFACTURING OVERHEAD

(2) 500	(4) 4,000
(3) 800	
(7) 280	
(8) 3,420	
Bal. 1,000	1,000

COST OF GOODS SOLD

(6) 5,600
1,000

By crediting the manufacturing overhead account by $1,000, the manufacturing overhead account will be left with a zero balance, and the cost of goods sold account will increase from $5,600 to $6,600. This shows that actual manufacturing costs incurred by Pine Furniture Manufacturer are eventually expensed on the income statement. If the transaction had not been recorded, cost of goods sold would have been understated and gross profit would have been overstated.

If, instead, Pine Furniture Manufacturer had *over-allocated* manufacturing overhead costs, then they would debit the manufacturing overhead account and credit the cost of goods sold account. Suppose manufacturing overhead was over-allocated by $300. A sample journal entry is shown below:

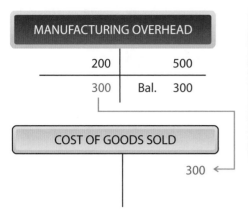

GENERAL JOURNAL			
DATE	**DESCRIPTION**	**DR**	**CR**
Mar 31	Manufacturing Overhead	300	
	Cost of Goods Sold		300
	To close over-allocated manufacturing overhead		

FIGURE 3.18

Note that with multiple jobs, the difference between the actual overhead and total allocated manufacturing overhead are written off the same way. The over or under-allocated amount can be written off using the cost of goods sold and proration methods.

Ethical Considerations

The valuation of inventory is vulnerable to significant manipulation. As stated previously in this chapter, a major component of the cost of manufactured inventory is direct labor, which is monitored through the use of time cards. Suppose that a plant manager of a manufacturer has a friend who works as an assembly line worker in the same factory. The friend has a history of missing days at work, and now is absent again. This latest absence has now surpassed the number of paid absent days the company policy allows, meaning the friend will not be paid for this missed day. The manager decides to punch the time card on behalf of his friend as a favor, thereby paying the employee while absent.

If this type of behavior is repeated many times, the implications can be far reaching. Managerial accountants may use the time cards to track the amount direct labor costs in producing a particular product. More direct labor costs will increase the cost of goods and reduce operating income. Also, this type of behavior could affect other employees whose bonuses are derived from profits, and might even affect the company's ability to borrow money. In short, this behavior is unethical.

If the accountant is aware of the situation and decides to ignore it, the accountant would be acting contrary to the standard of integrity in the *Statement of Ethical Professional Practice* (see chapter 1), which states that they must abstain from engaging in or supporting any activity that might discredit the profession. The plant manager is also likely acting contrary to the businesses own code of ethics.

There are several other possible ethical issues in the area of employee compensation. For example, suppose a hiring manager offers her niece a job for a wage of $15.00 per hour. However, other employees in the same job position as the manager's niece and with more experience are earning only $13.00 per hour. Overpaying for labor as a favor might not be illegal but is certainly unethical.

IN THE REAL WORLD

 Because of commitments in labor contracts, organizations often treat the wages paid to factory workers as fixed costs. The result is that many organizations only recognize materials costs as variable manufacturing costs.

In Summary

- **Job-order costing** is used when a product or service is provided that is customized to meet the needs of a particular customer.

- **Process costing** is used when the products or services provided cannot be distinguished from one another.

- **Subsidiary ledgers** are used to record detailed information regarding the balances in the general ledger accounts.

- The raw materials account is used to accumulate costs related to purchases of raw materials for production.

- The work-in-process (WIP) account is used to accumulate costs related to jobs or products that are being assembled or produced.

- The finished goods (FG) account is used to accumulate costs of goods or services that have been completed and are ready for sale.

- The cost of goods sold account is used to comply with the matching principle. Finished goods inventory is expensed through the COGS account when they are sold to customers.

- In job-order costing, a job card is used to accumulate costs.

- A **materials requisition form** is used to request materials to be transferred from the raw materials inventory to WIP.

- The **predetermined overhead rate** is used to allocate manufacturing overhead costs to particular jobs.

- The predetermined overhead rate is the ratio of total estimated manufacturing overhead costs to total estimated units of the cost allocation base.

- A **cost allocation base** is used to allocate overhead costs to products or services.

- In most manufacturing companies, either direct labor hours or machine hours are used as cost allocation bases.

- *Actual* manufacturing overhead costs are recorded on the debit side of the manufacturing overhead account.

- *Allocated* manufacturing overhead costs are recorded on the credit side of the manufacturing overhead account.

- At the end of the period, if the debit amounts recorded in the manufacturing overhead account exceed the credit amounts, then overhead has been under-allocated.

- At the end of the period, if the debit amounts recorded in the manufacturing overhead account are less than the credit amounts, then overhead has been over-allocated.

➪ There are two methods to account for under or over-allocated overhead:

   ✦ Cost of Goods Sold Method: write off the difference directly to cost of goods sold.

   ✦ Proration Method: prorate the difference to WIP, FG and COGS.

➪ Either method of accounting for under or over-allocated overhead can be used. However, most companies use the cost of goods sold method because it is simpler and the result does not significantly differ from the proration method.

Review Exercise

Gloricon Company manufactures chandeliers. Two of the company's largest clients requested customized chandeliers. These two requests were labeled as Job ID #808 and Job ID #910. Select information regarding the two jobs is provided below:

	Job ID #808	Job ID #910
Direct Materials Used	$200,000	$160,000
Direct Labor Required	$220,000	$230,000
Direct Labor Hours	11,000	12,500

The company allocated overhead cost to the jobs on the basis of direct labor hours worked. For the current year, the company estimated that it would require 16,000 direct labor hours and incur $400,000 of manufacturing overhead.

The following transactions were recorded for the year:

- Purchased $500,000 of raw materials on account.
- Ninety percent of raw materials purchased were put into production. These raw materials include $360,000 of direct materials and $90,000 of indirect materials.
- The company incurred $450,000 on direct labor and $205,000 on indirect labor.
- During the period, the company has also incurred the following factory costs: $95,000 on utilities, $25,000 on supplies and $94,500 on machine rental.
- The company recognized $70,000 in depreciation on factory equipment.
- $500,000 of Job ID #808 and $705,000 of Job ID #910 were completed by the end of the period.
- The chandeliers (Job ID #808 and Job ID #910) were sold on account for $1,900,000. The cost to manufacture these products was $1,035,000 ($435,000 for Job ID #808 and $600,000 for Job ID #910)

Required:

1. Calculate the total amount of manufacturing costs recorded in #808 and #910 job cards.
2. Based on the above information, prepare all the necessary journal entries.
3. Determine whether the manufacturing overhead has been over or under-allocated.
4. Prepare a journal entry to close any balance in the manufacturing overhead account to cost of goods sold.

Review Exercise – Answer

Part 1

$$\text{Predetermined Overhead Rate} = \frac{\text{Estimated Manufacturing Overhead}}{\text{Estimated Direct Labor Hours}} = \frac{\$400,000}{16,000} = \$25 \text{ per DLH}$$

	Job ID #808	Job ID #910
Direct Materials Used	$200,000	$160,000
Direct Labor Required	$220,000	$230,000
Allocated Manufacturing Overhead	$275,000*	$312,500**
Total Manufacturing Costs	$695,000	$702,500

*$25 × 11,000
** $25 × 12,500

Part 2

Total Allocated Manufacturing Overhead = (11,000 + 12,500) × $25 = $587,500

DATE	DESCRIPTION	DR	CR
	Raw Materials	500,000	
	Accounts Payable		500,000
	To record purchase of raw materials on account		
	WIP	360,000	
	Manufacturing Overhead	90,000	
	Raw Materials		$450,000
	Enter direct and indirect materials into production		
	WIP	450,000	
	Manufacturing Overhead	205,000	
	Wages Payable		655,000
	To apply direct and indirect labor		
	Manufacturing Overhead	214,500	
	Accounts Payable		214,500
	To record factory costs		
	Manufacturing Overhead	70,000	
	Accumulated Depreciation		70,000
	To record depreciation on factory equipment		

DATE	DESCRIPTION	DR	CR
	WIP	587,500	
	Manufacturing Overhead		587,500
	To record allocated manufacturing overhead		
	Finished Goods Inventory	1,205,000	
	WIP		1,205,000
	To transfer WIP to finished goods inventory		
	Accounts Receivable	1,900,000	
	Sales Revenue		$1,900,000
	To record sales revenue		
	Cost of Goods Sold	1,035,000	
	Finished Goods Inventory		1,035,000
	To record cost of goods sold		

Part 3

Actual Manufacturing Overhead = $90,000 + $205,000 + $214,500 + $70,000 = $579,500

Total Allocated Manufacturing Overhead = (11,000 + 12,500) × $25 = $587,500

Since actual manufacturing overhead is less than allocated manufacturing overhead, manufacturing overhead has been over-allocated by $8,000 ($587,500 - $579,500).

Part 4

DATE	DESCRIPTION	DR	CR
	Manufacturing Overhead	8,000	
	Cost of Goods Sold		8,000
	To close over-allocated overhead to cost of goods sold		

Appendix 3A: Manufacturing Overhead Control and Manufacturing Overhead Allocated Accounts

In chapter 3, we discussed the manufacturing overhead clearing account and how it is used to record *actual* manufacturing overhead costs as well as *allocated* manufacturing overhead costs. However, in reality, many companies choose to record actual overhead costs and allocated overhead costs in separate accounts. These companies record allocated overhead costs in a **manufacturing overhead allocated** account, and record actual overhead costs in a **manufacturing overhead control** account. Note that the same principles regarding manufacturing overhead costs apply when using these two accounts.

This appendix will show you how to track costs in the accounting system using these two accounts. The furniture example (Job ID #312) from chapter 3 will be used to demonstrate this process.

Recording Allocated Manufacturing Overhead Costs

Once the job is complete, Pine Furniture Manufacturer will multiply the predetermined overhead rate by the number of direct labor hours to estimate allocated manufacturing overhead costs. As shown in chapter 3, this amounted to $4,000 ($100/DLH × 40 hours). The journal entry to record this is shown below in figure 3A.1:

GENERAL JOURNAL

DATE	DESCRIPTION	DR	CR
Mar 21	WIP	4,000	
	Manufacturing Overhead Allocated		4,000
	To allocate manufacturing overhead		

FIGURE 3A.1

Notice that the manufacturing overhead allocated is decreased (credited) and WIP is increased (debited) when recording *allocated* manufacturing overhead costs.

Recording Actual Manufacturing Overhead Costs

Throughout the month, Pine Furniture Manufacturer records *actual* manufacturing overhead costs into its financial reporting system as they are incurred. Actual manufacturing overhead costs are recorded in the manufacturing overhead control account. This account is different from the manufacturing overhead allocated account used above.

Following are examples of transactions that Pine Furniture Manufacturer will record during the month in its manufacturing overhead control account.

In addition to the $1,000 direct materials being entered into production, Pine Furniture Manufacturer also uses $500 indirect materials from the raw materials inventory. Note that indirect material costs are part of the manufacturing overhead, which means they are added to the manufacturing overhead control account. A journal entry is made to decrease (credit) raw materials and increase (debit) manufacturing overhead control, as shown below in figure 3A.2.

GENERAL JOURNAL			
DATE	**DESCRIPTION**	**DR**	**CR**
Mar 13	WIP	1,000	
	Manufacturing Overhead Control	500	
	Raw Materials		1,500
	To enter direct and indirect materials into production		

FIGURE 3A.2

Pine Furniture Manufacturer also includes indirect labor costs in the manufacturing overhead control account. Similar to indirect materials, indirect labor costs are part of the manufacturing overhead and are included in the manufacturing overhead control account. The entry to record direct labor of $600 and indirect labor of $800 is shown in figure 3A.3.

GENERAL JOURNAL			
DATE	**DESCRIPTION**	**DR**	**CR**
Mar 19	WIP	600	
	Manufacturing Overhead Control	800	
	Wages Payable		1,400
	To apply direct and indirect labor		

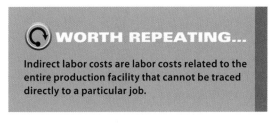

WORTH REPEATING...

Indirect labor costs are labor costs related to the entire production facility that cannot be traced directly to a particular job.

FIGURE 3A.3

Other costs such as depreciation of factory equipment and electricity expenses are also part of the manufacturing overhead, because they cannot be easily traced to a particular job. Therefore, Pine Furniture Manufacturer needs to include these costs in the manufacturing overhead control account as they incur.

Normally, the entries to record manufacturing overhead costs occur throughout the month. For simplicity, it is assumed that these transactions occur at the end of the period, March 31.

The entry to capitalize depreciation on factory equipment into the manufacturing overhead control account can be found in figure 3A.4.

GENERAL JOURNAL			
DATE	**DESCRIPTION**	**DR**	**CR**
Mar 31	Manufacturing Overhead Control	280	
	Accumulated Depreciation		280
	To record depreciation on factory equipment		

FIGURE 3A.4

The entry to capitalize factory electricity expenses into the manufacturing overhead control account can be found in figure 3A.5.

GENERAL JOURNAL			
DATE	**DESCRIPTION**	**DR**	**CR**
Mar 31	Manufacturing Overhead Control	3,420	
	Accounts Payable		3,420
	To record electricity expenses for the factory		

FIGURE 3A.5

Here is a quick summary of the manufacturing overhead control and manufacturing overhead allocated account balances:

MANUFACTURING OVERHEAD CONTROL		MANUFACTURING OVERHEAD ALLOCATED	
500			4,000
800			
280			
3,420			
Bal. 5,000			Bal. 4,000

FIGURE 3A.6

The difference between the manufacturing overhead control account ($5,000) and the manufacturing overhead allocated account ($4,000) is $1,000. The process of recording *actual* manufacturing overhead costs (using the manufacturing overhead control account) is entirely separate from the process of allocating *estimated* manufacturing overhead costs (using the manufacturing overhead allocated account).

Remember that the allocation of manufacturing overhead costs is based on the predetermined overhead rate. The predetermined overhead rate is based on total estimated manufacturing overhead costs and total estimated direct labor hours. If these estimates are different from the actual manufacturing overhead costs or the actual direct labor hours, then there will be a difference between actual and allocated manufacturing overhead costs.

Recall that the manufacturing overhead account is a temporary account. The same applies to the manufacturing overhead control and manufacturing overhead allocated account. Just as before, a difference between these two accounts indicate that inventory has not been accurately costed and therefore, the difference will have to be resolved.

In this particular case, since Pine Furniture Manufacturer has incurred more overhead costs ($5,000) than they have allocated ($4,000), they have **under-allocated** overhead. This means that during the month, Pine Furniture Manufacturer did not allocate enough overhead costs to WIP. On the other hand, if Pine Furniture Manufacturer had allocated more overhead costs than they had incurred, then they would have **over-allocated** overhead costs.

Following are two methods of accounting for under-allocated and over-allocated overhead when using the manufacturing overhead allocated and manufacturing overhead control accounts.

Cost of Goods Sold Method

In this method, the under or over-allocated overhead costs are simply expensed through the cost of goods sold account. The manufacturing overhead allocated account and the manufacturing overhead control account are cleared.

Since Pine Furniture Manufacturer had under-allocated their manufacturing overhead costs, they would record the entry shown in figure 3A.7.

GENERAL JOURNAL			
DATE	**DESCRIPTION**	**DR**	**CR**
Mar 31	Cost of Goods Sold	1,000	
	Manufacturing Overhead Allocated	4,000	
	Manufacturing Overhead Control		5,000
	To close under-allocated manufacturing overhead		

FIGURE 3A.7

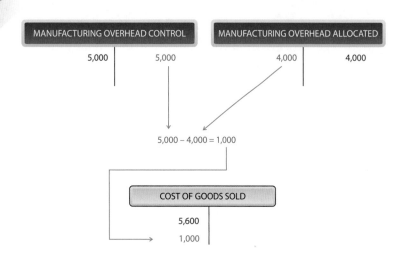

Since the manufacturing overhead allocated account has a credit balance ($4,000 CR), Pine Furniture Manufacturer will need to debit it to clear the account; and since the manufacturing overhead control account has a debit balance ($5,000 DR), Pine Furniture Manufacturer will need to credit it to clear the account. The difference is expensed through the cost of goods sold account.

FIGURE 3A.8

Suppose Pine Furniture Manufacturer had over-allocated manufacturing overhead costs instead. They would still debit the manufacturing overhead allocated account and credit the manufacturing overhead control account but would now have to credit cost of goods sold.

A sample journal entry can be seen in figure 3A.9.

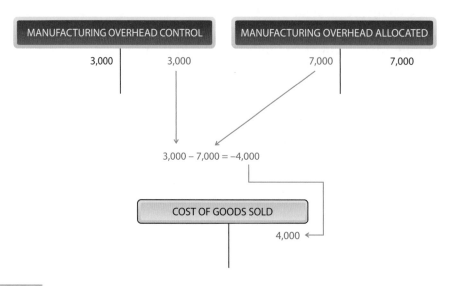

GENERAL JOURNAL			
DATE	DESCRIPTION	DR	CR
Mar 31	Manufacturing Overhead Allocated	7,000	
	Manufacturing Overhead Control		3,000
	Cost of Goods Sold		4,000
	To close over-allocated manufacturing overhead		

FIGURE 3A.9

Notice the difference between under-allocated overhead and over-allocated overhead. When overhead is under-allocated (estimated overhead costs are less than actual overhead costs), the cost of goods sold account is increased (debited). During the month, Pine Furniture Manufacturer's estimate of the cost of inventory was less than the actual costs. Therefore, the cost of inventory was understated. To reconcile this difference, cost of goods sold is increased.

When overhead is over-allocated (estimated overhead costs are greater than actual overhead costs), the cost of goods sold account is decreased (credited). During the month, if Pine Furniture Manufacturer allocated more overhead costs than were actually incurred, the cost of inventory would be overstated. To reconcile the difference between estimated and actual overhead costs, the cost of goods sold account would be decreased.

Proration Method

Another method of accounting for under- or over-allocated overhead involves allocating the difference between the manufacturing overhead control account and the manufacturing overhead allocated account to WIP, finished goods and cost of goods sold. Four steps have to be completed to prorate the under- or over-allocated overhead to WIP, FG and COGS.

Suppose that at the end of the year, Pine Furniture Manufacturer had the following balances in their records and have under-allocated their overhead by $1,000.

	End of Year Balance
WIP	$10,000
FG	20,000
COGS	20,000
	$50,000

At the end of the year, the balance in the WIP account amounts to $10,000. Finished goods inventory amounts to $20,000 and cost of goods sold for the year amounts to $20,000.

FIGURE 3A.10

Step 1: Determine how much overhead was allocated to each account.

	End of Year Balance	Allocated Manufacturing Overhead in Each Account
WIP	$10,000	$1,000
FG	20,000	1,000
COGS	20,000	2,000
Total	$50,000	$4,000

The company can determine this by reviewing their accounting records throughout the year. Assume the information presented in figure 3A.11.

FIGURE 3A.11

Step 2: Calculate the allocated manufacturing overhead for each account as a percentage of total allocated manufacturing overhead.

	(a) End of Year Balance	(b) Allocated Manufacturing Overhead in Each Account	(c) Percentage of Allocated Manufacturing Overhead in Each Account (b) ÷ $4,000
WIP	$10,000	$1,000	25%
FG	20,000	1,000	25%
COGS	20,000	2,000	50%
	$50,000	$4,000	100%

FIGURE 3A.12

Step 3: Use percentages to calculate the amount of under-allocated manufacturing overhead for each account.

	(a) End of Year Balance	(b) Allocated Manufacturing Overhead in Each Account	(c) Percentage of Allocated Manufacturing Overhead in Each Account. (b) ÷ $4,000	(d) Proration of Allocated Manufacturing Overhead (c) × $1,000
WIP	$10,000	$1,000	25%	$250
FG	20,000	1,000	25%	250
COGS	20,000	2,000	50%	500
	$50,000	$4,000	100%	$1,000

The percentages from step two are multiplied with the under-allocated amount of manufacturing overhead ($1,000) to determine how much of the under-allocation should be added to each of the accounts (WIP, FG, COGS).

FIGURE 3A.13

Step 4: Add prorated amounts back to ending balances of each account.

The prorated amounts are added back to the ending balances in column (a).

	(a) End of Year Balance	(b) Allocated Manufacturing Overhead in Each Account	(c) Percentage of Allocated Manufacturing Overhead in Each Account. (b) ÷ $4,000	(d) Proration of Allocated Manufacturing Overhead (c) × $1,000	(e) Account Balances Including the Prorated Amount (a) + (d)
WIP	$10,000	$1,000	25%	$250	$10,250
FG	20,000	1,000	25%	250	20,250
COGS	20,000	2,000	50%	500	20,500
	$50,000	$4,000	100%	$1,000	$51,000

FIGURE 3A.14

The journal entry to account for the under-allocated overhead is:

GENERAL JOURNAL			
DATE	DESCRIPTION	DR	CR
Mar 31	Work-In-Process	250	
	Finished Goods	250	
	Cost of Goods Sold	500	
	Manufacturing Overhead Allocated	4,000	
	Manufacturing Overhead Control		5,000
	To prorate under-allocated manufacturing overhead to WIP, FG and COGS		

FIGURE 3A.15

If Pine Furniture Manufacturer had instead over-allocated manufacturing overhead costs, the prorated amounts in column (d) would still be calculated in the same way. The exception would be that the prorated amounts would be subtracted from WIP, FG and COGS to reduce the ending balances. Therefore, column (e) would be (a)-(d). As a result, the journal entry would credit WIP, FG and COGS.

Companies can use either method when accounting for under or over-allocated overhead. However, a majority of companies use the cost of goods sold method over the proration method for the following reasons:

1. The cost of goods sold method is much simpler than the proration method and thus requires less resources from accounting personnel to administer. This results in time and cost savings.
2. In most cases, the difference between the two methods is not significantly material from each other.

In Summary

↪ *Allocated* manufacturing overhead costs can also be recorded in the **manufacturing overhead allocated** account.

↪ *Actual* manufacturing overhead costs can also be recorded in the **manufacturing overhead control** account.

↪ Both the manufacturing overhead allocated account and manufacturing overhead control account are clearing accounts, which means that they have to be closed and their ending balances have to be zero at the end of an accounting period.

↪ At the end of the period, if the ending balance of the manufacturing overhead control account is *greater* than the ending balance of the manufacturing overhead allocated account, then overhead has been **under-allocated.**

↪ At the end of the period, if the ending balance of the manufacturing overhead control account is *less* than the ending balance of the manufacturing overhead allocated account, then overhead has been **over-allocated.**

↪ There are two methods to account for under- or over-allocated overhead: the cost of goods sold method and the proration method.

↪ Under the cost of goods sold method, the under- or over-allocated overhead costs are simply expensed through the cost of goods sold account, and the manufacturing overhead allocated account and the manufacturing overhead control account are cleared.

↪ If the manufacturing overhead costs are under-allocated, then the cost of goods sold account is increased. If the manufacturing overhead costs are over-allocated, then the cost of goods sold account is decreased.

↪ Under the proration method, the under- or over-allocated overhead costs are allocated to WIP, finished goods and cost of goods sold.

↪ Under the proration method:

✧ Step 1: Determine how much overhead was allocated to each account.

✧ Step 2: Calculate the allocated manufacturing overhead for each account as a percentage of total allocated manufacturing overhead.

✧ Step 3: Use the percentages from step 2 to calculate the amount of under or over-allocated manufacturing overhead for each account.

✧ Step 4: Add or subtract the prorated amounts back to ending balances of each account.

↪ Either method of accounting for under- or over-allocated overhead can be used. However, most companies use the cost of goods sold approach because it is simpler to apply and the result usually does not significantly differ from the proration approach.

Review Exercise

PTR Company is a small equipment shop that uses the job costing system. The company allocates manufacturing overhead costs based on the number of machine hours worked. For each month, the company estimated that it would require 1,600 machine hours and incur $40,000 of manufacturing overhead costs. Manufacturing overhead is recorded using the manufacturing overhead allocated and control accounts.

The company provides the following information for the month of June:

- Beginning WIP account (June 1) was $2,00
- Beginning finished goods account (June 1) was $5,000
- No purchases were made
- The company incurred $55,000 on direct materials and $25,000 on indirect materials
- During the period, the company incurred direct and indirect labor costs of $30,000 and $20,000 respectively
- The company incurred $12,000 on other manufacturing overhead
- Transferred $134,000 from WIP to finished goods
- Sold finished goods with a cost of $120,000 for $200,000 on account
- Actual number of machine hours used was 2,000

After reviewing June's accounting records, the company determined that $1,000, $7,000 and $42,000 of manufacturing overhead was allocated to WIP, Finished Goods and COGS respectively.

Required:

1. Based on the above information, prepare all the necessary journal entries and determine if manufacturing overhead is over or under-allocated.
2. Using the proration method on the ending balances, allocate any over or under allocated overhead to WIP, Finished Goods and COGS.
3. Determine the ending balance of the WIP, Finished Goods and COGS accounts.

Review Exercise – Answer

Part 1

Predetermined overhead rate

= $40,000 ÷ 1,600 machine hours

= $25 per machine hour

Allocated manufacturing overhead

= $25 per machine hour × 2,000 machine hours

= $50,000

Actual manufacturing overhead

= Indirect materials + Indirect labor + Other MOH

= $25,000 + $20,000 + $12,000

= $57,000

Since actual manufacturing overhead is more than allocated manufacturing overhead, manufacturing overhead has been under-allocated by $7,000 ($57,000 - $50,000).

DATE	DESCRIPTION	DR	CR
	WIP	50,000	
	Manufacturing Overhead Allocated		50,000
	To record allocated manufacturing overhead		
	WIP	55,000	
	Manufacturing Overhead Control	25,000	
	Raw Materials		80,000
	To enter direct and indirect materials into production		
	WIP	30,000	
	Manufacturing Overhead Control	20,000	
	Wages Payable		50,000
	To apply direct and indirect labor		
	Manufacturing Overhead Control	12,000	
	Accounts Payable		12,000
	To record other manufacturing overhead costs		
	Finished Goods	134,000	
	WIP		134,000
	To transfer completed goods to finished goods inventory		
	Accounts Receivable	200,000	
	Sales		200,000
	Cost of Goods Sold	120,000	
	Finished Goods		120,000
	To record the sale of inventory on account		

Part 2

Ending balance of WIP

= \$2,000 + \$50,000 + \$55,000 + \$30,000 – \$134,000

=\$3,000

Ending balance of finished goods

= \$5,000 + \$134,000 – \$120,000

=\$19,000

Ending balance of cost of goods sold

=\$120,000

	(a) Ending Balance	(b) Allocated Manufacturing Overhead in Each Account	(c) Percentage of Allocated Manufacturing Overhead in Each Account (b) ÷ \$6,000	(d) Proration of Allocated Manufacturing Overhead (c) × \$7,000
WIP	\$3,000	\$1,000	2%	\$140
FG	19,000	7,000	14%	980
COGS	120,000	42,000	84%	5,880
Total	\$142,000	\$50,000	100%	\$7,000

DATE	DESCRIPTION	DR	CR
	WIP	140	
	Finished Goods	980	
	Cost of Goods Sold	5,880	
	Manufacturing Overhead Allocated	50,000	
	Manufacturing Overhead Control		57,000
	To prorate under-allocated overhead		

Part 3

	(a) Ending Balance	(b) Allocated Manufacturing Overhead in Each Account	(c) Percentage of Allocated Manufacturing Overhead in Each Account (b) ÷ \$6,000	(d) Proration of Allocated Manufacturing Overhead (c) × \$7,000	(e) Account Balances Including the Prorated Amount (a) + (d)
WIP	\$3,000	\$1,000	2%	\$140	\$3,140
FG	19,000	7,000	14%	980	19,980
COGS	120,000	42,000	84%	5,880	125,880
Total	\$142,000	\$50,000	100%	\$7,000	\$149,000

Notes

Chapter 4
PROCESS COSTING

LEARNING OUTCOMES:

❶ Describe the physical flow of units in process costing

❷ Describe components of WIP accounts

❸ Explain the concept of conversion costs

❹ Prepare journal entries for transferred units

❺ Calculate equivalent units of production

❻ Describe the effects of beginning and ending inventory balances on inventory valuation

❼ Perform inventory valuations using weighted-average cost

❽ Prepare a cost of production report

Appendix

❾ Perform inventory valuations using FIFO

❿ Understand the effects of transferred-in costs

Process Costing

In chapter 2, an overview for both job and process costing was provided. While job costing is best suited for special orders, process costing is used for similar goods manufactured in large quantities. Imagine operating a large popcorn machine at an amusement park. The machine continuously turns corn kernels, butter and salt (raw materials) into popcorn, which will then be sold in separate bags (finished goods: bags of popcorns). You would need time (labor) to put the kernels into the machines and bag the popcorn when it is produced. You will also need electricity (overhead) to operate the machine. Although the machine produces large quantities, you might be more interested in knowing how much it costs you to produce an individual bag of popcorn. If you start working at 9am, how much cost will you incur by 10am? How much finished goods will you have by 11am? Process costing will help you answer these questions not only for a popcorn machine but for certain manufacturing and service companies as well.

The previous chapter took an in-depth look at job-order costing using the example of Pine Furniture Manufacturer. Chapter 3 demonstrated how Pine Furniture Manufacturer tracked costs for one set of customized furniture. Now, assume that Pine Furniture Manufacturer receives an order to manufacture 10,000 identical chairs. In this case, it is impractical to track costs for each individual chair. Instead, it would be more efficient for managers to use process costing since all these chairs will undergo the exact same process when being produced. This chapter discusses how process costing is used to cost products.

Figure 4.1 shows the physical flow of materials in building generic chairs. Each set of raw materials (e.g. wood) goes through the following three processes to be converted into a chair:

- Process 1: Cutting department - carpenters work on the wood to cut and carve it into pieces that are ready to be assembled.
- Process 2: Assembling department - workers assemble the chairs with the use of screws and nails.
- Process 3: Painting department - laborers apply paint and perform finishing touches to the chairs. Once all three processes have been completed, the chair is considered completed and classified as finished goods inventory.

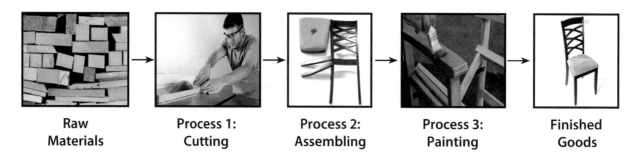

| Raw Materials | Process 1: Cutting | Process 2: Assembling | Process 3: Painting | Finished Goods |

FIGURE 4.1

As with all manufacturing companies, raw materials have to be purchased prior to production. These raw materials will be organized in the raw material sub-ledger accounts. After the raw materials are transferred to the factory, the manufacturing process begins. In process costing, costs of direct materials, direct labor and manufacturing overhead are accumulated for each process. Costs for the cutting department will be accumulated in an account named WIP-Cutting. Likewise, costs for the assembling and painting departments will be accumulated in their respective WIP accounts. This is in contrast to job-order costing where costs are accumulated for each specific job. Figure 4.2 and 4.3 illustrate the main difference between job costing and process costing. In figure 4.2, there is only one WIP account under job-order costing. All manufacturing costs (direct materials, direct labor, manufacturing overhead) related to that job are recorded into that one WIP account.

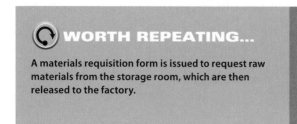

WORTH REPEATING...

A materials requisition form is issued to request raw materials from the storage room, which are then released to the factory.

Job-Order Costing

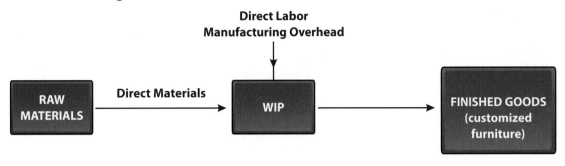

FIGURE 4.2

Figure 4.3 shows the accounts involved under process costing. Each process department (cutting, assembling and painting) has its own WIP account. Therefore, the costs are being tracked separately for each process under a separate WIP account.

Process Costing

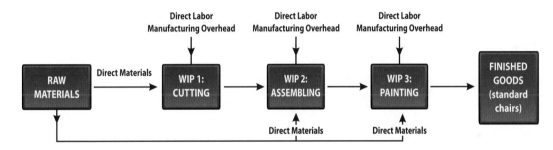

FIGURE 4.3

Figure 4.4 provides examples of the type of cost that goes into each WIP account.

	Direct Materials	Direct Labor	Manufacturing Overhead
WIP 1 - Cutting	Wood consumed when cutting chairs	Carpenters' wages	Depreciation of wood-cutting machinery
WIP 2 - Assembling	Cushions used in assembling chairs	Assemblers' wages	Rent for assembling department space
WIP 3 - Painting	Paint used on the chairs	Painters' wages	Painting supervisor's salary

FIGURE 4.4

While costs are accumulated for each process, costs also flow from one process to the next. In figure 4.3, the costs associated with the assembling process (WIP 2) include the direct materials, direct labor, and manufacturing overhead allocated to the department. As well, all the manufacturing costs from the cutting department (WIP 1) are also included in WIP 2. Notice that costs flow from WIP 1 (cutting department), to WIP 2 (assembling department) to WIP 3 (painting department) and then to finished goods inventory. Finished goods inventory only includes costs that flow from WIP 3. Once the finished goods are sold, the cost will be recorded as cost of goods sold (COGS) to match the revenue on the income statement.

In summary, each WIP account under process costing includes:

- The costs of direct materials related to the *current* process
- The costs of direct labor related to the *current* process
- The costs of manufacturing overhead allocated to the *current* process, AND
- All costs (direct material, direct labor, manufacturing overhead) from the *previous* process

From an accounting record keeping point of view, the WIP inventory will transfer from one WIP account to the other before reaching finished goods inventory. The journal entries will be illustrated in the forthcoming pages of the chapter.

IN THE REAL WORLD

In the service industry, many companies regularly spend a significant amount on labor. Fortunately, with automatic processing technology, they can reduce or possibly replace the time required to manually process customer orders. For instance, by offering automatic check-in terminals, airlines can decrease the number of check-in clerks and the amount of customers' wait time.

Determining the Cost of Inventory

In chapter 2, we briefly described how to accumulate costs using process costing. In our discussion we covered three scenarios. The first scenario (CarPainter Inc.) outlined the simplest case of process costing in which there was one process with no beginning or ending inventory. The second scenario (Tanya's Canoe Company) showed how process costing is applied when there is ending inventory and no beginning inventory. The third scenario is an example of how process costing is applied when there is both ending and beginning inventory. In that discussion, an overview of how the FIFO and weighted-average inventory valuation methods could affect inventory costs was provided. While chapter 2 covered the basic concepts behind process costing, the remaining portion of this chapter will analyze and discuss the details (e.g. journal entries) related to process costing.

It may be beneficial to review the concepts covered in chapter 2 before moving on with material in this chapter. Pay particular attention to the concept of beginning and ending inventory.

Equivalent Units of Production

It is important to learn how to account for partially completed products, since they will affect the cost of inventory. As a basic example, let us look at a surfboard manufacturing shop which shapes and paints surfboards. Assume that at the end of January, the shaping department received enough styrofoam material to make 50 surfboards for February. During February, the workers managed to fully shape 40 surfboards. These 40 surfboards will now be sent to the painting department at the end of the month. However, the remaining 10 surfboards, are still being worked on and are still part of the shaping WIP stage. As figure 4.5 shows, the shaping department did not have any surfboards in beginning inventory but had 10 surfboards in the ending inventory.

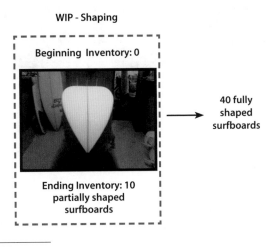

FIGURE 4.5

Suppose the shaping department incurred costs of $15,000 for the period. How does the manager determine the costs that will be allocated to each surfboard in the shaping department for the period? If 40 surfboards had been completed and 10 surfboards had not even been worked on, then total costs for the period will simply be divided by the total number of products completed ($15,000 ÷ 40). However, in this case, the 10 surfboards have been worked on. Therefore, $15,000 cannot simply be divided by 40 because part of the $15,000 applies to the 10 surfboards which have been partially completed. See figure 4.6.

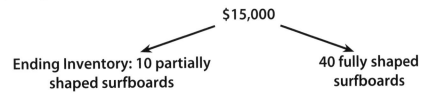

FIGURE 4.6

In order to calculate the costs belonging to the 10 surfboards (shaping department's ending inventory in February), the number of full units equivalent to the partially shaped surfboards need to be considered. Suppose each of the 10 surfboards is about half-way done (50% complete). Therefore, each partially completed surfboard can be considered to be ½ of a completed surfboard. Altogether, it can be approximated that they would be equivalent to five (½ + ½ + ½ + ½ + ½+ ½ + ½ + ½ + ½ + ½) completely shaped surfboards. See figure 4.7. This calculation is based on the concept of **equivalent units of production**. The equivalent units of production approximates the number of completed units based on the number of partially completed units and their percentage of completion.

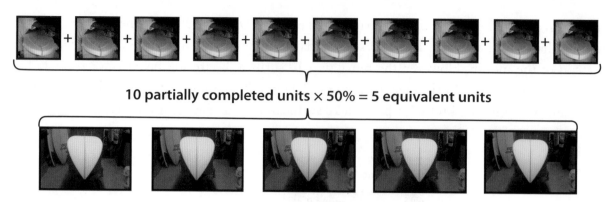

10 partially completed units × 50% = 5 equivalent units

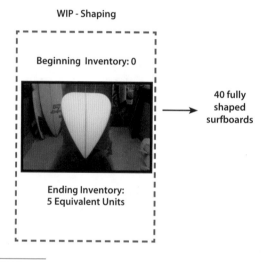

FIGURE 4.7

As another example, suppose the 10 surfboards are only ¼ shaped (25% complete). Therefore, the 10 surfboards together would represent 2.5 (¼ + ¼ + ¼ + ¼ +¼ + ¼ +¼ + ¼ +¼ + ¼) equivalent units of surfboards.

Going back to the previous scenario, since each of the 10 surfboards are 50% complete, this implies five equivalent units of production as shown in figure 4.8.

WIP - Shaping

Beginning Inventory: 0

40 fully shaped surfboards

Ending Inventory: 5 Equivalent Units

FIGURE 4.8

Total costs for the period ($15,000) is divided by 45 (40 + 5) to get the unit cost for the shaping department. Therefore, the equivalent unit cost is approximately $333.33/unit.

$$\frac{\$15,000}{40 + 5} = \$333.33/unit$$

The dollar value of the 40 shaped surfboards leaving the department during the period is $13,333 ($333.33/unit × 40 surfboards) and the dollar value of ending inventory (10 partially completed surfboards in WIP at the end of the period) is $1,667 ($333.33/unit × 5 equivalent surfboards).

One of the objectives of process costing is to determine the cost of inventory transferred to the next process and to determine the cost of ending inventory. Therefore, it is important to understand the purpose and principle behind the calculation of equivalent units.

A Simple Example of Process Costing

The simplest example of process costing involves only one process with no beginning or ending inventory. All department costs for the period belong to the finished goods produced in the period. Recall the CarPainter example from chapter 2, where CarPainter received 100 cars to be painted in the period. In that situation, the cost per unit could be found by dividing total costs incurred during the period ($30,000) by the number of finished goods (100). Therefore, each car had an average cost of $300/unit. In this very simple case, the cost of each unit is the average cost of the process.

However, in reality, this scenario rarely occurs. It is much more likely that a process has beginning inventory, ending inventory or both. The remainder of this chapter will show how to accumulate costs and update accounting records when beginning and/or ending inventory exists.

Accounting for Conversion Costs

Total manufacturing costs consist of direct materials, direct labor and manufacturing overhead. In practice, organizations often group direct labor costs and manufacturing overhead costs into a separate category called **conversion costs**. Conversion costs are important since it is what converts raw materials into finished goods. Conversion costs include all manufacturing costs except for direct materials.

Consider the following examples for the chairs manufactured by Pine Furniture Manufacturer:

Example 1: For the cutting department, conversion costs are the costs required to convert wood into cut pieces that are ready for the assembling department. In this case, some examples of conversion costs are the carpenters' wages and the depreciation of the cutting tools for the department.

Example 2: For the assembling department, conversion costs are the costs required to convert the pieces of wood into an assembled chair. Some examples are the assembly workers' wages and rental costs for the department's space.

Example 3: For the painting department, conversion costs are the costs required to paint the assembled chair and transform it into a completed product. Some examples are the wages of the painters and painting department supervisor.

Figure 4.9 shows that conversion costs in any department are made up of direct labor costs and manufacturing overhead costs.

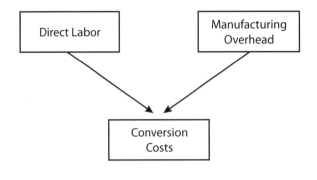

FIGURE 4.9

Determining the Cost of Goods When There is Ending WIP Inventory

Let us show how process costing principles are applied in the month of January for the first processing department at Pine Furniture Manufacturer. The cutting process is where carpenters shape, cut and carve the wood into pieces to be assembled into a chair. The materials are transferred from the raw materials inventory account to the cutting departments WIP 1 - Cutting account.

Assume that on January 1st, wood that was purchased from suppliers for $40,000 is entered into production to be worked on by the carpenters.

To record the journal entry, the WIP account related to the cutting department is increased (debited) and the raw materials account is decreased (credited). The journal entry to transfer direct materials to production is:

GENERAL JOURNAL			
DATE	**DESCRIPTION**	**DR**	**CR**
Jan 1	WIP 1 – Cutting	40,000	
	Raw Materials		40,000
	Enter direct materials into production		

The balance of the inventory account is $40,000.

FIGURE 4.10

On January 15, labor costs of $30,000 for the cutting department were incurred by Pine Furniture Manufacturer. In addition, $10,000 of manufacturing overhead was allocated to the cutting department at month-end.

To record the journal entry, the cost of labor wages in the cutting department is capitalized into WIP 1 because they form part of the inventory cost. The WIP 1 account is debited and wages payable is credited.

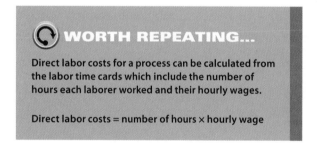

GENERAL JOURNAL			
DATE	**DESCRIPTION**	**DR**	**CR**
Jan 15	WIP 1 – Cutting	30,000	
	Wages Payable		30,000
	Add labor to WIP 1		

The balance of the inventory account is now $70,000 ($40,000 + $30,000).

WORTH REPEATING...

Direct labor costs for a process can be calculated from the labor time cards which include the number of hours each laborer worked and their hourly wages.

Direct labor costs = number of hours × hourly wage

FIGURE 4.11

Costs of manufacturing overhead allocated to the cutting department are also added to the process. Recall from the previous chapter that a variety of indirect and overhead costs were debited to the manufacturing overhead account. Then the amount of manufacturing overhead to allocate was estimated using the predetermined overhead rate and cost allocation base. Under process costing, separate overhead rates need to be calculated for each department. The journal entry is shown in figure 4.12.

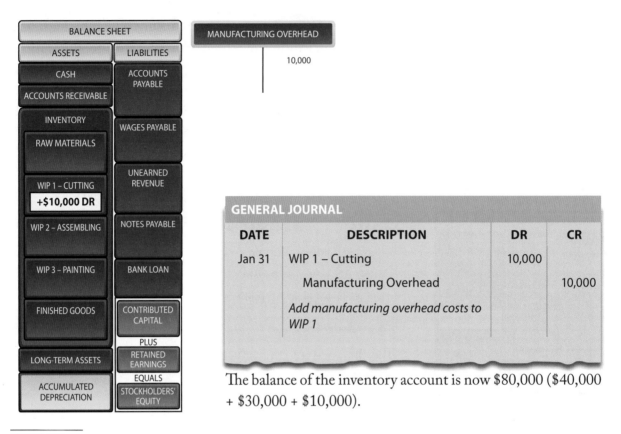

FIGURE 4.12

The balance of the inventory account is now $80,000 ($40,000 + $30,000 + $10,000).

Figure 4.13 gives a summary of the costs added to WIP 1 – Cutting department to this point. Recall that conversion costs are the sum of direct labor costs ($30,000) and manufacturing overhead costs ($10,000).

Total costs added during the month = Costs of direct materials during the month + Conversion costs added during the month

Total costs added during the month = Direct Materials + Conversion Costs

= $40,000 + ($30,000 wages + $10,000 manufacturing overhead)

= $80,000

FIGURE 4.13

The previous three journal entries show how costs are accumulated for a process during a month of operations. All costs that are associated with work done in the cutting department are added to the WIP account for the cutting department. Direct materials and conversion costs are accumulated and recorded in the accounting system in the WIP account.

However, to account for all activity in the cutting department, Pine Furniture Manufacturer has to determine how many units are completed and record the costs associated with the units transferred *out* of the department as well. In other words, the company needs to record the costs that follow the product from one department to another. Note that in this text, the terms "transferred out" and "completed" are used interchangeably when referring to units in WIP. This is because all units that are completed in a process are assumed to be transferred to the new process.

Pine Furniture Manufacturer currently does not know the number of units in ending inventory, or their cost. To determine the costs of these units, one must know the physical flow of units in a process. This will now be explained.

Physical Flow of Units

To illustrate the physical flow of units, consider the following case facts.

At the beginning of January, the cutting department at Pine Furniture Manufacturer started off without any inventory. During the month, enough direct materials to build 10,000 chairs were transferred from storage room to the cutting department. As the materials arrived, the carpenters were assigned their tasks and began working on the wood. By the end of the month the cutting department was able to complete and transfer out enough wood for 8,000 chairs to the assembling department. The wood (direct materials) for the remaining 2,000 chairs was still being worked on. Therefore, at the end of the month, the cutting department had 2,000 partially completed chairs in ending inventory.

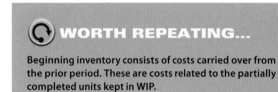

WORTH REPEATING...

Beginning inventory consists of costs carried over from the prior period. These are costs related to the partially completed units kept in WIP.

Another method to determine the physical flow of units would be to use the following formula:

# of Units in Beginning Inventory +   # of Units Completed (transferred out) +
# of Units Started During the period = # of Units in Ending Inventory

Using the same scenario, figure 4.14 shows how ending inventory can be calculated using the above formula. Since there is no beginning inventory, beginning inventory is zero. Ten thousand units were started during the month (since enough direct materials to build 10,000 chairs were transferred from storage room to the cutting department). By the end of the month, 8,000 units were completed and transferred out to the assembling department. Therefore, there are 2,000 units in the cutting department's ending inventory.

Units in Beginning Inventory + Units Started = Units Completed + Units in Ending Inventory
                                 0 + 10,000 = 8,000 + Units in Ending Inventory
                              10,000 - 8,000 = Units in Ending Inventory
                                       2,000 = Units in Ending Inventory

FIGURE 4.14

Pine Furniture Manufacturer must now determine the cost of the 8,000 units transferred out to the assembling department and of the 2,000 partially completed units remaining in inventory. Of the $80,000 total costs incurred by the cutting department in the month (see figure 4.13), a portion of those costs pertain to the 8,000 units transferred out. The remaining amount pertains to the 2,000 partially completed chairs in ending inventory. To determine these costs, Pine Furniture Manufacturer must first calculate the equivalent units of production for the month in the cutting department. Recall that equivalent units of production aid managerial accountants in determining the costs of inventory transferred out to the next department. Equivalent units also help in determining the cost of ending inventory.

Earlier in the chapter, we approximated the number of completed units based on partially-completed units. Recall that if there are 10 units which are each half-way done, this is equal to five equivalent units. The calculation was simplified because we assumed there was only one type of cost.

Now, let us make this calculation more advanced by recognizing that there are two types of costs involved – direct materials and conversion costs. Each chair that is produced in our example has both types of costs associated with it. Therefore, equivalent units for direct materials and conversion costs need to be calculated separately.

The formula to calculate equivalent units of production is as follows:

Equivalent Units of Production = # of Units × % Completion in Current Period

To calculate the equivalent units of production (EQU), Pine Furniture Manufacturer must determine how many full units the partially completed units are equivalent to. In other words, what percentage of the work has been completed for the partially completed units. EQU also has to be calculated separately for completed and ending inventory.

Calculation of Equivalent Units of Production

Step 1: Determine the equivalent units of production for completed inventory.

Eight thousand units were started and completed during the month. Since each chair is 100% completed, it will have consumed 8,000 chairs worth of both direct materials and conversion costs. Therefore, EQU for completed inventory is 8,000 for direct materials and 8,000 for conversion costs.

Step 2: Determine the equivalent units of production for ending inventory.

The cutting department supervisor indicated that the 2,000 units in ending inventory are 100% complete with respect to direct materials but only 80% complete with respect to conversion costs. Therefore, EQU with respect to direct materials is 2,000 (2,000 units × 100%). EQU with respect to conversion costs will be 1,600 (2,000 units × 80%)

Step 3: Calculate the number of total equivalent units of production for direct materials and conversion costs.

To find total EQU for direct materials, we add together the EQU for both completed and ending inventory with respect to direct materials. Likewise, we do a separate calculation for EQU with respect to conversion costs. Therefore, EQU for direct materials is **10,000** (8,000 + 2,000) and EQU for conversions costs is **9,600** (8,000 + 1,600).

Figure 4.15 summarizes the calculation of equivalent units of production for the month for the cutting department. The table shows that during the month, a total of 10,000 units have been accounted for. We see that there are 10,000 (8,000 + 2,000) equivalent units of production with respect to direct materials and that there are 9,600 (8,000 + 1,600) equivalent units of production with respect to conversion costs.

Summary of Equivalent Units for WIP 1 – Cutting			
	Physical Units	**Equivalent Units**	
		Direct Materials	**Conversion Costs**
Completed and Transferred Out (from WIP 1 to WIP 2)	8,000	8,000	8,000
Ending Inventory	2,000	2,000	1,600
Accounted For	10,000		
Total Equivalent Units		10,000	9,600

FIGURE 4.15

Note that the total equivalent units for conversion costs is less than for direct materials. This is because ending inventory is not 100% completed with respect to conversion costs. In other words, more conversion costs must be incurred in order to complete the units.

Now that the number of equivalent units of production has been calculated, it is possible for Pine Furniture Manufacturer to calculate the cost of both completed and ending inventory.

Calculation of Costs of Inventory

Step 1: Calculate the cost per equivalent unit.

In general, the formula to calculate cost per equivalent unit is as follows:

$$\text{Cost per Equivalent Unit} = \frac{\text{Costs*}}{\text{\# of Equivalent Units}}$$

*"Costs" refers to total direct material costs or total conversion costs

Recall from figure 4.13 that $40,000 was incurred for direct materials and $40,000 for conversion costs.

To calculate the cost per EQU for direct materials, Pine Furniture Manufacturer will divide total direct material costs by total direct material EQU. This gives cost per EQU for direct materials of **$4/unit** ($40,000 ÷ 10,000 EQU).

To find cost per EQU for conversion costs, Pine Furniture Manufacturer will divide total conversion costs by total conversion costs EQU. This gives cost per EQU for conversion costs of approximately **$4.17/unit** ($40,000 ÷ 9,600 EQU)

Step 2: Calculate the cost of completed units.

In general, the formula to calculate the cost of units is as follows:

Cost of Units = Cost per Equivalent Unit × # of Equivalent Units

The 8,000 equivalent units completed and transferred out are multiplied by the respective costs per EQU for direct materials and conversion costs. This means that **$65,333** (8,000 EQU × $4/EQU + 8,000 EQU × ~$4.17/EQU) of inventory was completed and transferred out to the assembling department.

Step 3: Calculate the cost of units in ending inventory.

The equivalent units in ending inventory are multiplied by the respective costs per EQU for direct materials and conversion costs. This means that **$14,667** (2,000 EQU × $4/EQU + 1,600 EQU × ~$4.17/EQU) of inventory remains in the cutting department at the end of the month.

Step 4: Ensure that all costs are accounted for.

Recall from figure 4.13 that total costs added during the month amount to $80,000. The purpose of calculating equivalent units and costs per equivalent unit was to find a way to allocate these costs between completed and ending inventory. Total costs of completed and ending inventory is **$80,000** ($65,333 + $14,667). All costs have been accounted for.

After all the costs in the cutting department have been calculated, Pine Furniture Manufacturer will then prepare a **cost production report**.

Cost of Production Report

A **cost of production report** is prepared to summarize the activity of a processing department. It will report on all costs transferred in from earlier processing departments as well as all direct material, direct labor and manufacturing overhead costs that are added during the period.

The cost of production report will have two main sections. One section deals with units and the other section deals with costs. The units section will show how many units must be accounted for, and follow up with a proof to show the flow of units through the department. The cost section is similar in that it shows the costs that must be accounted for and then follows up with proof to show the flow of costs through the department.

After collecting the data and performing the cost calculations in the above four steps, a completed cost of production report can be prepared for the cutting department as shown in figure 4.16. Each numbered item on the production report will be explained based on the detailed calculations shown earlier.

UNITS	Whole Units	Equivalent Units	
		Direct Materials	Conversion
Units charged to production			
Beginning inventory	-		
Units started	10,000		
Total Units accounted for	10,000		
Units to be assigned cost			
Units completed and transferred out	8,000	8,000	8,000
Ending inventory - 100% material, 80% CC	2,000	2,000	1,600
Total equivalent units	10,000	10,000	9,600

**Pine Furniture Manufacturer
Cutting Department
Cost of Production Report for January**

(a)

COST	Cost		
	Direct Materials	Conversion	Total Cost
Unit cost			
Beginning inventory	$ -	$ -	$ -
Costs added	40,000	40,000	80,000
Total cost to account for	$40,000	$40,000	$80,000
Total equivalent units	10,000	9,600	
Cost per equivalent unit	$4.00	$4.17	
Assign cost			
Costs transferred out	$32,000	$33,333	$65,333
Cost of ending inventory	8,000	6,667	14,667
Total cost accounted for			$80,000

(b)
(c)
(d)
(e)

FIGURE 4.16

(a) The two total figures under the Whole Units column must match. This will ensure that all units are accurately tracked as they flow through the department. The information in the top half of this report is the same information as shown in figure 4.15.

(b) To calculate the cost per equivalent unit for direct materials and conversion costs, divide the total cost to account for by the total equivalent units. This was shown in step one of calculating the cost of inventory.

(c) The costs transferred out is calculated by multiplying the cost per equivalent unit by the number of units completed. The cost of production report shows the total transferred out costs and the separate cost transferred out for direct material and conversion. This was shown in step two of calculating the cost of inventory.

(d) The cost of ending inventory is calculated by multiplying the cost per equivalent unit by the number of equivalent units in ending inventory. Again, the cost of production report shows the separate costs for direct materials and conversion as well as the total. This was shown in step three of calculation the cost of inventory.

(e) The total cost accounted for, which is $80,000, must equal the total costs added during the month. All costs added during the month are shown as total costs to account for and is also $80,000. This proves that all costs have been accounted for.

Effect on WIP Accounts

The costs of transferring the inventory out of the cutting department have been calculated. Next, this will be recorded in a journal entry.

Figure 4.17 outlines the journal entry to move costs related to completed inventory from WIP 1 – Cutting to WIP 2 – Assembling. The WIP 1 account has been decreased (credited) and the WIP 2 account has been increased (debited).

GENERAL JOURNAL			
DATE	DESCRIPTION	DR	CR
Jan 31	WIP 2 – Assembling	65,333	
	WIP 1 – Cutting		65,333
	Transfer completed goods from the cutting dep't to assembling dep't		

The balance of the inventory account is still $80,000. When costs are transferred from one WIP to another, the total cost of inventory does not change.

FIGURE 4.17

In figure 4.18 you will find the changes to the WIP 1 and WIP 2 T-accounts for the month. The figure shows how direct materials and conversion costs were added during the year to WIP 1. It also shows the transfer of costs related to the goods transferred ($65,333) to WIP 2. There is a balance of $14,667 in the WIP 1 account which represents the cost of ending inventory in WIP 1.

FIGURE 4.18

Determining the Cost of Goods When There is Beginning and Ending WIP Inventory

In the previous example in the cutting department, there was no beginning inventory. Let us now add more depth to our example by applying process costing principles when both beginning and ending inventory exist. The discussion will focus on cost accumulation in the cutting department in the following month, February (in the previous section we considered costs that occurred in the cutting department during January).

Assume Pine Furniture Manufacturer's beginning inventory in February is carried over from ending inventory at the end of January. Therefore, for the month of February, the cutting department has 2,000 units in beginning inventory that are 100% complete with respect to direct materials and 80% complete with respect to conversion costs. During the month, 10,000 chairs worth of raw materials are transferred from the storage room to the cutting department. By the end of the month, the cutting department was able to transfer 9,000 sets of cut chairs to the assembling department. This left them with remaining inventory of 3,000 partially cut chairs. A discussion with the cutting department supervisor indicated that the remaining chairs are 100% complete with respect to direct materials but only 20% complete with respect to conversion costs.

Recall from chapter 2 that first-in, first-out (FIFO) or weighted-average cost (WAC) valuation method can be used to determine the cost of inventory produced when there is beginning inventory in the process. Since process costing is generally used for products that are homogenous in nature and the product prices do not vary significantly in the long-run, most companies prefer using the weighted-average cost method. Also, it is much easier to administer the weighted-average cost method than the FIFO method. Note that the calculations for the WAC method will be covered in this chapter, while the FIFO method will be discussed in appendix 4A.

A CLOSER LOOK

Many organizations have adapted and streamlined their production processes to maintain a minimal amount of inventory. These organizations often use a costing method called backflush costing. In backflush costing no attempt is made to assign actual costs to work in process. Rather, standard costs are used to cost ending work in process using the equivalent unit calculations we have developed in this chapter. For example, if the standard cost of materials and conversion are $5.00 and $12.00 per equivalent unit respectively, these costs would be allocated to ending work in process and the balance charged to ending inventory.

Weighted-Average Cost Method (WAC)

The weighted-average cost (WAC) method takes the average of the costs in beginning inventory and the costs incurred in the current period. This method can be applied to Pine Furniture Manufacturer's cutting department for the month of February, if beginning inventory exists.

Equivalent units of production for direct materials and conversion costs have to be calculated. This amount will be calculated by taking the sum of total completed units and the amount of equivalent units in ending inventory.

Recall that at the beginning of February, the cutting department at Pine Furniture Manufacturer had 2,000 partially completed units in beginning inventory. Beginning inventory is 100% complete with respect to direct materials and 80% complete with respect to conversion costs. The costs associated to the beginning inventory are $8,000 and $6,667 for direct materials and conversion costs respectively. During the month, 10,000 chairs worth of raw materials was transferred to the cutting department. At the end of the month, 9,000 chairs worth of parts were cut and transferred to the assembling department. At the end of the month there were 3,000 partially cut chairs. The remaining inventory was 100% complete with respect to direct materials and 20% complete with respect to conversion costs. During the month, $16,000 of direct materials costs and $38,000 of conversion costs were incurred.

Calculation of Equivalent Units of Production

Step 1: Determine the equivalent units for inventory completed.

Since 9,000 units were completed during the month, there are **9,000** equivalent units each with respect to both direct materials (9,000 units × 100%) and conversion costs (9,000 units × 100%).

Step 2: Determine the equivalent units for ending inventory.

There are 3,000 partially completed units in the cutting department at the end of the month. The number of equivalent units of production for direct materials is **3,000** (3,000 units × 100%). The number of equivalent units of production with respect to conversion costs is **600** (3,000 units × 20%).

Step 3: Determine the total equivalent units with respect to direct materials and conversion costs.

To find total equivalent units for direct materials and conversion costs, take the sum of the number of units calculated in steps 1 and 2. Total equivalent units for direct materials are **12,000** (9,000 + 3,000). Total equivalent units for conversion costs are **9,600** (9,000 + 600). This information is summarized in figure 4.19.

Summary of Equivalent Units in WIP 1 - Cutting using WAC Method (February)			
	Physical Units	Equivalent Units	
		Direct Materials	Conversion Costs
Completed	9,000	9,000	9,000
Ending Inventory	3,000	3,000	600
Accounted For	12,000		
Total Equivalent Units		12,000	9,600

FIGURE 4.19

Now that the equivalent units of production are calculated, Pine Furniture Manufacturer will calculate the costs per equivalent unit. This unit cost will be used to determine the cost of inventory transferred out of the department and the cost of inventory remaining in the department.

Calculation of Cost of Inventory

Step 1: Calculate the cost per equivalent unit.

When calculating the costs per equivalent units, the costs incurred in the previous period for beginning inventory are treated the same as costs incurred in the current period. With respect to direct materials, total EQU are 12,000 and total costs are $24,000 ($8,000 + $16,000). Therefore, cost per equivalent unit is **$2/EQU** ($24,000 ÷ 12,000 EQU).

With respect to conversion costs, total EQU are 9,600 and total costs are **$44,667** ($6,667 + $38,000). Therefore, cost per equivalent unit is approximately **$4.65/EQU** ($44,667 ÷ 9,600 EQU).

Step 2: Calculate the cost of completed inventory.

To calculate direct materials or conversion costs related to completed inventory, the equivalent number of units is multiplied by the cost per equivalent unit with respect to direct materials or conversion costs. With respect to direct materials, the cost of completed inventory is $18,000 (9,000 EQU × $2/EQU). With respect to conversion costs, the cost of completed inventory is $41,875 (9,000 EQU × ~$4.65/EQU). Therefore, the total cost of completed inventory is **$59,875** (18,000 + $41,875).

Step 3: Calculate the cost of ending inventory.

There are 3,000 units in ending inventory which are 100% completed with respect to direct materials and 20% completed with respect to conversion costs. We can calculate that costs are $6,000 (3,000 EQU × $2/EQU) for direct materials and $2,792 (600 EQU × ~$4.65/EQU) for conversion costs. Therefore, the total cost of ending inventory is **$8,792** ($6,000 + $2,792).

Step 4: Ensure that all cost are accounted for.

The total costs of beginning inventory ($14,667) and costs added during the period ($54,000) amount to $68,667. The cost of units completed and transferred out ($59,875) plus the cost of ending inventory ($8,792) amounts to $68,667. Since this matches the total costs, the calculations have been performed accurately.

Figure 4.20 shows the cost of production report for the cutting department for the month of February with each numbered item explained.

Pine Furniture Manufacturer
Cutting Department
Cost of Production Report for February (WAC)

UNITS	Whole Units	Equivalent Units	
		Direct Materials	Conversion
Units charged to production			
Beginning inventory	2,000		
Units started	10,000		
Total Units accounted for	12,000		
Units to be assigned cost			
Units completed and transferred out	9,000	9,000	9,000
Ending inventory - 100% material, 20% CC	3,000	3,000	600
Total equivalent units	12,000	12,000	9,600

COST	Cost		
	Direct Materials	Conversion	Total Cost
Unit cost			
Beginning inventory	$8,000	$6,667	$14,667 ⓐ
Costs added	16,000	38,000	54,000
Total cost to account for	$24,000	$44,667	$68,667
Total equivalent units	12,000	9,600	
Cost per equivalent unit	$2.00	$4.65	
Assign cost			
Costs transferred out	$18,000	$41,875	$59,875
Cost of ending inventory	6,000	2,792	8,792
Total cost accounted for			$68,667 ⓑ

FIGURE 4.20

ⓐ Since there was beginning inventory, the costs associated with direct materials and conversion must be accounted for and included as part of the total cost to account for.

ⓑ The total cost accounted for, which is $68,667, must equal the total cost to account for. The total cost to account for combines the beginning inventory costs plus costs added during the month. This amounts to $68,667 and proves that all costs have been accounted for.

Although this chapter focused mainly on one manufacturing business, Pine Furniture Manufacturer, the concepts covered in process costing and job-order costing (chapter 3) can be applied to a wide range of companies. It is important for every student to understand the impact of inventory valuation and how it affects total costs. As you will see in the rest of this text, knowing the cost of inventory will help us in analyzing cost behavior and planning.

The following table summarizes the differences between the calculations for the WAC and FIFO methods. Note that the FIFO method will be discussed in appendix 4A.

	WAC	**FIFO** (see Appendix 4A)
Calculation of Equivalent Units of Production	1. Determine the equivalent units for inventory completed (both beginning inventory and inventory started during the month) 2. Determine the equivalent units for ending inventory 3. Calculate the number of equivalent units for: (a) direct materials and (b) conversion costs	1. Determine the equivalent units for beginning inventory 2. Determine the equivalent units for inventory started and completed during the month 3. Determine the equivalent units for ending inventory 4. Calculate the number of equivalent units for: (a) direct materials and (b) conversion costs
Calculation of Costs of Inventory	1. Calculate cost per equivalent unit for: (a) direct materials and (b) conversion costs 2. Calculate the cost of completed inventory 3. Calculate the cost of ending inventory 4. Ensure all costs are accounted for	1. Calculate cost per equivalent unit for: (a) direct materials and (b) conversion costs 2. Calculate the cost of completed inventory – sum of: i. Cost of Beg. Inv. ii. Cost to complete Beg. Inv. iii. Cost of inventory started and completed in the month 3. Calculate the costs of units in ending inventory 4. Ensure all costs are accounted for

IN THE REAL WORLD

When spoilage occurs in manufacturing organizations, management accountants are faced with the problem of how to allocate costs to spoilage. In effect, spoilage is simply another line in the Cost of Production Report. The Cost of Production Report will include spoilage as one of the uses of units of production. The equivalent units of inventory transferred in, materials, and conversion costs will be computed and costs are allocated to spoilage using the same approach as costs allocated to ending inventory and units transferred out. An additional complexity occurs when management accountants classify spoilage into normal and abnormal. Normal spoilage is usually calculated based on good units of production. For example, if 1,000 good units are produced, the normal spoilage rate is 2%, and the number of spoiled units was 25, then 20 (1,000 * 2%) units will be classified as normal and five (25-20) will be classified as abnormal. Normal spoilage is treated as a normal production cost and is added to inventory cost. Abnormal spoilage is charged to cost of goods sold in the period incurred.

Ethical Considerations

In some environments that use process costing, managers must calculate the amount of equivalent units in respect to direct materials and conversion costs. However, establishing the degree of completion of inventory in respect to conversion costs can be a challenge to management accountants. The reason is that it can be very difficult to accurately estimate how much conversion equivalent units are still in process.

Management accountants are encouraged to work with the production managers to obtain all the necessary information to properly make these estimates. If the production manager is trying meet a performance measurement by keeping conversion costs down, they may have the bias to estimate a higher percentage of completion. This would cause the equivalent units in ending inventory with respect to conversion costs to be overstated. Recall that under the WAC method, the cost per equivalent units with respect to conversion costs is calculated by dividing the total conversions costs for the period by the total conversion equivalent units for the period. If the conversion equivalent units are overstated, cost per equivalent unit would be understated. As a result, the production manager would be allocating a lower cost to the transferred units.

If this type of behavior continues, the implications can be significant. Managerial accountants would not have the accurate cost information for a particular process (or department). Sales prices may be set too low and cause a drop in profitability. If the managerial accountant wants the production managers' estimation to be sound, he or she need to ask detailed questions to get the proper answers.

In Summary

- ⟳ **Process costing** is the costing method applicable where goods or services result from a sequence of continuous or repetitive operations or processes. Costs are averaged over the units produced during the period.

- ⟳ In process costing, each process has a separate work-in-process (WIP) account.

- ⟳ Each WIP account includes the costs of direct materials and direct labor related to the process, the costs of manufacturing overhead allocated to the process and all costs (direct material, direct labor, manufacturing overhead) from the previous process.

- ⟳ **Conversion costs** are costs that are incurred while converting raw materials into finished goods.

- ⟳ Conversion costs are made up of direct labor and manufacturing overhead.

- ⟳ **Equivalent units of production** are the number of completed units that approximately equal the number of partially completed units based on their percentage of completion.

- ⟳ Equivalent units of production aid managerial accountants in determining the costs of ending inventory and the cost of inventory transferred to the next process.

- ⟳ Cost per EQU can be calculated by dividing costs with the number of EQU.

- ⟳ The **first-in-first-out (FIFO)** method of inventory valuation assumes that inventory received first is the first inventory to be consumed.

- ⟳ The **weighted-average cost (WAC)** method of inventory valuation averages the cost of inventory throughout the entire period.

- ⟳ In the FIFO method, the cost of completed inventory is first made up of costs from the beginning inventory before applying costs from the current period. Unlike FIFO, the WAC method does not treat costs that have incurred in different time periods differently. It simply averages the costs of inventory throughout the entire period.

- ⟳ The **cost of production report** provides a summary of cost information for a single process (i.e. department). The report shows how the manufacturing costs are allocated between a department's ending work in process inventory and the units completed and transferred out to the next department (or finished goods inventory).

Review Exercise

The Paladio Company uses the process costing system. The company provides the following information for a particular department:

	Whole Units	Direct Materials	Conversion Costs
Beginning WIP, October 1	10	$3,658	$5,589
Started in October	60		
Ending WIP, October 31	20		
Costs added during October		$23,758	$59,588

The ending inventory is 50% complete with respect to direct materials and 25% complete with respect to conversion. Assume the weighted-average method is used.

Required:

1. Calculate the total equivalent units with respect to direct materials and conversion costs.

2. Calculate the cost per equivalent unit for direct materials and conversion costs.

3. Prepare a cost of production report for October.

Review Exercise – Answer

Part 1

Beginning Inventory + Units Started = Completed Units + Ending Inventory

Rearrange the formula:

Completed Units

= Beginning Inventory + Units Started – Ending Inventory

= 10 + 60 - 20

= 50 units

	Whole Units	Direct Materials	Conversion Costs
Completed	50	50	50
Ending Inventory	20	10*	5**
Accounted for	70		
Total Equivalent Units		60	55

*20 × 50%
**20 × 25%

Part 2

	Direct Materials	Conversion Costs
Beginning inventory	$3,658	$5,589
Costs added during October	$23,758	$59,588
Total costs to account for [a]	$27,416	$65,177
Total Equivalent Units [b]	60	54
Cost per equivalent unit [a ÷ b]	$456.93	$1,185.04

Part 3

Paladio Company Cost of Production Report for October			
UNITS	**Whole Units**	**Equivalent Units**	
		Direct Materials	**Conversion**
Units charged to production			
Beginning inventory	10		
Units started	60		
Total Units accounted for	70		
Units to be assigned cost			
Units completed and transferred out	50	50	50
Ending inventory - 50% material, 25% CC	20	10	5
Total equivalent units	70	60	55

COST	**Cost**		
	Direct Materials	**Conversion**	**Total Cost**
Unit cost			
Beginning inventory	$3,658	$5,589	$9,247
Costs added	23,758	59,588	83,346
Total cost to account for	$27,416	$65,177	$92,593
Total equivalent units	60	55	
Cost per equivalent unit	$456.93	$1,185.04	
Assign cost			
Costs transferred out	$22,847	$59,252	$82,099
Cost of ending inventory	4,569	5,925	10,494
Total cost accounted for			$92,593

Appendix 4A: FIFO Cost Method

Under the FIFO method, the cost of completed inventory is first made up of costs from the beginning inventory before using costs from the current period. The important point to keep in mind when costing using the FIFO method is to keep costs from the previous month separate from the costs incurred in the current month. The same distinction should also be made for equivalent units.

Let us discuss the cutting department of Pine Furniture Manufacturer during the month of February again, this time using the FIFO method. Beginning inventory should be dealt with separately from inventory that was started and completed during February. Equivalent units of production should also be calculated separately. This is because units produced at different points in time will have different costs associated with it.

To determine the costs of inventory, Pine Furniture Manufacturer will have to calculate equivalent units of production for the month. Similar to the WAC method, equivalent units with respect to direct materials and conversion costs will have to be calculated. Total equivalent units are calculated by determining the extent of direct materials costs and conversion costs for:

- Beginning inventory
- Inventory that was started and completed during February, and
- Ending inventory

Calculation of Equivalent Units of Production

Step 1: Determine the equivalent units of production for beginning inventory.

The 2,000 units in beginning inventory are 100% complete with respect to direct materials and 80% complete with respect to conversion costs. No work has to be done with respect to direct materials' beginning inventory, while there is still 20% (100% - 80%) of work that has to be done with respect to conversion costs.

Therefore, there are **0** EQU (2,000 units × 0%) for beginning inventory with respect to direct materials. In terms of conversion costs, there are **400** EQU (2,000 units × 20%) of production in the beginning inventory.

Step 2: Determine the equivalent units of production for units started and completed during the month.

During the month, a total of 9,000 units were completed and transferred out to the next department. Since there was 2,000 units in beginning inventory, that means that 7,000 (9,000 - 2,000) units were started from scratch and completed. Therefore, there are **7,000** EQU (7,000 × 100%) of production with respect to both direct materials and conversion costs.

Step 3: Determine the equivalent units of production for ending inventory.

Ending inventory consists of 3,000 partially completed units that are 100% complete with respect to direct materials and 20% complete with respect to conversion costs. Therefore, there are **3,000** EQU (3,000 units × 100%) with respect to direct materials and **600** EQU (3,000 units × 20%) with respect to conversion costs.

Step 4: Determine the equivalent units of production for direct materials and conversion costs.

Total equivalent units for direct materials is **10,000** (0 + 7,000 + 3,000). Total equivalent units for conversion costs is **8,000** (400 + 7,000 + 600).

A summary of the equivalent units for February is shown in figure 4A.1.

Summary of Equivalent Units in WIP 1 - Cutting using FIFO Method (February)			
	Physical Units	**Equivalent Units**	
		Direct Materials	**Conversion Costs**
Beginning Inventory	2,000	0	400
Units Started and Completed	7,000	7,000	7,000
Ending Inventory	3,000	3,000	600
Accounted For	12,000		
Total Equivalent Units		10,000	8,000

FIGURE 4A.1

Remember that FIFO calculates equivalent units differently from the WAC method. The WAC method does not require a separation of beginning inventory from units started and completed.

Similar to the WAC method, after the equivalent units of production have been calculated, Pine Furniture Manufacturer can determine the costs of cut chairs transferred to the assembling department and the costs of remaining inventory in the cutting department.

Recall that Pine Furniture Manufacturer incurred a total cost of $54,000 ($16,000 of direct materials costs and $38,000 of conversion costs) in the cutting department during February. Let us now calculate the costs of inventory using the FIFO method.

Calculation of Costs of Inventory

Step 1: Calculate the cost per equivalent unit of production.

For the current period, cost per equivalent unit for direct materials is **$1.60/unit** ($16,000 ÷ 10,000 EQU). Cost per equivalent unit for conversion costs is **$4.75/unit** ($38,000 ÷ 8,000 EQU).

Note that only the costs that were added during the month ($54,000) are included in the cost per equivalent unit calculation. The costs related to beginning inventory are not added. This is because the cost of beginning inventory was incurred in the previous month. Under FIFO, these are kept separate from costs added during the current month.

Step 2: Calculate the cost of completed units.

Total costs of completed inventory is the sum of three amounts:
  (i) the costs of beginning inventory
  (ii) the cost to complete beginning inventory
  (iii) the cost of inventory started and completed in the month

(i) From January's ending inventory (figure 4.16), the cost of beginning inventory is **$14,667**.

(ii) Recall that since the beginning inventory was already complete with respect to direct materials, no more direct materials costs need to be added. However, beginning inventory was only 80% complete with respect to conversion costs, so 400 more units worth of conversion costs had to be incurred to complete it. Therefore, costs to complete beginning inventory amount to **$1,900** (400 EQU × $4.75/EQU).

(iii) From figure 4A.1, there are 7,000 equivalent units started and completed with respect to both direct materials and conversion costs. The costs associated with direct materials amount to $11,200 (7,000 EQU × $1.60/EQU) and the costs associated with conversion costs amount to $33,250 (7,000 EQU × $4.75/EQU). Therefore, total cost of inventory started and completed in the month amount to **$44,450** ($11,200 + $33,250).

To determine the cost of completed inventory, Pine Furniture Manufacturer will add the cost of beginning inventory ($14,667), the cost to complete the beginning inventory ($1,900), and the cost related to inventory started and completed in February ($44,450). This gives total costs of **$61,017** for inventory transferred out to the assembling department.

Step 3: Calculate the cost of ending inventory.

There are 3,000 EQU of direct materials and 600 EQU of conversion costs in ending inventory. Therefore, cost of ending inventory is $4,800 (3,000 EQU × $1.60/EQU) with respect to direct materials and $2,850 (600 EQU × $4.75/EQU) with respect to conversion costs. Total cost of ending inventory amounts to **$7,650** ($4,800 + $2,850).

Step 4: Ensure that all costs are accounted for.

Recall that the cost of beginning inventory is $14,667 and that the costs added during the month amount to $54,000. Therefore, total costs amount to **$68,667** ($14,667 + $54,000) and should be spread out over the inventory completed and ending inventory. The cost of completed inventory is $61,017, while the cost of ending inventory is $7,650. Their sum is equal to **$68,667** ($61,017 + $7,650) which matches the total costs that need to be accounted for. This also confirms that the calculations are accurate.

Figure 4A.2 shows the cost of production report for the cutting department for the month of February with each numbered item explained.

UNITS	Whole Units	Equivalent Units	
		Direct Materials	Conversion
Units charged to production			
Beginning inventory	2,000		
Units started and completed	7,000		
Ending inventory	3,000		
Total Units accounted for	12,000		
Units to be assigned cost			
Beginning inventory - 100% material, 80% CC	2,000	-	400
Units completed and transferred out	7,000	7,000	7,000
Ending inventory - 100% material, 20% CC	3,000	3,000	600
Total equivalent units	12,000	10,000	8,000

Pine Furniture Manufacturer
Cutting Department
Cost of Production Report for February (FIFO)

COST	Cost		
	Direct Materials	Conversion	Total Cost
Unit cost			
Beginning inventory			$14,667
Costs added	$16,000	$38,000	54,000
Total cost to account for			$68,667
Total equivalent units	10,000	8,000	
Cost per equivalent unit	$1.60	$4.75	
Assign cost			
Costs transferred out	$19,200	$41,817	$61,017
Cost of ending inventory	4,800	2,850	7,650
Total cost accounted for			$68,667

(a) (b) (c) (d)

FIGURE 4A.2

(a) Since there was beginning inventory, equivalent units must be calculated based on the percentage completed for direct materials and conversion costs. The top half of the cost of production report is taken from figure 4A.1.

ⓑ Cost per equivalent unit is calculated by dividing the costs added during the month by the total equivalent units. This was shown in step one of calculating the cost of inventory.

ⓒ The costs transferred out is the cost of beginning inventory ($8,000 for direct materials and $6,667 for conversion), the cost to complete beginning inventory ($1,900 for conversion) and the cost of inventory started and completed during the month ($11,200 for direct materials and $33,250 for conversion). This is shown in step two of calculating the cost of inventory.

ⓓ The total cost accounted for, which is $68,667, must equal the total cost to account for. The total cost to account for combines the beginning inventory costs plus costs added during the month. This amounts to $68,667 and proves that all costs have been accounted for.

The above scenario shows you how Pine Furniture Manufacturer would cost the inventory in the cutting department if there was beginning and ending inventory and if they used the FIFO method to value inventory.

Comparison of FIFO and WAC Methods

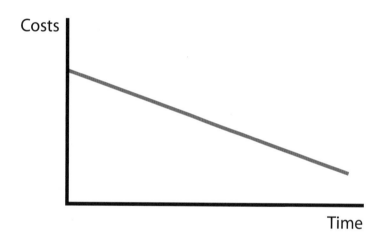

The ending inventory for the FIFO method amounted to $7,650 whereas the ending inventory under the WAC method amounted to $8,792. In the case of Pine Furniture Manufacturer, the WAC would result in higher gross profit and higher net income than the FIFO method. Recall that cost of goods sold is equal to beginning inventory plus purchases (or goods manufactured) less ending inventory. Therefore, the higher the ending inventory, the lower the cost of goods sold. A lower cost of goods sold would yield a higher gross profit.

A difference between the FIFO and WAC methods will exist if there are fluctuations in costs. For example, if the costs of production are decreasing, the FIFO method would yield a lower ending inventory amount than the WAC method. This is because under the FIFO method, the units produced first are transferred out first. Thus, the higher priced items will be completed and transferred out first, leaving the newer lower priced items in ending inventory. In the WAC method, however, the average cost of direct materials is used. This means that ending inventory contains a proportional mix of both higher-priced items and lower-priced items. If costs were decreasing, this would result in higher ending inventory using the WAC system than the FIFO system. The WAC method will also result in a lower cost of goods sold and higher gross profit in comparison to the FIFO method.

Review Exercise

SWEB Incorporated uses a process costing system. The manager of the forming department provides the following information for August:

| | Degree of Completion | | Costs | |
	WIP August 1, 2010	WIP August 31, 2010	WIP Beginning	Added in August
Physical Units	20,000	15,000		
Direct Materials	85%	75%	$50,300	$59,675
Conversion costs	20%	35%	$20,675	$37,975

The forming department started 55,000 units into production during the month and transferred 60,000 units to the next department.

Required:

1. If the company uses FIFO, what is the cost per equivalent unit with respect to direct materials? What is the cost per equivalent unit with respect to conversion costs?
2. Prepare a cost of production report.

Review Exercise – Answer

Part 1

Units started and completed

= Completed and Transferred – Beginning Inventory

= 60,000 - 20,000 = 40,000

| | | Equivalent Units | |
	Physical Units	Direct Materials	Conversion costs
Beginning Inventory	20,000	3,000[1]	16,000[2]
Units Started and Completed	40,000	40,000	40,000
Ending Inventory	15,000	11,250[3]	5,250[4]
Accounted for	75,000		
Total Equivalent Units		54,250	61,250

[1] $20,000 \times (1 - 0.85)$
[2] $20,000 \times (1 - 0.20)$
[3] $15,000 \times 0.75$
[4] $15,000 \times 0.35$

| | | Equivalent Units | |
	Physical Units	Direct Materials	Conversion costs
Costs Added [a]	20,000	$59,675	$37,975
EQU [b]	15,000	54,250	61,250
Cost per EQU [a ÷ b]	75,000	$1.10	$0.62

Part 2

<table>
<tr><td colspan="4" align="center">SWEB Incorporated
Forming Department
Cost of Production Report for August (FIFO)</td></tr>
<tr><td rowspan="2" align="center">UNITS</td><td rowspan="2" align="center">Whole Units</td><td colspan="2" align="center">Equivalent Units</td></tr>
<tr><td align="center">Direct Materials</td><td align="center">Conversion</td></tr>
<tr><td>Units charged to production</td><td></td><td></td><td></td></tr>
<tr><td>Beginning inventory</td><td>20,000</td><td></td><td></td></tr>
<tr><td>Units started and completed</td><td>40,000</td><td></td><td></td></tr>
<tr><td>Ending inventory</td><td>15,000</td><td></td><td></td></tr>
<tr><td>Total Units accounted for</td><td>75,000</td><td></td><td></td></tr>
<tr><td></td><td></td><td></td><td></td></tr>
<tr><td>Units to be assigned cost</td><td></td><td></td><td></td></tr>
<tr><td>Beginning inventory - 85% material, 20% CC</td><td>20,000</td><td>3,000</td><td>16,000</td></tr>
<tr><td>Units started and completed</td><td>40,000</td><td>40,000</td><td>40,000</td></tr>
<tr><td>Ending inventory - 75% material, 35% CC</td><td>15,000</td><td>11,250</td><td>5,250</td></tr>
<tr><td>Total equivalent units</td><td>75,000</td><td>54,250</td><td>61,250</td></tr>
</table>

<table>
<tr><td rowspan="2" align="center">COST</td><td colspan="3" align="center">Cost</td></tr>
<tr><td align="center">Direct Materials</td><td align="center">Conversion</td><td align="center">Total Cost</td></tr>
<tr><td>Unit cost</td><td></td><td></td><td></td></tr>
<tr><td>Beginning inventory</td><td></td><td></td><td>$70,975</td></tr>
<tr><td>Costs added</td><td>$59,675</td><td>$37,975</td><td>97,650</td></tr>
<tr><td>Total cost to account for</td><td></td><td></td><td>$168,625</td></tr>
<tr><td>Total equivalent units</td><td>54,250</td><td>61,250</td><td></td></tr>
<tr><td>Cost per equivalent unit</td><td>$1.10</td><td>$0.62</td><td></td></tr>
<tr><td></td><td></td><td></td><td></td></tr>
<tr><td>Assign cost</td><td></td><td></td><td></td></tr>
<tr><td>Costs transferred out</td><td>$97,600</td><td>$55,395</td><td>$152,995</td></tr>
<tr><td>Cost of ending inventory</td><td>12,375</td><td>3,255</td><td>15,630</td></tr>
<tr><td>Total cost accounted for</td><td></td><td></td><td>$168,625</td></tr>
</table>

Appendix 4B: Accounting for Transferred-in Costs

Now that we have learned about both the FIFO and WAC methods of costing for a single department (cutting), we can illustrate what happens to costing when products are transferred from process to process. Completed products from one processing department are transferred to the next processing department to undergo further work. This continues until no more work is needed on the product. Afterwards, it is transferred into finished goods inventory. A company can have one or more processing departments. In our example with Pine Furniture Manufacturers, there were three departments – cutting, assembling and painting.

Assume a company has two processing departments (A and B). Department A transfers completed units to department B in the middle of the month. The units that department B receives from department A are known as **transferred-in units**. The units have costs attached to them that are transferred from department A's WIP to department B's WIP. These are known as **transferred-in costs**, which consist of all costs attached to units received from a previous department.

Recall from our Pine Furniture Manufacturer example that in the month of February, the cutting department (WIP 1) worked on a total of 12,000 units with 2,000 units coming from beginning inventory. By the end of the month, the cutting department (WIP 1) had completed 9,000 units and transferred them to the assembling department (WIP 2). Figure 4B.1 shows that of the 12,000 physical units, 9,000 were transferred to the assembling department while 3,000 were still partially completed and included in the ending balance of WIP 1. Total costs of production in WIP 2 are partially allocated to the units transferred out to the painting department and partially to the units in its ending inventory. The following discussion will show these calculations in detail.

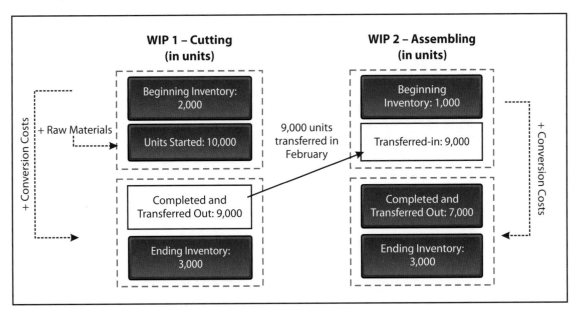

FIGURE 4B.1

In the month of February, the assembling department (WIP 2) will have received these 9,000 units and put them into production. Assume that WIP 2 had beginning inventory of 1,000 units.

If 9,000 units were transferred in and 7,000 units were completed and transferred out, this leaves 3,000 partially completed units in ending inventory. Further details are provided in figure 4B.2.

WIP 2 - Assembling		
	# of Chairs	% Completion
Beginning Inventory	1,000	
Transferred-in from cutting department	9,000	0%
Completed and transferred to painting department	7,000	100% transferred-in costs 100% materials 100% conversion costs
Ending Inventory	3,000	100% transferred-in costs 100% materials 50% conversion costs

FIGURE 4B.2

Recording Transferred-in Costs

Moving forward, we will use the WAC method to continue the example. Assume that on February 15th, the cutting department transferred 9,000 completed units worth $59,875 to the assembly department. These are the transferred-in costs, and must be accounted for by the assembling department. The journal entry is shown in figure 4B.3 below. All processing departments after the first will have transferred-in costs.

The journal entry is as follows:

GENERAL JOURNAL			
DATE	DESCRIPTION	DR	CR
Feb 15	WIP 2 – Assembling	59,875	
	WIP 1 – Cutting		59,875
	Transfer completed goods from the cutting department to assembling department		

FIGURE 4B.3

Calculation of Equivalent Units of Production

Similar to the cutting department, equivalent units of production for direct materials and conversion costs must first be calculated. Note that transferred-in costs are treated as a separate cost. Therefore, the equivalent units of production will also be calculated with respect to transferred-in costs. Once the equivalent units of production for each of the three costs (transferred-in, direct materials and conversion costs) are calculated, the equivalent cost per unit can be determined and applied to determine the costs of units transferred out and of ending inventory.

The following steps explain the calculation of equivalent units, followed by a summary of the calculation in figure 4B.4. Recall that the formula for equivalent units is as follows:

Equivalent Units of Production = # of Units × % Completion in Current Period

Step 1: Determine the equivalent units for inventory completed.

Since the units transferred out during February were 100% completed, the total physical units (7,000) is also the equivalent units (EQU) for each type of cost.

Step 2: Determine the equivalent units for ending inventory.

The 3,000 physical units to be accounted for are 100% complete with respect to transferred-in costs, 100% complete with respect to direct materials, but only 50% complete with respect to conversion costs. Therefore, if we apply the formula above, we get **3,000 EQU** (3,000 units × 100%) for transferred-in costs, **3,000 EQU** (3,000 units × 100%) for direct materials and **1,500 EQU** (3,000 units × 50%) for conversion costs.

Step 3: Determine the total equivalent units for each type of cost (transferred-in costs, direct materials, conversion costs).

The total equivalent units for each type of cost is the sum of the equivalent units for units completed and transferred out and units in ending inventory. Total equivalent units are **10,000** (7,000 + 3,000) for transferred-in costs, **10,000** (7,000 + 3,000) for direct materials and **8,500** (7,000 + 1,500) for conversion costs.

The above steps are summarized in figure 4B.4 below.

Summary of Equivalent Units in WIP 2 - Assembling using WAC with Transferred-in Costs (February)				
	Physical Units	**Equivalent Units**		
		Transferred-In Costs	**Direct Materials**	**Conversion Costs**
Beginning Inventory	1,000			
Transferred-in units (from Cutting)	9,000			
Total physical units to be accounted for	10,000			
Completed and transferred out during February	7,000	7,000	7,000	7,000
Ending Inventory	3,000			
Equivalent Units for Ending Inventory*		3,000	3,000	1,500
Total physical units accounted for	10,000			
Total Equivalent Units		10,000	10,000	8,500

* Transferred-in: 3,000 × 100%; Direct Materials: 3,000 × 100%; Conversion Costs: 3,000 × 50%

FIGURE 4B.4

Calculation of Cost of Inventory

We can now use the equivalent units determined above to calculate the costs allocated to the units transferred out and WIP 2's ending inventory.

Consider the following case facts.

We will now assume that the assembling department's total costs in beginning inventory amount to $18,000: $8,000 worth of transferred in units, $4,000 worth of direct materials and $6,000 of conversion costs. In addition, the assembly department incurred $10,000 worth of direct materials and $20,000 of conversion costs during the month of February. There are also $59,875 of transferred-in costs related to inventory coming in during the month.

The following steps show the process of calculating the cost of inventory transferred out of the assembly department and the cost of inventory remaining at the end of the month. Recall that the formula to calculate equivalent unit cost is as follows:

$$\text{Cost per Equivalent Unit} = \frac{\text{Costs*}}{\text{\# of Equivalent Units}}$$

*"Costs" refers to total direct material costs, or total conversion costs

Also recall that the formula to calculate costs from equivalent unit costs is as follows:

$$\text{Cost of Units} = \text{Cost per Equivalent Unit} \times \text{\# of Equivalent Units}$$

<u>**Step 1:**</u> <u>Calculate the cost per equivalent unit of production.</u>

The costs incurred for the beginning inventory include transferred-in costs, direct materials and conversion costs. Transferred-in costs have to be treated as a separate cost at the beginning of the process. Therefore, costs per equivalent units have to be calculated separately for each of the three types of costs.

The cost per EQU of transferred-in units is approximately **$6.79/EQU** ([$8,000 + $59,875] ÷ 10,000 EQU).

The cost per EQU of direct materials is **$1.40/EQU** ([$4,000 + $10,000] ÷ 10,000 EQU).

The cost per EQU of conversion costs is approximately **$3.06/EQU** ([$6,000 + $20,000] ÷ 8,500 EQU).

Step 2: Calculate the cost of inventory transferred out.

The 7,000 units completed and transferred out are 100% complete with respect to all three types of costs and therefore the equivalent units we use in each calculation is 7,000.

We multiply the EQU (7,000) by the cost per EQU with respect to each type of cost. We then take the sum of all three types of costs, yielding transferred-out costs of **$78,724** ([7,000 EQU × ~$6.79/EQU] + [7,000 EQU × $1.40/EQU] + [7,000 EQU × ~$3.06/EQU])

Step 3: Calculate the cost of ending inventory.

To calculate the costs associated with ending inventory, the number of equivalent units is multiplied by the cost per equivalent unit for each type of cost. We then take the sum of all three types of costs in ending inventory, yielding an amount of **$29,151** ([3,000 units × ~$6.79] + [3,000 units × $1.40] + [1,500 units × ~$3.06/unit])

Step 4: Ensure that all costs are accounted for.

The total costs of beginning inventory ($18,000) and costs added during the current period ($89,875) equal **$107,875**. The sum of cost of units transferred out ($78,724) and ending inventory ($29,151) also amounts to **$107,875**. Since all costs incurred have been accounted for, the calculations have been performed accurately.

Figure 4B.5 shows the cost of production report for the assembling department for the month of February.

Pine Furniture Manufacturer
Assembling Department
Cost of Production Report for February (WAC)

UNITS	Whole Units	Equivalent Units		
		Transferred-In	Direct Materials	Conversion
Units charged to production				
Beginning inventory	1,000			
Transferred-in units	9,000			
Total Units accounted for	10,000			
Units to be assigned cost				
Units completed and transferred out	7,000	7,000	7,000	7,000
Ending inventory - 100% transferred, 100% material, 50% CC	3,000	3,000	3,000	1,500
Total equivalent units	10,000	10,000	10,000	8,500

COST		Cost			
		Transferred-In	Direct Materials	Conversion	Total Cost
Unit cost					
Beginning inventory		$8,000	$4,000	$6,000	$18,000
Costs added		59,875	10,000	20,000	89,875
Total cost to account for		$67,875	$14,000	$26,000	$107,875
Total equivalent units		10,000	10,000	8,500	
Cost per equivalent unit		$6.79	$1.40	$3.06	
Assign cost					
Costs transferred out		$47,512	$9,800	$21,412	$78,724
Cost of ending inventory		20,363	4,200	4,588	29,151
Total cost accounted for					$107,875

FIGURE 4B.5

The major change for this cost of production report from the previous examples is the addition of the *Transferred-In* column. This is one extra item to track for equivalent units and costs.

See figure 4B.6 for an illustration of the flow of units under WAC.

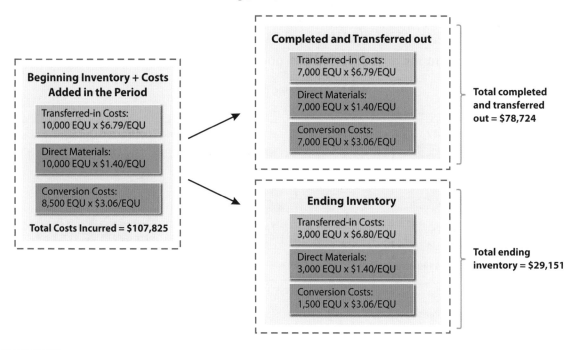

FIGURE 4B.6

In the WAC method, the costs associated with beginning inventory and those added during the period are lumped together. These costs are then averaged over the units that are transferred out and those that are left behind in ending inventory.

FIFO

The above calculation would be mostly the same if transferred-in costs are taken into account using the FIFO method instead of the WAC method. However, if using FIFO, it is important to note **when** the WIP was transferred in from the cutting department. Under FIFO, since goods purchased first must be consumed first, the units to be used in the calculation is generally as follows:

- Units to be accounted for:
    - Beginning WIP (started in the previous month)
    - Started and completed (transferred in during the current month)
- Units accounted for:
    - Ending inventory (only partially completed at month-end)

Recall that under WAC, we took the total of costs associated with beginning inventory and those that were incurred during the period, and then divided this amount by the total equivalent units of beginning inventory plus the units added in the period. However, under FIFO, we do not combine these two groups of units. Instead, we account for each set of costs separately.

This is shown in figure 4B.7, where beginning inventory and costs incurred during the period are separated. Note that unit cost $A corresponds to beginning inventory and unit cost $B corresponds to costs added during the period.

Also, notice that beginning inventory (shown with gray background) is consumed first. Then, units transferred in during the period (shown with green background) are consumed. Therefore, this illustrates the major difference between WAC and FIFO. Ending inventory under FIFO is mainly related to costs incurred in the *current* period and not from beginning WIP.

WIP 2 – Assembling (FIFO)

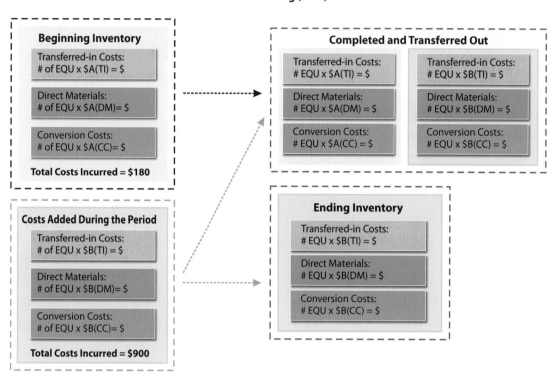

* Assume all units from beginning inventory were completed and transferred out. Ending inventory only contains units added during the period.

FIGURE 4B.7

FIFO vs. WAC

After taking transferred-in costs into account, it is still evident that the WAC method is relatively easier to administer. However, whether management chooses to use FIFO or WAC, the method must be consistently applied in future years in order to have comparative value and increased usefulness for decision-making.

In Summary

⤷ Partially completed products are transferred from one processing department to the next to undergo further work. This continues until no more work is needed on the product.

⤷ When a department receives units from another department, the units received are called **transferred-in units**.

⤷ Transferred-in units have costs attached to them that are also transferred from one department to the other. These are known as **transferred-in costs**, which consist of all costs attached to units received from a previous department.

⤷ Transferred-in costs are treated as separate from direct materials and conversion costs. Therefore, the equivalent units of production are also calculated with respect to transferred-in costs.

⤷ Once the equivalent units of production for each of the three costs (transferred-in, direct materials and conversion costs) are calculated, the equivalent cost per unit can be determined and applied to determine the costs of units transferred out and of ending inventory.

⤷ When a WIP account has beginning inventory, the FIFO or WAC method can be used to calculate the cost of beginning, transferred-out and ending inventory.

⤷ In the WAC method, the costs associated with beginning inventory and those added during the period are lumped together. These costs are then averaged over the units that are transferred out and those that are left behind in ending inventory.

⤷ Under FIFO, the costs associated with beginning inventory and those added during the period are not combined. Instead, each set of costs are accounted for separately. The beginning inventory is consumed first, and then the transferred-in units.

Review Exercise

Ajour Crème produces all types of lotion. Each product goes through two processes: mixing and packaging. Each department tracks direct materials and conversion costs. The mixing department will transfer product to packaging, and packaging will transfer the completed product to finished goods inventory.

Suppose the packaging department adds the direct materials (packing) at the beginningof the process and adds conversion costs evenly during the process. Beginning work-in-process inventory was 35% complete and ending work-in-process inventory was 25% complete with respect to conversion costs. Select information for the month of July in its packaging department is provided below.

Packaging Department				
	Physical Units	Transferred-In Costs	Direct Materials	Conversion Costs
Beginning WIP	4,200	$24,000	$24,600	$17,400
Transferred in	5,600			
Completed and transferred out	5,300			
Ending WIP	4,500			
Total costs added		$55,576	$44,000	$34,000

Required:

1. Calculate the total cost of the transferred out units using the weighted average method.

2. Prepare a cost of production report.

Review Exercise – Answer

Part 1

	Physical Units	Transferred-In Costs	Direct Materials	Conversion Costs
Completed and transferred out	5,300	5,300	5,300	5,300
Ending WIP	4,500	4,500	4,500	1,125
Accounted For	9,800			
Total EQU		9,800	9,800	6,425

	Transferred-In Costs	Direct Materials	Conversion Costs
Beginning	$24,000	$24,600	$17,400
Costs added	$55,576	$44,000	$34,000
Total Costs [a]	$79,575	$68,600	$51,400
Total EQU[b]	9,800	9,800	6,425
Cost per EQU [a ÷ b]	$8.12	$7.00	$8.00

Total cost of transferred-out units

= ($8.12 + $7.00 + $8.00) × 5,300

= $122,536

Part 2

		Ajour Crème Packing Department Cost of Production Report for July (WAC)			

UNITS	Whole Units	Equivalent Units		
		Transferred-In	Direct Materials	Conversion
Units charged to production				
Beginning inventory	4,200			
Transferred-in units	5,600			
Total Units accounted for	9,800			
Units to be assigned cost				
Units completed and transferred out	5,300	5,300	5,300	5,300
Ending inventory - 100% transferred, 100% material, 25% CC	4,500	4,500	4,500	1,125
Total equivalent units	9,800	9,800	9,800	6,425

COST	Cost			
	Transferred-In	Direct Materials	Conversion Costs	Total Cost
Unit cost				
Beginning inventory	$24,000	$24,600	$17,400	$66,000
Costs added	55,576	44,000	34,000	133,576
Total cost to account for	$79,576	$68,600	$51,400	$199,576
Total equivalent units	9,800	9,800	6,425	
Cost per equivalent unit	$8.12	$7.00	$8.00	
Assign cost				
Costs transferred out	$43,036	$37,100	$42,400	$122,536
Cost of ending inventory	36,540	31,500	9,000	77,040
Total cost accounted for				$199,576

Notes

Chapter 5
ACTIVITY-BASED COSTING

LEARNING OUTCOMES:

❶ Understand the purpose of activity-based costing (ABC)

❷ Calculate product and service cost using an ABC system

❸ Understand the difference between job-order and ABC systems

❹ Understand the concept of time driven ABC

❺ Understand and calculate unused capacity

❻ Describe how ABC and time-driven ABC is used in decision making

Activity-Based Costing: An Introduction

Understanding the cost of a service and producing a product is crucial for business success because it helps managers with decision-making. In the previous chapters, the costs of direct materials, direct labor and manufacturing overhead were included in the total product cost. Costs related to *direct* materials and *direct* labor can be easily tied to the product. However, *indirect* costs are difficult or too costly to trace to products. Therefore, a method using a single predetermined overhead rate has been developed in order to allocate these overhead costs to different products.

The predetermined overhead rate is the ratio of total budgeted overhead costs to the total budgeted cost allocation base:

$$\text{Predetermined Overhead Rate} = \frac{\text{Total Budgeted Overhead Costs}}{\text{Total Budgeted Cost Allocation Base}}$$

Generally, manufacturing companies use either direct labor hours or machine hours as a cost allocation base to assign overhead costs to products. In the past, this method of allocating overhead has served many companies well. In the earlier part of the 20th century, direct labor hours were mainly used to allocate overhead since manufacturing products was very labor-intensive and time cards were easy to track. When machines started replacing labor, companies switched to using machine-hours as their allocation base. However, in recent times, these two methods have become less accurate for the following reasons:

1. More and more companies are producing a variety of products in the same plant. Therefore, using one predetermined overhead rate can lead to incorrect costing.

2. In the past, the majority of costs in a company were related to direct costs, and only a small portion of costs pertained to indirect costs. However, with improved manufacturing technology (equipment that can be adjusted to work on different products with minimal downtime) and communication technology (e-mail, Enterprise Resource Planning (ERP) systems), indirect costs have come to represent a larger portion of total costs. Therefore, costing distortions become more material.

Allocating overhead costs using direct labor hours or machine hours is simple and easy to administer. However, it may not result in accurate costing of products if different products consume resources differently. To illustrate, assume a factory produces two products, product A and product B. Suppose product A uses ten direct labor hours, and product B requires more intricate work and takes 12 direct labor hours to produce. If a predetermined overhead rate is based on direct labor hours, then product B will have more allocated overhead costs than product A. This is because product B used more direct labor hours than product A. Recall, however, that overhead costs can include maintenance work done on machines that build the products. Suppose that when the machine is used to produce product A, the machine is stretched to its operating limits and requires a considerable amount of maintenance expense for each production run. However, machine use for product B utilizes the machine at its standard operating mode and requires minimal maintenance after a production run. Therefore, more overhead maintenance costs should be allocated to product A than to product B since it consumes more maintenance labor. However, with the predetermined overhead rate based on direct labor hours, product B would have been allocated a higher amount of overhead. The issue here is that costing systems which use a single predetermined overhead rate is easy and inexpensive to administer but it may not reflect the reality of the situation. As a result, managers could be pricing their products incorrectly.

The consequences of not being able to properly cost the products can be disastrous for a company. It would not be able to establish an accurate minimum selling price and have difficulty understanding how to improve operations. The company may also decide to remove an "unprofitable" product line that, in reality, was just allocated too many indirect costs.

Just from this simple example, it is evident that, in many cases, overhead in a company cannot be entirely based on one cost allocation base. There are many other factors to be considered when assigning costs to a product, such as the range of products, amount of batch setups, maintenance requirements for different products and the complexity of products produced. Therefore, costing methods need to be tailored for each specific organization in order to assign costs accurately.

Activity-Based Costing

Activity-Based Costing (ABC) is a method where managers can more accurately cost their products and services by minimizing the problems with overhead allocation. The ABC method is different from other costing systems in that it looks at specific activities that are performed in the process of making products or providing services. For example, in a tutoring company, one of the activities that the office administrator performs is tabulating and recording timesheets for the tutors employed by the company. The costs associated with this activity should be tracked because it requires the office administrator's time (a valuable resource), and is a crucial part of their service. The costs associated with this activity are then traced to each student. This way, managers can accurately determine how much of the timesheet preparation costs to allocate to each student.

In ABC, the idea is that products and services are produced by activities, and activities in turn consume resources. Often, ABC is used as a supplementary costing system for internal management and not for financial reporting purposes. This is because ABC takes into account all costs that affect the cost of a product, including non-manufacturing overhead like advertising, distribution, etc. In general, overhead costs are first allocated to activity pools, which are then allocated to the products themselves. See figure 5.1 for an illustration.

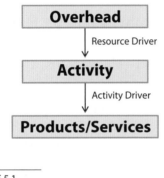

FIGURE 5.1

The following example will illustrate the steps for using activity-based costing in a manufacturing environment.

Activity-Based Costing at Print 4U

Print 4U Inc. is a printer of custom T-shirts and other clothing for both the fashion and advertising industries. The company prints single-colored and multi-colored shirts. The single-colored shirts are printed with higher quality materials to ensure that the colors do not fade. Consumers have the option to purchase multi-colored shirts that can be printed in any number of colors. They both use manual operated screen printing machines for small quantities and automated machines for larger production runs.

Using the ABC method, the following example will demonstrate the necessary steps to calculate overhead costs per unit for each product line. During the year, Print 4U printed 5,000 single-colored shirts and 4,000 multi-colored shirts.

Step 1: Identify activities.

Print 4U managers identify the following activities involved in producing printed shirts:

- *Order Processing*: When orders for shirts are received, the accounting department processes the orders and sends the requests to the factory.
- *Machine Setup*: This activity involves setting the machine for production runs for different styles. For example, the printing machine needs to be re-fitted when switching from printing single-colored to multi-colored shirts. This activity takes up the operator's time and, thus consumes resources.
- *Printing*: This activity involves printing pictures and logos onto the shirts.

By separating operations into activities, managers have created **activity cost pools**. Activity cost pools represent activities in businesses that are essential in providing goods or services to customers. These activities consume resources such as warehousing, labor time and machine time. This example has focused on only three activities but in reality there could be many more. Deciding on which activities are the most relevant to the operation of the business requires good judgment. That is why the design of an activity-based costing system requires input from all parts of the organization. Managers of various departments (e.g. marketing, production, engineering and sales) should work with upper management to identify significant activity cost pools.

Step 2: Identify the amount of overhead related to each activity.

Next, managers assign budgeted overhead costs to each activity cost pool. This is based on estimates. For example, suppose total budgeted overhead costs amount to $100,000. Managers assign 60% of overhead costs to printing, 30% of costs to machine setup and 10% of costs to process orders. Therefore, overhead costs associated with the printing activity amount to $60,000 (60% of $100,000). Overhead costs associated with machine setup amount to $30,000 (30% of $100,000). Overhead costs associated with order processing amount to $10,000 (10% of $100,000). Figure 5.2 outlines the costs associated with each activity cost pool.

	Printing	Machine Setup	Order Processing	Total
% of Overhead Associated with each Activity	60%	30%	10%	100%
Amount of Overhead Associated with each Activity	$60,000	$30,000	$10,000	$100,000

FIGURE 5.2

Step 3: Identify how much activity is used by each product.

Now that the overhead costs associated with each activity are identified, managers will have to determine the appropriate cost allocation bases to drive these activity costs to the different product lines. In this case, Print 4U has identified the cost allocation bases related to the three activities as follows:

Activity	Cost Allocation Base
Printing	Number of direct labor hours (DLH)
Machine Setup	Number of setups
Order Processing	Number of orders

Next, the amount of resources (i.e. cost allocation base) consumed by each product can be determined. Managers at Print 4U have estimated that the single-colored shirts will consume 4,000 direct labor hours, will involve 15 setups and will require 125 orders to be processed. They also estimate that the multi-colored shirts will consume 3,000 direct labor hours, involve 25 setups and require 200 orders to be processed. This information is outlined in figure 5.3. The totals for each activity have also been calculated.

	Printing	Machine Setup	Order Processing
Single	4,000 DLH	15 setups	125 orders
Multi	3,000 DLH	25 setups	200 orders
Total Activity	7,000 DLH	40 setups	325 orders

FIGURE 5.3

Step 4: Calculate the activity rate for each activity.

Managers now have enough information to calculate the activity rate for each activity. The **activity rate** is a measure of how much overhead costs are consumed by each unit of activity. This is calculated by dividing the amount of overhead associated with each activity (see figure 5.2) by the total activity for each pool (see figure 5.3). The activity rates are calculated in figure 5.4.

	Printing (DLH)	Machine Setup	Processing Orders
Amount of Overhead Associated with each Activity	$60,000	$30,000	$10,000
Total Activity	7,000 DLH	40 setups	325 orders
Activity Rate	$8.57 per DLH	$750 per setup	$30.77 per order

FIGURE 5.4

The activity rate for printing is calculated as $60,000 divided by 7,000 direct labor hours to give approximately $8.57 per DLH. The activity rate for setup is calculated as $30,000 divided by 40 setups to give $750 per setup. The activity rate for processing orders is calculated as $10,000 divided by 325 orders to give $30.77 per order.

Step 5: Use the activity rate to assign overhead costs to products.

Managers can now calculate the overhead costs for each unit of product. These calculations can be found in figure 5.5.

Single (5,000 units)	Printing	Machine Setup	Order Processing
Activity Used	4,000	15	125
Activity Rate	$8.57	$750	$30.77
Overhead Costs per Activity	$34,286*	$11,250	$3,846
Total Overhead Costs	$49,382		
Overhead Costs per Unit	$9.88		

*To avoid rounding errors, the calculation is 4,000 orders × ($60,000 ÷ 7,000 DLH)

FIGURE 5.5

Calculate costs associated with each product separately. For single-colored shirts, the printing activity consumed 4,000 direct labor hours. Multiplying this with the activity rate of approximately $8.57 for the printing activity gives a total cost of $34,286 for printing. Performing similar calculations for machine setups and processing orders, the total overhead costs for single-colored T-shirts become $49,382. Since 5,000 single-colored shirts are to be produced, the overhead cost per unit is equal to $9.88 ($49,382 ÷ 5,000).

Similar calculations can be made for the multi-colored shirts. These calculations can be found in figure 5.6.

Multi (4,000 units)	Printing	Machine Setup	Order Processing
Activity Used	3,000	25	200
Activity Rate	$8.57	$750	$30.77
Overhead Costs per Activity	$25,714*	$18,750	$6,154
Total Overhead Costs	$50,618		
Overhead Costs per Unit	$12.65		

*To avoid rounding errors, the calculation is 3,000 orders × ($60,000 ÷ 7,000 DLH)

FIGURE 5.6

Figure 5.6 shows that overhead cost per unit for the multi-colored shirts is $12.65. The ABC calculations for the assignment of indirect costs are summarized in figure 5.7 below.

SUMMARY OF ABC

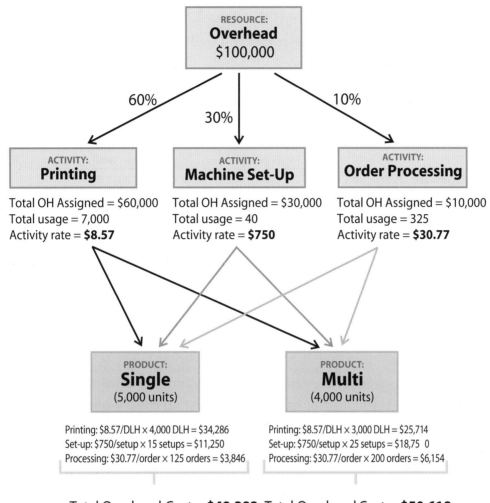

FIGURE 5.7

IN THE REAL WORLD

Activity-based costing can provide important insights for organizations where: a large component of total costs is made up of indirect costs; some resources consume significant amount of costs; different products use resources in very different proportions. An excellent example of an organization where all these conditions exist is a hospital. The services provided by a hospital can range from a routine procedure in an outpatients clinic to a major surgery. If the hospital is reimbursed by a government agency or an insurance company based on the cost of the services provided to the patients, understanding costs will be the fundamental part of the contractual relationship between the hospital and the funding agency. If the hospital is reimbursed based on a price for the services provided, the hospital needs to know its costs so that it can determine the relationship between its costs and the revenue it receives for its services.

Multiple POH Rates vs. Overall POH Rate

In the previous section, the overhead costs associated with single and multi-colored shirts have been calculated using the ABC method. If the ABC analysis is compared with the results determined using an overall predetermined rate, the reader will find that there are differences in the cost assigned to each product line.

Figure 5.8 outlines how unit overhead costs are calculated using an overall predetermined overhead rate.

	Overhead	
Total Estimated Overhead Costs	$100,000	
Total Estimated Direct Labor Hours	7,000	
Budgeted Overhead Rate	$14.29	
	Single (5,000 units)	Multi (4,000 units)
Direct Labor Hours	4,000	3,000
Overhead to Allocate	$57,143	$42,857
Overhead Costs per Unit	$11.43	$10.71

FIGURE 5.8

Let us assume that the costs related to activities such as printing, machine setup and ordering are not made distinct. Print 4U will now allocate the overhead to the two product lines on the basis of direct labor hours. To calculate the predetermined overhead rate, divide the total overhead cost of $100,000 by the total direct labor hours of 7,000. As a result, the predetermined rate is $14.29 per direct labor hour. This rate is then used to allocate overhead to each product. Since single-colored shirts consumed 4,000 direct labor hours, $57,143 ($14.29 × 4,000) of overhead will be allocated to the single-colored shirts. This amounts to a cost of $11.43 ($57,143 ÷ 5,000) per unit of a single-colored shirt. Similar calculations can be made for multi-colored shirts. The overhead cost per unit for multi-colored shirts is $10.71 ([$14.29 × 3,000] ÷ 4,000) per unit.

Figure 5.9 outlines the different unit overhead costs for each type of shirt.

	Single (5,000 units)	Multi (4,000 units)
Cost using Activity-Based Costing	$9.88	$12.65
Cost using Predetermined Overhead Rate	$11.43	$10.71

FIGURE 5.9

Notice that if the overall predetermined overhead rate is used, the single-colored shirts are over-allocated and the multi-colored shirts are under-allocated. The single-colored and multi-colored shirts use machine setup and order process cost overheads in a manner that is different from the way they use direct labor hours. Therefore, since the predetermined overhead rate is calculated based solely on direct labor hours, it does not take the machine setup and processing activity behaviors into account. Thus, in theory, the ABC method provides more accurate costing than the predetermined overhead rate.

In this case, only the overhead costs associated with the two product lines were considered. To calculate the cost per unit for single-colored and multi-colored shirts, managers will need to take the sum of the overhead cost, direct materials and direct labor costs per unit.

Activity-Based Costing and GAAP

In the above example, Print 4U Inc. included non-manufacturing costs (e.g. processing orders) into the cost of the printed shirts. According to GAAP, only costs related to the manufacturing of the product should be included into the cost of inventory. Therefore, the ABC method used in the example above does not comply with GAAP. However, this does not mean that the ABC method cannot be GAAP compliant. Since ABC is a method of allocating indirect costs to a product, it can be set up such that only manufacturing costs are allocated and non-manufacturing costs are not.

In general, most companies use the ABC method as a supplementary internal tool because they already have a costing system for external financial statement purposes. Because of this, companies will incorporate both manufacturing and non-manufacturing costs into their ABC system. In these cases, managers use information from the ABC system to help determine the 'true' cost of their products and to help make operational decisions. Using ABC information to manage the business operations to make them more efficient is referred to as **activity-based management**.

Drawbacks of Current Implementations of Activity-Based Costing

While ABC has been very beneficial for a variety of companies when analyzing their product costs, it is not without its drawbacks. Under the ABC system, overhead is assigned to the different activities based on the percentage of time spent on each activity. To determine these percentages, employees are surveyed and asked to estimate how much of their time they spend on each activity. Few employees will admit to having idle time, thus cost driver rates will be calculated assuming 100% capacity. In reality, operations do not operate at 100% capacity and, as a result, the cost driver rates are too high.

Another issue with traditional ABC is the time and costs involved with collecting employee surveys. This step of data collection is necessary to determine the percentages to allocate to each activity. As the company grows, it becomes increasingly difficult, causing ABC to be less effective in large-scale operations.

Fortunately, both these drawbacks have been addressed by a new method, time-driven ABC, as explained in the following section. However, before going into the details of this new method, the concept of capacity will first be discussed.

A CLOSER LOOK

Activity-based budgeting is a management tool that is closely related to activity based costing. Activity based budgeting exploits an understanding of how products or services consume costs, in order to identify the activity volumes required in an operating plan. These activity volumes can identify where the organization will have a surplus or shortage of resources for a given production plan. Enterprise resource planning (ERP) exploits knowledge of how products and services drive the consumption of activities (and therefore their cost) in the same way.

Using Time-Driven ABC to Identify Capacity Issues

Capacity in an organization refers to the extent to which a resource can be used. Examples of resources can include materials, warehouses, employees and machines. Consider the following example: You run a lawn mowing business for residents in the suburb of a large city. You have employed three workers. Every weekday they drive the company truck to customers' houses and mow their lawns. Assume that all lawns have a similar size, and under normal conditions (average temperature, no rain, lawnmowers working efficiently), it takes one hour to mow a lawn. If the employees work eight hours a day, they should be able to cut eight lawns a day. This is known as **theoretical capacity,** which is the amount of activity that is possible under ideal conditions. While it is possible to cut eight lawns a day, in reality, the employees only cut six lawns in an eight hour shift. This is because approximately two hours a day are lost, possibly due to:

- driving from one house to the next
- packing and unpacking the equipment on the truck
- taking a lunch break

Since these activities are unavoidable and are required to operate the business, it is only reasonable to expect that the employees cut six lawns in an eight hour shift. This is known as **practical capacity,** which is the reasonable level of activity that can actually be attained. Establishing the practical capacity can be achieved in various ways, such as basing performance on past history, performing a time study, interviewing people for their opinions or just making an educated guess. As mentioned earlier, cost accounting is not an exact science and estimates are often based on professional judgment. Practical capacities will often have to be adjusted due to many factors, such as employees becoming more experienced, more efficient equipment being used or larger sized jobs increasing efficiency.

One key measure that managers are interested in is **unused capacity**. Unused capacity refers to the difference between the current or budgeted operating level of activity and practical capacity. For example, suppose you know that the practical capacity for lawn cutting amounts to cutting six lawns per day. Currently, your employees are only cutting five lawns per day. Therefore, they are doing only five hours worth of work each day. Since there are six hours available in a practical day, this means that there is unused capacity of one hour per day (see figure 5.10).

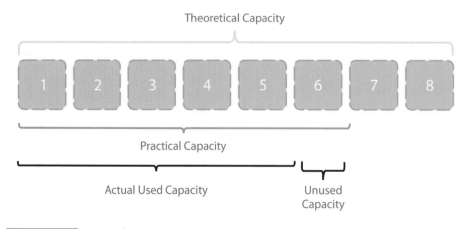

FIGURE 5.10

Alternatively, managers also want to identify areas which are functioning beyond capacity. If the employees are cutting seven lawns per day, they are being overworked. This will affect their productivity later on and would likely encourage you to hire another employee. Capacity is especially important in larger organizations where different departments may be experiencing different capacity issues. The ABC method can help identify such issues. This will be demonstrated next using an approach known as **time-driven ABC**.

Time-Driven ABC

The time-driven approach to ABC is an attempt to simplify the implementation of ABC and to provide a quick way of identifying capacity issues in an organization. This approach is endorsed by Robert S. Kaplan from Harvard Business School as a "new, innovative, time-driven methodology". Professor Kaplan has written a number of books and numerous papers on the subject of ABC costing. Let us now use the time-driven ABC approach to identify capacity issues at a government office.

Consider a government service department that issues birth, marriage and death certificates. The department has employed a total of ten employees, each earning $3,600 per month. This costs the government a total of $36,000 per month. There are three activities in the department: (1) data collection, (2) approval and (3) printing and mailing. Four employees are responsible for all the work related to data collection (e.g. organizing mail and documents). Four employees are responsible for the approval process (e.g. contacting references) and the remaining two employees are responsible for the printing and mailing (e.g. printing certificates and sending them to residences).

There are two vital pieces of information that are used to measure costs. These are the cost per unit of capacity and the time to carry out one unit of each kind of activity. The process to allocate costs under time-driven ABC is illustrated in the steps below. Note that the results of all calculations can be found in figure 5.11.

<u>**Step 1:**</u> <u>Determine the cost per time unit of capacity (i.e. cost per minute to supply the service).</u>

To determine the cost per time unit of capacity, the theoretical available amount of time that the employees can work needs to be calculated. In figure 5.11, column B highlights the number of employees available for each activity.

Column C shows the available minutes per month. Assume that the employees work eight hours each day. This will amount to 96,000 minutes per month (8 hours/day × 60 min/hr × 20 days/month × 10 employees). In other words, this is the total theoretical number of minutes available by all operators performing the function per month.

Column D highlights the practical supply capacity for the month. Given that employees have to take a lunch break, attend meetings and hold training seminars, they are only capable of working

80% of the time on the actual certificates. This amounts to 76,800 minutes (96,000 minutes × 80%) for the month. This is the practical capacity.

Since employees are paid $36,000 per month, the cost per time unit of capacity is **$0.469/min** ($36,000 ÷ 76,800 minutes).

Step 2: Determine the unit times of consumption of resource capacity (i.e. number of minutes required to perform each unit of work).

To determine the number of minutes required to perform each unit of work, employees or managers can be surveyed on how long it takes to collect data, approve then print and mail a certificate.

The results can be found in column E. It takes employees 15 minutes to collect data for a certificate, 20 minutes to approve a certificate and 12 minutes to print and mail a certificate. In this case, it is assumed that it takes similar times to perform these activities for any type of certificate.

Refer to the table below and the column descriptions to help you understand the logic of the process and its importance.

A	B	C	D	E	F	G	H	I	J	K
Activity	# of People	Available min/Month	Practical Supply Capacity	Unit Time (minutes)	Cost Assigned	Cost Driver Rate	Total Production Expected	Actual Production	Budgeted Costs given Actual Production	Unused Practical Capacity
Data Collection	4	38,400	30,720	15	$14,400	$7.03	2,048	2,100	$14,763	-$363
Approval	4	38,400	30,720	20	$14,400	$9.38	1,536	1,265	$11,866	$2,534
Printing & Mailing	2	19,200	15,360	12	$7,200	$5.63	1,280	1,130	$6,362	$838
Total	10	96,000	76,800		$36,000				$32,991	$3,009

FIGURE 5.11

In column F, the costs assigned to each activity are based on the number of personnel involved with the activity. Therefore, $14,400 ($3,600/employee × 4 employees) of overhead costs are assigned to the data collection activity. Since there are just as many people assigned to the approval activity (four people) $14,400 of overhead costs are also assigned to the approval activity. Using the same logic $7,200 ($3,600/employee × 2 employees) of overhead costs are assigned to the printing and mailing activity. Notice that the sum of the assigned costs amount to $36,000. This serves as a check that all costs have been assigned to the activities.

Step 3: Determine the cost driver rate.

Once the cost per time unit of capacity ($0.469/min) and the amount of time it takes to perform an activity is determined, it is possible to calculate the cost driver rates. In this case, the cost driver rate is defined as the cost of each activity per certificate.

This can be found in column G. The cost driver rate for data collection is $7.03/certificate ($0.469/min × 15 min/certificate). The cost driver rate for approval is $9.38/certificate ($0.469/min × 20 min/certificate) and $5.63/certificate ($0.469/min × 12 min/license) for printing and mailing.

Step 4: Determine the budgeted costs given actual production.

Columns H and I show the expected production and actual production, respectively, for each activity. Expected production is based on planning activities and is not used to evaluate operations. In column J, the budgeted costs given actual production are calculated. For the data collection activity, budgeted costs for actual production of 2,100 certificates amount to $14,763. This is calculated by multiplying the cost driver rate ($7.03) by actual production (2,100). Similarly, the budgeted costs for approval activities and printing & mailing activities amount to $11,866 ($9.38 × 1,265) and $6,362 ($5.63 × 1,130), respectively.

Step 5: Calculate unused capacity.

The difference between the costs assigned (column F) and the budgeted costs given actual production (column J) is the unused or overused practical capacity (Column K). Data collection activities exceeded capacity by $363. On the other hand, there was unused capacity relating to approval activities (of $2,534) and printing and mailing activities (of $838). Figure 5.12 illustrates a summary of the above calculations.

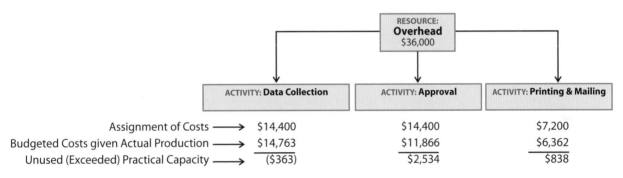

FIGURE 5.12

In a perfect world, the cost assigned would be equal to the budgeted cost for actual production. There would be no variance in capacity. However, in a real world, there will always be a difference. Performing this analysis helps managers understand how idle capacity could be used, thus increasing efficiency and profits. For example, if the supervisor from the data collection department suggested that she is understaffed, she will be in a strong position to support the hiring of another person since her department is over practical capacity. Using this model, the manager can tell that the other two departments are under-used with excess resources. This means that they can possibly transfer an individual from another department to data collection. The company can also replace an individual from the other departments with a new hire for data collection. This would reallocate capacity while keeping total labor costs the same.

After determining capacity issues with the help of time-driven ABC, a manager will be able to apply the *"move it, use it or lose it"* concept. If a manager determines that one department is under-resourced but another has too many resources, they can re-allocate resources from the department that has too many resources to the one that is under-resourced. In other words, the manager can *move* resources and *use* them elsewhere. Alternatively, if a department has too many resources and there is no room to use these resources in the other parts of the business, the manager can remove or reduce the resources to save money and become more efficient. In other words, they can *lose it*.

Analyzing and reporting of the cost of products and services is an important management tool that reveals the cost of doing business. This helps managers identify not only the true cost of products and services but also potential ways of saving costs. In other words, if you cannot measure it, you cannot manage it. Therefore, it is extremely important that the estimates used in this analysis are updated on a consistent basis.

Here, the time-driven ABC method has drawn out useful operational information from a government office that provides services to the public. This approach can also be used in manufacturing or retail organizations to identify capacity issues.

The following case study illustrates the usefulness of identifying capacity issues in an organization:

> *Adrian spent much of his professional career restructuring businesses. Once, during a consultation, he was approached by one of the bookkeepers who complained that she could not cope with the workload and asked if she could employ an assistant. Her primary role included processing accounts payable, reconciling the bank account each month, overseeing (but not processing) accounts receivable, processing bi-weekly payroll and generating various financial reports each month.*
>
> *Given that the business was having significant financial problems (hence the need to restructure), Adrian requested some information before agreeing to the new hire.*
>
> *1. How many incoming purchase invoices did she process per day and how long did each one take?*
>
> *2. How long did it take to complete the bank reconciliation each month?*
>
> *3. How much time did she typically take to oversee the outstanding accounts receivable accounts and how many times a week was she involved in this function?*
>
> *4. How long did it take to process bi-weekly salaries and how many salaried employees were there?*

5. *How long did it take to generate the monthly reports and how many reports did she have to generate?*

Adrian then performed a quick calculation based on company benchmarks and estimated that she was only productive for 18 hours a week. Adrian realized that even though she technically got paid for a 40 hour week (theoretical capacity), it would be unreasonable to assume that she could work that amount so he assumed with breaks, meetings, and other work related distractions, she could only be productive 75% of the time. Therefore, her practical capacity was 30 hours (75% × 40 hours) for the week. If she was only working 18 hours a week when she could have been working 30 hours then she was being productive only 60% of the time! He demonstrated that she had excess resource capacity of about $400 per week for which she was being paid but in fact was not being productive. After helping her to organize her work flow, they found that, in fact, she was perfectly capable of not just managing her current workload on her own but could actually take on more work. This exercise saved the company about $25,000 which would have been spent unnecessarily on the new hire.

This is an example of how identifying a resource's (in this case, an employee's) unused capacity benefitted the company. Organizations have many different types of resources (machines, warehousing, supervisors etc.). If managers are able to easily and accurately identify areas of unused or over-used capacity, the information can go a long way in helping the company to become more efficient and competitive.

Ethical Considerations

Although the ABC system provides a more accurate reporting, some managerial accountants continue to use a single predetermined overhead rate to allocate overhead costs to different products. These accountants may have entered the workforce when ABC was not introduced or was not popular. Therefore, they may not understand how the ABC system can be implemented. They may also not understand the costs and benefits of using an ABC system as opposed to a single allocation rate for overhead costs. The *Statement of Ethical Professional Practice* states under the standard of competence, that managerial accountants have a responsibility to maintain an appropriate level of professional expertise by continually developing knowledge and skills. According to this standard, accountants who avoid learning various cost management methods for whatever reasons (such as becoming accustomed to using one particular method) are behaving unethically.

In Summary

- **Total product costs** include the costs of direct materials, direct labor and manufacturing overhead.

- **Predetermined overhead rate** is the ratio of total budgeted overhead costs to the total budgeted cost allocation base.

- **Activity-based costing (ABC)** system determines the various activities and uses multiple cost allocation bases to assign overhead costs to products.

- Under the ABC method, both non-manufacturing and manufacturing overhead costs are included in the product cost. However, GAAP does not allow non-manufacturing overhead costs to be included in the cost of the inventory. As a result, the ABC method may not be GAAP compliant.

- Using ABC information to manage business operations to make them more efficient is referred to as **activity-based management**.

- The implementation of ABC system can be time consuming and costly.

- **Capacity** in an organization refers to how much a resource can be utilized.

- **Theoretical capacity** is the level of activity that can be attained under ideal operating conditions.

- **Practical capacity** is the reasonable level of activity that can actually be attained.

- **Unused capacity** refers to the difference between the current or budgeted operating level of activity and practical capacity.

- **Time-driven ABC** is a type of activity-based costing system that uses time and practical capacity to assign overhead costs to different activities.

- The purpose of time-driven ABC is to simplify the implementation of ABC for a large-scale organization and to quickly identify capacity issues.

Review Exercise

TWG Limited has a production department that uses activity based costing. The company identified the following estimated activity costs (i.e. budgeted overhead costs assigned to each activity) and estimated cost allocation bases for the period:

Activity	Activity Costs	Cost Allocation Base – Total
Materials handling	$60,000	25,000 pounds of material
Machine setup	16,000	10,000 machine setups
Machine maintenance	14,000	5,000 machine hours
Inspection	11,000	7,100 inspections

The following information is provided for the production of two product lines, X340 and Y500. The department produced 1,500 units of X340 and 1,450 units of Y500

	X340	Y500
Direct materials cost	$12,000	$22,500
Direct labor cost	$50,000	$35,000
Number of setups	1,400	5,300
Number of inspections	3,000	1,200
Number of machine hours	1,900	2,200
Pounds of material	10,000	16,000

Required:

Determine the unit cost for X340 and Y500. Which product line costs the least to manufacture?

Review Exercise – Answer

Activity		Activity Rate
Materials handling	$60,000 ÷ 25,000 pounds of material	$2.40 per pound of material
Machine setup	$16,000 ÷ 10,000 machine setups	$1.60 per machine set up
Machine maintenance	$14,000 ÷ 5,000 machine hours	$2.80 per machine hour
Inspection	$11,000 ÷ 7,100 inspections	$1.55 per inspection

Product X340

Machine setup	1,400 × $1.60	$2,240
Inspection	3,000 × $1.55	$4,650
Machine maintenance	1,900 × $2.80	$5,320
Materials handling	10,000 × $2.40	$24,000
Direct materials		$12,000
Direct labor		$50,000
Total costs		$98,210

Cost per unit = $98,210 ÷ 1,500 units = $65.47

Product Y500

Machine setup	5,300 × $1.60	$8,480
Inspection	1,200 × $1.55	$1,860
Machine maintenance	2,200 × $2.80	$6,160
Materials handling	16,000 × $2.40	$38,400
Direct materials		$22,500
Direct labor		$35,000
Total costs		$112,400

Cost per unit = $112,400 ÷ 1,450 units = $77.52

The per unit cost of the X340 is less than the per unit cost of the Y500, so the X340 costs the least to manufacture.

Chapter 6
COST-VOLUME-PROFIT ANALYSIS

LEARNING OUTCOMES:

❶ Understand the concept of cost behavior

❷ Describe relevant range, step fixed costs and step variable costs

❸ Separate mixed costs into fixed and variable costs

❹ Prepare and analyze a contribution margin statement

❺ Perform break-even analysis and target analysis

❻ Calculate contribution margin ratio

❼ Perform incremental analysis

❽ Summarize the basic cost-volume-profit (CVP) assumptions

❾ Calculate margin of safety

❿ Apply CVP analysis to a multi-product company

⓫ Perform sensitivity analysis

⓬ Explain cost structure and operating leverage

Cost Behavior Analysis: An Introduction

Many managerial accounting tools are applicable in your everyday life. Imagine your friend has recently decided to open a small candy store, offering a variety of candies. He believes that if he is able to attract enough customers, the store will make a generous profit. However, in the first week of operations, he ran into some problems. He did not understand why he was losing money even though the store was attracting a good amount of customers. So the question he asked himself is, "How many candies do I have to sell in order to fully cover my costs and obtain a profit?" At the same time, he wondered how his sales and costs would be affected if he decided to work shorter hours and sell fewer candies. Can he simply solve the problem by raising his prices by $1? What happens if the cost of producing candies increases? How would all of these factors affect his profits?

In order for your friend to make informed decisions, he must understand the behavior of his business' costs. In other words, he must be able to reasonably predict how total cost changes when the volume of activity (e.g. sales) changes. Analyzing cost behavior will allow him to gain a better understanding of how to manage costs and predict outcomes. This chapter will not only explain what cost behavior is, but also show how to perform a cost behavior analysis under different scenarios.

Cost Behavior and Relevant Range

Before analyzing cost behavior in depth, some key terminologies will be illustrated using the following example. Chocolaa Inc., a small local factory, produces various chocolate products for sale. Their products include white chocolate, dark chocolate, milk chocolate and more. Chocolaa Inc. has different types of costs:

1. **Variable costs** - Costs that change in relation to the change in production volume are considered variable costs. Some examples are cocoa powder, sugar, and wrappers for individual pieces of chocolates. These costs will vary according to the quantity of chocolates produced. Figure 6.1 shows the relationship between variable costs (vertical axis) and volume of production (horizontal axis). Notice that when no boxes of chocolate are produced, the total variable cost is equal to zero. As the volume of production increases, variable costs increase. If the variable cost per box of chocolate is $6, then for every box produced and sold, total variable cost will increase by $6. Thus, if 20,000 boxes are produced and sold, total variable cost will amount to $120,000 (20,000 boxes × $6).

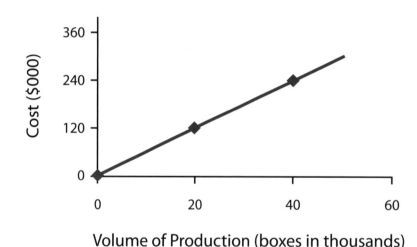

FIGURE 6.1

2. **Fixed costs** - Costs that do not change in relation to the volume produced are considered fixed costs. These costs remain constant regardless the quantity of chocolates produced. Some examples of these costs include rent, insurance and depreciation of machines. Figure 6.2 shows the relationship between the fixed costs (annual rent expense of $28,000 on the vertical axis) and volume of production (horizontal axis). It is assumed that fixed costs remain the same for all levels of production. Even when the company does not produce any chocolate, it will still incur the $28,000 of fixed cost.

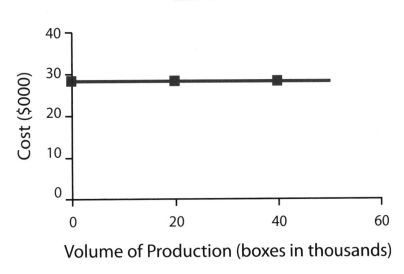

FIGURE 6.2

3.   **Mixed costs** - Those costs that contain both fixed and variable components. Suppose Chocolaa Inc. compensates its sales team with a base salary plus commission. The company's fixed costs would be the base salary, because the base salary is not dependent on the number of sales an employee makes. Sales commission would represent its variable costs because this amount would vary as the sales volume changes. As a result, this type of employee compensation is an example of a mixed cost.

Step Fixed and Variable Costs

In chapter 1, the concept of **relevant range** was introduced. Relevant range refers to a certain range of production where cost behaviors remain the same. For example, rent expenses would remain fixed at $28,000 if the production remained within the specific relevant range of 0-50,000 boxes. However, suppose the demand for chocolates suddenly doubled and the required production volume is beyond the capacity of the current factory. The business may have to rent out another factory to expand production capacity. If the cost of rent for the new factory is $12,000, this means that total rent expenses (a fixed cost in the relevant range) have been stepped up to $40,000. Since the rent expense will step up after a certain volume is reached, it is called a **step fixed cost**. Figure 6.3 gives a graphical representation of the step increase in rent if production doubled.

Step Fixed Costs

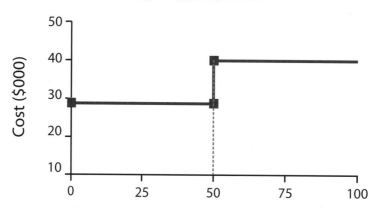

Volume of Production (boxes in thousands)

FIGURE 6.3

Consider another example. Steven is a supervisor in a plant where he can manage up to a maximum of five operators. Once the need arises to employ more operators, an additional supervisor is needed. The higher the volume of chocolate produced, the more operators required. As a result, the number of supervisors will vary (in steps) according to the amount of chocolate produced. In other words, the number of supervisors will have to be stepped up based on the volume of chocolate production. It is important to note that a company can also incur **step variable costs**.

Previously, the cost of direct labor is assumed to be a variable cost. However, direct labor differs from direct materials in terms of variable cost behavior. In the Chocolaa example, the direct materials, which include ingredients and wrappers for the chocolate, are true variable costs. If they are not used immediately, they can be stored and used at a later date. Direct labor, on the other hand, cannot be saved for a later date. If it is not used, it is lost.

Additionally, any one worker is capable of working on or producing products within a range. This means one worker is capable of making from zero to a certain quantity of products. Suppose each worker at Chocolaa Inc. can produce up to 2,000 boxes of chocolate and is being paid $30,000 per year. If Chocolaa produces 5,000 boxes, the company will need to hire three workers for $90,000 (direct labor costs). These three workers are capable of producing up to 6,000 boxes. Since only 5,000 boxes of chocolate are needed, these workers will not be working at full capacity. However, if the demand was 6,000 boxes, the workers would be working at full capacity. Only if production went above 6,000 boxes would a fourth worker be required and would the company incur an additional $30,000 in direct labor costs. This illustrates a relevant range for the cost of direct labor. A relatively small change in the quantity produced does not necessarily mean more workers must be hired or fired. Only if the quantity produced changes by a large enough margin does the quantity of workers need to change. This is referred to as step variable costs and is shown in figure 6.4.

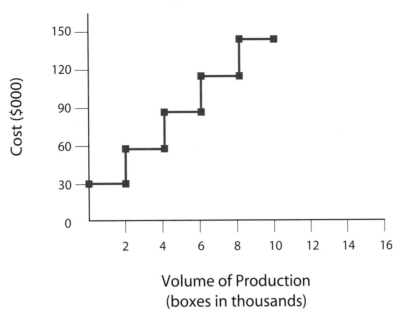

FIGURE 6.4

Thus what may initially appear to be a variable cost actually has a relevant range and behaves similar to a step fixed cost. The difference is that the relevant range for step variable costs is much smaller than the relevant range for step fixed costs. If a step variable cost has a very small relevant range and would step up frequently, most managers will likely treat it as a true variable costs to make calculations and decision making easier.

Mixed Costs Calculation

Not all mixed costs are as simple to separate into fixed and variable costs as the salary plus commission example. Costs, such as the maintenance of machines, may have a portion of fixed costs and variable costs that are not easily separated. The fixed portion of maintenance may include specialized equipment and tools or payments to maintenance employees. The variable portion may include parts and other items to repair the machines. Determining fixed and variable costs is important to properly calculate contribution margin.

Referring back to Chocolaa Inc., we are given the total maintenance costs over the last eight months as shown in figure 6.5. The assumption is that the cost of maintenance is related to the number of boxes produced. The maintenance costs are a combination of fixed and variable expenses. Two ways of separating the fixed from the variable costs are the high-low method and the least-square regression method.

Month	Volume of Production (boxes in thousands)	Maintenance Costs
January	2,000	$5,600
February	8,000	$7,200
March	16,000	$19,000
April	5,000	$5,900
May	6,000	$6,500
June	11,000	$7,900
July	15,000	$9,500
August	9,000	$7,700

FIGURE 6.5

The High-Low Method

The high-low method is a quick and easy way to factor out the fixed costs and the variable costs per unit of production. Let us use the information from figure 6.5 to show the high-low method calculations. Also, assume that there is a strong relationship between the maintenance costs and the number of boxes produced.

Step 1: Determine the periods that have the highest and lowest amount of production

In this case, March has the highest production and January has the lowest production.

Step 2: Calculate the change in production and the change in costs between the highest and the lowest amount of production.

Let us now take the difference between March and January's volume of production and maintenance costs.

March	16,000 units	$19,000
January	-2,000 units	-5,600
Change	14,000 units	$13,400

From the lowest to the highest volume of production, there was a change of 14,000 units and $13,400 in costs.

Step 3: Calculate variable costs

Variable costs can be calculated by dividing the change in cost by the change in production.

$$\text{Variable Cost per Unit} = \frac{\text{Change in Cost}}{\text{Change in Production}}$$

$$Variable\ Cost\ per\ Unit\ =\ \frac{\$13,400}{14,000\ units}$$

$$=\ \$0.96\ per\ unit$$

From this calculation, it is found that each box of chocolate that is produced incurs $0.96 of maintenance costs.

Step 4: Calculate the fixed costs component

Using the variable cost per unit of production and either the high or the low level of production, calculate the fixed costs component of the maintenance expense.

Fixed costs = High Production Cost − (Variable Cost per Unit × High Production Units)

OR

Fixed costs = Low Production Cost − (Variable Cost per Unit × Low Production Units)

Here, let us illustrate by using the high production cost information:

Fixed costs = $19,000 − ($0.96 × 16,000 units)
Fixed costs = $3,640

Using this information, the mixed cost is shown to include $3,640 of fixed costs. This is the cost that will be incurred by maintenance regardless of the level of production. The cost of $0.96 per unit is incurred for each unit that is produced and is considered a variable cost. Thus, for any level of production, total maintenance costs can be calculated as:

Total Maintenance Costs = $3,640 + ($0.96 × Number of Units Produced)

There is one major drawback in using the high-low method. A graph of the data in figure 6.5 is shown in figure 6.6. A straight line connects the high and the low production points that were used in the calculation. Notice how the line connecting the two points is nowhere near any of the other points on the graph. This suggests the high-low method will provide inaccurate results if there are any extremely high or low levels of production or extremely high or low costs associated with these levels of production. A straight line that runs closer to the majority of the points on the graph would provide a more accurate result for both the fixed cost and the variable cost per unit.

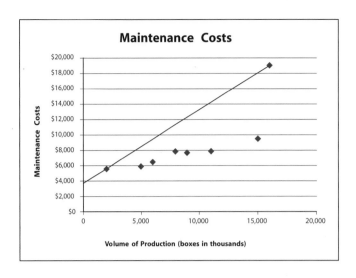

FIGURE 6.6

The Least-Square Regression Method

Compared to the high-low method, the least-square regression method calculates the fixed cost and the variable cost per unit more accurately. This method attempts to find a straight line that crosses, or is close to, as many data points on a graph as possible. This method uses statistical calculations, which can be cumbersome if done manually. Spreadsheet software, such as Excel, can easily calculate the fixed cost and variable cost per unit. Figure 6.7 presents a graph for the Chocolaa Inc.'s maintenance costs using the least-square regression method.

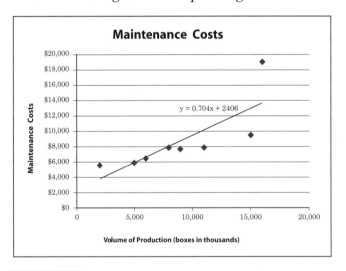

FIGURE 6.7

Notice that the straight line no longer connects the high and low points on the graph. The line is now closer to all the points on the graph. The formula, y=0.7049x + 2406.1, is automatically calculated by the software and provides the fixed costs and variable cost per unit. In this case, fixed costs are $2,406.10 and variable costs per unit of production are approximately $0.70 per unit. Thus, for any level of production, total maintenance costs can be calculated as:

$$\text{Total Maintenance Costs} = \$2,406.10 + (\$0.70 \times \text{Number of Units Produced})$$

This is very different from the cost figures from the high-low method and more accurately represent the fixed and variable cost components of the maintenance expense mixed cost.

Variable costs, fixed costs, and mixed costs represent three types of cost behavior patterns. **Cost behavior** refers to how costs change as volume of production or sales changes. In cost behavior analysis, costs are first classified as variable, fixed or mixed. Once these costs are classified, it is possible to perform **cost-volume-profit (CVP)** analysis. CVP analysis is a tool that managerial accountants use to understand how production volume affects profits and costs.

Contribution Margin Statement

Chapter 1 demonstrated how a contribution margin income statement can be prepared once its costs are classified as either variable or fixed. Recall that the contribution margin statement is a detailed report that separates variable costs and fixed costs. A conventional income statement groups all the variable and fixed product costs into either cost of goods sold or other operating expenses. Even though a conventional income statement provides useful information about a company's revenues and expenses for external reporting purpose, it does not provide all the information managers need for internal decision making. This is because the costs are not grouped by their behavior on a conventional income statement.

A contribution margin statement demonstrates how much revenue, less variable costs, is available to contribute to covering fixed costs. Once fixed costs are completely paid for, the remaining amount represents operating income. Separating the variable costs from fixed costs provides managers with useful information, because fixed costs are generally not affected by the volume of production with a given relevant range. For example, suppose a company experienced a decrease in sales orders. By preparing a contribution margin income statement, the company would realize whether the current sales revenue can still cover its fixed costs (e.g. rent and advertisement costs).

Figure 6.8 is Pine Furniture Manufacturer's contribution margin statement for the month of May. The second column of the table illustrates the calculation in total (e.g. $100,000 represents the amount of total revenue). The third column illustrates the calculation per unit (e.g. $10.00 represents the revenue per chair). The forth column illustrates the calculation of each cost as a percentage of revenue (e.g. total variable costs as a percentage of revenue is calculated by $72,000 ÷ $100,000 = 72%).

Pine Furniture Manufacturer Contribution Margin Statement For the Month Ending May 31, 2010						
	Total		Per Unit		Percentage	
Sales		$100,000		$10.00		100%
Less Variable Costs						
Wood	$50,000		$5.00		50%	
Paint & Screws	7,000		0.70		7%	
Labor	15,000	72,000	1.50	7.20	15%	72%
Contribution Margin		28,000		$2.80		28%
Less Fixed Costs						
Rent		15,000				
Operating Income		$13,000				

FIGURE 6.8

The calculation in total provides a big picture for total costs associated with each cost category. The total contribution margin is the difference between total revenue and total variable costs. It is important to remember that the total variable costs and total fixed costs include all types of costs incurred by the company. In other words, a contribution margin statement includes both product costs and period costs.

WORTH REPEATING...

The costs related to the manufacturing phase of a product are called product costs (e.g. direct materials, direct labor and manufacturing overhead). All other costs are called period costs (e.g. selling and administrative expenses).

The breakdown of the contribution margin statement into unit values for sales and variable costs simplifies analysis and break-even calculations which will be discussed in the next section. For example, the contribution margin statement tells us that the sales price per unit is $10 and total variable costs per unit amount to $7.20. This means that for every unit sold, it costs $7.20 to make that unit. The difference between the sales price per unit and the variable cost per unit gives the **contribution margin per unit**. The contribution margin per unit for Pine Furniture Manufacturer during the month of May is $2.80 ($10.00/unit - $7.20/unit). In other words, for every additional chair produced and sold, $2.80 is available to cover fixed costs and contribute towards profit.

Expressing sales and variable costs as a percentage of sales also provides some meaningful information. Figure 6.8 shows that wood costs 50% of the selling price of a chair, while paint and screws only cost 7% of the selling price. The percentage of sales that is left over to cover fixed costs is 28%.

The contribution margin statement will help managers at Pine Furniture Manufacturer understand what will happen if sales volume, variable costs or fixed costs change. For example, assume the managers at Pine Furniture Manufacturer predict that the sales will likely increase if they advertise the chairs in a magazine. The cost of advertising is $4,000 per month and the estimated increase in sales volume is 10%. Should the managers proceed with advertising?

The contribution margin statement with the above assumption is illustrated in figure 6.9. The increase in sales volume would increase sales revenue, variable costs and contribution margin by 10% (e.g. $100,000 × 10% + $100,000 = $110,000). However, the contribution margin will not increase enough to cover the new fixed cost therefore operating income will decrease. In this case, management will likely not proceed with the advertisement.

If Pine Furniture Manufacturer only sells one chair during the month of May, they will have a contribution margin of $2.80 which will have to be used to pay the fixed cost of rent. With only one chair sold, this will leave the company with an operating loss of $14,997.20. For each extra chair they sell during the month, the total contribution margin will increase and the operating loss will continue to decrease. To determine the amount of sales required in order to reach an operating income of $0, Pine Furniture Manufacturer should perform a break-even analysis.

Pine Furniture Manufacturer Contribution Margin Statement For the Month Ending June 30, 2010		
		Total
Sales		$110,000
Less Variable Costs		
Wood	$55,000	
Paint & Screws	7,700	
Labor	16,500	79,200
Contribution Margin		30,800
Less Fixed Costs		
Advertising		4,000
Rent		15,000
Operating Income		$11,800

FIGURE 6.9

Break-Even Analysis

Break-even analysis can be used by companies for planning purposes and for decision-making. Recall from chapter 1 that the break-even point is defined as the number of units produced where there is no profit or loss (i.e. total sales equal total expenses). The break-even point can be determined using either the graphical method or the equation method.

Graphical Method

One way to determine the break-even point is through the graphical method. Two types of graphs can be used to figure out this point: profit-volume graph and cost-volume-profit graph.

The first type is called the **profit-volume graph**, which requires plotting the operating income for different numbers of product sold. Managers can use this graph to determine the operating profit (or loss) at various levels of production.

Steps in creating the profit-volume graph:

1. The horizontal axis is labeled as number of units produced and sold, while the dollar amounts of operating profit and loss are indicated along the vertical axis.

2. If no units are produced and sold, the maximum operating loss is equal to the total fixed costs. This is the first point on the graph when drawing the profit line. This point will cross the vertical axis below zero (operating loss) at an amount equal to the fixed costs.

For Pine Furniture Manufacturer, this is point A in figure 6.10. Operating loss is equal to total fixed costs of $15,000 when no units are produced and sold.

3. Choose a level of production and calculate the amount of operating profit. Then, plot this point on the graph.
   Point B in figure 6.10 shows that if Pine Furniture Manufacturer produces and sells 14,000 units, their operating profit becomes $24,200 (14,000 × $2.80/unit – $15,000).

4. Connect these points (step 2 and 3) and this will become your profit line.
   In figure 6.9, the profit line is created by connecting point A and B.

Figure 6.10 illustrates Pine Furniture Manufacturer's production in a profit-volume graph.

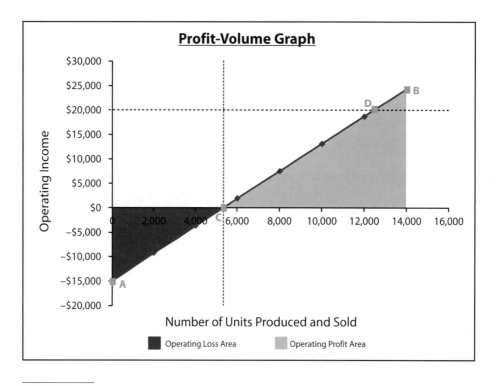

FIGURE 6.10

Notice that in figure 6.10, operating income increases as more products are produced and sold. The section above the horizontal axis (green area) indicates operating income for the company. The section below the horizontal axis (red area) indicates an operating loss. Using this graph, managers can determine where the line crosses the horizontal axis. Break-even (i.e. total revenue = total expenses) is shown on the graph where the vertical axis equals $0 at point C. From the figure, one can see that the line crosses the horizontal axis when the company produces and sells approximately 5,300 units (the exact point of intersection is 5,358).

Similarly, the manager can determine the volume of production to yield a target operating profit. For example, if the manager wants to determine the number of units that need to be produced and sold to reach an operating profit of $20,000, point D in figure 6.10 suggests the company should produce and sell 12,500 units.

Another approach to the graphical method is through the **cost-volume-profit graph**, as shown in figure 6.11. This graph helps managers understand how costs, sales and operating profit (or loss) are related.

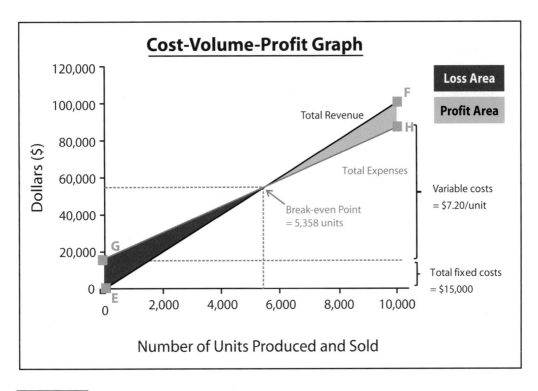

FIGURE 6.11

Steps in creating the cost-volume-profit graph:

1. The horizontal axis is labeled as number of units produced and sold. The vertical axis is labeled as dollars.

2. Plot the total revenue line:
   a) *First point*: zero units produced and sold.
      This is where cost and units produced are equal to 0. This point simply means that you will generate zero revenue if you do not produce and sell any units.
      First point for the Pine Furniture Manufacturer example is indicated as point E in figure 6.11.

   b) *Second point*: chosen level of production.
      This is determined by multiplying the selling price by a chosen level of production.
      For Pine Furniture Manufacturer, this is point F in figure 6.11 where the company will generate $100,000 ($10 per unit × 10,000 units) worth of revenue if it produces and sells 10,000 units.

c) *Connect the two points* (2a and 2b).

This line shows total revenues for any level of production.

Figure 6.11 shows that the total revenue line is produced by connecting point E and F together.

3. Plot the total expenses line:

a) *First point:* zero units produced and sold.

When zero units are produced and sold, total expenses will be equal to fixed costs. Even if no unit is produced and sold, this amount will still have to be paid. This point is located on the vertical axis.

For Pine Furniture Manufacturer, this is point G ($15,000 of fixed cost) in figure 6.11.

b) *Second point:* chosen level of production.

The second point is determined by multiplying a chosen level of production by unit variable costs and adding the fixed costs.

Figure 6.11 indicates that at point H, the company will incur $87,000 ($7.20 per unit × 10,000 units + $15,000) worth of expenses if it produces and sells 10,000 units.

c) *Connect the two points* (3a and 3b).

This line shows total expenses for any level of production.

The total cost line is produced by connecting point G and H, as shown in figure 6.11.

By determining where the total revenue and expenses lines intersect, one can determine the break-even point. The area between the two lines represents the difference between total revenue and total expenses. To the left of the break-even point, total expenses exceed total revenue. This is the loss area (red shaded triangle). To the right of the break-even point, total revenue exceeds total expenses. This represents the profit area (green shaded triangle). The horizontal line at $15,000 represents the total fixed costs.

As you can see, the profit-volume and cost-profit-volume graphs can both be used to determine the break-even point. While the cost-volume-profit graph focuses on revenues and costs, the profit-volume graph shows how the level of production affects profits. Moreover, managers can use the profit-volume graph to easily determine the number of units required to obtain a certain operating profit.

A CLOSER LOOK

Many people believe that it was the development of computer spreadsheets that triggered the explosion in sales of personal computers in the early 1980s. These spreadsheets were used by decision makers primarily to evaluate and present the type of cost volume profit analyses we have discussed in this chapter. This use of spreadsheets reflects the critical importance of this management accounting tool for managers.

Equation Method

Let us now move on to the second method, the equation method. Following is the basic formula that is used in the contribution margin statement:

Sales – Variable Costs – Fixed Costs = Operating Income

This formula shows that operating income is equal to the amount that is left over after both fixed and variable costs are subtracted from total sales.

Sales amount is equal to the sales price per unit multiplied by the amount of units sold; and variable costs are equal to the variable costs per unit multiplied by the number of units sold. Therefore, the formula can be re-written as:

(Sales Price per Unit × Number of Units) – (Variable Costs per Unit × Number of Units) – Fixed Costs = Operating Income

This can be re-arranged as follows:

(Sales Price per Unit – Variable Costs per Unit) × Number of Units = Fixed Costs + Operating Income

Since the difference between the sales price and the variable costs results in the contribution margin, this information can be substituted into the above formula as follows:

$$\text{Number of Units} = \frac{(\text{Fixed Costs} + \text{Operating Income})}{\text{Contribution Margin per Unit}}$$

To determine the number of units needed to break-even, we substitute operating income of $0 and solve for the number of units. This is because break-even point is reached when total revenues equal total expenses, which results in an operating income of $0. The fixed costs of $15,000 can be found on the contribution margin statement (figure 6.8). The contribution margin per unit can be found by dividing contribution margin ($28,000) by number of units (10,000) to get $2.80 per unit.

Break-Even Point in Units = (Fixed Costs + $0) ÷ Contribution Margin per Unit

= ($15,000 + $0) ÷ $2.80 per unit

= 5,358 units (rounded up)

Therefore, Pine Furniture Manufacturer will break-even if 5,358 chairs are built and sold. Break-even units are always rounded because the company can not make and sell a fraction of a product. The units are always rounded up to ensure the company will at least make $0 operating profit. If the units were rounded down to 5,357 units, the company would experience a negative operating income.

To prove the break-even calculation works, the contribution margin statement can be recreated using the sales and variable costs per unit, and multiply by the break-even figure of 5,358 units. The contribution margin statement has been recreated in figure 6.12. Notice that the sales and variable costs per unit, as well as the percentage of variable costs to sales, have not changed. The $2.40 operating income is due to rounding up the break-even units to 5,358. As noted earlier, rounding down the break-even units would result in a negative operating income. Using 5,357 units for this example would result in a loss of $0.40.

Pine Furniture Manufacturer Contribution Margin Statement May 31, 2010						
	Total		**Units**		**Percentage**	
Sales		$53,580		$10.00		100%
Less Variable Costs						
Wood	$26,790		$5.00		50%	
Paint & Screws	3,751		0.70		7%	
Labor	8,037	38,578	1.50	7.20	15%	72%
Contribution Margin		15,002		2.80		28%
Less Fixed Costs						
Rent		15,000				
Operating Income		$2.40				

FIGURE 6.12

Target Analysis

Although the break-even analysis determines the amount of units sold in order to break even, most companies often target an operating income that is greater than $0. Management often wants to know how many units of a product must be sold to achieve a certain target operating income.

Suppose Pine Furniture Manufacturer would like to generate an operating income of $20,000. Using the equation method shown earlier, let us replace operating income with $20,000. Thus:

$$\text{Number of Units to Yield }\$20{,}000\text{ Operating Income} = \frac{\text{(Fixed Costs} + \$20{,}000)}{\text{Contribution Margin per Unit}}$$

$$= \frac{(\$15{,}000 + \$20{,}000)}{\$2.80}$$

$$= 12{,}500 \text{ units}$$

Therefore, to achieve a target operating income of $20,000, Pine Furniture Manufacturer will have to build and sell 12,500 chairs.

Both the equation and graphical method arrive at the same conclusion (i.e. break-even point is 5,358 units and the business needs to sell 12,500 units to yield $20,000 in operating profit).

So far, the example of a manufacturing company has been used to demonstrate the break-even concept. However, the break-even analysis can be used for essentially any industry. Let us use an example of a hair salon called Stylair, which specializes in providing different types of haircuts. The fixed costs incurred by the salon are the rent, depreciation of equipment and staff salaries. The variable costs include hair dye, shampoo, conditioner and other product costs. Stylair charges $50 and incurs $20 of variable cost for each haircut, and has annual fixed costs of $40,000. Using the break-even formula, Stylair will have to provide 1,334 haircuts in a year to break-even.

$$\text{Number of Haircuts (to break-even)} = \frac{\$40{,}000}{\$30^*}$$

$$= 1{,}334 \text{ haircuts}$$

*$50 - $20 = $30

Income Tax Implications for CVP

The discussion of CVP, break-even analysis and targeting operating income has ignored income taxes to keep the calculations as simple as they can be. Often, managers must meet a target of net income, which is operating income less income taxes. By taking income taxes into account, the managers will be able to see the result of decisions once taxes are paid. This can be especially important if there are certain favorable tax consequences that can be taken advantage of.

Contribution Margin Ratio

Another useful tool in CVP analysis is the **contribution margin ratio**. The contribution margin ratio presents contribution margin as a percentage of total sales and is given by the following formula:

$$\text{Contribution Margin Ratio} = \frac{\text{Contribution Margin}}{\text{Revenue}}$$

Managers can use the contribution margin ratio to determine how contribution margin changes with changes to revenue. This concept will be demonstrated using Pine Furniture Manufacturer as an example.

As shown in figure 6.8, the contribution margin ratio for Pine Furniture Manufacturer for the month of May 2010 is:

$$\text{Contribution Margin Ratio} = \$28{,}000 \div \$100{,}000$$

$$= 0.28$$

$$= 28\%$$

This means that a $1 increase in revenues will result in a $0.28 increase in contribution margin. In addition, if fixed costs remain the same, this will also result in a $0.28 increase in operating income. This formula is especially useful because it tells managers how the company's operating income changes as its revenue changes. For example, if managers know that sales will increase by $40,000 in the following month, they can use the contribution margin ratio to calculate a corresponding increase in operating income of $11,200 ($40,000 × 28%).

On some occasions, managers would also like to know the amount of revenue needed to achieve a certain level of profit. To accomplish this, they can re-arrange the contribution margin formula and substitute contribution margin with fixed costs plus target operating income to get:

$$\text{Revenue Needed to Obtain Target Operating Income} = \frac{\text{(Fixed Costs + Target Operating Income)}}{\text{Contribution Margin Ratio}}$$

Therefore, if Pine Furniture Manufacturer wanted to know how much revenue is needed to achieve an operating income of $20,000, they would perform the following calculation:

$$\text{Revenue Needed to Obtain Operating Income of } \$20,000 = (\$15,000 + \$20,000) \div 28\%$$
$$= \$125,000$$

Therefore, Pine Furniture Manufacturer would have to generate revenues of $125,000 to achieve an operating income of $20,000.

Incremental Analysis

Managers at Pine Furniture Manufacturer may also face the decision of expanding their operations by renting more space to increase production. Suppose the company estimated that this will increase rent cost by $10,000 and increase sales volume by 5,000 units. To decide whether to proceed with this expansion, managers can recreate the entire contribution margin statement with the new information to see if operating income increases. Using the per unit and percentage values from figure 6.8, keep in mind that sales, all variable costs and fixed costs will increase. The original contribution margin statement and the revised contribution margin statement are shown in figure 6.13.

Pine Furniture Manufacturer Original Contribution Margin Statement May 31, 2010		
Sales		$100,000
Less Variable Costs		
Wood	$50,000	
Paint & Screws	7,000	
Labor	15,000	72,000
Contribution Margin		28,000
Less Fixed Costs		
Rent		15,000
Operating Income		$13,000

Pine Furniture Manufacturer Revised Contribution Margin Statement May 31, 2010		
Sales		$150,000
Less Variable Costs		
Wood	$75,000	
Paint & Screws	10,500	
Labor	22,500	108,000
Contribution Margin		42,000
Less Fixed Costs		
Rent		25,000
Operating Income		$17,000

FIGURE 6.13

There should be no change in contribution margin ratio, which means it will remain at its original 28% ($42,000 ÷ $150,000). Figure 6.13 shows an increase in operating income of $4,000, and assuming that there are no other factors to consider, this expansion should be implemented.

If there are many components in the contribution margin statement, creating a brand new contribution margin statement can be time-consuming. A quicker method is to simply examine the items that have changed. This is referred to as **incremental analysis**. In this example, sales volume would increase by 5,000 units. At a sale price of $10 per unit, this means sales would increase by $50,000. Additionally, fixed expenses will increase by $10,000. Since we already determined that the contribution margin ratio will not change, we can use the contribution margin ratio of 28% to assist in the calculation.

Incremental contribution margin ($50,000 × 28%)	$14,000
Less incremental rent expense	10,000
Incremental increase in operating income	$4,000

Based on the above calculation, operating income will increase by $4,000, which is the same increase found by comparing the two contribution margin statements. By only examining the items that have changed, an incremental analysis can provide information quicker to decision makers.

Assumptions for CVP Analysis

Up until now, the chapter has focused on showing how companies use selling price, variable costs per unit and quantity sold to calculate their break-even point and contribution margin. For Pine Furniture Manufacturer, all the ratios are calculated by using the selling price of $10.00/unit and variable costs of $7.20/unit. Would the ratios provide the same answers if the selling price was to increase from $10.00 to $11.00 or decrease from $10.00 to $9.00? The answer is no. This is because these CVP tools were developed with some critical underlying assumptions. The assumptions are as follows:

1. **Constant selling prices**: Throughout the relevant range, even if the volume changes, it is assumed that the selling price remains the same. This is important because the CVP analysis requires the manager to calculate the contribution margin. This contribution margin is then used to calculate the break-even point and contribution margin ratio. If the selling price changes, the contribution margin will change, and the previously calculated break-even point and contribution margin ratio will no longer apply. Therefore, the selling price is assumed to remain constant throughout the relevant range.

2. **Constant variable costs per unit**: It is assumed that the variable costs per unit remain constant throughout the relevant range. This is important for the same reason as above. If variable costs per unit change, then the contribution margin and entire CVP analysis is affected.

3. **Constant fixed costs**: Changes in fixed costs would affect the break-even point calculation. Therefore, it is assumed that the fixed costs remain constant throughout the relevant range.

4. **Units produced equal units sold**: It is assumed that the number of units produced is always equal to the number of units sold. This is an important assumption because if the company produces goods but does not sell any of them, it would incur all the costs related to the products and receive none of the benefits (sales). This will affect the contribution margin and the resulting CVP analysis. Therefore, it is assumed that all units produced are also sold.

Margin of Safety

It is important for a company to know by how much the current sales can drop before the company starts experiencing losses. This question can be answered by using another tool called the margin of safety. The **margin of safety** represents the excess of sales over break-even revenues. Since the break-even point is where the profits are zero, sales can drop until the break-even point is reached before the company starts experiencing an operating loss.

The margin of safety is calculated as follows:

$$\text{Margin of Safety (in dollars)} = \text{Current Sales} - \text{Break-Even Sales}$$

The margin of safety can also be expressed in terms of units, and in percentage form.

$$\text{Margin of Safety (in units)} = \text{Current Output} - \text{Break-Even Output}$$

$$\text{Margin of Safety Percentage} = \frac{\text{Margin of Safety (in dollars)}}{\text{Current Sales}}$$

Let us analyze the margin of safety for Pine Furniture Manufacturer. As calculated earlier, Pine Furniture Manufacturer reaches its break-even point when 5,358 chairs are sold with revenues of $53,580. It was also determined that in order to reach a target of $20,000 operating income, 12,500 chairs must be sold. Selling the chairs at $10 each, Pine Furniture Manufacturer will generate sales of $125,000. By inputting this information in the margin of safety formulas, we are able to calculate the margin of safety and margin of safety percentage for Pine Furniture Manufacturer. The calculations are provided in figure 6.14.

	Dollars	Units
Sales	$125,000	12,500
Break-Even Sales	53,580	5,358
Margin of Safety	71,420	7,142
Margin of Safety Percentage	57.14%	57.14%

FIGURE 6.14

The calculation shows that a 57.14% reduction in sales will result in Pine Furniture Manufacturer just breaking even. In other words, the company's sales can drop by $71,420 or 7,142 units before it starts incurring a loss. This also shows that at the current level of output and sales, Pine Furniture Manufacturer can incur $71,420 of additional costs before they start incurring an operating loss. These calculations show that the margin of safety can provide useful information about the riskiness of a business. Generally, a low margin of safety will indicate that the business is at risk of generating an operating loss if sales decrease just slightly. The higher the margin of safety, the more comfortable the business is.

Sales Mix

In the Pine Furniture Manufacturer example, it is assumed that the company made only one product. However, in reality, companies usually produce and sell multiple types of products. For example, Pine Furniture Manufacturer may also produce and sell wooden nightstands along with wooden chairs. **Sales mix** refers to the relative quantities of the types of products that are produced by a company. For example, if 8,000 chairs are built and sold while 2,000 nightstands are built and sold, the sales mix would be 80% (8,000 ÷ (8,000 + 2,000)) chairs and 20% (2,000 ÷ (2,000 + 8,000)) nightstands.

Since the nightstands have a different selling price and variable cost per unit than the chairs, the inclusion of nightstands would affect Pine Furniture Manufacturer's break-even analysis. Therefore, when two or more products are being produced, companies can still perform CVP analysis using what is known as the **weighted-average contribution margin**. The weighted-average contribution margin takes the weighted average of each of the product contribution margins based on the number of units sold.

The formula to determine the weighted average contribution margin is:

$$\text{Weighted-Average Contribution Margin} = \begin{array}{l}(\text{Contribution Margin per Nightstand} \times \text{Sales Mix for Nightstands}) \\ + (\text{Contribution Margin per Chair} \times \text{Sales Mix for Chairs})\end{array}$$

Assume the Pine Furniture Manufacture has the following information regarding nightstands and chairs (figure 6.15).

	Contribution Margin	Sales Quantity	Sales Mix
Nightstand	$3.50	2,000 units	20%
Chair	$2.80	8,000 units	80%

FIGURE 6.15

The weighted-average contribution margin per unit would amount to:

$$\text{Weighted Average Contribution Margin per Unit} = (\$3.50 \times 20\%) + (\$2.80 \times 80\%)$$
$$= \$2.94/\text{unit}$$

To determine the break-even point, the following formula it used:

$$\text{Break-Even Point} = \frac{\text{Fixed Cost}}{\text{Weighted-Average Contribution Margin}}$$
$$= \frac{\$15,000}{\$2.94 \text{ per unit}}$$
$$= 5,103 \text{ units}$$

Since these 5,103 units are made up of both nightstands and chairs, the break-even number of units for each product can also be calculated. To determine the number of nightstands and chairs that have to be produced and sold to break-even, we multiply each of the sales mix percentages with this break-even point.

$$\begin{aligned}\text{Number of Nightstands to Break-Even} &= \text{Break-Even Point} \times \text{Sales Mix for Nightstands} \\ &= 5,103 \times 20\% \\ &= 1,021 \text{ nightstands}\end{aligned}$$

$$\begin{aligned}\text{Number of Chairs to Break-Even} &= \text{Break-Even Point} \times \text{Sales Mix for Chairs} \\ &= 5,103 \times 80\% \\ &= 4,083 \text{ chairs}\end{aligned}$$

Therefore, Pine Furniture Manufacturer will have to produce and sell 1,021 nightstands and 4,083 chairs to break even. Notice that the total nightstands and chairs to be produced amounts to 5,104, yet the break-even calculation stated that 5,103 units needed to be made. This is due to always rounding up to the nearest whole unit, as discussed earlier in this chapter.

Sensitivity Analysis

There are many uncertainties involved in business operations, as there are often unexpected changes to variables. In order to plan strategically, managers will want to know how certain changes will impact the company's profitability. This introduces us to the topic of sensitivity analysis.

Sensitivity analysis is a type of analysis that helps managers answer "what if?" questions. For example, managers may want to know the answer to following questions:

- *What* will happen to operating income *if* sales drop by 5%?
- *What* might happen to the contribution margin *if* variable costs decrease by 10%?
- *What* might happen to operating income *if* they offer a 5% discount on their products?

These are the types of questions that sensitivity analysis attempts to answer.

For example, suppose Pine Furniture Manufacturer would like to know how operating income is affected if sales drop by 5%. Sales for May are currently $100,000. A drop of 5% would reduce sales to $95,000. Pine Furniture Manufacturer can use the contribution margin ratio to determine the decrease to operating income.

The contribution margin ratio of 28% (that was calculated earlier) shows that for every $1.00 change in revenue, operating income will change by $0.28.

$$\begin{aligned} \text{Decrease in Operating Income} \quad &= \text{Contribution Margin Ratio} \times \text{Decrease in Revenue} \\ &= 28\% \times \$5,000 \\ &= \$1,400 \end{aligned}$$

Therefore, a decrease of 5% in sales will decrease operating income by $1,400.

Performing a series of "what-if" analyses using the contribution margin statement will help managers become more responsive to changes in operations. They can also use sensitivity analysis to develop strategies and assess other planning devices.

A CLOSER LOOK

In practice, sensitivity (or "what if") analysis is usually undertaken using a computer based spreadsheet. Analysts will develop a financial model of the organization on a spreadsheet. The analysts will then use simulation software to model the effect of changes in assumptions about prices, costs, and volume on financial results. It is without question that these management accounting tools, which are elaborations of the CVP ideas described in this chapter, are among the most important used in practice.

Cost Structure and Operating Leverage

The **cost structure** of a company refers to the portion of a company's costs that are fixed versus variable. Managers have the ability to control the cost structure of their company. For example, Pine Furniture Manufacturer currently pays a fixed rent of $15,000 per month. However, initially the company was offered three payment options when signing the lease. The three options were:

1. Fixed fee of $15,000 (current option)
2. Fixed fee of $8,000 plus $0.60 per chair produced and sold
3. Pay $1.60 per chair produced and sold

Option 1

The first option is made up entirely of fixed costs. No matter how many chairs Pine Furniture Manufacturer sells, they will always pay $15,000 for rent. Therefore, if Pine Furniture Manufacturer has a bad month and sells no chairs, they will still have to pay $15,000.

Option 2

The second option consists of mixed costs, or a combination of fixed and variable costs. The fixed portion amounts to $8,000. This amount will always have to be paid no matter how many chairs are produced and sold. The variable portion amounts to $0.60 per chair produced and sold. Therefore, the more chairs Pine Furniture Manufacturer produces and sells, the more rent it will have to pay. Conversely, the fewer chairs it produces and sells, the less rent it will have to pay. Since there is a fixed portion, if Pine Furniture Manufacturer produces no chairs, it will still have to pay $8,000 in rent.

Option 3

The last option is made up entirely of variable costs. If option 3 is chosen, Pine Furniture Manufacturer would have to pay $1.60 for every chair produced and sold. In this option, the more chairs Pine Furniture Manufacturer produces and sells, the more rent it would have to pay. Similarly, the fewer chairs it produces and sells, the less rent it would have to pay. Note that if Pine Furniture Manufacturer did not produce and sell any chairs, they would not be obligated to pay any rent for the month.

The operating income for the above mentioned options has been calculated using different production volumes (4,000 chairs, 10,000 chairs and 16,000 chairs). The results are outlined in the figure 6.16 and plotted in figure 6.17.

Remember that the contribution margin ratio in this example is 28% and chairs are sold for $10 each. The contribution margin for each chair is, therefore, $2.80 (28% × $10/chair).

Method of Payment	Operating Income Based on the Number of Chairs Produced and Sold		
	4,000	10,000	16,000
$15,000 fixed fee	($3,800)	$13,000	$29,800
$8,000 fixed fee plus $0.60 per chair	$800	$14,000	$27,200
$1.60 per chair	$4,800	$12,000	$19,200

FIGURE 6.16

Option 1

If option 1 is selected, a fixed fee of $15,000 has to be paid. The operating income for this option can be found by solving the following equation:

$$\text{Operating Income for Option 1} = \$2.80/\text{chair} \times \text{Number of Chairs} - \$15,000$$

If Pine Furniture Manufacturer sells 4,000 chairs, Pine Furniture Manufacturer will suffer an operating loss of $3,800 ($2.80/chair × 4,000 chairs - $15,000). If 10,000 chairs are produced, operating income will be $13,000 ($2.80/chair × 10,000 chairs − $15,000). If 16,000 chairs are produced, operating income will be $29,800 ($2.80/chair × 16,000 - $15,000).

Option 2

If option 2 is selected, the payment will involve fixed costs of $8,000 and variable costs of $0.60 per unit. Therefore, the contribution margin will decrease to $2.20 per chair ($2.80/chair - $0.60/chair). The operating income for this option can be found by solving the following equation:

$$\text{Operating Income for Option 2} = \$2.20/\text{chair} \times \text{Number of Chairs} - \$8,000$$

If 4,000 chairs are produced, Pine Furniture Manufacturer will have an operating income of $800 ($2.20/chair × 4,000 chairs - $8,000). If 10,000 chairs are produced and sold, the company's operating income will be $14,000 ($2.20 × 10,000 - $8,000). If 16,000 units are produced, operating income will be $27,200 ($2.20 × 16,000 - $8,000).

Option 3

If option 3 is selected, Pine Furniture Manufacturer is required to pay the rent based on variable costs of $1.60 per chair. This will drop the contribution margin from $2.80 per chair to $1.20 per chair ($2.80/chair - $1.60/chair). The operating income for this option can be found by solving the following equation:

$$\text{Operating Income for Option 3} = \$1.20/\text{chair} \times \text{Number of Chairs}$$

If 4,000 chairs are produced and sold, operating income amounts to $4,800 ($1.20/chair × 4,000 chairs). If 10,000 chairs are produced, operating income will be $12,000 ($1.20/chair × 10,000 chairs). Similarly, if 16,000 chairs are produced, operating income will be $19,200 ($1.20/chair × 16,000 chairs).

These results are plotted in figure 6.14.

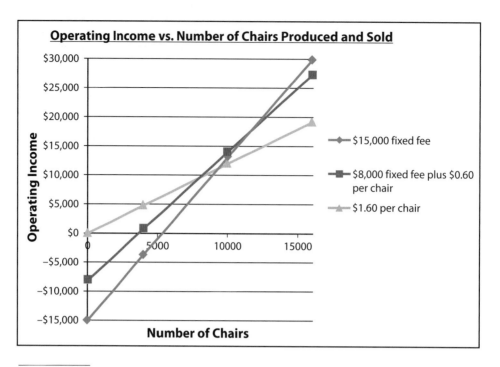

FIGURE 6.17

In figure 6.17, the vertical axis shows the operating income under the three different options for the three different output volumes (4,000 chairs, 10,000 chairs and 16,000 chairs).

At 4,000 units

When 4,000 chairs are produced and sold, it is the 3rd option ($1.60 per chair) that results in the highest operating income ($5,200). The 1st option ($15,000 fixed fee) results in an operating loss of $3,800. The 2nd option ($8,000 fixed fee plus $0.60 per chair) results in an operating income of $800, which is in between option 1 and 3.

At 10,000 units

When 10,000 chairs are produced and sold, it is the 2nd option ($8,000 fixed fee plus $0.60 per chair) that results in the highest operating income ($14,000). The 3rd option ($1.60 per chair) results in the lowest operating income and the 1st option ($15,000 fixed fee) leads to operating income of $13,000 which is in between option 2 and 3.

At 16,000 units

When 16,000 chairs are produced and sold, the 1st option ($15,000 fixed fee) results in the highest operating income ($29,800). The 3rd option ($1.60 per chair) results in the lowest operating income ($19,200). The 2nd option will result in an operating income of $27,200 which is in between option 1 and 3.

Points of Intersection

Pine Furniture Manufacturer will now determine the points of intersection between the three lines. Determining these points of intersection will allow Pine Furniture Manufacturer managers to determine which option is ideal for a given output volume. For example, managers can ask themselves, if 11,000 chairs are produced and sold, which option will yield the highest operating income? Identifying the points of intersection will help answer this question. These intersection points have been identified in figure 6.18.

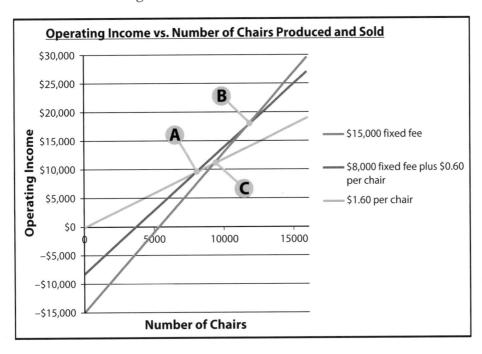

FIGURE 6.18

Intersection point A represents the point at which the operating income of option 2 is the same as the operating income of option 3. This will occur when 8,000 chairs are produced and sold. This amount can be determined either from the graph or by solving a linear system of equations. Pine Furniture Manufacturer can use the equations they developed earlier to determine the volume at which option 2 and option 3 intersect.

$$
\begin{aligned}
\text{Operating Income for Option 2} &= \text{Operating Income for Option 3} \\
\$2.20/\text{chair} \times \text{Number of Chairs} - \$8,000 &= \$1.20/\text{chair} \times \text{Number of Chairs} \\
\text{Number of Chairs} &= 8,000
\end{aligned}
$$

Point B represents the point at which the operating income of option 1 is the same as the operating income of option 2. This will occur when 11,667 chairs are produced and sold. To determine the volume at which option 1 and option 3 intersect, Pine Furniture Manufacturer can use the equations developed earlier:

$$
\begin{aligned}
\text{Operating Income for Option 1} &= \text{Operating Income for Option 2} \\
\$2.80/\text{chair} \times \text{Number of Chairs} - \$15,000 &= \$2.20/\text{chair} \times \text{Number of Chairs} - \$8,000 \\
\text{Number of Chairs} &= 11,667
\end{aligned}
$$

Point C represents the point at which the operating income of option 1 is the same as the operating income of option 3. This will occur when 9,375 chairs are produced and sold. This can be determined by solving the following equation:

$$\text{Operating Income for Option 1} = \text{Operating Income for Option 3}$$

$$\$2.80/\text{chair} \times \text{Number of Chairs} - \$15,000 = \$1.20/\text{chair} \times \text{Number of Chairs}$$

$$\text{Number of Chairs} = 9,375$$

For production volume to the left of point A (less than 8,000 chairs), option 3 will yield the highest operating income. For any production volume between points A and B (between 8,000 chairs and 11,667 chairs), option 2 will yield the highest operating income and for production volume to the right of point B (greater than 11,667 chairs), option 1 will yield the highest operating income. This information is summarized in figure 6.19.

Volume of Production	Less than 8,000 chairs (to the left of point A)	Between 8,000 and 11,667 chairs (in between points A and B)	Greater than 11,667 chairs (to the right of point B)
Option that yields the highest operating income	Option 3	Option 2	Option 1

FIGURE 6.19

Interpreting the results

Notice that option 1 (fixed fee only) results in the highest operating income if more than 11,667 chairs are produced and sold. However, once volume drops below 9,375 chairs, this option will result in the lowest operating income compared to the three options. This makes the first option the riskiest option because of the high quantity of chairs that has to be sold. The least risky option is the third option (all variable costs). This is because if no units are produced and sold, no rent will have to be paid. This will save rent costs. However, once the company starts to produce more than 8,000 chairs, option 2 will yield a higher operating income than option 3.

This example illustrates the old business adage, "no risk, no return". In this particular case, Pine Furniture Manufacturer has chosen the riskiest option.

Note that the concept of an appropriate cost structure can be applied to any industry and is not just limited to the manufacturing sector.

Operating Leverage

How a company devises its cost structure affects what is known as its **operating leverage**. Operating leverage refers to the effect of fixed costs on overall operating income as production volume changes. The higher the portion of fixed costs, the higher the company's operating leverage. The higher a company's operating leverage, the greater the fluctuations in operating income from changes in volume. In other words, operating leverage measures how sensitive operating income is to a change in sales. The degree of operating leverage can be calculated by using the following formula:

$$\text{Degree of Operating Leverage} = \frac{\text{Contribution Margin}}{\text{Operating Income}}$$

Let us now calculate the degree of operating leverage for each of Pine Furniture Manufacturer's rental options when 10,000 chairs are produced. To calculate the degree of operating leverage, contribution margin is divided by operating income. The results can be found in figure 6.20.

Options	Contribution Margin (a)	Operating Income (b)	Degree of Operating Leverage (a)÷(b)
(1) $15,000 fixed fee	$28,000	$13,000	2.15
(2) $8,000 fixed fee plus $0.60 per chair	$22,000	$14,000	1.57
(3) $1.60 per chair	$12,000	$12,000	1.00

FIGURE 6.20

Notice that the first option has the highest operating leverage since it has the highest portion of fixed costs. Option 3 has the lowest operating leverage because it has the lowest portion of fixed costs. The degree of operating leverage helps managers evaluate a company's riskiness due to variations in production and sales volumes. Managers can also calculate how much operating profit would increase with an increase in sales. For example, option 1 has a degree of operating leverage of 2.15. This means that for every 1% increase in sales, operating profit will increase by 2.15%. Suppose that under option 1, the company experienced a 10% increase in sales. This would amount to a 21.5% increase in operating profit.

A high degree of operating leverage signals a riskier situation for a company. However, it also indicates a greater potential for profit if sales are at a high enough level. A low degree of operating leverage suggests a less risky situation for a company. However, at the same time, it suggests a lower potential for profit when sales volumes are high.

CVP analysis provides a framework to approach cost behavior analysis. Many of the tools introduced in this chapter are used together to help management in decision making. By performing CVP analysis, a business can determine which set of costs, volume and products best suit their profit model. In the following chapters of this text, other methods of analysis will be discussed that are also used by management to plan and control.

IN THE REAL WORLD

Consider the cost structure of a company that produces hydroelectricity. Once the generating stations are built, virtually all costs incurred by the company will be fixed. Since costs are mostly fixed, there is a high risk involved in building and operating these facilities. For this reason, governments are often involved in building and operating hydroelectric utilities. Once these facilities are built, income increases dramatically because the contribution margin ratio is very high. However, low variable costs often tempt organizations into damaging price wars. Because capacity is fixed and variable costs are low, companies tend to pick any price that is needed to increase sales volume in order to fully use the capacity. This pricing method is not aligned with the company's overall strategy and is chosen without an in-depth cost analysis. In the long run, this method often limits the company's ability to cover the fixed operation costs. If this continues, it will lead to bankruptcy.

Ethical Considerations

Offering discounts in order to increase sales volume is a common sales technique, but it can lead to unethical behavior in certain scenarios. Assume that a company pays commissions to its sales people based on gross sales. Gross sales is the total sales amount before discounts or returns of products are deducted. Net sales is the sales amount after discounts and returns, and is used to calculate profits. Since discounts reduce the value of gross sales and ultimately profits, the higher the discount, the lower the contribution margin per unit. To compensate for the decreased contribution margin, a much higher volume of sales is required to meet a target profit level.

Based on the company's compensation method, a sales person is often tempted to offer discounts to customers. The discount does not affect the gross sales price per unit, but will decrease the selling price the customer has to pay. Sales volume will likely increase, thereby increasing gross sales and potentially paying handsome commissions to the sales person. Unfortunately, a large increase in sales volume is required to compensate for discounts. If this large increase in sales volume is not realized, business profits will decrease.

Price controls are important to ensure that discounts are only awarded to eligible customers and according to agreed prices. Frequent comparisons of the invoiced values with price lists are common controls that are easy to implement. Another way to address this issue is to pay commissions based on net sales as opposed to gross sales.

In Summary

↬ **Variable costs** are costs that vary in relation to the change in volume produced.

↬ **Fixed costs** are costs that do not change in relation to volume produced.

↬ **Mixed costs** are costs that contain both fixed and variable components. Mixed costs can be separated into these components using the following methods:

♦ The **high-low method** uses the change in production and change in costs between the highest and the lowest level of production to separate mixed costs.

♦ The **least-square regression method** uses statistical calculations to separate mixed costs. Spreadsheet software, such as Excel, can perform this calculation.

↬ **Relevant range** refers to the specific range of production where cost behavior remains the same.

↬ **Step fixed costs** are fixed costs that will change once the volume of production exceeds the relevant range. **Step variable costs** are variable costs that change in increments.

↬ **Cost behavior** refers to how costs change as volume of production changes.

↬ The purpose of **cost-volume-profit (CVP)** is to help managerial accountants analyze how the production volume affects the company's profits and costs in the short-run.

↬ **Break-even point (BEP)** determines the number of units that needs to be produced and sold in order for total revenues to equal total expenses.

↬ The equation and the graphical methods are used to calculate BEP and targeted income.

♦ **The equation method's** formula for calculating number of units for BEP and targeted income is: the sum of fixed costs and operating income divided by contributed margin per unit.

♦ The **graphical method** involves both the profit-volume and the cost-volume-profit graphs. The **profit-volume graph** determines BEP and targeted income by plotting the operating income for different number of products sold. BEP would be the point where the line crosses the horizontal axis, the number of units produced and sold. The **cost-volume-profit graph** determines break-even by the intersection of the total revenue and total expense lines.

↬ **Target analysis** is a form of CVP analysis where companies target an operating income greater than zero. For example, managers often want to know how many units of a product must be sold to achieve a certain target operating income.

↬ **Incremental analysis** quickly determines the financial impact by examining only the items that have changed.

↬ The assumptions for the chapter's CVP analysis are as follows: selling price, variable costs, and fixed costs are constant throughout the relevant range and units produced equal units sold.

↪ **Contribution margin ratio (CM ratio)** can be determined by dividing the contribution margin by revenue. The CM ratio provides information on how contribution margin changes with changes in revenue, and determines the amount of revenue needed to obtain a target operating income.

↪ The **margin of safety** represents the excess of sales over break-even revenues. It can be represented in terms of dollars, units, or a percentage. The margin of safety show how much sales can drop before a net loss is incurred.

↪ **Sales mix** refers to the relative quantities of the types of products produced by a company.

↪ When two or more products are being produced, companies perform CVP analysis using **weighted-average contribution margin**. The weighted-average contribution margin takes the weighted average of each of the product contribution margins based on the number of units sold.

↪ **Sensitivity analysis** is a type of analysis that helps managers answer "what if?" questions and helps them become more responsive to changes in operations. The CM ratio can assist in answering these questions.

↪ The **cost structure** of a company refers to the portion of a company's costs that are fixed versus variable. When given with several payment options, consider how each option will affect operating income and the amount of risk surrounding each alternative.

↪ **Operating leverage** refers to the effect of fixed costs on overall operating income as production volume changes. **Degree of operating leverage** is determined by dividing contribution margin by operating income.

Review Exercise

Plasticator Inc. makes and sells plastic containers for prescription medication. The plastic material costs $0.03 for each container and labor used to produce each container costs $0.15. The selling price of each container is $0.25. Plasticator incurs a rent expense of $52,000 per month.

In order to continue at the peak performance level, the machines used to produce the containers must be regularly maintained. The more containers made, the more maintenance is required. Plasticator considers the maintenance costs to be a mixed cost. This month (August), Plasticator spent $74,000 on maintenance and needs to determine the fixed and variable portions. The production volume and maintenance costs for the past seven months are presented below. Assume that the volume produced is equal to the volume sold for each month.

Month	Volume of Production (Units)	Maintenance Costs
February	5,900,000	$43,000
March	6,000,000	$55,000
April	5,200,000	$61,000
May	7,600,000	$85,000
June	7,500,000	$84,000
July	7,200,000	$72,000
August	6,500,000	$74,000

Required:

1. Use the high-low method to calculate the fixed and variable portion of the maintenance cost.
2. Create the contribution margin statement for August.
3. Calculate the break-even point for Plasticator Inc. in units.
4. How many units must Plasticator Inc. sell to have an operating income of $400,000?
5. Calculate the degree of operating leverage for Plasticator Inc. at their current operating level. What does the degree of operating leverage indicate?

Review Exercise – Answer

Part 1

	Volume of Production	Maintenance Costs
May	7,600,000 units	$85,000
April	- 5,200,000 units	- $61,000
Change	2,400,000 units	$24,000

$$\text{Variable Cost per Unit} = \frac{\text{Change in Cost}}{\text{Change in Production}}$$

$$= \frac{\$24,000}{2,400,000 \text{ units}}$$

$$= \$0.01 \text{ per unit}$$

Using the high level of production:

Fixed Cost = $85,000 - (7,600,000 × $0.01) = $9,000

Alternatively, using the low level of production:

Fixed Cost = $61,000 - (5,200,000 × $0.01) = $9,000

Whether the high or low level of production is used to determine the fixed cost portion, it is estimated to be $9,000.

Part 2

Plasticator Inc. Contribution Margin Statement For the Month of August		
Sales		$1,625,000
Less Variable Costs		
Plastic	$195,000	
Labor	975,000	
Maintenance	65,000	1,235,000
Contribution Margin		390,000
Less Fixed Costs		
Rent	52,000	
Maintenance	9,000	61,000
Operating Income		$329,000

Part 3

Contribution Margin per Unit = $0.25 - ($0.03 + $0.15 + $0.01) = $0.06 per unit

$$\text{Break-Even Point in Units} = \frac{\text{Fixed Costs}}{\text{Contribution Margin per Unit}}$$

$$= \frac{(\$52{,}000 + \$9{,}000)}{\$0.06}$$

$$= 1{,}016{,}667 \text{ units}$$

Plasticator must sell 1,016,667 units to break even.

Part 4

$$\begin{array}{c}\text{Units to Yield \$400,000}\\\text{Operating Income}\end{array} = \frac{\text{Fixed Costs} + \text{Operating Income}}{\text{Contribution Margin per Unit}}$$

$$= \frac{(\$52{,}000 + \$9{,}000) + \$400{,}000}{\$0.06}$$

$$= 7{,}683{,}334 \text{ units}$$

Plasticator Inc. must sell 7,683,334 to reach a target operating income of $400,000.

Part 5

$$\text{Degree of Operating Leverage} = \frac{\text{Contribution Margin}}{\text{Operating Income}}$$

$$= \frac{\$390{,}000}{\$329{,}000}$$

$$= 1.19$$

Since Plasticator has a degree of operating leverage of 1.19, this means that for every 1% increase in sales, they will experience a 1.19% increase in operating income.

Notes

Chapter 7
COSTING AND PRICING STRATEGIES

LEARNING OUTCOMES:

❶ Understand the concept of absorption costing

❷ Understand the concept of variable costing

❸ Prepare an income statement under absorption costing

❹ Prepare a contribution statement under variable costing

❺ Explain the maximum profit pricing strategy

❻ Calculate the selling price using the cost-plus pricing method

❼ Calculate the maximum allowable cost using the target costing method

Costing Approaches: An Introduction

Lawrence and Claudia each rent a separate portable cotton candy stand that they operate at various carnivals in their hometown. They buy the sugar ingredients and cones, and pay for the electricity based on how many kilowatt-hours they consume. Lawrence believes that the cost of producing his cotton candy only includes the cost of sugar ingredients, cones and electricity. On the other hand, Claudia believes that the cost of producing the cotton candy also includes an appropriate portion of the rent in addition to the costs included by Lawrence. Lawrence asked her, "Why do you think the cost of producing a cone of cotton candy includes a portion of the rent? I mean, I can make one more cone of my fine cotton candy right now without paying any additional for rent." Claudia replies, "Without paying rent, I can't even make one cotton candy cone because I wouldn't have a stand in the first place. So it's definitely part of the cost of producing a cone. Lawrence, you clearly do not understand the true cost of making a cotton candy cone." Lawrence and Claudia both assigned a slightly different set of costs to each cotton candy cone. Both had their reasons for using their own approach.

Who is correct in their reasoning? Well, both are correct since both options can be used. Each option provides the owner with valuable information that can be used to help assess the costs of running the cotton candy stand. Similarly, businesses managers can use either option when analyzing costs internally in order to make informed decisions.

Absorption Costing

You have learned so far that all manufacturing costs are included in the cost of a product. These costs are recorded as inventory on the balance sheet. The inventory is then expensed in the form of cost of goods sold when the goods are sold. This matches the product cost with the revenue it helped generate and is in compliance with GAAP.

This method of costing, which you have been using since you commenced your accounting classes, is called **absorption costing** because all manufacturing costs are *absorbed* into the value of inventory. In the cotton candy example,

WORTH REPEATING...

All manufacturing costs include direct materials, direct labor and all manufacturing overhead (both variable and fixed).

Claudia chose to use this approach and includes all manufacturing costs (sugar ingredients, cones, electricity and the rent of the cotton candy stand) in the cost of the cotton candy.

Assume Claudia produces 100 cones of cotton candy per day which costs her $100 ($20 for sugar ingredients, $20 for cones, $10 for electricity and $50 for renting the stand). To prepare for a carnival, she would like to produce 20 more cones and would like to know how much more it would cost her. The stand can produce at least 300 cones per day, so the capacity is not a problem. Based on her historical numbers, it seems each cone costs $1 ($100 ÷ 100 cones). Does that mean producing 20 additional cones would cost $20 more?

The answer is no because the $50 cotton candy stand rental fee does not change regardless of whether 100 or 120 cones are produced. To produce the additional 20 cones, only the variable components of the manufacturing costs (sugar ingredients, cones and electricity) will increase. Although Claudia knows the true cost of producing her cotton candy, she cannot easily see how her costs would change if she produces an extra 20 cones.

In reality, managers face the same situation when analyzing product cost under absorption costing because the fixed and variable components of costs are not separated. In other words, the product costs are not separated by cost behavior. To resolve this problem, another approach has been developed to better judge product costs based on cost behavior.

Variable Costing

Variable costing assigns only variable manufacturing costs (i.e. direct materials, direct labor and variable manufacturing overhead) to a product. Variable costing is also known as marginal costing. It is performed for internal analysis purpose only and does not conform to GAAP. In other words, this costing approach cannot be used to prepare any formal financial statements (e.g. balance sheet and income statement). The fundamental difference between absorption

WORTH REPEATING...

Period costs are expensed in the accounting period in which they are incurred without going through the inventory account.

costing and variable costing is the method in which fixed manufacturing overhead is dealt with when calculating the cost of a product.

Under variable costing, the cost of fixed manufacturing overhead is not viewed as part of the product cost. Instead, it is treated as a period cost (an expense). The logic behind this approach is that fixed manufacturing overhead is considered as part of the cost of running a business. In some managers' point of view, this type of cost expires once a period ends and the entire amount should be expensed right away.

Figure 7.1 illustrates how fixed manufacturing overhead is treated under absorption costing and variable costing.

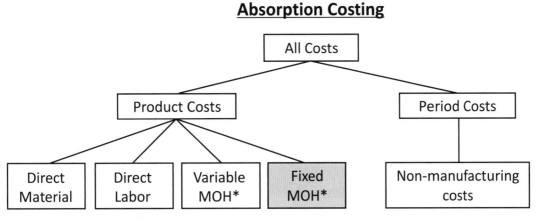

*MOH = Manufacturing Overhead

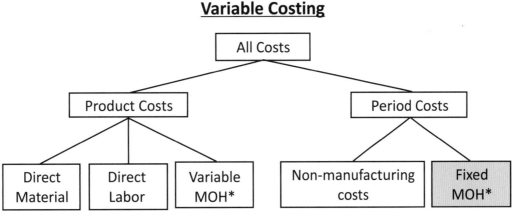

*MOH = Manufacturing Overhead

FIGURE 7.1

Refer back to the cotton candy example. Lawrence chose to use the variable costing approach because he only included the variable manufacturing costs (sugar ingredients, cones and electricity) in the cost of the cotton candy. The cost of renting the cotton candy stand, a fixed manufacturing overhead cost, is excluded from the cost of the products. If his output level increases, he can easily estimate how much product costs will increase with the level of output.

A primary benefit of variable costing is that it helps users separate the costs of production that vary with the level of output from the costs that do not change within the relevant range. All costs that do not vary with the level of output (fixed costs) are irrelevant when calculating the change in the cost of production.

WORTH REPEATING...

Relevant range refers to cost behavior remaining the same within a certain range of production.

The differences between absorption costing and variable costing are summarized in figure 7.2.

Variable vs. Absorption Costing	
Variable Costing	**Absorption Costing**
• Product costs only include direct materials, direct labor and variable manufacturing overhead costs	• Product costs include direct materials, direct labor, variable manufacturing overhead and fixed manufacturing overhead costs
• Not used for external reporting purposes	• Used for external reporting purposes

FIGURE 7.2

Absorption Costing: Bright Ideas

To help illustrate the difference between absorption costing and variable costing, consider Bright Ideas, a company that manufactures chandeliers. Its annual production data and costs are shown below in figure 7.3.

Selling Price per Unit Sold	$30
Manufacturing Costs:	
Direct Materials Cost per Unit	$6
Direct Labor Cost per Unit	$8
Variable Manufacturing Overhead per Unit	$5
Fixed Manufacturing Overhead	$45,000
Non-Manufacturing Costs:	
Rent (for Head Office)	$15,000
Sales Department Salaries	$21,500

FIGURE 7.3

Assume for now that Bright Ideas manufactured and sold 15,000 units in year 2010, and had no beginning inventory. Based on the production data, Bright Ideas consumed $90,000 ($6 per unit × 15,000 units produced) of direct materials, $120,000 ($8 per unit × 15,000 units produced) of direct labor, $75,000 ($5 per unit × 15,000 units produced) of variable manufacturing overhead and $45,000 of fixed manufacturing overhead (e.g. machine depreciation). The company also incurred non-manufacturing related costs such as head office rent and salaries paid to employees of the sales department.

If Bright Ideas chooses to use the absorption costing approach, the product cost would include all manufacturing costs as shown in figure 7.4.

Direct Material	$90,000
Direct Labor	120,000
Variable Manufacturing Overhead	75,000
Fixed Manufacturing Overhead	45,000
Total Cost of Goods Manufactured	$330,000

FIGURE 7.4

Since the absorption approach conforms to GAAP, the cost information can be used to prepare a formal income statement. For the year 2010, Bright Ideas generated revenue of $450,000 ($30 selling price per unit × 15,000 units sold). The cost of goods sold can be calculated by adding beginning inventory and cost of goods manufactured, then subtracting ending inventory. Bright Ideas had no beginning inventory, and since all units produced in 2010 were also sold during the year, there is no ending inventory. Therefore, cost of goods sold amounts to $330,000. The completed income statement is shown in figure 7.5.

Bright Ideas Income Statement - Absorption Costing For the Year Ending December 31, 2010		
Sales Revenue		$450,000
Cost of Goods Sold:		
Beginning Inventory	$0	
Cost of Goods Manufactured	330,000	
Less: Ending Inventory	0	
Cost of Goods Sold		330,000
Gross Profit		120,000
Operating Expenses:		
Rent	15,000	
Sales Department Salaries	21,500	
Total Operating Expenses		36,500
Operating Income		$83,500

FIGURE 7.5

In this statement, the amount of costs of goods sold includes direct materials, direct labor and all manufacturing overhead. Once the cost of goods sold is deducted from sales revenue, Bright Ideas shows a gross profit of $120,000. After the non-manufacturing (i.e. operating) expenses are further subtracted, the company shows an operating income of $83,500.

Variable Costing: Bright Ideas

Although the income statement prepared above by Bright Ideas provides the full cost of the product, it may not satisfy the needs of management. Internally, managers may wish to determine the behavior of their product costs as sales volume changes.

If Bright Ideas chooses to use the variable costing approach, the product cost would include only the variable manufacturing costs as shown in figure 7.6.

Direct Material	$90,000
Direct Labor	120,000
Variable Manufacturing Overhead	75,000
Variable Cost of Goods Manufactured	$285,000

FIGURE 7.6

In the above calculation, the cost of goods manufactured includes variable manufacturing costs only. The fixed manufacturing overhead is excluded (i.e. not treated as a product cost). Since variable costing separates product costs by their cost behavior, a contribution margin statement can easily be prepared. Remember, this statement is not compliant with GAAP and will not be part of the financial statements available to the external stakeholders of Bright Ideas. The purpose of this statement is to assist management in analyzing cost behavior. The contribution margin statement is shown in figure 7.7.

Bright Ideas **Contribution Margin Statement - Variable Costing** **For the Year Ending December 31, 2010**		
Sales Revenue		$450,000
Variable Costs:		
Beginning Inventory	$0	
Variable Cost of Goods Manufactured	285,000	
Less: Ending Inventory	0	
Variable Cost of Goods Sold:		285,000
Contribution Margin		165,000
Fixed Costs		
Fixed Manufacturing Overhead	45,000	
Rent	15,000	
Sales Department Salaries	21,500	
Total Fixed Costs		81,500
Operating Income		$83,500

FIGURE 7.7

Unlike the income statement illustrated under absorption costing, both cost of goods manufactured and cost of goods sold under variable costing include variable manufacturing costs only. Fixed manufacturing overhead is not included as part of the cost of inventory. Instead, it is treated as an expense in the period incurred in the same way as all the other non-manufacturing costs. Once the cost of goods sold is deducted from sales revenue, Bright Ideas shows a contribution margin of $165,000. After the fixed expenses are further subtracted, the company has an operating income of $83,500.

Bright Ideas Summary

To further examine the differences between absorption costing and variable costing, the two statements are compared side by side as shown in figure 7.8.

Bright Ideas Contribution Margin Statement - Variable Costing For the Year Ending December 31, 2010		
Sales		$450,000
Variable Costs:		
Variable Beginning Inventory	$0	
Variable Cost of Goods Manufactured	285,000	
Less: Variable Ending Inventory	0	
Variable Cost of Goods Sold:		285,000
Contribution Margin		165,200
Fixed Costs:		
Fixed Manufacturing Overhead	45,000	
Rent	15,000	
Sales Department Salaries	21,500	
Total Fixed Costs		81,500
Operating Income		$83,500

Bright Ideas Income Statement - Absorption Costing For the Year Ending December 31, 2010		
Sales		$450,000
Cost of Goods Sold:		
Beginning Inventory	$0	
Cost of Goods Manufactured	330,000	
Less: Ending Inventory	0	
Cost of Goods Sold		330,000
Gross Margin		120,000
Operating Expenses:		
Rent	15,000	
Sales Department Salaries	21,500	
Total Operating Expenses		36,500
Operating Income		$83,500

FIGURE 7.8

The only difference between the two approaches is how the fixed manufacturing overhead is treated. As highlighted in figure 7.8, absorption costing includes the fixed manufacturing overhead as part of the product cost while variable costing does not. Under variable costing, the cost of inventory includes variable manufacturing costs only.

The two costing approaches may serve different purposes when analyzing product costs and making decisions. The absorption costing calculation demonstrates to users how much the products really cost. In other words, the variable costing calculation shows which components of the product costs will actually change as production volume changes. People who favor absorption costing feel that product costs should fully reflect their true costs. People who favor variable costing feel that fixed manufacturing overhead would be incurred as part of operating the business and, therefore, is not truly a cost incurred by producing an additional unit of product.

Variable Costing and Mixed Costs

The above example assumed that all variable costs are manufacturing related. However, it is possible for a company to incur variable costs or mixed costs (which include a variable component) outside of the manufacturing function. Assume the compensation for the sales team is a mixed cost instead of fixed cost. That is, the $21,500 total compensation is actually comprised of both a fixed salary and commissions based on sales (i.e. a variable cost). Bright Ideas determines that the fixed portion (salaries) amounts to $8,000 and that the variable portion (commissions) is $0.90 for each item sold. Therefore, $8,000 will be recognized as a fixed cost and $13,500 ($0.90 per unit × 15,000 units sold) will be recognized as a variable cost. Since these costs are non-manufacturing in nature, they will not impact the variable product cost. However, they will be presented separately when the contribution margin statement is prepared. A new contribution margin statement with this mixed cost is shown in figure 7.9.

Bright Ideas Contribution Margin Statement - Variable Costing For the Year Ending December 31, 2010		
Sales		$450,000
Variable Costs:		
Beginning Inventory	$0	
Variable Cost of Goods Manufactured	285,000	
Less: Ending Inventory	0	
Variable Cost of Goods Sold:		285,000
Variable Commissions		13,500
Contribution Margin		151,500
Fixed Costs:		
Fixed Manufacturing Overhead	45,000	
Rent	15,000	
Sales Department Salaries	8,000	
Total Fixed Costs		68,000
Operating Income		$83,500

FIGURE 7.9

This change will not impact the income statement in figure 7.5 at all because the income statement is not meant to reflect the cost behavior.

Income Differences Under Absorption and Variable Costing

In the previous section, we demonstrated how variable costing impact inventory costs and facilitate cost behavior analysis. Another important aspect of insight variable costing provides is income interpretation. Assume you were a manager at Bright Ideas. You generated the same sales revenue and incurred the same costs every year for three years. Intuitively, you would expect to see the same operating income for all three years. However, if the production volume is different from the sales volume in a given period, absorption costing would not present operating income the way you expect. Let us first look into why this situation may arise.

The examples in figure 7.5 and figure 7.6 are relatively simple because Bright Ideas sells as many chandeliers as it produces. In reality, production volume will usually not equal to sales volume for a given period. If production is greater than sales, there will be unsold items in inventory (an asset) at the end of a period. Under absorption costing, these unsold inventory items will carry fixed manufacturing overhead costs with them. The fixed manufacturing overhead costs will only be expensed when the inventory is sold. *Stated another way, fixed manufacturing overhead follows the product under absorption costing.*

On the other hand, under variable costing, fixed manufacturing overhead is always viewed as a period cost (an expense) in the period they occur regardless when the inventory is sold. *Stated another way, fixed manufacturing overhead follows the period under variable costing.* This difference in accounting for fixed manufacturing overhead under the two costing approaches is illustrated using a simple scenario (figure 7.10)

Absorption Costing

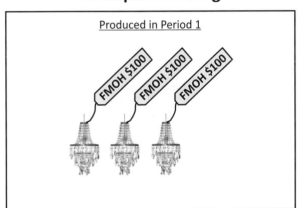

Variable Costing

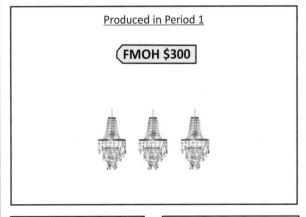

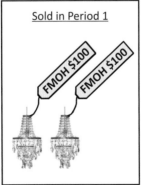

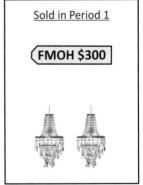

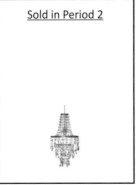

*FMOH = Fixed Manufacturing Overhead

FIGURE 7.10

Figure 7.10 illustrates the situation when three chandeliers are produced in period 1, two are sold in period 1 and one is sold in period 2. The total fixed manufacturing overhead incurred amounts to $300. Under absorption costing, the fixed manufacturing costs follow the product. Thus, $200 is expensed in period 1 and $100 is expensed in period 2. Under variable costing, the fixed manufacturing costs follow the period. Thus, all $300 is expensed under period 1 when incurred whether or not all products are sold in period 1. Since the two approaches account for different amounts of expenses under each period, we would expect to see a difference in operating income. We will now examine two detailed examples when production is different from sales in a given period.

Production is Greater Than Sales in a Given Period

Assume for 2011 Bright Ideas produces 18,000 units in anticipation of higher sales, but only sells 15,000 units during the year. This leaves them with 3,000 units in ending inventory. Assume that the sales price does not change, all cost items remain unchanged and salaries and commission is treated as a mixed cost as illustrated in figure 7.9. Refer back to figure 7.3 to see the pricing and cost information. For comparison, the absorption statement and variable statement with the current production and sales level are presented in figure 7.11.

Bright Ideas Contribution Margin Statement - Variable Costing For the Year Ending December 31, 2011		
Sales		$450,000
Variable Costs:		
Beginning Inventory	$0	
Variable Cost of Goods Manufactured	342,000	
Less: Ending Inventory	57,000	
Variable Cost of Goods Sold:		285,000
Variable Commissions		13,500
Contribution Margin		151,500
Fixed Costs:		
Fixed Manufacturing Overhead	45,000	
Rent	15,000	
Sales Department Salaries	8,000	
Total Fixed Costs		68,000
Operating Income		$83,500

Bright Ideas Income Statement - Absorption Costing For the Year Ending December 31, 2011		
Sales		$450,000
Cost of Goods Sold:		
Beginning Inventory	$0	
Cost of Goods Manufactured	387,000	
Less: Ending Inventory	64,500	
Cost of Goods Sold		322,500
Gross Margin		127,500
Operating Expenses:		
Rent	15,000	
Sales Department Salaries	21,500	
Total Operating Expenses		36,500
Operating Income		$91,000

FIGURE 7.11

Absorption costing shows a higher operating income of $7,500 ($91,000 - $83,500). There is also a difference in the values of cost of goods manufactured and ending inventory, which is highlighted in figure 7.11. The difference is caused by the treatment of fixed manufacturing overhead and its impact on ending inventory.

Under absorption costing, remember that fixed manufacturing overhead follows inventory. Therefore, a portion of this overhead will be attributed to the unsold items remaining in ending inventory and will not be recorded as an expense on the income statement. The absorption costing calculation for the value of ending inventory is shown in figure 7.12.

Direct Material	$6 × 3,000 units	$18,000
Direct Labor	$8 × 3,000 units	24,000
Variable Manufacturing Overhead	$5 × 3,000 units	15,000
Fixed Manufacturing Overhead	($45,000 ÷ 18,000 units) × 3,000 units	7,500
Total Ending Inventory		$64,500

FIGURE 7.12

Since ending inventory needs to be subtracted from cost of goods manufactured to arrive at cost of goods sold, the higher the value of ending inventory, the lower the cost of goods sold. This explains why absorption costing shows a higher operating income.

Under variable costing, the value of ending inventory includes only variable manufacturing overhead. Figure 7.13 shows the calculation for ending inventory under this approach.

Direct Material	$6 × 3,000 units	$18,000
Direct Labor	$8 × 3,000 units	24,000
Variable Manufacturing Overhead	$5 × 3,000 units	15,000
Total Ending Inventory		$57,000

FIGURE 7.13

All fixed manufacturing overhead are treated as expenses in the current period. Since expenses need to be deducted from revenue to calculate operating income, the higher the expenses, the lower the operating income. This explains why variable costing shows a lower operating income.

If a manager uses absorption costing to analyze profits, he or she would see that profits increased from last year. An initial reaction may be the company was able to cut costs somewhere or was managing operations more efficiently. However, the true reason for the increase in profit in this case is simply because more items were manufactured than were sold in this period. It can be difficult to discern this cause if the variable costing statement is not prepared. Variable costing shows profits more in line with what a manger would expect when sales remain constant.

Production is Less Than Sales in a Given Period

In year 2012, Bright Ideas cuts production to 12,000 units to compensate for the overproduction from the previous year. The ending inventory of 3,000 units from last year now becomes the beginning inventory for this year. In total, they have 15,000 units that can be sold. This year, sales are again 15,000 units. As with the last two years, sales price, variable cost per unit and fixed costs remain the same. Refer back to figure 7.3 to see the pricing and cost information.

For comparison, the absorption statement and variable statement with the current production and sales level are presented in figure 7.14.

Bright Ideas Contribution Margin Statement - Variable Costing For the Year Ending December 31, 2012		
Sales		$450,000
Variable Costs:		
Beginning Inventory	$57,000	
Variable Cost of Goods Manufactured	228,000	
Less: Ending Inventory	0	
Variable Cost of Goods Sold:		285,000
Variable Commissions		13,500
Contribution Margin		151,500
Fixed Costs:		
Fixed Manufacturing Overhead	45,000	
Rent	15,000	
Sales Department Salaries	8,000	
Total Fixed Costs		68,000
Operating Income		$83,500

Bright Ideas Income Statement - Absorption Costing For the Year Ending December 31, 2012		
Sales		$450,000
Cost of Goods Sold:		
Beginning Inventory	$64,500	
Cost of Goods Manufactured	273,000	
Less: Ending Inventory	0	
Cost of Goods Sold		337,500
Gross Margin		112,500
Operating Expenses:		
Rent	15,000	
Sales Department Salaries/Commission	21,500	
Total Operating Expenses		36,500
Operating Income		$76,000

FIGURE 7.14

This time, variable costing shows a higher operating income of $7,500 ($83,500 - $76,000). There is also a difference in the values of beginning inventory and cost of goods manufactured, which is highlighted in figure 7.14. The difference is caused by the treatment of fixed manufacturing overhead and its impact on beginning inventory.

The absorption costing method carried over $7,500 of fixed manufacturing overhead from the previous year (2011). This amount is expensed during this year (2012) when the goods were sold. Also, since all the goods produced this year were also sold, the entire amount of this year's fixed manufacturing overhead is also expensed this year. In other words, the absorption costing statement this year expensed a portion of the fixed manufacturing overhead from last year and the amount incurred this year.

On the other hand, all the fixed manufacturing overhead incurred last year was expensed last year under variable costing. The variable costing statement this year expensed the amount fixed manufacturing cost incurred this year only. This explains why absorption costing shows a smaller operating income than variable costing since the expenses under absorption costing are in higher amounts.

If a manager uses absorption costing to analyze profits, he or she would see that profits decreased substantially from last year. An initial reaction may be the company incurred more costs or became less efficient in their operations. However, the true reason for the decrease in profit this year is simply because fewer items were manufactured than were sold. Variable costing shows profits more in line with what a manger would expect when sales remain constant.

Impact of Production and Sales Volume

It is worth emphasizing that the timing of expensing fixed manufacturing overhead is what results in the differences reported in operating income between variable and absorption costing. The overall effect is that fixed manufacturing overhead will eventually be recorded as an expense and impact operating income; it is just a question of when that will happen. If we compare the operating income reported by the two approaches over the three years, notice that the overall operating income is the same.

	Year	Operating Income	
		Absorption Costing	Variable Costing
Figure 7.8	2010	$83,500	$83,500
Figure 7.11	2011	91,000	83,500
Figure 7.14	2012	76,000	83,500
	Total	$250,500	$250,500

FIGURE 7.15

Since the sales volume remained constant over the three years, the operating income reported under variable costing more closely represents what managers would expect to see. If managers only used absorption costing to monitor operating profit, they might view 2011 as an exceptional year, but show concern in 2012 when operating income drops dramatically. If only the income statement is relied upon, management may end up making bad decisions, such as mistakenly discontinuing a profitable product line.

The difference between the production and sales volume in a given year will contribute to the operating income variance between the two approaches. If the number of units manufactured during the year is equal to the number of units sold (as in year 2010 in the example), then both approaches would show the same operating income.

If the number of units manufactured during the year is greater than sales volume (as in year 2011 in the example), absorption costing would show a higher operating income than variable costing. If the number of units manufactured during the year is less than the number of units sold (as in year 2012 in the example), absorption costing would have a lower operating income than variable costing.

Our example assumed that sales volume always remained constant while production volume fluctuated. Similar variations in operating income would occur if production volume remained constant and sales volume fluctuated. The relationship of the production and sales volumes to the operating income reported under the two costing approaches is shown in figure 7.16. Whatever relationship production volume has with sales volume (greater than, less than or equal to), that will also be the relationship absorption operating income has with variable operating income.

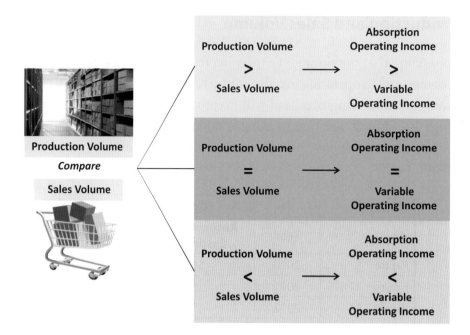

FIGURE 7.16

As in the cotton candy example that started this chapter, there are some that feel absorption costing is the best way to cost a product, since it represents all the manufacturing costs on a per unit basis. There are also some that feel variable costing is the best way to cost a product, since fixed manufacturing overhead is not really a cost of making an additional unit of a particular product. Whichever method is used by management internally to assign costs to their products, the selling price must be high enough to cover the costs and generate a profit.

Pricing Methods

Before establishing a selling price, businesses typically spend a considerable amount of time trying to understand the market for their product. Are identical or similar products available to potential customers from other companies? What is the demand for the product? What are customers willing to spend on the product?

If a business sells raw materials like precious metals or agricultural items, the business is in competition with other companies that are selling an identical commercial product. There will be a market for the product with a set price that all business must sell at. If one company were to charge a higher price than its competitors for the product, customers would simply stop buying from the company and start buying from the competitors. If one company were to charge a lower price than its competitors, it would lose money.

A more common situation is where a business sells a product that is similar to other products that companies sell, but included additional features to make it stand out. Clothing items, toothpaste and household cleaners are examples where businesses attempt to make their product different from their competitors. In this situation, companies must establish their own selling price for their product. Consider the following business case for an illustration of pricing methods.

Jordan studied fashion and design in college. In his final year, he created a preliminary business plan for a line of baseball caps as a school project. The line consisted of ten unique designs which all cost approximately the same amount to manufacture. Jordan was able to estimate the cost of sourcing his raw materials (plain baseball cap) and the cost of designing and stitching the embroidery on his baseball caps. Jordan wants to implement his business plan and decides that he will perform the embroidery design and stitching processes in-house. He will need to purchase the necessary equipment and hire his friends to help him. After reviewing the alternatives for sales channels, Jordan decides to start his business by establishing an online store. Jordan has to complete his business plan to apply for a small start-up loan. This would be his only source of start-up financing. To complete his budgets, Jordan needs to determine what price he should charge customers for his baseball caps.

Through the encouragement of his friends, Jordan set up social media accounts which featured his preliminary designs. He has received a number of emails and positive feedback about the unique styles and designs featured in his new line. Jordan needs to determine the price level that his target customers would be willing to pay. If the price is set too high, there may be less interested customers. If it is set too low, the company's costs and required returns may not be covered. Businesses must be aware of the true costs of their products in order to set an appropriate price level. Establishing the right price level is important as businesses strive to maximize revenues and profitability. Understanding these concepts will help Jordan set the appropriate selling price for his baseball caps. In this section, three different pricing methods will be discussed: maximum profit pricing, cost-plus pricing and target costing.

Maximum Profit Pricing

Generally, customers' willingness to buy a product is dependent on its price. Usually, if the price of an item is lower, greater quantities will be demanded by customers. If the price is higher, fewer items will be demanded by customers. You can observe this general rule by watching crowds at a store that has a good sale. This is the foundation of the law of demand from economics. Understanding this relationship between price and quantity demanded means that if a company can accurately forecast the volume of items sold at any particular price, they will be able to set a price that will provide them with the highest operating income possible.

For example, if a company set their selling price at $1, three people would purchase their product and the company would generate $3 in profit. If the company set their selling price at $3, two people would purchase their product and the company would generate $6 in profit.

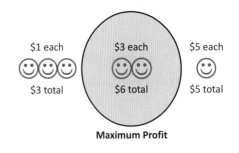

FIGURE 7.17

Finally, if the company set their selling price at $5, only one person would purchase their product and the company would generate $5 in profit. This is illustrated in figure 7.17. In this example, the company should set their selling price at $3 to maximize their profits.

Returning to the baseball caps example, suppose Jordan has calculated variable costs per baseball cap to be $9. Fixed costs for the year will be $9,000. He has estimated the quantity demanded at various selling prices and has created a table illustrating the basic contribution margin statement as shown in figure 7.18.

Price per Unit	Quantity Demanded	Sales	Variable Costs	Contribution Margin	Fixed Costs	Operating Income
$16	1,500	$24,000	$13,500	$10,500	$9,000	$1,500
18	1,200	21,600	10,800	10,800	9,000	1,800
20	1,000	20,000	9,000	11,000	9,000	2,000
22	800	17,600	7,200	10,400	9,000	1,400
24	700	16,800	6,300	10,500	9,000	1,500
26	500	13,000	4,500	8,500	9,000	(500)
28	400	11,200	3,600	7,600	9,000	(1,400)

FIGURE 7.18

It is assumed in the above table that Jordan can produce and sell (i.e. supply) enough baseball caps to meet any level of demand. Notice that the highest price shown in the table does not generate the highest operating income. In fact, the highest price would cause an operating loss. The highest operating income will be generated if the selling price is set at $20 per baseball cap.

The challenge with using this pricing scheme is determining an accurate relationship between the price and the quantity demanded. Jordan could use his social media account to ask people to indicate how much they would be willing to pay for one of his caps, and count how many people would pay which price. The data collected could then be used to estimate the relationship between the price and demand for his entire market, thus creating the table in figure 7.18. Jordan could also experiment by selling the baseball caps at various prices to determine the demand. Again, he would have to estimate the relationship between the price and demand for the entire market based on the data he collects. An easier method to set a selling price would be to use the cost-plus pricing method or the target costing method.

Cost-Plus Pricing

The most common method to pricing is applying a markup to cost, which is the **cost-plus pricing** method. A **markup** is the difference between a product's selling price and its cost, and is often expressed as a percentage of cost. The formula for cost-plus pricing is as follows:

$$\text{Selling Price} = \text{Cost} \times (1 + \text{Markup Percentage})^*$$

*An alternative way to calculate selling price is: Cost + (Cost × Markup Percentage)

For example, if a company's markup is 30%, it adds 30% to the total cost of the product to obtain the selling price. Therefore, for a product that costs $100, the company would calculate the selling price to be $130, as shown below.

$$
\begin{aligned}
\text{Selling Price} &= \text{Cost} \times (1 + \text{Markup Percentage})^* \\
&= \$100 \times (1 + 0.30) \\
&= \$130
\end{aligned}
$$

*or: Cost + (Cost × Markup Percentage) = $100 + ($100 × 30%) = $130

However, the above formula for cost-plus pricing requires two inputs (i.e. cost and mark-up percentage). Therefore, the key questions for a company are: which cost amount should be used and what is the appropriate markup percentage?

Cost-Plus Pricing

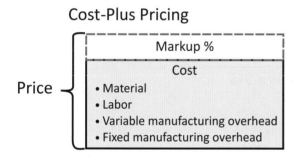

Earlier in the chapter, we discussed two methods to determine the total cost assigned to a unit of a product: absorption and variable costing. To successfully implement cost-plus pricing, the full (absorption) cost to produce a product is often used. As mentioned previously, this includes the variable product costs (i.e. direct materials, direct labor, and variable manufacturing overhead), as well as the fixed manufacturing overhead costs. Once the full cost is determined, the markup is then added to the cost to provide the business with a selling price.

Let us return to our business case with Jordan's baseball caps. Jordan has prepared a breakdown of the estimated costs of manufacturing and selling the baseball caps for the upcoming year (figure 7.19). He has estimated that he will be able to manufacture and sell 1,000 baseball caps during the year.

	Per Unit	Total (1,000 units)
Direct materials	$4	
Direct labor	$3	
Variable manufacturing overhead	$2	
Fixed manufacturing overhead	-	$6,000
General and administrative expenses	-	$3,000

FIGURE 7.19

By using the information in figure 7.19, the full cost of a baseball cap is determined to be $15 ($4 + $3 + $2 + $6,000 ÷ 1,000 units). It is important to note that general and administrative expenses are not included in the full cost since it is always considered a period cost (i.e. it is not a product cost).

Now that we have determined a cost on which to apply the markup, the next step is to determine an appropriate markup percentage. Many companies often resort to using a markup rate that is deemed as a standard in the industry or one that is determined by the use of professional judgment. Another popular method is to use a calculated markup that is large enough to cover general and administrative (G&A) expenses and provide a sufficient rate of return. This markup percentage also takes the unit product cost into account. This method of determining the markup percentage will be referred to as the formula method. It can be calculated using the following formula:

$$\text{Markup Percentage} = \frac{(\text{Required Rate of Return} \times \text{Investment}) + \text{G\&A Expenses}}{\text{Sales Volume} \times \text{Unit Product Cost}}$$

Assume that Jordan must take out a bank loan of $13,500 to startup the business (i.e. investment). If a 20% rate of return is required on the investment, then the markup can be calculated as follows:

$$\text{Markup Percentage} = \frac{(20\% \times \$13,500) + \$3,000}{1,000 \times \$15} = 38\%$$

After marking up the full cost of $15 by 38%, the selling price is determined to be $20.70 ($15 × 1.38). The calculation of the selling price is summarized below.

Price Quote Sheet (Full Cost)	
Direct materials	$4.00
Direct labor	3.00
Variable manufacturing overhead	2.00
Fixed manufacturing overhead (based on 1,000 units)	6.00
Product cost per unit	15.00
Markup (38% of product cost)	5.70
Selling price	$20.70

FIGURE 7.20

Jordan's Baseball Caps Forecasted Contribution Margin Statement For the Year Ending December 31, 2011		
Sales		$20,700
Variable Costs		
Direct Material	$4,000	
Direct Labor	3,000	
Variable Overhead	2,000	9,000
Contribution Margin		11,700
Fixed Costs		
Fixed manufacturing Overhead	6,000	
General & Administrative	3,000	9,000
Operating Income		$2,700

FIGURE 7.21

If Jordan prepares a contribution statement based on the quantity he plans to sell (1,000 units), his selling price of $20.70 and the costs he has estimated, he finds that he ends up with an operating income of $2,700. The operating income is 20% of his initial investment ($2,700 ÷ $13,500). Therefore, Jordan has priced his product properly to generate a profit and the return he is looking for. From this contribution margin statement, he can also perform a break-even analysis to determine how many baseball caps he must sell to break even.

The main advantage of cost-plus pricing is that the business can ensure that it covers the product costs and earns a profit. There is a disadvantage to cost-based pricing as well. It was previously mentioned that in order to establish a price, businesses must gather information to understand their market and their customers. However, this pricing model does not take the market and customer information into consideration.

By establishing his business in the social media, Jordan learned that his target customers enjoy the unique styles and designs featured in his line. By adding unique features to products that customers enjoy, businesses can set a premium price. Assume similar baseball cap designers charges $25 per baseball cap. By failing to understand the market and consumer behavior, it is unlikely that potential customers will view the relatively low selling price ($20.70) to be a premium product or even comparable to the other products in the market.

Target Costing

An alternative to cost-based pricing is target costing. **Target costing** is the process of using the anticipated market price to calculate the maximum costs the business can incur. This means the manufacturing and other costs cannot exceed the maximum allowable cost. The maximum allowable cost is also known as the **target cost**. The target cost is determined using the following formula:

Target Cost = Predetermined Selling Price – Desired Profit

The above formula can also be used to analyze sales and costs and profit on a per unit basis.

Target costing is often used when a company believes it has little or no control over the product's selling price. In these situations, the market determines the selling price based on supply and demand.

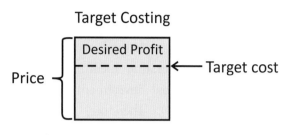

Target Costing

For example, suppose a company wishes to introduce a brand new toilet bowl cleaner. There are already a number of different brands available on the market, each with their own twist that makes them different. The prices of these cleaners range from $3.50 to $5.00 per bottle. The company management feels that to keep competitive in this market, they cannot charge more than the high end of $5.00 per bottle. Management may ultimately decide that the selling price should fall midway between the high and low prices, so they set the selling price to be $4.25 per bottle.

Another reason some companies use target costing is because they believe a significant portion of the product cost occurs in the design and development stage of the value chain. The design and development stages can ensure that inexpensive, yet reliable parts are used. Proper design of the production process can be implemented to minimize costs. Also, only the features that customers view as valuable are added. In this scenario, it is believed that once a product has been designed and developed, little can be done to significantly reduce its cost in the production phase. In target costing, the product is designed, developed and produced with the maximum allowable cost kept in mind and not exceeded. An effective implementation of target costing requires a strong understanding of what the customer truly values and encourages the company to avoid spending on activities that add minimal value from the customers' perspective.

Let us return to Jordan's baseball cap business to illustrate target costing. Suppose Jordan knows that similar baseball cap designers are charging $25 per baseball cap. At this selling price, it allows for a suitable premium to be charged for their unique designs and the quality of materials used. Therefore, Jordan sets the unit selling price of his baseball caps at $25. Recall that Jordan projects he can sell 1,000 baseball caps for the upcoming year and that an investment of $13,500 is required to design, develop, and produce the caps. He desires a rate of return of 20% on his investment. The target cost is calculated as follows:

Estimated sales	$25,000	(1,000 units × $25/unit)
Less: Desired profit	2,700	(20% × $13,500)
Target cost (for 1,000 units)	$22,300	
Absorption cost	$15,000	(1,000 units × $15/unit)
Plus: Administrative costs	3,000	General & Administrative
Total cost (for 1,000 units)	$18,000	

FIGURE 7.22

Therefore, the target cost for the 1,000 baseball caps is $22,300. Jordan's total costs amount to $18,000. Therefore, at this target selling price and desired profit, Jordan can easily meet the desired profit of $2,700. In fact, there is a buffer of $4,300 ($22,300 - $18,000) by which his total costs could increase. For example, Jordan can consider increasing the quality of his materials used in the production of his baseball caps to further satisfy his customer base. He could also consider spending more on advertising to try and increase the demand for his product.

An advantage of target costing is that it is a proactive approach to managing costs and helps minimize the use of non-value added activities. It also makes use of information available in the market and allows companies to avoid the burden of determining an acceptable selling price. A key disadvantage is it can reduce the quality of products, since management is pressured to not exceed the maximum allowable cost. This may lead to the use of cheap components in the production phase of the product, which reduces the product's overall quality. In addition, the implementation of target costing requires very detailed cost data.

Once the price is established using a suitable pricing method, Jordan can test his business model by performing cost-volume-profit analysis, which was introduced in chapter 6. These include break-even calculations, determining the volume of baseball caps he must sell before earning a given profit level, and so forth.

Ethical Considerations

When managers are measured against the department profitability, or have bonuses tied to the profits of a department, it can be tempting to try and use the manufacturing of products to increase profitability in the short-run. As was shown in the chapter, when production is greater than sales, absorption costing shows a higher operating profit. This is because some of the fixed manufacturing overhead is not expensed during the period. Instead, it is recorded in inventory. Unfortunately, engaging in over production just to show better profits is a short term solution and can lead to serious issues.

One serious issue revolves around cash. Overproduction causes inventory to buildup. As production increases, more material, labor and variable manufacturing overhead must be used. These things cost money. Thus, overproduction uses up the organization's cash, and this cash will be tied up in unsold inventory. If the organization then does not have enough cash to pay for future expenses such as labor, they may have to resort to borrowing money to pay their bills. There is also the risk that the unsold inventory will become obsolete (i.e. computer components).

Another serious issue involves how the manager will behave during the next period. As shown in the chapter, the fixed manufacturing overhead that is deferred from one period will be expensed in the next. This will cause operating profit to drop in the next period. To avoid the drop in profit, the manager can increase production yet again, ensuring there is enough overproduction to record a desirable profit. This can lead to a cycle of constantly overproducing just to maintain profitability.

In Summary

⇨ **Variable costing** only assigns direct material, direct labor and variable overhead costs to inventory.

⇨ **Absorption costing** will assign direct material, direct labor, variable overhead and fixed manufacturing overhead costs to inventory.

⇨ **Full cost** (or absorption cost) is the unit product cost determined using the absorption costing method.

⇨ Absorption costing is permitted under GAAP and IFRS for reporting purposes, variable costing is not permitted.

⇨ Under variable costing, fixed manufacturing overhead is treated as a period cost. Absorption costing treats fixed manufacturing overhead as a product cost.

⇨ Income statements prepared under variable costing will differ from income statement prepared under absorption costing if production units and sales units differ.

⇨ If manufactured units are greater than sales, absorption operating income will be greater than variable operating income.

⇨ If manufactured units are less than sales, absorption operating income will be less than variable operating income.

⇨ If manufactured units are equal to sales, absorption operating income will be equal to variable operating income.

⇨ Maximum profit pricing examines the relationship between price and quantity demanded to find the price that will provide the most operating income.

⇨ A **markup** is the difference between a product's selling price and its cost.

⇨ **Target costing** is the process of using the anticipated market price to calculate the maximum allowable cost for a product.

⇨ Target costing is often used when a company believes it has little or no control over the product's selling price.

⇨ The maximum allowable cost is also known as the **target cost**.

Review Exercise 1

WIA Limited manufactures and sells a single product. During the first year of operations in 2010, the company produced 100,000 units and sold 80,000 units. The selling price for the product is $600 per unit. The following costs were incurred during the company's first year of operations:

Direct Materials	$190 per unit
Direct Labor	$250 per unit
Variable Manufacturing Overhead Costs	$90 per unit
Variable Selling and Administrative Costs	$50 per unit sold
Fixed Manufacturing Overhead Cost	$590,000
Fixed Selling and Administrative Costs	$90,000

Required:

1. Assume that the company uses the absorption costing method:
   a) Calculate the unit product cost.
   b) Prepare an income statement for the year.
2. Assume that the company uses the variable costing method:
   a) Calculate the unit product cost
   b) Prepare a contributed income statement.
3. Why is there a difference in the operating income amounts calculated in parts 1 and 2?

Review Exercise – Answer

Part 1

a) Under the absorption costing method, the unit product cost includes all manufacturing costs (including fixed manufacturing overhead).

Fixed manufacturing overhead rate

= FMOH ÷ Production Volume

= $590,000 ÷ 100,000 units

= $5.90 per unit

Unit Product Cost

= DM per unit + DL per unit + VMOH per unit + FMOH rate

= $190 + $250 + $90 + $5.90

= $535.90 per unit

b)

WIA Limited		
Income Statement		
For the Year Ended on December 31, 2010		
Revenues		$48,000,000[1]
Cost of Goods Sold:		
Beginning Inventory	$0	
Cost of Goods Manufactured	53,590,000[2]	
Less: Ending Inventory	10,718,000[3]	
Cost of Goods Sold		42,872,000
Gross Margin		5,128,000
Operating Expenses:		
General and Administrative Costs		4,090,000[4]
Operating Income		$1,038,000

[1]$600/unit × 80,000 units

[2]($190 + $250 + $90 + $5.90) per unit × 100,000 units

[3]($190 + $250 + $90 + $5.90) per unit × (100,000 units - 80,000 units)

[4]($50/unit × 80,000 units) + $90,000

Note that since the company is in its first year of operations, there is no beginning inventory.

Part 2

a) Under the variable costing method, the unit product cost includes only the variable manufacturing costs.

Unit Product Cost

= DM per unit + DL per unit + VMOH per unit

= $190 + $250 + $90

= $530 per unit

b)

WIA Limited Contributed Margin Statement For the Year Ended on December 31, 2010		
Revenues		$48,000,000[1]
Variable Costs		
Variable Beginning Inventory	$0	
Variable Cost of Goods Manufactured	53,000,000[2]	
Less: Variable Ending Inventory	10,600,000[3]	
Variable Cost of Goods Sold		42,400,000
Variable General and Administrative Costs		4,000,000[4]
Contributed Margin		1,600,000
Operating Expenses:		
Fixed Manufacturing Overhead Costs	590,000	
Fixed General and Administrative Costs	90,000	680,000
Operating Income		$920,000

[1] $600/unit × 80,000 units

[2] ($190 + $250 + $90) per unit × 100,000 units

[3] ($190 + $250 + $90) per unit × (100,000 units - 80,000 units)

[4] $50/unit × 80,000 units

c) The difference in operating income arises from the variance in the treatment of the fixed manufacturing overhead costs between the two methods. Absorption costing only recognizes 80% (80,000 units sold/100,000 units produced) of the fixed manufacturing overhead cost, whereas the variable costing method expenses the full amount.

Operating income difference:

= Absorption Operating Income – Variable Operating Income

= $1,038,000 - $920,000

= $118,000

Operating income difference:

FMOH not expensed in the absorption costing income statement

= $5.90 × (100,000 – 80,000)

= $118,000

Or:

FMOH not expensed in the absorption costing income statement

=(100% - 80%) × $590,000

=$118,000

Review Exercise 2

Linwood Company recently began production of a new navigation device, which required a capital investment of $650,000. Linwood is currently considering establishing a selling price for this new device that will ensure a 20% return on the capital investment. The engineering and the sales department compiled the following estimates for producing and selling 80,000 devices:

	Total (80,000 units)
Variable Costs Per Unit:	
Direct Materials	$11 per unit
Direct Labor	$24 per unit
Variable Manufacturing Overhead	$15 per unit
General And Administrative Expenses	$16 per unit sold
Fixed Costs:	
Fixed Manufacturing Overhead	$240,000
General And Administrative Expenses	$74,000

Required:

1. Calculate the markup percentage.

2. The company has a cost-plus pricing policy that uses the absorption (full) cost as the cost base and the markup percentage calculated in part 1. How much would the company charge for its new navigation device?

3. Based on a recent consumer report, the company predicts that its device cannot be priced higher than $65. At this particular price, the company believes it can sell 85,000 units and assumes the fixed costs will remain the same. Using the target costing method, would the company exceed the maximum allowable cost?

Review Exercise – Answer

Part 1

Absorption Cost

= Direct Materials + Direct Labor + Variable Manufacturing Overhead + Fixed Manufacturing Overhead Cost per unit

= $11 + $24 + $15 + ($240,000 ÷ ÷ 80,000 units)

= $53 per unit

Markup Percentage

= [(Required Rate of Return × Investment) + G&A Expenses] ÷ [Sales Volume × Unit Product Cost]

= [(0.2 × 650,000) + ($16 per unit sold × 80,000) + $74,000] ÷ (80,000 × $53 per unit)

= 0.35 or 35%

Part 2

Selling Price

= Absorption Cost × (1 + Markup)

= \$53 × (1 + 0.35)

= \$71.55

The selling price is \$71.55.

Part 3

Target Cost

= Estimated Sales − Desired Profit

= (\$65 per unit × 85,000) − (0.2 × \$650,000)

= \$5,395,000

Manufacturing Costs based on 85,000 units

= [(\$11 + \$24 + \$15) × 85,000] + \$240,000 + \$74,000 + (\$16 × \$85,000)

= (\$50× 85,000) + \$240,000 + \$74,000 + (\$16 × \$85,000)

= \$5,924,000

Since the total manufacturing costs is greater than the target cost, the company will exceed the maximum allowable cost. If they are unable to price the product at more than \$65, they should not manufacture the product.

Notes

Chapter 8
SEGMENT REPORTING AND TRANSFER PRICING

LEARNING OUTCOMES:

❶ Explain the different type of responsibility centers

❷ Explain the concept of segment reporting

❸ Differentiate between traceable and common fixed costs

❹ Explain the concept of transfer pricing

❺ Apply market based transfer pricing

❻ Apply cost-based transfer pricing

❼ Apply negotiated transfer pricing

Segment Reporting: An Introduction

Consider the composition of a professional football team. The team as a whole is comprised of many smaller, essential parts, two of which are the offensive team and the defensive team. The head coach cannot effectively manage the entire team on his own and call every single play. Therefore, he assigns the responsibility of managing the offensive team to the offensive coordinator and the responsibility of managing the defensive team to the defensive coordinator.

Similarly, when an organization continues to grow, it becomes more and more difficult for the manager at the top to make all the decisions. For instance, it is unreasonable to expect the CEO of a national hotel chain to decide whether a particular hotel guest at one of the hotels in a major city can check out thirty minutes late. These decisions should instead made by employees at the lower levels of the organization (such as department managers and supervisors).

When more and more decisions are being delegated to lower level managers and employees, the company is working towards becoming a fully decentralized organization. A **decentralized organization** is an organization in which the power to make decisions is not held by a few top managers or executives, but instead is spread throughout the company to people with various decision-making roles at lower levels. In other words, more autonomy is given to managers and employees positioned at lower levels of the organizational structure. **Autonomy** is the right or power to govern oneself without external control and constraint. Not only do lower level employees of decentralized organizations have more power in decision-making, but they are also held accountable for the decisions they make.

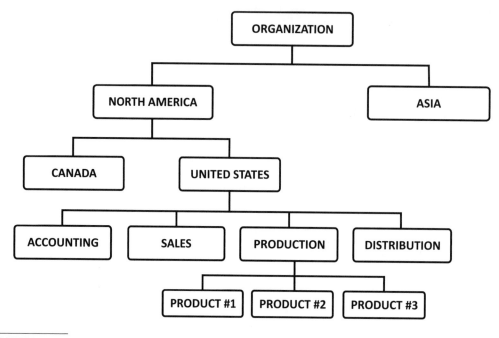

FIGURE 8.1

Depending on the size of the organization, there can be many levels of accountability for managers. For example, a large international corporation may first divide its business into geographic regions (e.g. North America and Asia) and then division by country (e.g. Canada and the United States). The next level may involve breaking down each country division into functional departments (e.g. accounting, sales, production and distribution). The production department can be further divided into various product lines.

Each of the areas that managers will be accountable for can be called a responsibility center. A **responsibility center** is one in which a manager is responsible or held accountable for the performance of a department. **Responsibility accounting** is a system that measures the plans and actual performances of each responsibility center. There are four types of responsibility centers: cost, revenue, profit and investment centers.

A **cost center** is a part of the company where the manager is responsible for controlling costs only. In figure 8.1, the accounting department can be viewed as a cost center, since it only incurs costs and does not directly generate revenue. Other examples include maintenance, marketing and human resource departments. It is important that the costs that the manager is responsible for are controllable by the manager. It would be unreasonable to hold the manager of the accounting department responsible for the rate paid on the electricity used or the amount of taxes that are paid by the organization.

Assume the sales segment in figure 8.1 has control over revenues (i.e. the United States sales volume). In other words, the sales department is an example of a **revenue center**. A revenue center is held accountable for the revenues only. Again, it is important that revenue center managers are only held responsible for revenue that is controllable. Sales volume is controllable, whereas government grants are not. Holding a revenue center manager responsible for the amount of a government grant received would be unreasonable.

Looking at figure 8.1, the United States segment can be viewed as a **profit center**. The country division manages both the costs (e.g. distribution and production departments) and revenues (e.g. sales department), and is therefore measured based on profits. A profit center is accountable for the revenues and the costs. Other examples of profit centers include restaurant branches that are part of a restaurant chain, such as corporate-owned Starbucks or Pizza Hut. Each of these branches controls revenues through prudent advertising and improving customer service. They also control costs such as payroll and maintenance. Profit centers can be used as evaluative tools for senior managers or area managers to assess one branch (profit center) against another of similar size. In these cases, a percentage of expenses relative to sales or profits would be used.

While cost centers are measured against the costs they incur and profit centers are measured on the difference between their revenues and costs, **investment centers** are evaluated on how well they use available capital. For example, investment centers may be evaluated by how

WORTH REPEATING...

Return on investment (ROI) measures how well an organization or center creates income relative to the amount of resources they have available.

much they improve their return on investment (ROI) ratio. The North American regional manager would be responsible for approving capital investments and held responsible for how well the investments perform.

IN THE REAL WORLD

Organizations often have a difficult time developing performance standards for profit centers, because the profit centers' performance can be affected by many uncontrollable and local circumstances. As a result, some organizations use the concept of relative performance evaluation, which compares the performance of a profit center to a comparable organization unit or a comparable competitor.

There is often a strong interdependence between revenues and expenses. For example, if a profit center incurs $3,000 in expenses to generate $10,000 of revenue, they have spent 30% ($3,000 ÷ $10,000) of their sales on costs. If revenue were to increase while expenses remained fixed, the profit center has done well. Conversely, if revenue were to increase to $11,000 but expenses increased to $5,000, the profit center has spent 45% ($5,000 ÷ $11,000) of their sales on costs. In this case, the profit center has not done well. Therefore, holding managers accountable for controllable revenues and expenses can be a great way to evaluate performance.

However, there are drawbacks in responsibility accounting. For example, if a company experiences a decrease in sales, the sales manager will be held accountable. However, in reality, the reduction in sales may have been due to the poor product quality. As a result, the production manager should be held accountable in this situation. Therefore, it is important to recognize that even specific measurements of a company's performance are a result of the efforts of a number of people and departments. At certain times, this may result in conflicts and situations where it is difficult to assign responsibility. Managers must be prepared for these situations.

Managers can monitor and control a decentralized organization using a variety of techniques. One of these techniques is segment reporting. In general terms, the word segment is synonymous with section or part. In accounting, a **segment** is a portion of a company that operates separately from other parts of the company and has separate performance reports created. Because the segment is separate, managers can collect data regarding cost, revenue or profit for that particular segment. **Segment reporting** is the process by which a company separates and reports financial information based on the business segments. Based on figure 8.1, the United States country division and all the responsibility centers below it could be considered one segment.

A CLOSER LOOK

Although having a decentralized organization has its benefits by giving more employees decision making responsibilities, it can create inefficiencies. The United States division and the Canadian division may have the same department structure (i.e. each has an accounting, sales, production and distribution department). The departments will report to the divisional manager; however, there may be minimal communication between the same departments in the different divisions (e.g. the production department in the United States may not communicate with the production department in Canada). In this case, best practices are not shared and the performance of the organization as a whole is not optimized.

Segment Reporting: Hearty Desserts Shop

Tanya is the owner-manager of the Hearty Desserts Shop, a dessert shop that currently sells only two types of products: ice cream and cakes. In addition to Tanya, the store has the following employees:

- A baker who makes the cakes (direct labor)
- A cashier who accepts payments for both the ice cream and cakes
- An ice cream server who spends most of her time serving ice cream and some of her time operating the ice cream maker machine
- A cake server who supports the baker and serves the cake
- A janitor responsible for cleaning the entire premise on a daily basis

The baker is paid an hourly wage and the rest of the employees are paid a salary. According to the facility rent agreement, no portion of the premise that Tanya rents out can be subleased to another party under any circumstance. Also, the company's administration and advertising costs are incurred with respect to the store as a whole.

Tanya asked her accountant to report on the company's profits. Tanya is not only interested in knowing how the store is performing as a whole, but is also interested in comparing the financial performance of each of the product lines. Figure 8.2 shows the financial data compiled by her accountant that illustrates the contribution generated from both the ice cream and cake product lines for the past year. The total column is the combined, or consolidated, amount of the entire business.

Hearty Desserts Shop Segmented Contribution Margin Statement For the Year Ended December 31, 2010			
		Segment (Product Line)	
	Total (Store)	Ice Cream	Cake
Sales	$239,000	$150,000	$89,000
Less: Variable Costs	92,100	60,000	32,100
Contribution Margin	146,900	90,000	56,900
Less: Traceable Fixed Costs	44,000	21,000	23,000
Segment Margin	102,900	$69,000	$33,900
Less: Common Fixed Costs	87,500		
Operating Income	$15,400		

FIGURE 8.2

The accountant decided that the segmented contribution margin statement would prove to be the most useful report for Tanya. The above form of the contribution margin statement is used to evaluate the performance of a business's segments. The contribution margin for a segment is calculated by beginning with revenue and deducting variable costs. There is a change in the process at this point to establish the overall segment margin. In the contribution margin statement, the accountant separated the fixed costs that are attributable (traceable) to each of the two business segments from costs that are not. Once the contribution margin is calculated, the **segment margin** is then calculated by deducting fixed costs that are traceable to the particular segment from the segment's contribution margin. Fixed costs common to all of the segments (or untraceable to particular segments) are not deducted to calculate the segment margin. The distinction between traceable and common costs will be discussed in detail later in the chapter.

WORTH REPEATING...

Contribution margin statement is a detailed report that separates variable costs and fixed costs.

Examples of Segments

As mentioned previously, a business segment represents a division of business that generates profits from its own unique type of activities. For Hearty Desserts, the ice cream and cake product lines are ideal business segments for reporting purposes. Other examples of business segments are:

- For a small airline, the segments may be based on flights: domestic and international flights
- The segments in an electronics store could be based on how the products are sold: retail, catalogue and online
- For a large grocery chain, the segments may be based on geographical locations: northern, central and southern.
- The segments in a service business such as an accounting firm could be based on the types of clients served: individuals, small businesses and large corporations

Sales and Contribution Margin

Sales represent revenues from each of the business segments. Variable costs are those costs for each segment that vary with the level of sales activity for that segment. In other words, within a segment, if there are no sales then there will be no variable costs incurred by the segment. For example, the materials used in production are variable because if there are no sales, no materials would be used (assuming that the volume of production is always equal to the volume of sales). Conversely, the higher the sales, the higher the usage of materials. Contribution margin represents the portion of sales that is left to pay for all fixed expenses. It is clear that in the case of Hearty Desserts, the ice cream segment is generating a much higher sales amount and contribution margin than the cake segment.

Calculating the contribution margin is important to calculate the break-even point. More specifically, when the contribution margin is equal to all the fixed expenses, the business will not make a profit nor incur a loss. When the contribution margin exceeds the fixed expenses, the business will be profitable.

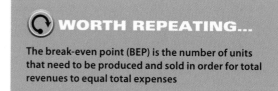

WORTH REPEATING...

The break-even point (BEP) is the number of units that need to be produced and sold in order for total revenues to equal total expenses

Before describing traceable and common fixed costs, it would be useful to examine a more detailed version of the segmented contribution margin as shown in Figure 8.3.

Hearty Desserts Shop Segmented Contribution Margin Statement (Detailed) For the Year Ended December 31, 2010		Segment (Product Line)	
	Total (Store)	Ice Cream	Cake
Sales	$239,000	$150,000	$89,000
Less: Variable Costs	92,100	60,000	32,100
Contribution Margin	146,900	90,000	56,900
Less: Traceable Fixed Costs			
Ice Cream Server's Salary	19,000	19,000	
Cake Server's Salary	22,000		22,000
Depreciation of Equipment	3,000	2,000	1,000
Total Traceable Fixed Costs	44,000	21,000	23,000
Segment Margin	102,900	$69,000	$33,900
Less: Common Fixed Costs			
Rent	10,000		
Tanya's Salary	40,000		
Cashier's Salary	18,000		
Janitor's Salary	15,000		
Administration and Advertising	4,500		
Total Common Fixed Costs	87,500		
Operating Income	$15,400		

FIGURE 8.3

Traceable and Common Fixed Costs

Fixed costs are those expenses that remain the same for any given level of activity (within a relevant range). **Traceable fixed costs** are those fixed expenses that can be directly linked to a business segment. In other words, a traceable fixed cost is a fixed cost related to a particular segment that would no longer be incurred by the company if the segment was eliminated. For example, in the case of Hearty Desserts, the ice cream server's salary is directly related to the ice cream segment. If Tanya decides to stop serving ice cream and discontinue the entire segment, then the business will not employ an ice cream server to whom a salary will be paid. Therefore, the ice cream server's salary is a traceable fixed cost. More specifically, this expense is traceable to the ice cream product line segment. For similar reasons, the cake server's salary is also a traceable fixed cost. It is traceable to the cake product line.

The equipment depreciation is listed as a traceable fixed cost. The preparation of each type of final product (ice cream or cake) uses different equipment. For instance, Tanya uses an industrial ice cream maker, which would obviously not be related to the cake product line. If the ice cream segment was dropped, it would be reasonable to assume that Tanya would sell the ice cream maker. Similarly, making cakes requires the use of the oven and other kitchen equipment.

On the other hand, a **common fixed cost** is a fixed cost that supports more than one segment, but is not traceable in whole or in part to a single segment. In other words, even if a segment was eliminated, the common fixed costs would remain the same. For instance, Tanya's entire fixed salary will be paid to her even if one of the segments (ice cream or cake) is discontinued. Therefore, Tanya's salary is a common fixed cost. The cashier and janitor's salary are also common fixed costs. It would be reasonable to assume that if one of the product lines were discontinued, the cashier and janitor would still be required to work in the dessert shop.

Rent expense is also a common fixed cost. It was mentioned earlier that no portion of the rented premise can be subleased. Therefore, if Tanya were to discontinue one of the product lines, she would still be subject to the entire $10,000 annual rent expense. Lastly, the fixed costs for administration and advertising are common since it was mentioned that these costs were incurred on a store-wide basis as opposed to a segment-by-segment basis.

Segment Reporting: Reflections Entertainment

Let us take a look at another example of segment reporting. This time, a larger company will be analyzed— one which is more likely to be decentralized and segmented in the real world. Reflections Entertainment is a private company that distributes new music and film to both brick-and-mortar and online retailers. Competition in the industry is fierce, so it is important for management to track sales based on product segments and sales channels in order to continuously update and improve the business strategy.

Shown in figure 8.4 are the monthly revenues and expenses for Reflections, based on the company's product lines.

Reflections Entertainment
Segmented Contribution Margin Statement
For the Month Ended December 31, 2010

	Total (Company)	Divisions	
		Music	Film
Sales	$80,000	$50,000	$30,000
Less: Variable Costs	40,000	25,000	15,000
Contribution Margin	40,000	25,000	15,000
Less: Traceable Fixed Costs	20,000	15,000	5,000
Segment Margin	20,000	$10,000	$10,000
Less: Common Fixed Costs	15,000		
Operating Income	$5,000		

FIGURE 8.4

Based on the segmented contribution margin statement, the music and film division generate the same amount of segment margin. Let us use the segment margin percentage to determine how much out of every dollar in segment sales each segment keeps in earnings. This ratio can be calculated using the following the equation:

$$\text{Segment Margin Percentage} = \frac{\text{Segment Margin}}{\text{Segment Sales}} \times 100\%$$

Therefore, the segment margin percentages for the music and film divisions are 20% and 33% respectively. Although the music division generates a higher revenue and contribution margin, it also generates higher expenses and a lower segment margin percentage than the film division. Notice that only the fixed expenses that are traceable are included in the calculation of the segment margins of the music and film divisions. This could include the salary of each of the divisional managers and sales staff, as well as rental fees for storage space required for stock of each product line (if the space is clearly segregated for the two product lines).

Levels of Segmented Statements

Reflections segments their business based on product lines initially. However, they are also interested in the sales channels used to distribute their products. The hierarchy for Reflections Entertainment is shown in figure 8.5.

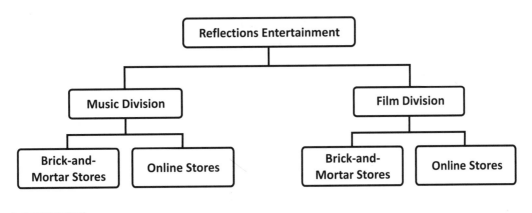

FIGURE 8.5

Management would like to take a closer look at the music division. To provide more information for decision making purposes, the manager of the music division asked the accountant to prepare a segmented contribution margin statement for another level of segments. (figure 8.6). Since distribution efforts include both brick-and-mortar stores and online distribution, the management of the music division is interested in learning where its sales team should direct its focus in order to grow the business.

Reflections Entertainment - Music Division Segmented Contribution Margin Statement For the Month Ended December 31, 2010			
		Segments	
	Total (Music Division)	Brick-and-Mortar Store	Online Stores
Sales	$50,000	$30,000	$20,000
Less: Variable Costs	25,000	20,000	5,000
Contribution Margin	25,000	10,000	15,000
Less: Traceable Fixed Costs	7,500	5,000	2,500
Segment Margin	17,500	$5,000	$12,500
Less: Common Fixed Costs	7,500		
Operating Income	$10,000		

FIGURE 8.6

The music division segment has its own segments: brick-and-mortar stores and online stores. This further separation of the music division demonstrates that though the sales to the physical retail store (brick-and-mortar) currently generates higher revenue, the online distribution channel is more profitable due to lower expenses. This is proven when the music division manager calculates the segment margin percentage for both segments. He finds that the brick-and-mortar stores provide a 16.7% segment margin ($5,000 ÷ $30,000) and the online stores provide a 62.5% segment margin ($12,500 ÷ $20,000). The management of Reflections can make key decisions with such a detailed knowledge of the business.

For example, assume that the traceable fixed costs for brick-and-mortar are related to the salary of a sales professional dedicated specifically to selling from brick-and-mortar stores. Conversely, Reflections only has a part-time sales professional dedicated to making online sales. Given the profitability of online stores is higher, management at Reflections should dedicate more sales staff to this division.

When multiple levels of segments exist, fixed costs that are traceable to a particular segment can become a common fixed cost when that segment is examined in detail. Note that from figure 8.4, traceable fixed costs for the music division was $15,000. Once the music division is segmented, the $15,000 traceable fixed costs is now split between traceable fixed costs for the brick-and-mortar and the online segments, and common fixed costs for the music division as a whole.

For instance, the salary of the music division's manager is considered a traceable fixed cost to the music division in figure 8.4. That is, if the music division were to be discontinued entirely, the music division's manager would be out of a job and the company would no longer pay that particular payroll expense. However, it is a common cost in figure 8.6 because within the music division, if either one of the brick-and-mortar or the online store segments were discontinued, it would be reasonable to assume that the music division would still exist. Therefore, the music division manager would still have his current job and be paid.

Segment Reporting and Financial Accounting

The segmented contribution margin statement is useful for management analysis and decision making. For external financial reporting purposes, a company may be required to provide segmented profit reports similar to those used for internal decision making by management. As studied in financial accounting, a publicly traded company must compile an income statement to report profits to external users in its annual report. The income statement must combine (i.e. consolidate) all the profits from the various divisions or segments of the business. GAAP states that a business segment must be separately reported on the income statement if it represents a 10% or greater portion of the company's:

i)   total revenue
ii) total operating profit, or
iii) total assets

Other requirements include: all reported segments must represent a majority (75% or more) of the company's total revenue, a maximum of 10 segments are to be displayed, and the exception that if 90% of a company's revenue is derived from one industry, segments need not be disclosed.

The purpose of segment reporting in the financial statements for external users (e.g. investors) is to provide important details about the potential profit and risk associated with each line of business. The external users can then make a more informed decision regarding their involvement with the business. For instance, suppose a company with two segments has reported a zero operating income amount for the past few years. A further investigation reveals that one segment consistently showed a very high positive operating income, whereas the other segment always showed an offsetting negative operating income. Management is planning for the discontinuance of the poor performing segment in the near future. Once this segment is discontinued, the company may prosper because of the strong financial performance of the other segment. If the income statement was not presented with segments, a potential investor may immediately turn down an opportunity of investing in the business while the investment might be worthwhile in reality. Ultimately, the purpose of segment reporting in financial statements is to help external users make more informed decisions and judgments with respect to the entity as a whole.

For publicly traded companies, the segmented reports prepared for internal purposes is closely aligned with those required for external reporting according to US GAAP standard SFAS 131 and the corresponding IFRS standard (IFRS 8). In fact, the externally reported segment information will be based on the segment reports used internally by management. In this chapter, given that Reflections Entertainment is a private company, segment reporting is not a requirement based on GAAP. This tool can still be implemented and used for internal decision-making, as it provides the management team with useful information.

Transfer Pricing: An Introduction

Suppose Hearty Desserts Shop has expanded its business. Each product line (ice cream and cake) has its own factory to manufacture the products and is responsible for selling the products to various supermarkets. Each product line is now operating as a segment (or division) of the business. The divisions will be evaluated individually based on their ability to maximize revenues and control costs. Currently, the cake division plans to introduce ice cream cakes. The manager of the cake division has two choices in purchasing ice cream, it can either purchase from the ice cream division of Hearty Desserts or from an independent supplier in the market.

It is important to point out that the ice cream division would like to charge as high a price as possible to maximize revenue, and the cake division would like to pay as low a price as possible to minimize expenses. If the cake division manager decides to purchase from the ice cream division, this will impact the operating income of each segment, but ultimately Hearty Desserts as a whole will experience no change in profitability before tax. It is like taking money from your left pocket and putting it in your right pocket.

So, if the cake division will buy from the ice cream division, what price should the ice cream division charge? The price that will be charged is known as the **transfer price**. A transfer price is the price one division charges for a good or service sold to another division within the same company. **Transfer pricing** focuses on how to allocate an internal price to the good or service that can be agreed upon by managers at the divisions involved.

Upper management will usually decide a pricing method to be used for the business. Once the method has been chosen, managers of each division will have to use that method to calculate the transfer price. Although divisional managers may not be able to set the pricing method, they may be able to decide whether to go through with the transfer or not. The following section will discuss the three types of transfer pricing methods: market-based, cost-based and negotiated transfer prices.

Market-Based Transfer Prices

In making transfer pricing decisions, upper management may resort to setting the transfer price equal to the market price. The **market price** is the price charged for a product or service on the outside market. Using a market price will only work if there is an **intermediate market** for the product. That is, the product is currently being sold in a competitive market to outside customers. Applying a market price works easily if:

- the product and price is identical to other products on the market
- the segments are not closely linked together
- there is no difference in costs or benefits between selling to the market and transferring internally

FIGURE 8.7

If the above situations are present, the market price is easy to determine. However, in the real world, it is rare that the product and price are perfectly identical to others on the market. In this situation, the market price is more challenging to determine. Negotiation may have to take place between the two divisions to arrive at an agreeable market price, or upper management may have to choose an alternative transfer pricing strategy.

Cost-Based Transfer Prices

Companies can also use a cost-based approach to setting transfer prices. The transfer price is set using the variable costs of the selling division, and may also include fixed costs allocated to the units produced. This method is useful if a market price is too costly to determine, or if the

 WORTH REPEATING...

Full costing is absorption costing. It will assign direct material, direct labor, all variable overhead and all fixed overhead costs to inventory. In this case, the total cost includes both product costs and period costs.

product being sold is unique and not available elsewhere. The only challenge may be determining the true cost of the product being transferred.

To illustrate cost-based transfer prices, assume the headphones manufacturing division is a business segment at Mega Music Manufacturing (MMM). The company has a divisional structure which also includes the media player manufacturing division, a business segment that produces MP3 players for private labels. The headphones manufacturing division (headphones division) makes a single product, which it sells to outside customers and supplies the media player manufacturing division with.

If upper management has directed that the cost-based method for transfer pricing be used, the headphones division will sell to the media player division at the full cost of the headphones. If the full price of the headphones is $5.17, then this will be the price paid by the media player division to the headphones division.

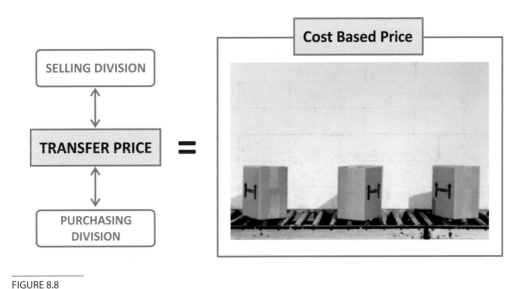

FIGURE 8.8

An issue arises regarding the profits of the selling (headphones) division. By transferring at cost, the headphones division will not record any profit on the transfer to the media player division. In a situation like this, upper management may implement a **cost plus** pricing scheme. A cost plus price will add a percentage to the transfer price to allow the selling division to record some profit on the transfer. For example, cost plus 15% on the full cost of $5.17 would mean the transfer price would be $5.95 ($5.17 × 1.15). This will allow the headphones division to record a $0.78 profit on each headphone transferred to the media player division.

Calculating Negotiated Transfer Prices

A **negotiated transfer price** is a transfer price mutually agreed on between the buying and selling divisions. The managers involved in the negotiation will meet to discuss the terms and conditions of the transfer. The managers may end up not going through with the transfer if an agreeable price cannot be reached. However, if a transfer price can be agreed upon, it is generally true that the following two statements should hold:

1. The selling division will agree to a transfer price that increases its own profits.
2. The purchasing division will also agree to a transfer price that increases its own profits.

The above two statements imply that if the transfer price is less than the selling division's cost, the selling division will not agree to the transfer since it would be incurring a loss on the transaction. On the other hand, if the transfer price is set too high, the purchasing division will not make a profit on the transaction. Therefore, a range of acceptable transfer prices can be determined. The **range of acceptable transfer prices** is the range of prices for which the transfer will be profitable for both the selling and purchasing divisions.

Returning to the Mega Music Manufacturing example, what is the acceptable range of transfer prices for the headphones division's sale of headphones to the media player division? Some more information is required to calculate the range.

Headphones Division (Seller):		
Headphones production capacity per year	300,000	headphone sets
Variable manufacturing cost per headphone set	$4.50	per headphone set
Commission on each headphone set sold	$0.50	per headphone set
Shipping on each headphone set sold	$1.00	per headphone set
Fixed costs per year	$200,000	
Selling price of MMM headphone set on outside market*	$11	per headphone set
Media Player Division (Purchaser):		
Price per headphone set if outsourced	$10	per headphone set
Required number of headphone sets per year	50,000	headphone sets

* Includes selling costs (commission and shipping)

FIGURE 8.9

Note that the selling price of the headphones on the outside market is set at $11 per set. This price includes the costs of commission and shipping per set. If the headphones division sells to the media player division, the commission and shipping will not have to be charged and the selling price will drop to $9.50 each.

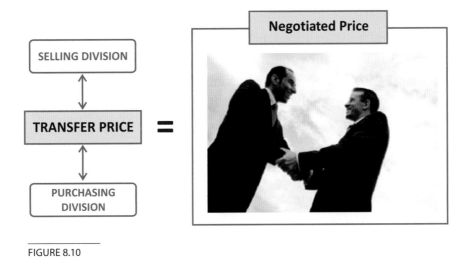

FIGURE 8.10

First, the selling division's (headphones division's) lowest acceptable transfer price must be determined. If the transfer impacts sales to the outside market, then the transfer price must cover both the variable manufacturing costs as well as any lost profits from lost sales. The lost profits are called **opportunity costs**. An opportunity cost is the value of the next best alternative that is foregone in order to accept a particular alternative. The lost sales arise from having to forgo sales to the outside market in order to fill the purchasing division's order.

The purchasing division (media player division) would only accept the transfer if the division's profit increases. Since the purchaser will likely have an outside supplier, the purchaser will buy the product from the internal supplier only if the transfer price is less than the price offered by the outside supplier.

Case #1: Selling Division with Idle Capacity

Assume that the selling division (headphones division) has enough idle capacity to fulfill the entire order of headphones from the purchasing division (media player division) without interfering with sales of headphones to its regular outside customers. Assume that the headphones division is selling only 230,000 sets of headphones per year to outside customers. As shown in figure 8.9, the headphones production capacity is 300,000 units. Therefore, the unused capacity is 70,000 sets of headphones, which is enough to meet the media player division's requirement of 50,000 headphone sets per year. If 50,000 headphone sets are made and transferred, what range of transfer prices would be acceptable for both divisions?

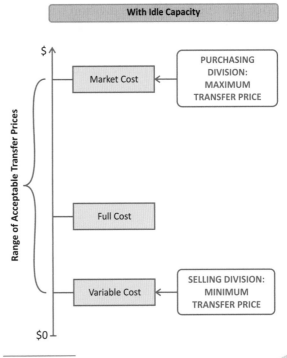

FIGURE 8.11

The headphones division will need to cover the variable manufacturing costs, which amounts to $4.50. From their perspective, any price set above that amount is acceptable. The media play division will look for any price that is less than the current price they pay, which is $10. Therefore the acceptable range is anywhere from $4.50 and $10. The final selling price will depend upon the negotiation skills of each divisional manager. Since both divisions will benefit from this business transaction, they should be able to agree on a transfer price.

Case #2: Selling Division with No Idle Capacity

Assume that the headphones division has *zero* idle capacity. From figure 8.9, it is shown that the headphones division has a capacity of 300,000 sets. Zero idle capacity means it is manufacturing and selling 300,000 sets of headphones per year to customers in the outside market at $11 per set. This selling price can be dropped to $9.50 per set for the internal customer (media player division) because the commission and shipping costs will not be incurred.

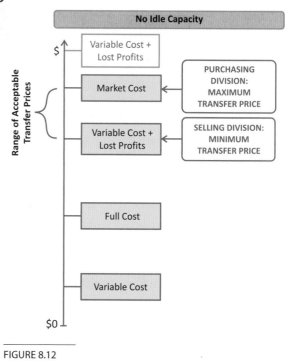

FIGURE 8.12

To fulfill the order from the media player division, the headphones division will need to forego sales of 50,000 units to outside customers. The headphones division will need to cover the lost sales from not selling to the outside customers. The internal transfer price of $9.50 is the minimum acceptable price that the headphones division will accept. The media player division will only accept a transfer price of less than $10. Therefore the acceptable range is anywhere from $9.50 and $10.

In some cases, an acceptable range may not exist if the minimum transfer price the seller will accept is greater than the maximum transfer price the buyer will accept. In the case of the headphones, if the shipping cost must be charged because the two divisions are in two different locations, the minimum acceptable selling price set by the headphones division will be $10.50. In this situation, the media player division will choose to purchase from the outsourced supplier. This scenario is illustrated in the transparent portion of figure 8.12.

IN THE REAL WORLD

In a multinational organization, income taxes from different countries can impact the after tax profit of the division and the organization as a whole. The divisions of a multinational corporation must pay taxes to the government of the country in which they operate. If a division is operating in a country with a high corporate income tax rate and must purchase from a division operating in a country with a low corporate income tax rate, the transfer price should be set relatively high. The reasoning behind this has to do with taxable income. If the purchasing division with a high tax rate pays a high transfer price, the transfer price will be recorded as an expense and reduce taxable income, therefore reducing the income taxes paid. The selling division with the low tax rate will record the transfer price as revenue and increase taxable income; however the lower tax rate means that the amount of tax paid will be less than the tax savings of the purchasing division. Overall, the organization experiences a net tax saving.

Ethical Considerations

A department manager often faces a lot of pressure to meet performance goals. While reaching these goals, managers must remember that their actions can have an impact on other departments within the organization. Managers must also remember that the overall goal of the organization is to remain profitable and provide returns to the stockholders.

If the manager of the sales department consistently offers discounts in order to meet monthly gross sales targets, she must be aware that her actions to meet her goals may have an impact on another department. If there are not enough finished products available to sell, the production department will have to increase their output to meet the increase in sales. If the only way to meet this increase is production is to hire more staff or work overtime, the total costs incurred by the production department will increase.

Although revenue will increase, the cost of production has increased as well. Depending on the new sales figures and new costs, the organization may actually end up losing profit because of the sales manager's selfish actions.

In Summary

⇨ A **decentralized organization** is an organization in which decisions are not made exclusively by top managers, but are made by people with various decision-making roles at the lower levels.

⇨ **Autonomy** is the right or power to govern oneself without external control and constraint.

⇨ A **responsibility center** is one in which a manager is responsible or held accountable for the performance of a department.

⇨ **Responsibility accounting** is a system that measures the plans and actual performances of each responsibility center.

⇨ There are four types of responsibility centers: cost, revenue, profit and investment centers.

  ✧ A **cost center** is required to manage only costs.

  ✧ A **revenue center** is held accountable for the revenues only.

  ✧ A **profit center** is accountable for the revenues and the costs.

  ✧ An **investment center** is evaluated based on how well they use the available capital.

⇨ In accounting, a **segment** is a part of a company for which managers seek to collect information related to cost, revenue or profit.

⇨ **Segment reporting** is the process by which a company separates and reports financial information based on the business's segments.

⇨ **Traceable fixed costs** are those fixed expenses that can be directly linked to a segment of business.

⇨ A **common fixed cost** is a fixed cost that supports more than one segment, but is not traceable in whole or in part to any one segment.

⇨ When multiple levels of segments exist, fixed costs that are traceable to a segment can be a common cost of another segment.

⇨ The segment margin percentage determines how much out of every dollar of segment sales each segment keeps in earnings.

⇨ The segment reports for external reporting often look similar to the traditional income statement.

⇨ A **transfer price** is the price one department or division charges for a good sold or service rendered to another department or division within the same organization.

⇨ **Transfer pricing** focuses on how to allocate an internal price to the good or service that can be agreed upon by managers at the divisions involved.

⇨ **Market-based approach** sets transfer prices based on market price.

⇨ The **market price** is the price charged for a product or service on the outside market.

⇨ An **intermediate market** is an outside market in which the transferred product or service is sold in its present form.

➪ The market-based approach works well when the selling division has no idle capacity.

➪ A **cost-based approach** in setting transfer prices provides companies the option to either set the transfer price at the variable cost or full (absorption) cost.

➪ A **negotiated transfer price** is a transfer price agreed on between the buying and selling departments or divisions.

➪ The **range of acceptable transfer prices** is the range of prices for which the transfer will be profitable for both the selling and purchasing divisions.

➪ A range of acceptable transfer prices does not exist if the minimum transfer price the seller will accept is greater than the maximum transfer price the buyer will accept.

➪ The **opportunity cost** of an alternative is the value of the next best alternative that was foregone.

Review Exercise

Anville Systems Inc. manufactures and sells only two products to outside customers: pipes and engines. The company is segmented based on product lines. The pipes and engines are each produced in separate factories. All period costs incurred by the company are considered fixed costs. The company owns the head office which it purchased several years ago. The revenue and cost information for the year ended December 31, 2010 are presented below.

	Segment (Product)	
	Pipes	**Engines**
Selling price per unit	$32	$500
Variable manufacturing cost per unit	$20	$250
Traceable fixed costs	$800,000	$1,300,000

Anville Systems manufactured and sold 200,000 pipes and 12,000 engines for the year. The company incurs $600,000 in common fixed costs per year.

The engines produced by Anville Systems uses the same model of pipes that it produces internally. However, throughout 2010, the engines segment purchased these pipes from an external supplier at a cost of $26 per unit.

Required:

1. Indicate whether each of the following fixed costs are common or traceable:
   - Rent (for factories)
   - Depreciation of head office building
   - Salary of company's CEO

2. Prepare a segmented contribution margin statement for the past year.

3. It is now January 2011. The engines segment is considering purchasing the pipes by means of an internal transfer from the pipes segment. Determine a range of acceptable transfer prices for the pipes (if such a range exists), assuming that the pipes segment has sufficient idle capacity to fulfill the internal order. Explain your reasoning.

4. Assume that the pipes segment is operating at capacity instead. Suppose that the pipes segment's selling price includes a shipping cost of $3. However, internal transfers will not require the $3 shipping cost. What is the transfer price that will be agreed upon by the two segments, if any? Explain your reasoning.

Review Exercise – Answer

Part 1

Traceable/Common	Cost
Traceable	Factory rent
Common	Depreciation of head office building
Common	Salary of company's CEO

Part 2

	Total	Pipes		Engines	
Anville Systems Inc.					
Segmented Contribution Margin Statement					
For the Year Ended December 31, 2010					
		Segment (Product Line)			
	Total	Pipes		Engines	
Sales	$12,400,000	$6,400,000	(1)	$6,000,000	(3)
Less: Variable Costs	7,000,000	4,000,000	(2)	3,000,000	(4)
Contribution Margin	5,400,000	2,400,000		3,000,000	
Less: Traceable Fixed Costs	2,100,000	800,000		1,300,000	
Segment Margin	3,300,000	$1,600,000		$1,700,000	
Less: Common Fixed Costs	600,000				
Operating Income	$2,700,000				

(1) $32/pipe × 200,000 pipes

(2) $20/pipe × 200,000 pipes

(3) $500/engine × 12,000 engines

(4) $250/engine × 250 engines

Part 3

Since the seller (pipes segment) has enough idle capacity to fulfill the internal transfer to the buyer (engines segment), it does not have to sacrifice any sales to outside customers. The pipes segment will just need to cover its variable manufacturing costs. Therefore, the minimum acceptable price from the pipes segment's perspective is $20. The engines segment would look for any price that is less than the current price they pay to the external supplier. Therefore, the maximum acceptable price from the engines segment's perspective is $26. Combining these results, we obtain the range of acceptable transfer prices: $20 to $26.

Part 4

The seller has zero idle capacity. This implies that for every pipe unit sold to the engines segment, a unit of sale to an outside customer will be lost. Therefore, the minimum acceptable price is the price that would cover the lost sales from not selling to outside customers (adjusted for any selling costs on outside sales that would not be incurred by the pipes segment on the internal transfer). Therefore, the minimum acceptable price is $29 ($32 outside selling price - $3 shipping cost no longer incurred). The engines segment would look for any price that is less than the amount that they pay to the external supplier. Therefore, the maximum acceptable price from the engine segment's perspective is $26. Since the maximum acceptable price of $26 is less than the minimum acceptable price of $29, a range of acceptable transfer prices does not exist. Therefore, no internal transfer will occur.

Notes

Chapter 9
MASTER BUDGET

LEARNING OUTCOMES:

❶ Identify the benefits of budgeting

❷ Explain the different components of the master budget

❸ Prepare a budgeted income statement

❹ Prepare a capital expenditure budget

❺ Prepare a cash budget

❻ Prepare a budgeted balance sheet

❼ Describe the use of budgets for planning and controlling

❽ Explain the difference between zero-based and incremental budgeting

❾ Explain the difference between top-down and bottom-up budgeting

❿ Describe the concept and impact of budgetary slack

⓫ Describe the concept of budgeting variance

Budgets: An Introduction

Imagine embarking on a long journey in a foreign country without a map or a plan. It would be difficult, if not impossible, to reach your destination. However, if you had a map, you would be able to create a plan of directions to ensure you are heading the right way. In principle, the economic life of a company is no different from a journey. In order to reach your destination and goals you will need a plan.

Before devising a plan, businesses typically spend a considerable amount of time determining what they are good at and what opportunities exist in the market that will allow them to exploit their strengths. This assessment leads to the development of their strategy. A business' **strategy** focuses on its resources and allows managers to create business plans which outline the business' financial and non-financial goals. To ensure that a business reaches its financial and strategic goals, managers must design and develop a robust business plan. For example, a business plan may include goals to increase total sales or reduce total costs. **Budgets** are numerical tools that help managers decide what course of action to pursue in order to achieve the company's financial goals. This chapter will mainly focus on preparing budgets for manufacturing companies. However, these principles can also be used for merchandising and service businesses.

Benefits of Budgeting

Budgets give managers a more detailed picture of which goals need to be accomplished. Having a more detailed picture helps managers tailor their operations so that their financial goals can be achieved. Another benefit of budgeting is that once the financial period is over, comparisons can be made between the original budget and actual results. This analysis can then be used to improve operations for the following period and to evaluate employee performance.

A Simple Example of a Personal Budget

Budgets are essentially a forecast of expected revenues, expenses and cash flows. For example, in April, when Helga is preparing her personal budget for May, she knows that:

1. She will earn $3,000 cash in salary next month.
2. Her student loan payment (principal only) will amount to $1,000 cash. Assume that her monthly interest payment is $50.
3. Her rent will be $600 cash per month.

She also assumes the following:

4. Her living expenses will be approximately $1,100 cash per month.
5. Her car will need new tires next month. They will cost about $500.

Figure 9.1 shows her budgeted income statement for the next month (May, 2012). A budgeted income statement outlines the budgeted changes in net worth (i.e. revenues less expenses).

Helga Linderson	
Personal Budgeted Income Statement	
For the month ending May 31, 2012	
Budgeted Salary	$3,000
Budgeted Expenses:	
Rent	600
Other Living Expenses	1,100
Tires	500
Interest	50
Total Budgeted Expenses	2,250
Budgeted Personal Net Income	**$750**

FIGURE 9.1

The budgeted income statement shows that Helga's net worth will increase by $750 next month. Notice that the loan payment of $1,000 is not listed in the above budget. This is because reducing the principal amount of your student loan has no effect on net worth; therefore, it should not appear on the budgeted income statement. However, the $50 interest on the loan is an expense and is listed on the budgeted income statement.

Helga could have also prepared what is known as a **cash budget**. A cash budget outlines budgeted changes in cash, as opposed to net worth. Figure 9.2 outlines a basic cash budget for the situation above.

Helga Linderson
Personal Cash Budget
For the month ending May 31, 2012

Budgeted Inflows:	$3,000
Salary	
Budgeted Outflows:	
Rent	600
Other Living Expenses	1,100
Tires	500
Interest	50
Loan Payment	1,000
Total Budgeted Outflows:	3,250
Budgeted Inflow (Outflow)	**($250)**

 WORTH REPEATING...

Accrual accounting is used when preparing the financial statements. Accrual accounting matches expenses with revenues (an increase and decrease to net worth) in the period in which they occur and not necessarily when the cash is paid or received.

FIGURE 9.2

The cash budget includes the loan payment because it affects the flow of cash in and out of her bank account. Notice that even though her net worth is budgeted to increase next month (by $750), she will unfortunately have a negative cash flow of $250. This example shows that changes in cash do not always reflect changes in net worth.

Since a budget is prepared for a future period, some costs are unknown and have to be estimated. In the previous example, Helga's earnings, loan payment, interest and rent are costs that are known, while the cost of her living expenses and new tires are just approximations or assumptions.

The accuracy of a budget is largely dependent on the assumptions one makes. For example, suppose that Helga ends up spending more than $500 on new tires in May. Since her assumptions are different from the actual result, her cash flow is affected. The same is true for businesses. If businesses make poor assumptions when preparing their budgets, their expected profitability and cash flow can be far off from reality.

The following is an example of Abacus Inc.'s operating budget for one period of operations:

Abacus Inc.
Budgeted Income Statement
For the period ending March 31, 2011

Budgeted Revenues	$250,000
Budgeted Cost of Goods Sold	150,000
Budgeted Gross Profit	100,000
Budgeted Expenses:	
Administrative Costs	20,000
Selling Costs	15,000
Salaries	35,000
Rent	10,000
Total Budgeted Expenses	80,000
Budgeted Net Income	**$20,000**

FIGURE 9.3

Figure 9.3 outlines budgeted revenues and expenses for Abacus Inc. for the period ending March 31, 2011. Once the actual figures for revenues and costs are known, they can be compared against this budget. The difference between actual and budgeted amounts is called *variance*. The topic of variance analysis will be studied in the forthcoming materials.

Types of Budgets

There are many types of budgets that managers can prepare for different purposes. Different budgets provide different information. An overview and description of some budgets available to managers is provided below.

An **operating budget** outlines budgeted changes to the income statement during the period. All transactions that would impact profits on the income statement are regarded as part of the operating budget. An operating budget is made up of a series of budgets that are related to the income statement. For example, the operating budget includes the revenue budget, cost of goods sold budget and operating expenses budget.

Capital budgets involve changes in the company's financial resources and only impact the budgeted balance sheet. Capital budgets are those budgets that relate to the building or purchasing of long-term assets. These assets are recorded on the balance sheet and do not impact equity at the time of purchase. As these assets depreciate, equity decreases and the depreciation is recorded as an expense, at which time they will be recorded as part of the operating budget.

Cash budgets monitor cash flowing into and out of the bank account with no regard to profits. Transactions such as borrowing money, collecting accounts receivables, reducing debt and buying assets do not impact profits but they do impact cash flow. Cash budgets help a company analyze whether they have enough cash to operate the company (e.g. meet payroll and pay suppliers). Figure 9.4 shows how certain transactions affect the cash account.

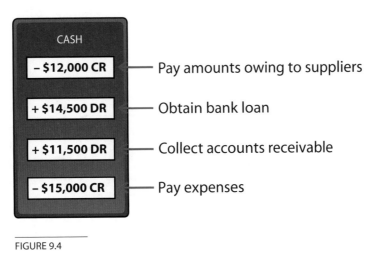

FIGURE 9.4

All the above budgets can be presented individually in one large combined budget called the **master budget**. The master budget encompasses all aspects of business operations. It includes various budgets, such as the operating budget, capital budget and cash budget.

We will now proceed using a manufacturing firm as an example. The budgets that will be prepared are:

1. The *sales budget* outlines the budgeted quantity and selling price of products or services sold.
2. The *production budget* outlines how much product needs to be produced.
3. The *purchases budget* outlines how much material needs to be purchased.
4. The *operating expenses budget* outlines the budgeted expenses not related to manufacturing activities.
5. The *capital budget* outlines the buying and selling of long-term assets.
6. The *cash flow budget* outlines cash flowing into and out of the business, regardless of profits.
7. The *master budget* represents the big picture reflected through all the organization's individual budgets.

Preparing an Operating Budget

There is no specific way to create budgets. It is more about "what works for you". Different financial controllers and managers require different information and therefore will require employees to use different tools and formats in creating their own budgets. However, the next section will provide you with a logical guideline and sequence to demonstrate the manner in which a budget can be prepared.

Since many resources are dependent on sales, it is a logical starting point. Once the revenue budget is created it is then possible to determine how many products have to be purchased or manufactured to meet the expected demand. This allows management to prepare the production and the purchases budget. Once the purchase budget is prepared, the operating expenses (non-manufacturing costs) budget is prepared. These budgets are then assembled to form the budgeted income statement. The sum of all these activities relate to the company's operating budget. Our example will involve preparing budgets for Pine Furniture Manufacturer Inc.

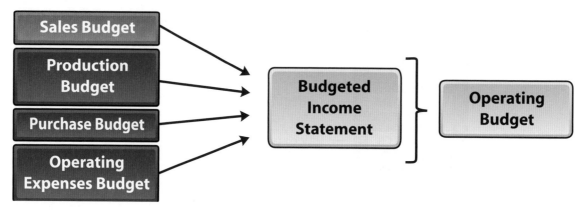

Step 1: Prepare a Sales Budget.

Since all other budgets are dependent on sales, the first step in creating an operating budget involves preparing a sales budget. The sales budget shows the estimated sales volume and selling price for a specific period. Management will first estimate the sales volume for each period. Pine Furniture Manufacturer has provided its sales volume forecast for the year 2012 in figure 9.5.

Pine Furniture Manufacturer Sales Volume Forecast For the year ending December 31, 2012					
	Q1	Q2	Q3	Q4	Total
Sales Volume	4,900	3,900	5,700	8,500	23,000

FIGURE 9.5

Figure 9.5 demonstrates how many chairs are likely to be sold in each quarter. Pine Furniture Manufacturer predicts that most chairs will be sold in the fourth quarter and that the second quarter will have the slowest sales. This information was developed from past performance and existing or potential customers. Analyzing expected sales is important for production planning, because the more chairs expected to sell, the more chairs will need to be manufactured.

Keep in mind that it is much easier to forecast sales when patterns can be seen from historical performance. For example, if the business has experienced a steady increase in sales for the past three years, and if the economic conditions are likely to remain unchanged, it is reasonable to assume that the sales will continue to increase in the upcoming year. However, if a competitor comes out with a new product or service, it will likely impact future sales and make the forecast less accurate. In addition, significant research and thought is necessary to gauge forecasted sales when new or modified products are created, whether it be in the current or new geographic markets.

Using the budgeted selling price of $50 per chair and the budgeted sales volume, Pine Furniture Manufacturer can now determine the budgeted revenue for 2012. The first quarter (Q1) sales volume of $245,000 was calculated by multiplying the sale price per chair ($50) by the number of budgeted units to be sold (4,900) in Q1. Figure 9.6 shows the sales volume in dollars broken down for each quarter. Total budgeted sales for the upcoming year are $1,150,000.

Pine Furniture Manufacturer Sales Forecast For the year ending December 31, 2012					
	Q1	Q2	Q3	Q4	Total
Chairs	$245,000	$195,000	$285,000	$425,000	$1,150,000

FIGURE 9.6

The above sales budget in figure 9.6 was made based on a number of assumptions regarding demand. However, actual sales volumes can differ from the budgeted amounts for a number of reasons such as:

- Customers may switch to competitors because of cheaper prices, better service or other incentives
- The quality of the products or services may not meet customers' expectations, causing them to cancel their order or demand a refund
- An economic downturn may reduce demand

Now that Pine Furniture Manufacturer has determined their sales budget, it is possible to determine their production and purchases budget. The production budget outlines how many chairs to produce to meet the budgeted sales demand and the purchase budget outlines how much material must be purchased to meet the budgeted production schedule.

Step 2: Prepare a Production Budget

The next logical step in the budget process should be forecasting how much product needs to be produced to fill the expected orders.

Assume that Pine Furniture Manufacturer has 3,000 chairs in finished goods inventory at the beginning of the year. At times, the company experiences unusual increases in customer orders. As a result company managers decided to maintain a certain amount of inventory at the end of each quarter. For quarters 1 to 4, its targeted ending finished goods inventories are 3,100, 4,200, 4,500 and 1,000 units respectively. Next, to determine the amount of production units for each period, the following formula will be used:

$$\text{Budgeted Production Units} = \text{Budgeted Sales} + \text{Budgeted Ending Inventory} - \text{Beginning Inventory}$$

Using the sales forecast and the information provided above, Pine Furniture Manufacture can now prepare the production budget for the year 2012. Based on the calculations in figure 9.7, it is now able to approximate how many chairs to produce in order to meet the sales and ending inventory targets. For example, it will need to produce 5,000 units in the first quarter in order to satisfy the sales volume of 4,900 units and the ending inventory of 3,100 units. Note that the ending inventory for one quarter becomes the beginning inventory for the following quarter. We will also assume there are no partially completed units for each quarter. Therefore, Pine Furniture Manufacturer should budget to build 21,000 chairs (5,000 + 5,000 + 6,000 + 5,000).

Pine Furniture Manufacturer Production Budget For year ending December 31, 2012	Q1	Q2	Q3	Q4
Budgeted Sales Volume (Figure 9.5)	4,900	3,900	5,700	8,500
Budgeted Ending Inventory (Given)	3,100	4,200	4,500	1,000
Budgeted Beginning Inventory	(3,000)	(3,100)	(4,200)	(4,500)
Budgeted Production Units	5,000	5,000	6,000	5,000

FIGURE 9.7

To ensure the budgeted production units is calculated correctly, Pine Furniture Manufacturer can double check that the closing inventory for each quarter equals the target ending inventory amount. First, let us determine the amount of units available for sale for each quarter. This can be done by taking the sum of the budgeted beginning inventory and budgeted production units. Then, the closing inventory balance is simply the difference between the units available for sale and the budgeted sales volume. Since figure 9.8 shows that the ending inventory is the same as the target amount, the budgeted production units is calculated correctly.

	Q1	Q2	Q3	Q4
Budgeted Beginning Inventory in Units	3,000	3,100	4,200	4,500
Budgeted Production Units	5,000	5,000	6,000	5,000
Budgeted Units Available for Sale	8,000	8,100	10,200	9,500
Budgeted Sales Volume	(4,900)	(3,900)	5,700	8,500
Budgeted Ending Inventory in Units	3,100	4,200	4,500	1,000

FIGURE 9.8

Step 3: Prepare the Purchasing Budget

The budgeted number of units to manufacture from the production budget is crucial in preparing the purchasing budget. Based on Pine Furniture Manufacturer's historical data, five square feet of direct materials are needed to produce one chair. As a result, the company can now determine how much direct materials need to be purchased for each quarter. Pine Furniture Manufacturer managers can calculate this amount by multiplying the direct materials needed per chair by the number of budgeted production units.

Using the information provided by the production budget (figure 9.9), let us calculate the amount of budgeted direct materials required:

	Q1	Q2	Q3	Q4	Total
Budgeted Production Units	5,000	5,000	6,000	5,000	21,000
Direct Materials (sq. ft.) per Chair	5	5	5	5	5
Budgeted Direct Materials to be Used (sq. ft.)	25,000	25,000	30,000	25,000	105,000

FIGURE 9.9

Pine Furniture Manufacturer has budgeted for 105,000 sq. ft. of direct materials to be used during the upcoming year. Next, Pine Furniture Manufacturer can now determine the amount of direct materials to be purchased for each quarter. Figuring out the amount of direct materials to purchase is similar to creating the production budget. Assume Pine Furniture Manufacturer has 100,000 sq. ft. of direct materials in beginning inventory. For quarters 1 to 4, it expects the ending inventory to have 80,000, 75,000, 60,000 and 50,000 sq. ft. of direct materials respectively.

The formula to calculate how much direct material should be purchased is:

> Purchases of Direct Materials = Direct Materials to be Used + Budgeted Ending Direct Materials - Beginning Direct Materials

Using the above formula, Pine Furniture Manufacturer can determine the amount of direct materials needs to be purchased for each quarter as shown in figure 9.10.

	Q1	Q2	Q3	Q4
Direct Materials to be Used (Figure 9.7)	25,000	25,000	30,000	25,000
Budgeted Ending Inventory (Given)	80,000	75,000	60,000	50,000
Budgeted Beginning Inventory	(100,000)	(80,000)	(75,000)	(60,000)
Direct Materials to be Purchased (sq. ft.)	5,000	20,000	15,000	15,000

FIGURE 9.10

Lastly, to determine the dollar amount of purchases that have to be made, Pine Furniture Manufacturer multiplies the cost per sq. ft. of direct materials by the amount of direct materials that need to be purchased. Assume the company estimates direct materials costs to be $0.80/sq. ft. Figure 9.11 is Pine Furniture Manufacturer's purchasing budget.

Pine Furniture Manufacturer
Purchasing Budget
For year ending December 31, 2012

	Q1	Q2	Q3	Q4
Direct Materials to be Purchased (sq. ft.)	5,000	20,000	15,000	15,000
Budgeted Direct Material Cost per Chair	$0.80	$0.80	$0.80	$0.80
Budgeted Purchase Cost	$4,000	$16,000	$12,000	$12,000

FIGURE 9.11

Therefore, Pine Furniture Manufacturer expects to purchase a total of 55,000 sq. ft. (5,000 + 20,000 + 15,000 + 15,000) of direct materials for $44,000 ($4,000 + $16,000 + $12,000 + $12,000) in 2012. Note that at the end of the year, there will be 50,000 sq. ft. of material in ending inventory with a value of $40,000 (50,000 × $0.80).

Step 4: Prepare the Direct Labor Budget

The calculation of direct labor cost is based on estimated production units and the estimated labor cost per chair. The labor cost for each chair is calculated by multiplying the number of estimated direct labor hours for each chair by the direct labor cost per hour. Assume Pine Furniture Manufacturer estimates it takes two direct labor hours (DLH) per chair at $12 per DLH. Similar to direct material to be purchased calculations, figure 9.12 calculates budgeted direct labor hours for each quarter by.

	Q1	Q2	Q3	Q4	Total
Budgeted Production units	5,000	5,000	6,000	5,000	21,000
DLH per Chair	2	2	2	2	2
Budgeted Direct Labor Hours	10,000	10,000	12,000	10,000	42,000

FIGURE 9.12

The next step is to calculate the budgeted direct labor costs. This can be done by multiplying the budgeted direct labor hours by the direct labor cost per DLH ($12 per DLH). Pine Furniture Manufacturer can now prepare its direct labor budget as shown in figure 9.13.

Pine Furniture Manufacturer
Direct Labor Budget
For year ending December 31, 2012

	Q1	Q2	Q3	Q4
Budgeted Direct Labor Hours	10,000	10,000	12,000	10,000
Direct Labor Cost per DLH	$12.00	$12.00	$12.00	$12.00
Budgeted Direct Labor Costs	$120,000	$120,000	$144,000	$120,000

FIGURE 9.13

In 2012, Pine Furniture is expected to spend \$504,000 (\$120,000 + \$120,000 + \$144,000 + \$120,000) for direct labor.

Step 5: Prepare the Manufacturing Overhead Budget

In addition to direct materials and direct labor, manufacturing overhead costs must be considered. Pine Furniture Manufacturer estimates the manufacturing overhead costs for 2012 is \$126,000.

In order to determine the manufacturing overhead for each quarter, a predetermined overhead rate will be used. Pine Furniture Manufacture allocates budgeted manufacturing overhead costs based on the estimated number of direct labor hours (DLH).

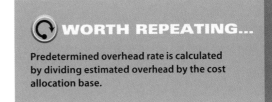

WORTH REPEATING...

Predetermined overhead rate is calculated by dividing estimated overhead by the cost allocation base.

Therefore, the predetermined overhead rate is:

$$\text{Predetermined Overhead Rate} = \frac{\text{Estimated Manufacturing Overhead}}{\text{Direct Labor Hours}}$$

$$= \frac{\$126,000}{42,000 \text{ DLH*}}$$

$$= \$3$$

*The 42,000 DLH was calculated in Figure 9.12

Using the predetermined overhead rate and the budgeted direct labor hours for each quarter, the manufacturing overhead costs will be allocated according to figure 9.14.

Pine Furniture Manufacturer Manufacturing Overhead Budget For year ending December 31, 2012					
	Q1	Q2	Q3	Q4	Total
Budgeted Direct Labor Hours (Figure 9.12)	10,000	10,000	12,000	10,000	42,000
Predetermined Overhead Rate	\$3.00	\$3.00	\$3.00	\$3.00	\$3.00
Budgeted Manufacturing Overhead	\$30,000	\$30,000	\$36,000	\$30,000	\$126,000

FIGURE 9.14

Step 6: Prepare Ending Finished Goods Inventory Budget

First, we will determine the cost of producing a single chair. Figure 9.15 shows the unit product cost is calculated by taking the sum of the direct material cost per unit, direct labor cost per unit and manufacturing overhead cost per unit.

		Unit Costs
Direct Materials Cost per Unit	$0.80 per sq. ft. × 5 sq. ft. per chair	$4
Direct Labor Cost per Unit	$12 per DLH × 2 DLH per chair	24
Manufacturing Overhead Cost per Unit	$3 per DLH × 2 DLH per chair	<u>6</u>
Cost per Chair		$34

FIGURE 9.15

Since there are 1,000 chairs in finished goods inventory at the end of the year (step 2), the cost of the ending finished goods inventory is $34,000 ($34 per chair × 1,000 chairs). Note that this amount will be recorded in the budgeted balance sheet. Figure 9.16 summarizes Pine Furniture Manufacturer's ending finished goods inventory budget.

Pine Furniture Manufacturer Ending Finished Goods Inventory Budget December 31, 2012	
Ending Inventory (Number of Chairs)	1,000
Cost per Chair	<u>$34</u>
Ending Inventory (Dollar Amount)	<u>$34,000</u>

FIGURE 9.16

Step 7: Prepare the Cost of Goods Sold Budget

Before preparing the cost of goods sold budget, we need to determine the cost of the direct materials used. Recall that the budgeted direct materials used for 2012 is 105,000 sq. ft. (figure 9.9) and the budgeted price for direct materials is $0.80 per sq. ft. Therefore, the cost of direct materials used is $84,000 (105,000 sq. ft. × $0.80 per sq. ft.).

Now that we have determined the budgeted cost of direct materials used, budgeted direct labor costs and budgeted manufacturing overhead costs, we can prepare the cost of goods sold budget. The cost of goods sold budget will be used when preparing the budgeted income statement. The formula for determining the budgeted cost of goods sold (COGS) is:

COGS = Cost of Direct Material Used + Direct Labor Cost + Budgeted Manufacturing Overhead Costs + Beginning Finished Goods Inventory – Ending Finished Goods Inventory

Assuming the cost of beginning finished goods inventory is $102,000, Pine Furniture Manufacturer can budget COGS to be $782,000 ($84,000 + $504,000 + $126,000 + $102,000 - $34,000).

Pine Furniture Manufacturer Cost of Goods Sold Budget December 31, 2012	
Direct Material Used (Step 7)	$84,000
Direct Labor Costs (Step 4)	504,000
Manufacturing Overhead Costs (Step 5)	126,000
Beginning Finished Goods (Given)	102,000
Ending Finished Goods (Step 6)	(34,000)
Cost of Goods Sold	$782,000

FIGURE 9.17

Now that Pine Furniture Manufacturer has budgeted for sales and cost of goods sold, the company will prepare budgets for the remaining items on the income statement (i.e. operating expenses).

Step 8: Prepare an Operating Expenses Budget

Pine Furniture Manufacturer will now prepare the operating expenses budget for non-production costs. The operating expenses budget outlines the period costs (those costs that are incurred in each period but are not related to manufacturing) that Pine Furniture Manufacturer is expecting to incur as a result of operations in the upcoming period. These period costs are made up of both variable and fixed costs. Figure 9.18 outlines the variable and fixed costs that are budgeted for the upcoming year.

Pine Furniture Manufacturer Operating Expense Budget For year ending December 31, 2012	
Variable Costs:	
Delivery	$11,500
Commissions	57,500
Office supplies	400
Total Variable Costs	69,400
Fixed Costs:	
Accounting and professional services	2,000
Admistration staff salaries	42,000
Advertising	8,000
Depreciation	12,000
Computer leases	1,200
Printing collateral	2,000
Insurance	2,000
Interest on loans	800
Rent & utilities	16,000
Sales personnel salaries	120,000
Total Fixed Costs	206,000
Total Operating Expenses	$275,400

FIGURE 9.18

The operating expenses budget is generally quite simple since each expense is straightforward. For example, most of the larger expenses such as rent, administrative staff salaries and insurance are usually known. On the other hand, smaller expenses such as office supplies are not always determined accurately. However, they are usually relatively immaterial expenses and would not make a large impact to the budget if they are not estimated accurately.

Step 9: Prepare the Budgeted Income Statement

Now that revenues and expenses have been calculated, all the data can be combined into one income statement. Figure 9.19 combines all the data from the budgets prepared in steps one through eight.

Pine Furniture Manufacturer Budgeted Income Statement For the Year Ending December 31, 2012	
Revenue:	$1,150,000
Cost of Goods Sold	782,000
Gross Profit	368,000
Operating Expenses:	
Delivery	11,500
Commissions	57,500
Accounting and professional services	2,000
Admistration salaries	42,000
Advertising	8,000
Depreciation	12,000
Computer leases	1,200
Printing collateral	2,000
Insurance	2,000
Interest on loans	800
Office supplies	400
Rent & utilities	16,000
Sales Salaries	120,000
Total Operating Expenses	275,400
Net Income	$92,600

FIGURE 9.19

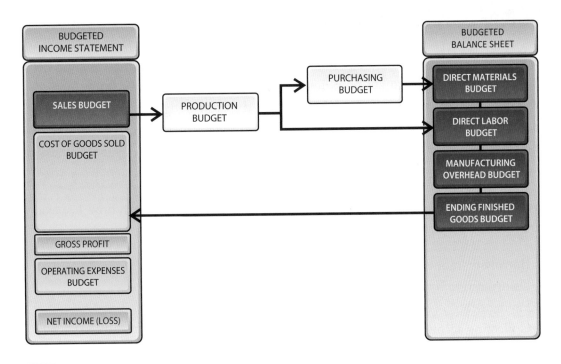

FIGURE 9.20

Figure 9.20 shows a summary of all the steps in the budgeting process that have been discussed so far.

Preparing a Capital Budget

Before preparing the cash budget, Pine Furniture Manufacturer will also have to consider what equipment purchases and sales it will have to make in the upcoming year. Decisions related to whether an asset should be purchased or not depends on a variety of factors such as the initial investment, profitability and financing requirements. Capital budgeting provides the tools necessary to determine how attractive a capital investment might be. This will be covered in chapter 12. For now, let us assume that Pine Furniture Manufacturer has determined that next year they will need to purchase $65,000 worth of equipment (cash outflow) and can sell the old equipment for $20,000 (cash inflow). Therefore, the total capital expenditure amounts to $45,000. See figure 9.21.

Pine Furniture Manufacturer Capital Budget For the Year Ending December 31, 2012	
Capital Expenditures	$65,000
Less: Sale of Capital Assets	(20,000)
Total Capital Expenditures	$45,000

FIGURE 9.21

Preparing a Cash Budget

Suppose you are a manager at Pine Furniture Manufacturer. In addition to estimating net income, you will also want to approximate how much cash you have to spend in future periods. This is where the cash budget comes into use. You can use the cash budget to plan for Pine Furniture Manufacturer's short term and long term credit needs. You can also use it to determine how much you can invest in capital expenditures. Cash budgeting is an integral part of your business' planning and control.

You have learned in financial accounting that profits are different from cash flow. For example, the following transactions increase or decrease the bank account without impacting equity:

- Borrowing money
- Using cash to buy assets
- Paying debts
- Collecting accounts receivable

Conversely, revenues and expenses may or may not impact cash flow due to the accrual system of accounting. For example, sales made on account will increase equity, but does not affect the cash account. Similarly, expenses will reduce equity and have no effect on cash.

The timing of activities relating to cash budgets and operating budgets are quite different. Figure 9.22 illustrates some examples of transactions where cash can increase or decrease without any impact on equity.

		Value	New Cash Balance	Owner's Equity
	Opening Balances		**5,000**	**10,000**
1	Pay cash for fixed assets	2,000	3,000	10,000
2	Borrow cash from the bank	5,000	8,000	10,000
3	Pay back the principal amount of a loan	2,000	6,000	10,000
4	Collect accounts receivable	4,000	10,000	10,000
5	Deposit unearned revenue	10,000	20,000	10,000
6	Sell a machine	1,000	21,000	10,000
7	Refund a customer deposit	3,000	18,000	10,000
8	Prepay insurance	1,000	17,000	10,000

FIGURE 9.22

Figure 9.23 illustrates some examples of transactions where cash remains the same while equity changes under accrual accounting.

		Value	New Cash Balance	Owner's Equity
	Opening Balances		**5,000**	**10,000**
1	Bill customer for services - pay next month	8,000	5,000	18,000
2	Charge expenses to your credit card	5,000	5,000	13,000
3	Recognize unearned revenue as earned	2,000	5,000	15,000
4	Recognize prepaid expenses	1,000	5,000	14,000
5	Depreciate assets	3,000	5,000	11,000
6	Record a bad debt	1,000	5,000	10,000
7	Record cost of goods sold	2,000	5,000	8,000
8	Record interest due for loans	1,000	5,000	7,000

FIGURE 9.23

Since cash flow is the lifeblood of a business, it is crucial to maintain a cash budget to forecast cash requirements before running out of cash. Once a business runs out of cash, it is often too late to borrow money on such short notice. Banks and suppliers do not want to provide credit to a business that cannot pay its bills. If cash shortages are anticipated, a manager can plan ahead by altering operations, obtaining financing or issuing stock. Essentially, a cash budget tracks all cash flowing into and out of the bank account. Cash flow forecasts are usually done on a monthly basis to help determine the financing needs for the particular period.

Because the cash budget is an internal document, there is no real standard format in which it should be presented. The format in this text represents a common format that is used by many businesses.

Businesses often prepare cash budgets on a monthly or quarterly basis. Figure 9.24 demonstrates the receipts portion of the cash budget on a quarterly basis.

Pine Furniture Manufacturer **Excerpt of Cash Budget** **For the year ending December 31, 2012**					
Receipts:	**Q1**	**Q2**	**Q3**	**Q4**	**Total**
Cash sales	$183,750	$146,250	$213,750	$318,750	$862,500
Collections from credit customers	58,950	50,138	67,163	99,938	276,188
Total Cash Receipts	242,700	196,388	280,913	418,688	1,138,688

FIGURE 9.24

The figure demonstrates estimated cash receipts (cash flows into the business) from cash sales and collections from credit customers every quarter. Notice that Q3 and Q4 have the highest cash inflows. This is largely due to the fact that Pine Furniture Manufacturer does most of its business at the end of the year. Cash inflows are lowest during Q1 and Q2, when business is at its slowest.

Estimating Cash Receipts

Cash receipts represent all cash that the company receives during a period. As part of regular operations, cash is received through the sale of products or services. Sales are either made to customers who pay cash immediately or customers who will pay later. Customers who pay later are buying on account and will eventually pay cash. Thus, there are two main categories of cash receipts: 1) cash sales and 2) cash collections from customers.

Cash Sales

In order to create the budget, managers must estimate the amount of cash sales that will occur each period. One way to estimate the cash sales is to examine the sales budget and, based on past trends, estimate how much of the total sales will be cash and how much will be on account (credit sales). In Pine Furniture Manufacturer's case, managers referred back to the sales budget (figure 9.6) and found the total budgeted sales for each quarter. Based on past trends, they estimate that 75% of a quarter's sales will be made in cash and the remaining 25% are sales made on account. We can determine cash sales and credit sales for each quarter as follows:

Pine Furniture Manufacturer Forecasted Cash Sales and Credit Sales For the year ending December 31, 2012					
	Q1	Q2	Q3	Q4	Total
Sales	$245,000	$195,000	$285,000	$425,000	$1,150,000
Cash sales (@ 75% of quarter's sales)	183,750	146,250	213,750	318,750	862,500
Credit sales (@ 25% of quarter's sales)	61,250	48,750	71,250	106,250	287,500

FIGURE 9.25

Notice that of the $245,000 sales in Q1, $183,750 will be cash and the remaining sales will be on account (credit sales). This basic calculation is performed for each quarter, eventually showing that total cash sales for the year will amount to $862,500.

Collections from Credit Customers

Collecting cash from customers who bought on account does not necessarily occur in the same period as the original sale. The timing of the collection will affect the cash receipts shown in the cash budget. Just as examining sales trends to determine cash sales can be used, examining collection trends can be used to estimate how long it takes to collect cash from credit customers. For example, Pine Furniture Manufacturer's historical trends suggest that the collections are made throughout the quarter of sale and in the following quarter. With that information, Pine Furniture Manufacturer can assume the following with regards to credit sales:

- 84% of credit customers pay during the quarter in which the sale took place
- 15% pay in the quarter following the sale
- The remaining 1% of credit sales are uncollectible

Therefore, a formula for Pine Furniture Manufacturer can be derived for cash collections from credit sales:

$$\text{Cash collections from credit sales in current quarter} = \text{84\% of current quarter's credit sales} + \text{15\% of previous quarter's credit sales}$$

Assuming that credit sales in the fourth quarter of 2011 for Pine Furniture Manufacturer totalled $50,000, we can obtain the budgeted cash collections from credit sales for the first quarter of 2012 using the above formula.

- 84% of 2012 Q1 credit sales = 0.84 × $61,250 = $51,450 (where $61,250 is taken from figure 9.25)
- 15% of 2011 Q4 credit sales = 0.15 × $50,000 = $7,500
- Cash collections from credit sales for 2012 Q1 = $51,450 + $7,500 = $58,950

Similarly, for 2012's Q2, budgeted cash collections from credit sales = (0.15 × $61,250) + (0.84 × $48,750) = $50,138. Following the same calculations, Q3 and Q4 will collect $67,163 and $99,938 respectively.

Thus, for Q1, total cash receipts will be $242,700. This is calculated by combining the cash sales of $183,750 plus the collections from customers of $58,950. Figure 9.26 illustrates how cash receipts are combined.

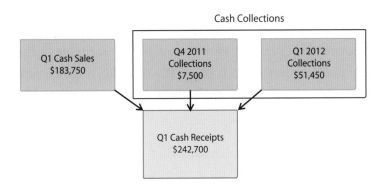

Cash Collections

Q1 Cash Sales $183,750

Q4 2011 Collections $7,500

Q1 2012 Collections $51,450

Q1 Cash Receipts $242,700

A CLOSER LOOK

Another way to estimate collections is to examine individual customers and their payment history. If a significant number of sales are credit customers, the company should examine how long each customer takes to pay.

FIGURE 9.26

Estimating Cash Disbursements

Figure 9.27 outlines the budgeted cash disbursements for each quarter. The process of estimating cash disbursements is similar to estimating cash receipts. To make proper estimations, managers need to consider the operation, production volume and invoicing terms. For example, a manager will know the payment terms for purchases made from their suppliers. Based on the production budget, the manager can determine the amount of material that needs to be purchased. With the sales budget, they will know the sales volume for a particular period. This will help determine when to make the purchases, when those payments are due and how to update the cash budget for payments to suppliers and for operating expenses.

Pine Furniture Manufacturer Excerpt of Cash Budget For the year ending December 31, 2012					
Disbursements:	Q1	Q2	Q3	Q4	Total
Payments for materials to suppliers	22,000	8,000	10,000	10,000	50,000
Payments towards operating expenses (payroll, rent etc.)	226,350	226,350	226,350	226,350	905,400
Capital Expenditure	0	45,000	0	0	45,000
Dividends	0	0	0	3,000	3,000
Total Cash Payments	248,350	279,350	236,350	239,350	1,003,400

FIGURE 9.27

For larger companies, this level of detail may be too time-consuming. As a quick method, many companies have noticed that cash payments for inventory are related to cost of goods sold. For example, they notice, on average, the cash payments for inventory are based on a percentage of the budgeted cost of goods sold in the current and previous periods (e.g. 70% of COGS for current quarter plus 30% of COGS in the previous quarter). They then apply these percentages to update the cash budget.

From the purchasing budget, Pine Furniture Manufacturer calculated that they would purchase $44,000 of material during the year. These purchases are on account (credit) and are going to spread out during the year, with more material being purchased in the last two quarters as sales increase. The "payment for materials to suppliers" row in figure 9.27 shows the payments for the purchases of materials for each quarter. Since the purchases are on account, the first quarter will include cash payments on materials bought in previous periods.

Similarly, cash payments towards operating expenses can be estimated using historical data to identifying when payments are actually made. This would be similar to the way that collections from customers are calculated. Historical data would indicate when these expenses are paid and by how much.

From the direct labor budget, the manufacturing overhead budget and the operating expenses budget, Pine Furniture Manufacturer estimates that each of these amounts will be paid evenly throughout the year. These amounts are recorded as payments towards operating expenses.

The cash disbursements will also include items such as capital expenditures, dividend payments, income tax instalments and interest on long-term loans. Pine Furniture Manufacturer is planning on purchasing new capital in the second quarter and paying dividends in the fourth quarter.

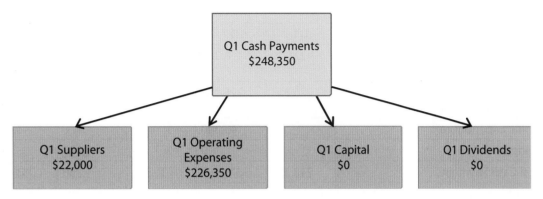

FIGURE 9.28

The payments for material, operating expenses, capital expenditure and dividends are combined to calculate the estimated cash payments for each quarter, as shown in figure 9.28.

Completing the Cash Budget

Once the estimates for cash receipts and cash payments are complete, they can be combined into the cash budget. The cash budget will also show how the cash balance will change each period based on the receipts and payments made during the period. Figure 9.29 is a complete cash budget for Pine Furniture Manufacturer for the upcoming fiscal year end.

Pine Furniture Manufacturer Cash Budget For the Year Ending December 31, 2012					
Receipts:	**Q1**	**Q2**	**Q3**	**Q4**	**Total**
Cash Receipts from Sales	$183,750	$146,250	$213,750	$318,750	$862,500
Collections from Credit Customers	58,950	50,138	67,163	99,938	276,188
Total Cash Receipts	242,700	196,388	280,913	418,688	1,138,688
Disbursements:	**Q1**	**Q2**	**Q3**	**Q4**	**Total**
Payments for Raw Materials to Suppliers	22,000	8,000	10,000	10,000	50,000
Payments Towards Operating Expenses (payroll, rent etc.)	226,350	226,350	226,350	226,350	905,400
Capital Expenditure	0	45,000	0	0	45,000
Dividends	0	0	0	3,000	3,000
Total Cash Payments	248,350	279,350	236,350	239,350	1,003,400
Opening Cash Balance	23,000	17,350	(65,613)	(21,050)	
Cash Inflow	242,700	196,388	280,913	418,688	
Less: Cash Outflow	248,350	279,350	236,350	239,350	
Ending Cash Balance	$17,350	(65,613)	(21,050)	$158,288	

FIGURE 9.29

Notice in Q1, the opening cash balance is $23,000. After taking into account the cash inflow of $242,700 and cash outflow of $248,350, Pine Furniture Manufacturer is left with an ending cash balance of $17,350 at the end of Q1. This amount is carried to the opening cash balance of the following period (Q2). Notice that the ending cash balance for the year (Q4) is $158,288 which is a positive balance. In fact, this is an increase in the cash balance of $135,288 from the beginning of the year. You can see, however, that there are two periods (Q2 and Q3) where there will be a cash deficit. This shows the usefulness of preparing a cash budget on a quarterly basis. If Pine Furniture Manufacturer managers had prepared a cash budget on an annual basis, they would not be able to identify the quarters in which they are predicted to have cash shortages. As a result, business operations would falter.

Now that they know they will be short of cash in Q2 and Q3, managers will have to figure out how to cope with the shortfall. There are a number of options:

1. They can consider obtaining more financing from the bank in the form of a credit line or term loan. This will help them operate successfully during the cash poor period.
2. They can also try to negotiate extended payment terms with suppliers as this will increase their cash flow.

3. Managers can consider improving operations to reduce inefficiencies (i.e. costs). If operational changes are going to be made, this essentially requires managers to revise the operating budgets.
4. Another option is to reduce inventory to free up more cash for operations.
5. Alternatively, managers could work on collecting cash from credit customers more quickly. This would increase the cash flow and make more cash available for use.
6. Pine Furniture Manufacturer owners can also consider issuing more stock to raise financing. Typically, though, this option is exercised as a last resort because issuing stock requires giving up ownership of the company.

Options 2 to 5 are all management issues and would require major changes within the organization. These changes may take time to implement and would not help with the rather immediate cash shortfall that will happen in the second quarter. The last option changes the financial structure of the company and may not be feasible. Thus, the first option to obtain short term financing from a bank is usually the choice to cover cash shortfalls.

The analysis of cash flow needs is highly dependent on how well the cash budget was prepared and how robust the assumptions were. Ideally, budgets are created with realistic expectations and all members of management can agree on the numbers. Any time actual sales are lower than budgeted sales, cash receipts will be lower as well. This will reduce cash flow and may increase financing requirements.

The managers at Pine Furniture Manufacturer decide to approach the bank with their budgeted cash flow to arrange for a loan to cover the cash shortfall in Q2 and Q3. The bank promised to make a loan available to them during the year. The bank loan should be greater than the anticipated cash shortfall. This will allow for more flexibility as actual cash receipts and payments differ from the budget. Pine Furniture Manufacturer will also want to keep a minimum cash balance of $10,000 in their bank account.

Pine Furniture Manufacturer will now update this loan information on the cash budget (see figure 9.30).

Pine Furniture Manufacturer Cash Budget For the Year Ending December 31, 2012					
Receipts:	**Q1**	**Q2**	**Q3**	**Q4**	**Total**
Cash Receipts from Sales	$183,750	$146,250	$213,750	$318,750	$862,500
Collections from Credit Customers	58,950	50,138	67,163	99,938	276,188
Total Cash Receipts	242,700	196,388	280,913	418,688	1,138,688
Disbursements:	**Q1**	**Q2**	**Q3**	**Q4**	**Total**
Payments for Raw Materials to Suppliers	22,000	8,000	10,000	10,000	50,000
Payments Towards Operating Expenses (payroll, rent etc.)	226,350	226,350	226,350	226,350	905,400
Capital Expenditure	0	45,000	0	0	45,000
Dividends	0	0	0	3,000	3,000
Total Cash Payments	248,350	279,350	236,350	239,350	1,003,400
Financing Requirements:					
Loan Borrowings	0	75,613	0	0	75,613
Loan Repayments	0	0	44,563	31,050	75,613
Opening Cash Balance	23,000	17,350	10,000	10,000	
Cash Inflow	242,700	272,000	280,913	418,688	
Less: Cash Outflow	248,350	279,350	280,913	270,400	
Ending Cash Balance	$17,350	$10,000	$10,000	$158,288	

FIGURE 9.30

The new information regarding the loan has been shaded in gray. In Q2, Pine Furniture Manufacturer will borrow $75,613 so that they can meet their cash requirements and have a remaining cash balance of $10,000. In reality, they may round the amount that is borrowed to the next highest multiple of $1,000 to try and keep things simple. During Q3 and Q4, they will pay back the entire amount of the loan and have an ending cash balance of $158,288 at the end of Q4 (i.e. end of the year). Interest charges on the short-term loan have been ignored to keep the example simple, but would be included in the loan repayment section.

As an extension of the cash budget analysis, Pine Furniture Manufacturer may feel that the ending balance of $158,288 is too much cash to keep in their bank account. Cash that just sits in a bank account does not earn interest and is not a productive asset. Thus, any amount of cash that is over a certain amount may be invested in short-term investments. Short-term investments allow the company to earn interest and can be easily converted back to cash as needed.

Even though the particular cash budget above is prepared on a quarterly basis, companies may instead choose to prepare a cash budget every month. In a given month, there may be many transactions that significantly effect the cash balance.

A CLOSER LOOK

Many analysts conclude that accounting principles provide management with so many options for external reporting that they render financial statements unreliable. In fact, these analysts focus more on an organization's cash flow statement. They argue that cash flow statements are subject to fewer manipulations potential, and therefore are more reliable.

Budgeted Balance Sheet

The budgeted income statement is used to plan or forecast operations for the upcoming year. The cash budget is used to plan and forecast cash changes for the upcoming year. The next step in preparing the master budget is to prepare a budgeted balance sheet. The budgeted balance sheet provides a concise summary of how expected operations in the upcoming year will affect the financial position of the company. It will outline the company's expected amount of assets, liabilities and owner's equity at the end of the year.

We can use the information in our budgets to help prepare the budgeted balance sheet for the year (see figure 9.31).

Pine Furniture Manufacturer Budgeted Balance Sheet As at December 31, 2012	
Assets	
Cash	$158,288
Accounts Receivable	345,000
Inventory	74,000
Building	404,712
Equipment	85,000
Accumulated Depreciation	(24,000)
Total Assets	**$1,043,000**
Liabilities	
Accounts Payable	300,680
Bank Loan	255,000
Total Liabilities	555,680
Stockholder's Equity	
Contributed Stock	202,400
Retained Earnings	284,920
Stockholder's Equity	487,320
Total Liabilities and Stockholder's Equity	**$1,043,000**

FIGURE 9.31

Notice that the cash balance in the budgeted balance sheet is taken from the cash budget (figure 9.30). The remaining amounts on the balance sheet can be determined by applying relationships based on historical data and by using the budgets already prepared. This is similar to what was done when preparing the cash receipts and cash disbursements sections in the cash budget. Always remember that there are multiple ways for managers to estimate the budgeted amounts on the budgeted balance sheet. These methods depend on the operations of the business and on historical trends. Below we will go into depth on how accounts receivable, inventory, equipment and accounts payable can be estimated.

Accounts Receivable

Pine Furniture Manufacturer knows the accounts receivable amount is usually proportional to the amount of sales incurred during the year, similar to the cash budget. Assuming the credit policies do not change significantly during the upcoming year, Pine Furniture Manufacturer estimated that accounts receivable should amount to 30% of total sales. Therefore, 30% of $1,150,000 is $345,000. This percentage is based on historical trends that Pine Furniture Manufacturer managers have noticed throughout the years. The sales amount of $1,150,000 is taken from the sales budget found in figure 9.6.

Inventory

Amounts for inventory can be calculated based on the purchasing and production budgets prepared earlier in this chapter. Inventory includes costs related to materials, WIP and finished goods. Ending inventory for direct materials amounts to $40,000 (see step 3 from preparing the operating budget). Since there are no partially completed units, there is no ending WIP inventory. Finished goods ending inventory amounts to $34,000 (see figure 9.16). Therefore, ending inventory is $74,000 ($40,000 + $0 + $34,000).

Equipment

Recall from the capital budget that Pine Furniture Manufacturer expects to increase capital assets by $45,000 in the upcoming year. This information will be taken into account when estimating the equipment amount on the budgeted balance sheet. Assume at the end of last year, Pine Furniture Manufacturer had $40,000 worth of equipment. With the anticipated increase of $45,000, the ending balance in the upcoming year is estimated to be $85,000 ($40,000 + $45,000).

Accounts Payable

Since Pine Furniture Manufacturer knows their payment terms and how many purchases they make during the year, they can estimate the amount of accounts payable remaining at end of the year. For larger companies, however, this process may be too time-consuming. Therefore, they may develop other methods to estimate accounts payable. For example, they can take a percentage of budgeted operating expenses or cost of goods sold.

The rest of the amounts on the balance sheet can be determined using similar methods and reasoning as described above.

Budgeted Cash Flow Statement

The budgeted cash flow statement is the formal version of the cash budget and is completed after the budgeted income statement and balance sheet are prepared. Similar to the cash budget, it outlines the budgeted sources and uses of cash relating to operating, investing and financing activities for the upcoming period. All inputs to the budgeted cash flow statement in figure 9.32 below are taken from the cash budget (figure 9.30).

Pine Furniture Manufacturer Budgeted Cash Flow Statement For the Year Ending December 31, 2012	
Cash Flow from Operations:	
Cash receipts from sales	$862,500
Collections from credit customers	276,188
Total Cash Receipts	1,138,688
Payments to suppliers	(50,000)
Payment of salaries and other operating expenses	(905,400)
Total Cash Payments	(955,400)
Net Cash Flow from Operating Activities	183,288
Cash Flow from Investing:	
Sale of Equipment	(45,000)
Net Cash Flow from Investing Activities	(45,000)
Cash Flow from Financing:	
Proceeds from Bank Loan	75,613
Payment of Bank Loan	(75,613)
Dividends	(3,000)
Net Cash Flow from Financing Activities	($3,000)
Net Increase in Cash	135,288
Opening Cash Balance, Jan 1, 2012	23,000
Ending Cash Balance, Dec 31, 2012	$158,288

FIGURE 9.32

Master Budget

Recall that the master budget represents the big picture reflected through the budgeted income statement, budgeted balance sheet and the budgeted cash flow statement. Figure 9.33, visually depicts the relationships between the different types of budgets for a manufacturing business.

Flow of Budgets

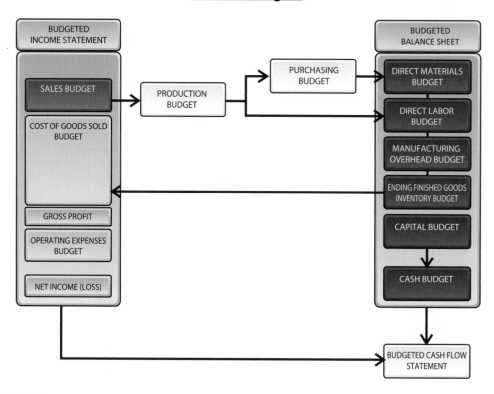

FIGURE 9.33

The budgeted income statement includes the sales budget which is used to prepare the production, purchasing, direct materials, direct labor, manufacturing overhead and cost of goods sold budgets. After the operating expenses budget is prepared, Pine Furniture Manufacturer can put together all this information to form the budgeted income statement. Pine Furniture Manufacturer also prepares the capital budget which is used in the preparation of the cash budget. Along with the direct materials, direct labor and manufacturing overhead budgets, Pine Furniture Manufacturer managers use the cash budget to prepare the budgeted balance sheet. The budgeted cash flow statement is then prepared using information from various budgets.

Effective Planning and Controlling

Planning and controlling a budget are key to keeping a business on track to remain liquid and profitable. The strategy of a company will state its long-term and short-term goals or objectives.

Long-term objectives involve broad strategic planning and will impact the entire organization. Usually this type of planning will look up to five years into the future. The strategy can include selling or closing a division of the company, product line expansion, geographic expansion, etc. For any of these strategies, very broad budgets can be created. The budgets are typically broad because attempting for forecast with any accuracy five years into the future can be challenging, time consuming and the budget will likely have to be changed as circumstances change. As an example, Pine Furniture Manufacturer may set a long-term strategy of growing operating income by 25% over the next five years and create some broad budgets to plan for this growth.

Short-term objectives involve planning the operations of the company to meet the long-term strategy. Budgets that are created for short-term objectives typically cover a one year period and are much more detailed than the long-term budgets. Figures for the revenue and the various expenses are all planned with as much detail as possible. This budget now becomes the plan for the year and actual results will be compared to this plan. So, after Pine Furniture Manufacturer creates their five-year budget, they would need to create short-term operational budgets. They may develop a budget for the upcoming year which shows an increase in operating income of 5%. This particular budget is a short-term step to achieving the long-term goal of 25% growth in operating income.

To properly control the business, managers compare actual results to the budget. Changes may be made to the budget to adjust for any deviation as needed. For example, if Pine Furniture Manufacturer spent more than expected to add a new chair model to its range of products, the short-term operational budget may not be met. To ensure that the company is still on pace to achieve the short-term goal of increasing operating income by 5% this year, the managers will have to cut other costs or increase revenue and adjust the operating budget accordingly.

Planning and Controlling Budgets

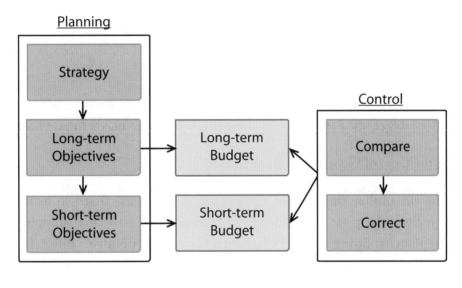

FIGURE 9.34

A well planned budget that is not controlled will likely lead to poor results. On the other hand, attempting to control an organization without a plan or goal to provide direction can be a frustrating endeavor. Lack of a plan or lack of control leads to wasted effort. Therefore, it is important to have good planning and effective control at the same time to ensure that the budgeting system turns out to be a valuable tool for management.

Budgeting for a Merchandising Firm

Up until now, we have discussed the different components of a master budget for a manufacturing firm. In this section, we will discuss how a master budget for a merchandising firm is put together. While there are many similarities between the two processes, there are also some key differences. For example, merchandising firms will not include direct materials, direct labor or manufacturing overhead into the cost of their products because they do not manufacture anything. Instead, the cost of their merchandising inventory will include the cost to purchase those items and, if applicable, the associated freight costs.

For example, consider Buffy's Beautiful Belts Inc. Buffy purchases brand name belts from overseas and sells them in her store. Let us now outline how Buffy will prepare a master budget for her company. These steps are also relevant for other merchandising firms.

Step 1: Prepare a Sales Budget.

She will forecast the amount of belts that she is expecting to sell, as well as the selling price of each belt.

Step 2: Prepare a Purchasing Budget.

Based on her sales budget, she can determine how many belts she needs to purchase.

Step 3: Prepare the Cost of Goods Sold Budget.

This is where she will outline the product costs of the merchandise that will be sold. The cost of goods sold will include the price she paid for the belts and the associated shipping costs. Notice that this is where merchandising and manufacturing firms master budgets differ. To prepare a cost of goods sold budget, merchandising companies have to only consider finished goods inventory. Manufacturing firms, however, have to consider raw materials, WIP and finished goods inventory when preparing the COGS budget. To determine the cost of goods sold for a merchandising firm the following formula can be used.

Cost of Goods Sold   =   Beginning Inventory + Purchases – Ending Inventory

Step 4: Prepare an Operating Expenses Budget.

Buffy will estimate the period costs (both fixed and variable) she expects to incur such as rent, salaries and depreciation.

Step 5: <u>Prepare a Budgeted Income Statement, Capital Expenditure Budget, Cash Budget and Budgeted Balance Sheet.</u>

She will compile the budgets from steps one to four and prepare a budgeted income statement. The formation of the capital expenditure budget, cash budget, budgeted balance sheet and budgeted cash flow statement will follow the same process that is used in a manufacturing firm.

Approaches to Budgeting

Up to this point, we have discussed the different budgets that are prepared in the budgeting process and how they fit together to form the master budget. This section will discuss approaches regarding how the budget is estimated. Consider managers at Pine Furniture Manufacturer who are putting together the sales budget for the upcoming year. There are many ways in which they can go about estimating sales volume. They can perform a detailed analysis and consider each customer and their expected sales volume during the year (this is the approach used earlier in this chapter). Alternatively, they can base their estimates on sales amounts from the previous year. For example, if sales in the prior year amounted to $500,000 and they generally increase by 2% per year, the company can budget an amount of $510,000 ($500,000 × 1.02) for sales. The two approaches used for budgeting are incremental and zero-based budgeting.

Incremental Budgeting

The term incremental refers to increasing or gaining something. **Incremental budgeting** involves creating a new budget that is based on gradual changes from the previous year's budget. For example, when budgeting an amount for salaries, the budgeted amount can be based on an annual increment to salaries paid in the prior year. For example, if salaries in the previous year amounted to $50,000, and management expects a 5% increase every year, this amounts to salaries of $52,500 ($50,000 + $50,000 × 5%) for the current year. This type of increase can be applied to any expense such as rent, utilities and administrative costs. It can also be applied to revenues, assets and liabilities.

Since the incremental budget is based on the previous budget or performance figures, this type of budgeting is relatively easy to administer. In addition, changes from the prior year are easy to identify and can be applied consistently across multiple departments within an organization.

However, problems with incremental budgeting can arise if the previous budget (the budget that the new budget is based on) was:

1. Not prepared properly: For example, if the previous budget included excessive amounts of selling costs, then the new budget may also have excessive amounts of selling costs since it is based on inaccurate figures.
2. Prepared under different circumstances: For example, if a company is going to substantially increase their recruiting efforts, applying a constant year-over-year increase to the previous recruiting expenses, will result in a much lower budgeted expenses than the actual expenses. This will affect the variance and employee performance analysis at the end of the year.

Another problem with incremental budgeting is that it does not provide any incentive for managers to reduce costs because costs in the upcoming budget are based on changes to the figures from previous years. Also, since the allocations of budgeted expenditures generally remain the same year after year, changes in the business are not as easily reflected in the budgets.

Another major problem of incremental budgeting is the tendency for departments to spend up to the budget so that the budget will not be decreased next year. This encourages wasteful spending and budgetary slack. Over time, all these factors will likely make the company less competitive.

Zero-Based Budgeting

Zero-based budgeting requires that managers create budgets from scratch and justify their budget requests in detail, regardless of the amounts spent in previous years. This approach ensures that past mistakes or unnecessary expenditures are not repeated. Suppose a company was preparing a sales budget for the upcoming year. In the incremental approach, the sales budget for the upcoming year would be based on last year's sales budget. However, in the zero-based budgeting approach, the budget would start off with $0 revenue and possible client sales would be added to it. The company would consider both new and old revenue streams and the amount of orders they expect to make during the year. Zero-based budgeting does not use any reference for expenditures. This means that every expense has to be evaluated and approved before it is included in the budget.

One of the advantages of zero-based budgeting is that it forces managers to perform a comprehensive analysis of all aspects of their operations, without taking historical costs for granted. This will make it easier to identify areas for improvement. For example, if a manager is in the process of determining the advertising budget using the zero-based approach, he or she will have to re-visit contracts with the previous agencies and may notice that some agencies have better pricing options than others. This will help the manager reduce costs in the future. These costs would not have been re-visited if the manager had used the incremental approach.

On the other hand, a disadvantage of zero-based budgeting is the difficulty of preparation. Since it forces managers of every department to critically examine their expenditures, it is very time-consuming and costly. Zero-based budgeting also benefits some departments more than others. For example, it is easier for a production department (where results are known) to justify their costs as opposed to the research department (where results are unknown).

As you can see, due to the extra work that must be performed, the zero-based approach is cumbersome to use compared to the incremental approach. However, the zero-based approach has more potential to improve the business and detect inefficiencies than the incremental approach.

While preparing budgets, companies can use a blend of both approaches: use past performance as a guide (incremental budgeting), while using the zero-based approach for calculations. However, it is well worth the effort to use the zero-based approach because it tends to be more accurate than the incremental approach.

Different Budgeting Methods

The success of a budget is largely dependent on employee buy-in. In other words, a budget is only useful if lower management and employees are attempting to meet its targets. Two types of budget creation are top-down and bottom-up. **Top-down**, or **imposed budgeting**, is a budgeting process where all the figures are determined by upper management and imposed throughout the organization. This method may result in resentment from the employees.

Another type of budgeting is **bottom-up**, or **participative budgeting**. In this case, managers of all levels fully co-operate and contribute to budget creation. Any disagreements with upper management are discussed to find a mutual agreement. This method is generally more effective because it encourages teamwork and allows managers to feel like they have more control in the decision-making process. This approach will also result in better estimates of different costs because upper-management is unlikely to be as familiar with the day-to-day operations of each department.

While budgets can be top-down or bottom-up, most organizations in practice choose to use a mix of both.

Budgetary Slack

A significant problem in budgeting is that managers will try to build in budgetary slack, also called buffers. **Budgetary slack** represents the tendency of employees to intentionally underestimate revenues and overestimate expenses in the budgeting process. This is because budgets usually form a large part of performance evaluation (e.g. many organizations will not give a bonus unless the budget has been met or exceeded). Therefore, if employees are able to build in a budget with higher expenses and lower revenues, it will make it easier for them to meet the projections. This will also allow employees to hedge against any unforeseen circumstances during the year.

Having budgetary slack also means that the organization will not be operating at maximum efficiency. Therefore, it is important for upper management to understand the importance of a fair budget and to not put too much emphasis on cost reduction. Since budgeting is meant to motivate employees and coordinate efforts, managers must ensure that they encourage positive behavior and not use the budget as a tool for punishment. The participative budget, as we discussed above, is a great way for management to improve employees' commitment to the budgeting process.

Although every employee of a company should share the same goals for the organization, their different roles sometimes lead them to have different incentives during the budgeting process. Thus, upper management also needs to take the human impact of budgeting into consideration.

Preparing Variance Reports

In the same way you would check your map while traveling, a manager must continually compare the budget to actual figures to ensure that operations are moving in the right direction. A **variance report** shows numerically how actual amounts differ from budgeted amounts. For example, a variance sales report will provide information such as:

- Total actual sales during the month or quarter.
- The variance of actual sales from budgeted sales.
- A cumulative total of actual sales each month or quarter.
- A cumulative variance by month or quarter.

These figures are useful in providing a snapshot of where the business stands financially compared to its budget. An example of a Pine Furniture Manufacturer sales variance report can be found in figure 9.35. Notice that this report outlines the expected sales volumes for Q1 and Q2 (from figure 9.5 and 9.6). Pine Furniture Manufacturer managers include actual sales for each quarter and compare these amounts to the budgeted amounts.

Pine Furniture Manufacturer Sales Variance For Quarter 1 and Quarter 2	Q1 (units)	Q1 (dollars)	Q2 (units)	Q2 (dollars)
Budgeted	4,900	$245,000	3,900	$195,000
Actual	5,200	$260,000	3,800	$190,000
Variance	300	$15,000	(100)	($5,000)

FIGURE 9.35

Notice that the budgeted sales forecast in Q1 was $245,000 versus the actual sales performance of $260,000. In other words, there was a favorable variance of $15,000 ($260,000 - $245,000). In the second quarter, Pine Furniture Manufacturer's actual sales are $5,000 ($190,000 - $195,000) less than the budgeted sales. Once significant variances have been identified, it is extremely important to investigate their cause. Identifying the source of variances will help managers improve their operations and prepare accurate budgets in the future. The primary objective of a variance report is to identify where the organization might be heading off course (away from the target). This will allow sufficient time to take corrective action and avoid further problems. For example, after investigation Pine Furniture Manufacturer managers concluded that the decrease in sales in the second quarter was due to a cancelled contract by a customer, thus fewer units were sold than were expected. Managers can now follow up with the sales representatives to determine why the customer cancelled the order. This information can be used to improve customer service and pricing options available to customers. Note that some variances are a result of circumstances that are unpredictable and unavoidable, such as:

- A change in the currency exchange rates, which could influence earnings
- An act of war (9/11 for example)
- A new competitor enters the market, cuts prices and steals part of your market share

From this chapter, it is evident that financial budgeting is a great tool for a company to reach its plans and goals. Not only does it promote continuous improvement, but it also helps managers make decisions for future periods. In the business world, having a budget is like having a financial map which will help guide your organization to future success. In the following chapters, we will be extending the budgeting concepts introduced here.

IN THE REAL WORLD

In the 1960s, Sam Walton, the founder of Walmart, decided to increase their sales volume by maintaining sales prices lower than their competitors (i.e. reducing profit margin). In order to assess the effectiveness of the strategy, the company compared their actual performance with their expected performance. However, given the small business size and the absence of computers, the budgets were likely not prepared in great detail.

Today, however, Walmart is the largest private employer in the US and Mexico, and one of the largest in Canada with estimated sales in 2010 of $405B. Walmart prepares budgets that are used in small businesses such as budgeted income statements and balance sheets, but it also prepares budgets for different divisions and departments. Some examples include budgets for marketing, advertising, training and even various charities. The budget and actual results in each region will be populated into regional budgets, which ultimately roll up into the Walmart Corporation in a form of a Master Income Statement, Balance Sheet and Cash Flow Statement. Like any other company, the management of Walmart is held accountable to ensure performance meets or exceeds expectation. Without a doubt, Walmart's current budgetary process is extremely sophisticated, and has certainly contributed to their great success.

Ethical Considerations

Recall that budgetary slack is the tendency to underestimate revenues and overestimate expenses when preparing a budget. This would be considered unethical if performance bonuses are related to how well the budgeted amounts are met or exceeded. Unethical behavior can also arise by overestimating revenues and underestimating expenses. There is a fine line between making a poor judgement when estimating revenues and expenses and when a manager intentionally (unethically) uses inaccurate numbers.

The motivation for this practice is widespread. For example, a manager who might have experienced a poor sales season is warned that he will be fired if sales do not increase in the near future. To help save his job for the time being, he may prepare an overly optimistic sales budget for the upcoming year knowing that it is unlikely to be met. This is only a short-term solution, since actual sales will eventually prove his budget to be wildly inaccurate.

This inaccurate budget can potentially cause a number of problems for the company. For example, the business owner may take the sales forecast to the bank when applying for an operating loan. The bank may award the loan based on a good history of accurate forecasting. If the sales do not meet expectations, it will affect the credibility of the business and its ability to borrow money in the future. The overly optimistic sales volume can cause a build-up of excess inventory which can lead to cash flow problems. As a result, managers who prepare sales and expense budgets should be challenged with regard to their logic and justify how they established their estimates.

In Summary

- **Budgets** are numerical tools that help managers reach the financial goals in their business plans.

- Budgets help managers tailor their operations to meet their financial goals. They also improve operations by allowing comparisons of budgeted and actual results.

- The **operating budget** outlines budgeted changes to the income statement during the period. The budgeted income statement is used to plan or forecast operations for the upcoming year.

- **Capital budgets** involve changes in the company's financial resources and only impact the budgeted balance sheet.

- The **budgeted balance sheet** provides a concise summary of how expected operations in the upcoming year will affect the financial position of the company (i.e. asset, liabilities and equity).

- **Cash budgets** monitor cash flowing into and out of the bank account with no regards to profits.

- The budgeted cash flow statement is a formal version of the cash budget. It outlines the budgeted sources and uses of cash relating to operating, investing, and financing activities for the upcoming period.

- The **master budget** encompasses all aspects of business operations, which include all organization's individual budgets.

- The **sales budget** outlines the budgeted quantity and selling price of products or services sold.

- The **production budget** outlines how much product needs to be produced.

- The **purchases budget** outlines how much product needs to be purchased.

- The **operating expenses budget** outlines the budgeted expenses not related to manufacturing activities.

- Planning involves setting short-term objectives that align with the company's long-term strategy. Budgets are created to support these objectives.

- To properly control the business, actual results are compared to the budget. Changes may be made to the budget to adjust for any deviation.

- Budgeting for a merchandising firm is very similar to budgeting for a manufacturing firm, except that merchandising inventory includes the cost of purchasing the products as opposed to production costs (i.e. direct materials, direct labor, and manufacturing overhead).

- **Zero-based budgeting** requires managers to justify their budget requests in detail from scratch, regardless of the previous amounts spent.

- **Incremental budgeting** involves creating a new budget which is based on gradual changes from the previous year's budget.

⇨ **Top-down**, or **imposed budgeting**, is a budgeting process where all the figures are determined by upper management and imposed throughout the organization.

⇨ **Bottom-up**, or **participative budgeting**, is a budgeting process where managers of all levels fully co-operate and contribute to budget creation.

⇨ **Budgetary slack** represents the tendency of employees to intentionally underestimate revenues and overestimate expenses in the budgeting process.

⇨ A **variance report** shows, numerically, how actual amounts differ from budgeted amounts.

Review Exercise

SteelCorp Inc. makes steel filing cabinets for offices. They are in the process of preparing an operating budget and a cash budget for 2012. The yearly budget will be broken into quarters to provide more details. The details required for the 2012 budget are given below:

2012 Quarter	Budgeted Sales Volume
Q1	4,300
Q2	4,600
Q3	4,500
Q4	4,800

- Each filing cabinet sells for $500.
- There are 800 filing cabinets in finished goods inventory at the end of 2011 with a value of $360,000. At the end of each quarter, SteelCorp wishes to have 600 units in finished goods inventory.
- Each cabinet uses 50 sq. ft. of steel (direct material) during the manufacturing process. The cost of steel for 2012 is estimated to be $8.00 per sq. ft.
- SteelCorp currently has 30,000 sq. ft. of steel (direct material) in beginning inventory. At the end of each quarter, SteelCorp wants to have to have 40,000 sq. ft. of ending inventory.
- Each cabinet requires four machine hours and two direct labor hours to manufacture.
- Direct labor costs $14 per direct labor hour.
- SteelCorp allocates manufacturing overhead costs based on the estimated number of machine hours. Estimated manufacturing overhead costs for 2012 are $630,000.
- For each quarter, it is estimated that 40% of sales will be cash and 60% will be credit. Of the credit sales, 80% of customers pay in the quarter of the sale and 20% pay in the following quarter. Credit sales from Q4 of 2011 were $1,300,000.
- Direct labor costs and manufacturing overhead costs are paid for in cash in the quarter they are incurred.
- Assume operating expenses occur evenly throughout the year and are all paid fully in cash.
- For each quarter, 70% of material purchases are paid for in cash in the quarter of the purchase and 30% are paid for in the following quarter. Purchases of materials from Q4 2011 were $1,500,000.
- SteelCorp will purchase a new machine worth $700,000 and will make two equal payments. The first payment will be made in Q1 and the second will be made in Q3.
- SteelCorp will pay $60,000 in dividends in Q4.
- Currently, the cash balance in the bank is $15,000. SteelCorp wants to maintain a minimum cash balance of $10,000 in the bank at the end of each quarter.

The operating expenses are:

Variable Costs:	
Delivery	$5,200
Commissions	6,500
Office supplies	2,300
Fixed Costs:	
Accounting and professional services	1,800
Administration staff salaries	35,000
Advertising	9,000
Computer leases	4,200
Printing collateral	1,400
Insurance	1,200
Interest on loans	500
Rent	20,000
Utilities	3,000
Sales staff salaries	42,000

Required:

1. Prepare the following budgets for 2012:
   a) Sales budget for each quarter
   b) Production budget for each quarter
   c) Purchasing budget for each quarter
   d) Direct labor budget for each quarter
   e) Manufacturing overhead budget for each quarter
   f) Ending finished goods inventory budget
   g) Cost of goods sold budget
   h) Operating expenses budget
2. Prepare a budgeting income statement for 2012.
3. Prepare the 2012 cash budget for each quarter.

Review Exercise – Answer

Part 1

a) Firstly, prepare the sales volume forecast.

SteelCorp Inc. Sales Volume Forecast For the Year Ending December 31, 2012					
	Q1	**Q2**	**Q3**	**Q4**	**Total**
Cabinets	4,300	4,600	4,500	4,800	18,200

Next multiply the forecasted amount by the selling price per unit to create the sales budget.

SteelCorp Inc. Sales Budget For the Year Ending December 31, 2012					
	Q1	**Q2**	**Q3**	**Q4**	**Total**
Cabinets	$2,150,000	$2,300,000	$2,250,000	$2,400,000	$9,100,000

b) Use the sales volume and the beginning and ending finished goods inventory amounts to create the production budget.

SteelCorp Inc. Production Budget For the Year Ending December 31, 2012				
	Q1	**Q2**	**Q3**	**Q4**
Budgeted Sales Volume	4,300	4,600	4,500	4,800
Budgeted Ending Inventory	600	600	600	600
Budgeted Beginning Inventory	(800)	(600)	(600)	(600)
Budgeted Production Units	4,100	4,600	4,500	4,800

c) First, calculate how much material must be used based on the budgeted production units.

	Q1	**Q2**	**Q3**	**Q4**
Budgeted Production Units	4,100	4,600	4,500	4,800
Direct Materials per Cabinet	50	50	50	50
Budgeted DM to be Used (sq. ft.)	205,000	230,000	225,000	240,000

Note that the cost of the direct materials to be used is (205,000 + 230,000 + 225,000 + 240,000) × $8.00/sq. ft. = $7,200,000

Next, calculate the quantity (in sq. ft) of material to be purchased, taking into account beginning and ending direct materials inventory.

	Q1	**Q2**	**Q3**	**Q4**
Budgeted DM to be Used (sq. ft.)	205,000	230,000	225,000	240,000
Budgeted Ending Inventory	40,000	40,000	40,000	40,000
Budgeted Beginning Inventory	(30,000)	(40,000)	(40,000)	(40,000)
DM to be Purchased (sq. ft.)	215,000	230,000	225,000	240,000

Finally, prepare the purchasing budget.

SteelCorp Inc. Purchasing Budget For the Year Ending December 31, 2012				
	Q1	Q2	Q3	Q4
DM to be Purchased (sq. ft.)	215,000	230,000	225,000	240,000
Budgeted DM Cost (per sq. ft.)	$8.00	$8.00	$8.00	$8.00
Budgeted Purchase Cost	$1,720,000	$1,840,000	$1,800,000	$1,920,000

d) First, calculate how many direct labor hours are required.

	Q1	Q2	Q3	Q4	Total
Budgeted Production Units	4,100	4,600	4,500	4,800	18,000
Direct Labor Hour per Cabinet	2	2	2	2	2
Budgeted Direct Labor Hours	8,200	9,200	9,000	9,600	36,000

Then, create the direct labor budget.

SteelCorp Inc. Direct Labor Budget For the Year Ending December 31, 2012				
	Q1	Q2	Q3	Q4
Budgeted Direct Labor Hours	8,200	9,200	9,000	9,600
Direct Labor Cost per DLH	$14.00	$14.00	$14.00	$14.00
Budgeted Direct Labor Cost	$114,800	$128,800	$126,000	$134,400

e) Since manufacturing overhead is allocated based on machine hours, calculate how many machine hours are budgeted.

	Q1	Q2	Q3	Q4	Total
Budgeted Production Units	4,100	4,600	4,500	4,800	18,000
Machine Hours per Cabinet	4	4	4	4	4
Budgeted Machine Hours	16,400	18,400	18,000	19,200	72,000

Next, calculate the predetermined overhead rate:

$$\text{Predetermined Overhead Rate} = \frac{\text{Estimated Manufacturing Overhead}}{\text{Machine Hours}}$$

$$= \frac{\$630,000}{72,000 \text{ machine hours}}$$

$$= \$8.75 \text{ per machine hour}$$

Finally, create the manufacturing overhead budget.

SteelCorp Inc. Manufacturing Overhead Budget For the Year Ending December 31, 2012	Q1	Q2	Q3	Q4
Budgeted Machine Hours	16,400	18,400	18,000	19,200
Predetermined Overhead Rate	$8.75	$8.75	$8.75	$8.75
Budgeted Manufacturing Overhead	$143,500	$161,000	$157,500	$168,000

f) First, calculate the cost per unit.

		Unit Cost
Direct Material Cost per Cabinet	$8.00 per sq. ft. × 50 sq. ft. per cabinet	$400
Direct Labor Cost per Cabinet	$14.00 per DLH × 2 DLH per cabinet	28
Manufacturing Overhead Cost per Cabinet	$8.75 per machine hour × 4 machine hours	35
Cost per Cabinet		$463

Then, create the ending finished goods inventory budget.

SteelCorp Inc. Ending Finished Goods Inventory Budget December 31, 2012	
Ending Inventory (# of Cabinets)	600
Cost per Cabinet	$463
Ending Inventory (Dollar Amount)	$277,800

g) Compile the cost of goods sold budget from the previous budgets created.

SteelCorp Inc. Cost of Goods Sold Budget December 31, 2012	
Direct Materials Used	$7,200,000
Direct Labor Costs	504,000
Manufacturing Overhead Costs	630,000
Beginning Finished Goods Inventory	360,000
Ending Finished Goods Inventory	(277,800)
Cost of Goods Sold	$8,416,200

h) Compile the given information into an operating expense budget.

SteelCorp Inc. Operating Expenses Budget For the Year Ending December 31, 2012	
Variable Costs:	
Delivery	$5,200
Commissions	6,500
Office supplies	2,300
Total Variable Costs	14,000
Fixed Costs:	
Accounting and professional services	1,800
Administration staff salaries	35,000
Advertising	9,000
Computer leases	4,200
Printing collateral	1,400
Insurance	1,200
Interest on loans	500
Rent	20,000
Utilities	3,000
Sales staff salaries	42,000
Total Fixed Costs	118,100
Total Operating Expenses	$132,100

Part 2

Use the sales budget, the cost of goods sold budget and the operating expenses budget to create the budgeted income statement.

SteelCorp Inc. Budgeted Income Statement For the Year Ending December 31, 2012	
Revenue	$9,100,000
Cost of Goods Sold	8,416,200
Gross Profit	683,800
Operating Expenses	
Delivery	5,200
Commissions	6,500
Office supplies	2,300
Accounting and professional services	1,800
Administration staff salaries	35,000
Advertising	9,000
Computer leases	4,200
Printing collateral	1,400
Insurance	1,200
Interest on loans	500
Rent	20,000
Utilities	3,000
Sales staff salaries	42,000
Total Operating Expenses	132,100
Net Income	**$551,700**

Part 3

Firstly, separate the sales into cash and credit sales.

SteelCorp Inc. Forecasted Cash Sales and Credit Sales For the Year Ending December 31, 2012					
	Q1	Q2	Q3	Q4	Total
Sales	$2,150,000	$2,300,000	$2,250,000	$2,400,000	$9,100,000
Cash Sales (40% of quarter's sales)	860,000	920,000	900,000	960,000	3,640,000
Credit Sales (60% of quarter's sales)	1,290,000	1,380,000	1,350,000	1,440,000	5,460,000

Next, calculate collections from credit customers.

Collections for Q1 = ($1,290,000 × 80%) + ($1,300,000 × 20%) = $1,292,000

Collections for Q2 = ($1,380,000 × 80%) + ($1,290,000 × 20%) = $1,362,000

Collections for Q3 = ($1,350,000 × 80%) + ($1,380,000 × 20%) = $1,356,000

Collections for Q4 = ($1,440,000 × 80%) + ($1,350,000 × 20%) = $1,422,000

Next, calculate payments for material purchases.

Payments for Q1 = ($1,720,000 × 70%) + ($1,500,000 × 30%) = $1,654,000
Payments for Q2 = ($1,840,000 × 70%) + ($1,720,000 × 30%) = $1,804,000
Payments for Q3 = ($1,800,000 × 70%) + ($1,840,000 × 30%) = $1,812,000
Payments for Q4 = ($1,920,000 × 70%) + ($1,800,000 × 30%) = $1,884,000

Now, complete the cash budget.

SteelCorp Inc. Cash Budget For the Year Ending December 31, 2012					
Receipts:	**Q1**	**Q2**	**Q3**	**Q4**	**Total**
Cash receipts from sales	$860,000	$920,000	$900,000	$960,000	$3,640,000
Collections from credit customers	1,292,000	1,362,000	1,356,000	1,422,000	5,432,000
Total Cash Receipts	2,152,000	2,282,000	2,256,000	2,382,000	9,072,000
Disbursements:					
Payment for material purchases	1,654,000	1,804,000	1,812,000	1,884,000	7,154,000
Payments for labor	114,800	128,800	126,000	134,400	504,000
Payments for overhead	143,500	161,000	157,500	168,000	630,000
Payments for operating expenses	33,025	33,025	33,025	33,025	132,100
Capital Expenditure	350,000	0	350,000	0	700,000
Dividends	0	0	0	60,000	60,000
Total Cash Payments	2,295,325	2,126,825	2,478,525	2,279,425	9,180,100
Financing Requirements:					
Loan Borrowings	138,325	0	205,675	0	344,000
Loan Repayments	0	(138,325)	0	(102,575)	(240,900)
Opening Cash Balance	15,000	10,000	26,850	10,000	
Cash Inflow	2,290,325	2,282,000	2,461,675	2,382,000	
Less: Cash Outflow	2,295,325	2,265,150	2,478,525	2,382,000	
Ending Cash Balance	$10,000	$26,850	$10,000	$10,000	

Chapter 10
VARIANCE ANALYSIS AND STANDARD COSTING

LEARNING OUTCOMES:

❶ Explain the importance of variance analysis

❷ Describe the difference between a static budget and a flexible budget

❸ Use a flexible budget to analyze variances

❹ Describe and calculate sales-volume variance

❺ Describe and calculate flexible budget variance

❻ Describe and calculate static budget variance

❼ Calculate the price, efficiency, spending variances

Variance Analysis: An Introduction

Ana was recently promoted to the district manager position at a large pharmaceutical company. She has a strong background in pharmacy, but limited experience in managing sales and costs. At the beginning of the first month in her new role, she created a budget for the district's revenues, costs and profits. Her performance evaluation is based on her ability to meet the budgeted amounts. Unfortunately, at the end of the month, Ana noticed that actual spending was significantly greater than her budgeted amounts. Also, actual sales and profits were substantially less than what was budgeted. In other words, there were significant variances, which refer to the differences between actual and budgeted amounts. By recognizing the variances, she was immediately able to target the areas that needed improvement. In addition, Ana anticipates that drug prices and sales volume will change next month. How would Ana prepare a budget taking all this information into account?

Management control is the process by which managers set targets for performance, measure actual performance and address differences between actual and targeted performance. To do this effectively, it is important for every manager to understand their revenues and costs and implement a strong budgeting system. However, comparing actual performance with budgeted performance can become complex when actual activity fluctuates from what was planned. The concepts covered in this chapter will help managers like Ana to better evaluate their costs and performance.

Recall from chapter 9 that a budget is a planning tool used to map out future financial activity. Given that a budget is a quantitative forecast of anticipated activities and goals, it needs to be prepared prior to the start of the period. At the end of a given period, the comparison of the budgeted and actual results provides valuable information about performance. Budgets can be used to plan and evaluate the performances of businesses, departments and employees. It is very unlikely that a business predicts actual results perfectly. Therefore, it is imperative that managers monitor the budgeted inputs and outputs very carefully on a regular basis.

At different points throughout the fiscal period, managers compare budgets with actual results. This process of analyzing variances that occur between budgeted amounts and actual amounts is called *management by exception*. In this process, managers attempt to determine the root causes of the variances. They also develop methods to ensure that such variations are not repeated. The managerial accounting tools used to analyze these variances are illustrated in the following section.

Static and Flexible Budgets

You are the owner of Delish Hot Dog Stand and have been in business for a number of years near your town's largest baseball stadium. You need to prepare a budget in order to place orders for hot dogs, buns and condiments. Given past experience, you budgeted to sell 3,000 hot dogs for the month of July at $2.50 per hot dog. The budgeted variable costs, fixed expenses and budgeted income can be found in figure 10.1.

Delish Hot Dog Stand Budgeted Contribution Margin Statement For the Month Ending July 31, 2010			
	Budgeted Amount per Hot Dog	**# of Hot Dogs**	**Total**
Revenue	**$2.50**	3,000	$7,500
Variable Costs			
Hot dogs	0.50	3,000	1,500
Buns	0.10	3,000	300
Condiments	0.05	3,000	150
Total Variable Costs	**0.65**		1,950
Contribution Margin			5,550
Fixed Costs			
Part time helper			800
Operating licence			500
Car lease			300
Gas			200
Insurance			50
Total Fixed Costs			1,850
Operating Income			$3,700

FIGURE 10.1

Examine figure 10.1. If everything goes according to plan and you sell exactly 3,000 hot dogs for $2.50 each, you will expect to incur total variable costs of $1,950 (which is $0.65 per hot dog), fixed costs of $1,850 and make an operating income of $3,700. This budget is called a **static budget** because it is prepared for a fixed level of output. A static budget is the typical budget that is prepared prior to the start of the period (i.e. the original budget). Management normally predicts that a certain number of units will be sold for the upcoming period and prepares a budget based on this prediction. For example, in the Delish Hot Dog Stand example, it is prepared under the assumption that you will produce and sell exactly 3,000 hot dogs in July. However, during the month of July, you record *actual* sales and *actual* costs. It turns out that your planned sales were too optimistic and aggressive. In addition, the outdoor hot dog stand suffered sales losses due to heavy rainfall in July. You also experimented with the selling price by slightly changing the price depending on demand on the particular day. All these factors resulted in sales being less than expected. The comparison between estimated and actual performance is illustrated in figure 10.2 below.

Delish Hot Dog Stand Static (Original) Budget Variance Report For the Month Ending July 31, 2010	(A) Budgeted	(B) Actual	(C) = (B) - (A) Variance
Revenue	$7,500	$6,875	-$625
Variable Costs			
Hot dogs	1,500	1,250	-250
Buns	300	250	-50
Condiments	150	125	-25
Total Variable Costs	1,950	1,625	-325
Contribution Margin	5,550	5,250	-300
Fixed Costs			
Part time helper	800	800	-
Operating licence	500	500	-
Car lease	300	300	-
Gas	200	200	-
Insurance	50	50	-
Total Fixed Costs	1,850	1,850	-
Operating Income	$3,700	$3,400	-$300

FIGURE 10.2

In figure 10.2, column A shows the budgeted amounts previously calculated in figure 10.1. Column B shows the actual sales and costs for the month of July. Column C shows the difference between budgeted and actual amounts. This demonstrates a static budget variance because it calculates the differences between the (static) budgeted contribution statement and the actual results. Actual revenue is $625 less than budgeted revenue.

As a responsible manager, you are interested in knowing how this variance came about. You come up with two possible reasons:

1. You did not sell exactly 3,000 hot dogs during July
2. You did not sell each hot dog for an average selling price of $2.50

Note that option 1 relates to volume and option 2 relates to price. If the actual number of hot dogs sold or actual selling price per hot dog is different from the budgeted amounts, it could lead to differences between budgeted and actual revenue. Based on the static budget variance alone (figure 10.2), it is impossible to tell if the difference in revenue is due to a difference in volume or a difference in price. Luckily, managerial accountants have developed a method known as flexible budgeting to solve this problem.

Before illustrating flexible budgets, the following concept should be explained.

Favorable vs. Unfavorable

In chapter 9, positive and negative values were used to analyze the variances between budgeted and actual amounts. However, this method of analysis does not show whether the negative variance is good or bad. A negative variance is not necessarily bad, and a positive variance is not necessarily good. For example, if a company's costs for the current period increased from the previous period, the reported variance is a positive amount. However, incurring more costs is obviously not desired by an organization. As a result, managerial accountants use a labeling scheme to solve this problem.

Variances are labeled as either "F" or "U". "F" stands for "favorable" and "U" stands for "unfavorable". Generally, it is always favorable to have a higher income. Therefore, if a variance leads to an increase in income, it is considered favorable and is labeled with an "F". Similarly, if a variance leads to a reduction in income, it is labeled with a "U" because it is unfavorable to have a lower income.

Figure 10.3 shows the same amounts as figure 10.2, except the variances have been labeled with an "F" or "U" instead of positive or negative signs.

Delish Hot Dog Stand
Static (Original) Budget Variance Report
For the Month Ending July 31, 2010

	Budgeted	Actual	Variance
Revenue	$7,500	$6,875	$625 U
Variable Costs			
Hot dogs	1,500	1,250	250 F
Buns	300	250	50 F
Condiments	150	125	25 F
Total Variable Costs	1,950	1,625	325 F
Contribution Margin	5,550	5,250	300 U
Fixed Costs			
Part time helper	800	800	-
Operating licence	500	500	-
Car lease	300	300	-
Gas	200	200	-
Insurance	50	50	-
Total Fixed Costs	1,850	1,850	-
Operating Income	**$3,700**	**$3,400**	**$300 U**

FIGURE 10.3

Notice that since revenues are less than expected (which has contributed towards a lower income), the $625 difference is considered unfavorable. Also notice that since the total variable costs are lower by $325, they have been labeled with an "F" since lower costs lead to a higher income.

Flexible Budget

To determine the root causes of the variances, we will prepare what is known as a flexible budget. A **flexible budget** is prepared using budgeted selling prices, budgeted costs and *actual* sales volume. This is different from a static budget because a static budget is prepared using budgeted selling prices, budgeted costs and *budgeted* sales volume. In chapter 9, all the budgets discussed were essentially static budgets because a single sales volume figure was budgeted for each period. These budgets were obviously not adjusted for actual results because actual results were not known at the time they were prepared. Once the budgeted period has ended and actual financial results are known, companies can prepare a flexible budget in order to adjust for changes in sales volume. The flexible budget would depict what the static budget would have looked like if the correct quantity of units sold was budgeted. This information is summarized in figure 10.4.

Static Budget	Flexible Budget
Budgeted Selling Prices	Budgeted Selling Prices
Budgeted Costs	Budgeted Costs
Budgeted Volume	*Actual* Volume

FIGURE 10.4

Recall that you had originally budgeted to sell 3,000 hot dogs. However, due to the weather and changes in the selling price, you only ended up selling 2,500 hotdogs. Therefore, the budgeted sales volume was 3,000 but the actual sales volume was 2,500. At the beginning of July, instead of preparing a static budget based on 3,000 hot dogs, a flexible budget could have been prepared based on varying numbers of hot dogs. Figure 10.5 below shows the flexible budget for Delish Hot Dog Stand, based on 2,500, 3,000, 3,500, and 4,000 hot dogs.

Delish Hot Dog Stand Flexible Budget For the Month Ending July 31, 2010					
	Budgeted Amount per Hot dog	Based on 2,500 Hot Dogs	Based on 3,000 Hot Dogs	Based on 3,500 Hot Dogs	Based on 4,000 Hot Dogs
Revenue	**$2.50**	$6,250	$7,500	$8,750	$10,000
Variable Costs					
Hot dogs	0.50	1,250	1,500	1,750	2,000
Buns	0.10	250	300	350	400
Condiments	0.05	125	150	175	200
Total Variable Costs	**0.65**	1,625	1,950	2,275	2,600
Contribution Margin		4,625	5,550	6,475	7,400
Fixed Costs					
Part time helper		800	800	800	800
Operating licence		500	500	500	500
Car lease		300	300	300	300
Gas		200	200	200	200
Insurance		50	50	50	50
Total Fixed Costs		1,850	1,850	1,850	1,850
Operating Income		**$2,775**	**$3,700**	**$4,625**	**$5,550**

FIGURE 10.5

Notice that in the flexible budget, the dollar amounts of revenues and costs are based on budgeted selling prices ($2.50 per hot dog), budgeted variables costs ($0.65 per hot dog), budgeted fixed expenses ($1,850), and different sales volumes (2,500, 3,000, 3,500 and 4,000 hot dogs).

In general, the following formulas can be used to calculate the flexible budget. Note that fixed costs remain the same within the relevant range.

Budgeted Revenues = Actual Sales Volume × Budgeted Price

Budgeted Costs = Budgeted Fixed Costs + (Actual Sales Volume × Budgeted Variable Cost per Unit)

Budgeted Operating Income = Budgeted Revenues – Budgeted Costs

Variance Analysis

Now, there are three reports to work with the static budget, flexible budget and actual results. A comparison of the information from these three reports will help identify and classify variances. This comparison can be found in the performance report provided below (see figure 10.6).

Delish Hot Dog Stand Performance Report For the Month Ending July 31, 2010					
	A	**B**	**C**	**D**	**E**
	Actual (2,500)	**Flexible Budget Variances (A - C)**	**Flexible Budget (2,500)**	**Sales-Volume Variance (C - E)**	**Static Budget (3,000)**
Revenue	$6,875	$625 F	$6,250	$1,250U	$7,500
Variable Costs					
Hot dogs	1,250	0	1,250	250 F	1,500
Buns	250	0	250	50 F	300
Condiments	125	0	125	25 F	150
Total Variable Costs	1,625	0	1,625	325 F	1,950
Contribution Margin	5,250	625 F	4,625	925 U	5,550
Fixed Costs					
Part time helper	800	0	800	0	800
Operating licence	500	0	500	0	500
Car lease	300	0	300	0	300
Gas	200	0	200	0	200
Insurance	50	0	50	0	50
Total Fixed Costs	1,850	0	1,850	0	1,850
Operating Income	$3,400	$625 F	$2,775	$925 U	$3,700

FIGURE 10.6

First, consider the flexible budget column (column C), the sales-volume variance column (column D) and the static budget column (column E). Recall that the static budget was prepared for a sales volume of 3,000 hot dogs, and the flexible budget was created for various levels of output. Because the actual level of output is 2,500 hot dogs, the flexible budget created for a sales volume of 2,500 hot dogs is the one used for the variance analysis. Since both static and flexible budgets use *budgeted* prices and costs, the variances between the flexible budget and static budget are entirely dependent on sales volume. Hence, the variance between the flexible budget and static budget is called the **sales-volume variance**.

Figure 10.6 shows that the sales volume variance for revenue is $1,250 U. This means that if the budgeted selling price is $2.50 and you sold 500 hot dogs less than expected, there will be an unfavorable sales difference of $1,250. Notice that the sales volume variance for operating income is $925 U. This suggests that the overall unfavorable operating income is partially caused by the difference between the actual and budgeted sales volume. This can be further explained by the case facts. Since there was heavy rainfall in July, it would have been less likely for people to go outdoors to enjoy a hot dog.

The next step in analyzing the variance is to compare the actual results (column A) with the flexible budget (column C). The differences between these two columns can be found in column B, which is called the **flexible budget variance**. The flexible budget variance is a useful measure because it provides insight on operating performance. Since the flexible budget (column C) is prepared using the actual sales volume, any differences are due to changes in operations.

For example, the flexible-budget variance for revenue shows that even with 2,500 hot dogs sold, revenue is $625 higher than predicted. If the flexible budget revenue is divided by the number of hot dogs, it results in a budgeted selling price of $2.50 ($6,250 ÷ 2,500). The actual selling price per hot dog is $2.75 ($6,875 ÷ 2,500). In fact, if the favorable flexible budget variance of $625 is divided by the 2,500 hot dogs, the result will be $0.25 per hot dog. Therefore, each hot dog was sold on average for 25 cents more than the budgeted price. Recall that during the month of July, you experimented with the selling price. This increase in selling price may have contributed to the decline in sales units, because the higher the price, the lower the quantity demanded.

So far, $925 of unfavorable sales volume variance is caused by selling 500 hot dogs less than budgeted, and $625 of favorable flexible budget variance is caused by selling each hot dog for 25 cents more than the budgeted price. By adding the two variances, we can get the overall difference between the actual and budgeted performance (i.e. static budget variance).

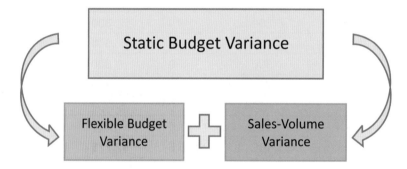

When analyzing only the revenue portion of the flexible budget variance, it is known as the **selling-price variance**. A selling-price variance occurs when there is a difference between the budgeted selling price and the actual selling price. The formula to calculate the selling-price variance is:

Selling-Price Variance = (Actual Selling Price per Unit − Budgeted Selling Price per Unit)
× Actual Units Sold

Using the amounts from our example, we can calculate the selling-price variance to be:

$$\text{Selling-Price Variance} = (\$2.75 - \$2.50) \times 2{,}500 \text{ hot dogs}$$
$$= \$625 \text{ F}$$

This shows that even though 2,500 hot dogs were sold, revenues for Delish were $625 greater than predicted because of a higher selling price.

Now that flexible budget variances have been calculated for revenues, the same can be done for the costs. Refer back to figure 10.6.

Notice that the flexible budget variances for variable costs (column B) are $0. This means that variable costs behaved as they were supposed to, given that only 2,500 hot dogs were sold. The same is true for the fixed expenses.

The differences between the static budget (column E) and actual results (column A) are due to differences in sales volume (sales-volume variance) and selling price (flexible budget variance). From Delish Hot Dog Stand example, the static budget variance for operating income amounted to $300 U (see figure 10.3). The static budget variance can be broken down into a sales-volume variance and a flexible budget variance. In this case, the sales-volume and flexible budget variance for operating income amounted to $925 U and $625 F respectively. The sum of these two variances is $300 U ($925 U + $625 F), which matches the static-budget variance for operating income. Figure 10.7 outlines the relationship between the static-budget variance, sales-volume variance and the flexible-budget variance.

	A	B	C	D	E
Delish Hot Dog Stand Performance Report For the Month Ending July 31, 2010					
	Actual (2,500)	**Flexible Budget Variances (A - C)**	**Flexible Budget (2,500)**	**Sales-Volume Variance (C - E)**	**Static Budget (3,000)**
Revenue	$6,875	$625 F	$6,250	$1,250 U	$7,500
Variable Costs					
Hot dogs	1,250	0	1,250	250 F	1,500
Buns	250	0	250	50 F	300
Condiments	125	0	125	25 F	150
Total Variable Costs	1,625	0	1,625	325 F	1,950
Contribution Margin	5,250	625 F	4,625	925 U	5,550
Fixed Costs					
Part time helper	800	0	800	0	800
Operating licence	500	0	500	0	500
Car lease	300	0	300	0	300
Gas	200	0	200	0	200
Insurance	50	0	50	0	50
Total Fixed Costs	1,850	0	1,850	0	1,850
Operating Income	$3,400	$625 F	$2,775	$925 U	$3,700

FLEXIBLE BUDGET VARIANCE   SALES-VOLUME VARIANCE

STATIC BUDGET VARIANCE

FIGURE 10.7

This particular example focused on the variance between actual and budgeted sales. In other situations, a variance in costs should also be analyzed. For Delish Hot Dog Stand, there were no flexible budget variances with respect to costs.

Let us now address a situation where cost variances are applicable. Remember that the analysis is very similar to revenue variances in that the differences between actual costs and budgeted costs at budgeted quantity are made up of two components, one that is caused by the difference between actual and budgeted volume, and the other is caused by the difference between actual and budgeted price. The concept of standard costing will begin the discussion of cost variances.

Standard Costing: A Manufacturing Example

It is common practice for many manufacturing companies to use standards to help prepare their budgets and to investigate variances. Consider Finoola Inc., a company that manufactures socks.

Finoola's manufacturing process includes costs related to materials (e.g. yarn), labor (e.g. floor workers required to operate high-speed machinery to stitch socks) and manufacturing overhead (e.g. rent, depreciation and utilities). Remember that a standard can refer to the ideal cost of an input. For example, the standard cost of yarn for the above company could be $0.006 per gram. This represents how much each gram of yarn *should* cost. This is an example of a **price standard**. A price standard sets a cost for an operating activity that is considered ideal by the company. Standard costing systems also require the use of **quantity standards**. Quantity standards are set to identify *how much* input *should* be used. For example, a standard quantity of yarn for a pair of socks may be 100 grams. This means that each pair of socks should ideally require 100 grams of yarn at $0.006 per gram. This means that the standard cost of yarn for a pair of socks is $0.60 ($0.006 per gram × 100 grams × 1 pair of socks). This is an example of a standard cost and standard quantity related to direct materials.

Standards can also be developed for direct labor and manufacturing overhead. For example, the company can set the standard direct labor rate of $15 per direct labor hour and the direct labor quantity of 0.05 direct labor hours for each pair of socks. Therefore, the standard direct labor cost for each pair of socks would be $0.75 ($15/direct labor hour × 0.05 direct labor hours).

With regards to manufacturing overhead, assume the company has set a standard price of $20 per direct labor hour and the standard quantity of manufacturing overhead hours for each pair of socks to be 0.05 direct labor hours. Therefore, the standard cost related to manufacturing overhead is $1.00 for each pair of socks ($20/direct labor hour × 0.05 direct labor hours). The sum of the standard costs of direct materials, direct labor and manufacturing overhead for one pair of socks amounts to $2.35. These amounts are summarized in figure 10.8.

	Direct Material	Direct Labor	Manufacturing Overhead	Total
Standard Price	$0.006 per gram	$15 per DLH	$20 per DLH	
Standard Quantity	100 grams	0.05 DLH	0.05 DLH	
Total Cost for each pair of socks	$0.60	$0.75	$1.00	$2.35

FIGURE 10.8

One purpose of developing standards is to compare them to actual operations and eliminate inefficiencies. Other purposes include price setting, budgeting and production planning. Any organization that employs a standard costing system must also keep track of actual costs accurately. This is important when comparing the budgeted amounts (calculated using standard costs) with the actual amounts.

Developing Standards

How do managers at organizations develop standards? Typically, standards are set with the input of many different members of the organization. For example, the operations manager, production manager and upper management may all be involved in setting the standards related to machine operations. With enough discipline and creativity, it is believed that these standards should be achievable. However, setting standards too high might demotivate employees, and thus hurt productivity. At the same time, standards that are too easily achieved will cause budgetary slack. Some organizations rely on past costs to develop standards for upcoming periods. While this may be a quick way of developing standards, it is possible that past costs included inefficiencies, design changes or equipment upgrades that might become a part of standard costs for upcoming periods. It is up to the standard setters to exercise their good judgment when developing standards.

A CLOSER LOOK

When setting performance standards, management must be careful not to motivate the employee to sacrifice important unmeasured performance for measured performance. This is because unmeasured performance can affect the company's financial position in the long-run. For example, if a production manager is evaluated based on their ability to control manufacturing costs, they might avoid incurring the overtime charges necessary to meet delivery commitments to an important customer.

Manufacturing Cost Variances

Previously, the difference between the flexible budget and the actual results was analyzed. However, the flexible budget variance only examined the difference in revenues based on a set quantity of products sold. This analysis is now taken to a more detailed level as the cost portion of the flexible budget variance is separated into Direct Materials, Direct Labor, Variable Overhead and Fixed Overhead Flexible Budget Variances.

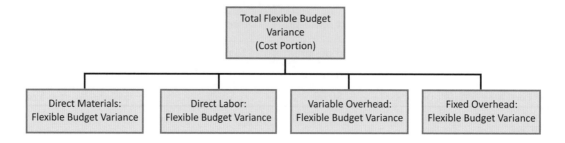

Fixed overhead flexible budget variance will not be discussed as the calculations are beyond the scope of this course. To determine the flexible budget variance for direct materials, direct labor, and variable overhead, the socks manufacturer case will be used. Refer back to figure 10.8 for the standard costs of a pair of socks.

Direct Materials

Suppose actual direct materials costs related to the production of 10,000 pairs of socks amounted to $7,350. Using the standard costs from figure 10.8, the standard (budgeted) direct materials costs can be calculated for the actual output of 10,000 pairs of socks. This amounts to $6,000 of direct materials costs and is calculated by multiplying the actual output of 10,000 pairs by the $0.60 standard cost for direct materials.

At the end of the period, the actual cost of yarn (direct materials) was $0.007 per gram and that 105 grams of yarn was used for each pair of socks. Therefore, the total direct material variance in this case is $1,350 U ($7,350 - $6,000). Given the output of 10,000 pairs, Finoola spent $1,350 more on direct materials than the standard (budgeted) costs. Similar to the revenue variances discussed in the first half of this chapter, cost variances can also be broken down into two components. One component is the **price variance**, which relates to the difference between actual costs and standard costs. The other component is the **efficiency variance**, which looks at the difference between actual quantity and standard quantities for actual output. Normally, direct materials price variance takes into account actual quantity of input *purchased* whereas direct materials efficiency variance takes into account actual quantity of input *used*. However, for simplicity, we will always assume that the actual quantity of input purchased equals actual quantity of input used.

The following formula is used to calculate the price variance for direct materials:

Price Variance DM* = (Actual Price of Input – Standard Price of Input)
                                × Actual Quantity of Input

* Direct Materials

Price Variance (DM) = ($0.007/gram – $0.006/gram) × 10,000 pairs × 105 grams/pair

= $1,050 U

To determine the price variance, the difference between the actual price and the standard price is multiplied by the actual quantity. Since the actual cost of $0.007 per gram is greater than the standard cost of $0.006 per gram, the $1,050 price variance is considered as unfavorable. This is because higher costs would lead to lower income.

The formula to calculate the efficiency variance for direct materials is as follows:

$$\text{Efficiency Variance DM*} = (\text{Actual Quantity of Input} - \text{Standard Quantity for Actual Output}) \times \text{Standard Price}$$

* Direct Materials

$$\text{Efficiency Variance (DM)} = (105 \text{ grams/pair} - 100 \text{ grams/pair}) \times 10{,}000 \text{ pairs} \times \$0.006/\text{gram}$$

$$= \$300 \text{ U}$$

To determine the efficiency variance, the difference between the actual quantity of yarn used and the standard quantity of yarn used (for 10,000 pairs) is multiplied by the budgeted price. Since 105 grams per pair were used instead of the standard 100 grams, the $300 efficiency variance is considered as unfavorable. At this level of output, more materials were used which incurred more costs and lowered the operating income.

The above variance analysis concluded that Finoola experienced a $1,050 unfavorable price variance and a $300 unfavorable efficiency variance. By adding the two variances, the flexible budget variance for direct materials amounted to $1,350 U. This relationship is shown in figure 10.9.

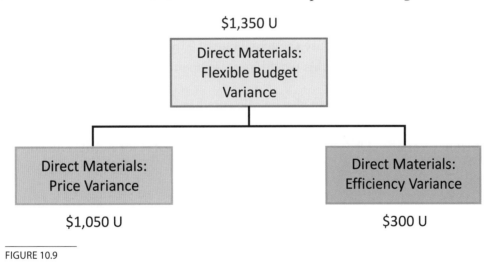

FIGURE 10.9

By identifying the price and efficiency variance, managers can ask informed questions and investigate the cause of these differences. For example, the purchasing manager may question why the yarn costs are $1,050 more than expected. A possible follow-up procedure may include discussing the price increase with their current supplier. Moreover, the $300 of unfavorable efficiency variance can trigger production managers to investigate the manufacturing process and identify where the loss in efficiency occurs. Perhaps, more materials have been wasted or the quality of the materials purchased was not up to par and had to be thrown away. This would therefore increase the amount of materials used in the process.

Direct Labor

The direct labor variance can also be separated into its price and efficiency components. Suppose the actual direct labor costs to manufacture 10,000 pairs of socks amounted to $9,100. Using the standard costs from figure 10.8, the standard (budgeted) direct labor costs for the actual output of 10,000 pairs of socks amount to $7,500 (10,000 pairs × $0.75/pair).

At the end of the period, the actual direct labor rate was $13 per direct labor hour (DLH) as opposed to the standard of $15 per DLH. The actual DLH per pair was 0.07 (as opposed to the standard of 0.05 DLH). The total direct labor variance in this case is $1,600 U ($9,100 - $7,500). The variance is unfavorable because Finoola Inc. spent $1,600 more on direct labor than the budgeted cost for an actual output of 10,000 pairs. The $1,600 unfavorable variance can be broken down into its price variance and efficiency variance. This analysis is very similar to the analysis of direct materials.

The formula to calculate the price variance for direct labor is:

> Price Variance DL* = (Actual Labor Rate – Standard Labor Rate)
>   × Actual Direct Labor Hours Used
>
> * Direct Labor

$$\text{Price Variance (DL)} = (\$13/\text{DLH} - \$15/\text{DLH}) \times 10{,}000 \text{ pairs} \times 0.07 \text{ DLH/pair}$$
$$= \$1{,}400 \text{ F}$$

The $1,400 variance is favorable because the actual rate of $13 is less than the budgeted rate of $15. If all other factors remain the same, this would increase operating income.

The direct labor efficiency variance can also be calculated as follows:

> Efficiency Variance DL* = (Actual DLH – Standard DLH for Actual Output)
>   × Standard Rate
>
> * Direct Labor

$$\text{Efficiency Variance (DL)} = (0.07 \text{ DLH/pair} \times 10{,}000 \text{ pairs} - 0.05 \text{ DLH/pair}$$
$$\times 10{,}000 \text{ pairs}) \times \$15/\text{DLH}$$
$$= (700 \text{ DLH} - 500 \text{ DLH}) \times \$15/\text{DLH}$$
$$= \$3{,}000 \text{ U}$$

The $3,000 variance is unfavorable because the actual labor hours (700 hours) are greater than the budgeted amounts (500 hours). Since more hours are used than necessary to build 10,000 pairs, this would result in lower operating income.

The above analysis has determined that the price and efficiency variance for direct labor are $1,400 F and $3,000 U respectively. The sum of these two variances will result in a direct labor flexible budget variance of $1,600 U. This relationship is illustrated in figure 10.10.

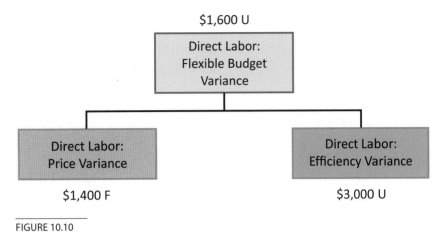

FIGURE 10.10

Variable Manufacturing Overhead

In terms of manufacturing overhead, the calculation of overhead variance is usually limited to variable costs. This is because fixed costs are constant in the relevant range. Variable overhead variances can be separated into the spending variance and the efficiency variance. The **spending variance** holds the actual activity constant to find the variance caused by differences in overhead rates. The **efficiency variance** holds the standard rate constant to find the variance caused by differences in activity.

Assume that in the case of Finoola Inc., the predetermined overhead rate is calculated by using direct labor hours as the cost allocation base. Recall from chapter 3 that cost allocation base refers to the activity used as the basis to allocate manufacturing overhead costs to products. Figure 10.8 shows that the standard price per DLH is $20. The standard DLH per pair is 0.05. Therefore, the total variable overhead cost per pair of socks is $1.00 ($20 per DLH × 0.05 DLH per pair). At the end of the period, it was found that total actual variable manufacturing overhead costs to manufacture 10,000 pairs amounted to $12,600. Using the amounts above, the spending variance and the efficiency variance can be calculated.

The formula for the variable overhead spending variance is as follows:

Variable Overhead Spending Variance = (Actual Rate – Standard Rate) × Actual Quantity

Variable Overhead Spending Variance = ($18/DLH* - $20/DLH) × 700 DLH

= $1,400 F

* $12,600 ÷ 700 DLH = $18/DLH

This variance is favorable because the actual rate of $18 per DLH is less than the budgeted rate of $20. All other factors remaining constant, this would result in lower costs and higher operating income.

The formula for the variable overhead efficiency variance is as follows:

$$\text{Variable Overhead Efficiency Variance} = (\text{Actual Quantity} - \text{Standard Quantity for Actual Output}) \times \text{Standard Rate}$$

$$\text{Variable Overhead Efficiency Variance} = (700\ \text{DLH} - 500\ \text{DLH}) \times \$20/\text{DLH}$$

$$= \$4,000\ \text{U}$$

This variance is unfavorable because the actual quantity of hours used (700 DLH) is greater than budgeted (500 DLH).

The variances calculated above conclude a favorable spending variance of $1,400 and an unfavorable efficiency variance of $4,000. The sum of these two variances is the flexible budget variance for variable overhead (i.e. the overall difference between the actual and standard variable overhead costs.) This relationship is illustrated in figure 10.11.

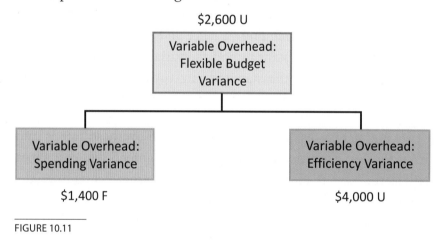

FIGURE 10.11

In order to properly plan and control, managers need to understand the reasons behind the variances. Compared to direct labor and direct materials, understanding the manufacturing overhead variance is relatively more complicated. This is because the variance can reflect inefficiencies in the cost allocation base rather than variable overhead itself. In this example, since overhead is based on direct labor hours, the 200 additional hours used resulted in an unfavorable overhead efficiency variance of $4,000. At the same time, the actual rate of overhead was only $18, compared to the budgeted amount of $20. Therefore, the unfavorable flexible budget variance is caused by using more direct labor hours and not by the overhead rate.

Variable manufacturing overhead is also made up of many different costs. This means that it will be affected by several other factors, such as indirect materials, indirect labor, prices for energy, etc. A manager would need to know *where* the source of the variance is in order to improve it for the future.

Note on Variance Analysis

It is important to realize that not all favorable variances are good, and not all unfavorable variances are bad for the organization. It is possible to create favorable variances by hiring incompetent supervisors at lower wages, or purchasing poor-quality materials at cheaper prices. However, this would be detrimental for the organization because incompetent leadership and inferior quality products will eventually lead to decreased profits, lower morale or a hurt company reputation. Thus, managers should focus on keeping quality at the desired level and reducing the amount of waste and spoilage in their system.

Standard Costing: A Service Example

Michael Stott is the manager of Merv's Telemarketing Services which provides telemarketing for various corporate clients. The company employs ten people who are constantly on the phone calling potential customers on behalf of the clients. For each call an employee makes, Merv's Telemarketing will bill the client $1.50. At the end of 2010, a budget was made for the first six months of 2011. Michael has standard prices and quantity for direct labor and variable overhead.

	Direct Labor	Variable Overhead
Standard Quantity	0.05 DLH*	0.05 DLH
Standard Price	$10.00 per DLH	$2.80 per DLH
Total cost per call	$0.50 per call	$0.14 per call

*DLH = Direct Labor Hours

Since each employee should work 7.5 hours a day, five days a week, over the six months the employees should have worked for 9,000 hours (7.5 hrs/day × 5 days/week × 4 weeks/month × 6 months × 10 employees). At $10 per hour, total labor costs should be $90,000. Also, each employee is supposed to make 20 calls per hour, so there should be 180,000 calls made in the six month period. The variable overhead covers items such as the cost of the phone bill and maintenance on the phone system. The overhead is applied based on direct labor hours, so it should be $25,200 (9,000 hours × $2.80) over six months. The company budgets fixed costs for $40,300. These costs include rent, insurance, electricity and manager's salary.

Based on the above information, Michael was able to create the following static budget (Figure 10.12).

Merv's Telemarketing Services Static Budget For the 6 Months Ending June 30, 2011		
	Per Call	Static Budget
Revenue	$1.50	$270,000
Variable Costs		
Direct Labor	0.50	90,000
Variable Overhead	0.14	25,200
Total Variable Costs	0.64	115,200
Contribution Margin		154,800
Fixed Costs		
Rent		12,000
Insurance		900
Hydro		2,400
Manager's Salary		25,000
Total Fixed Costs		40,300
Operating Income		$114,500

FIGURE 10.12

On June 30, 2011, Michael prepared a performance report to analyze revenue and costs. He noticed fixed costs did not change; however there are a number of differences from the original budget.

- The 10 employees worked 9,450 hours over the six months
- An average of 21 calls per hour were made
- Clients were billed at $1.30 per call
- The company's total revenue amounted to $257,985
- The 10 employees were paid $100,265 over the six months
- Total variable overhead was $23,247
- Rent, insurance, hydro and manager's salary remained at $12,000, $900, $2,400 and $25,000 respectively

Michael uses the actual results and the standard (or budgeted) prices to create a flexible budget. The flexible budget is created using budgeting prices and actual volume. Actual volume was 198,450 calls (9,450 hours × 21 calls per hour). The static budget, actual results and flexible budget are shown in figure 10.13.

Merv's Telemarketing Services Performance Report For the Six Months Ending June 30, 2011			
	Actual	Flexible Budget	Static Budget
Revenue	$257,985	$297,675[1]	$270,000
Variable Costs			
Direct Labor	100,265	99,225[2]	90,000
Variable Overhead	23,247	27,783[3]	25,200
Total Variable Costs	123,512	127,008	115,200
Contribution Margin	134,473	170,667	154,800
Fixed Costs			
Rent	12,000	12,000	12,000
Insurance	900	900	900
Hydro	2,400	2,400	2,400
Manager's Salary	25,000	25,000	25,000
Total Fixed Costs	40,300	40,300	40,300
Operating Income	$94,173	$130,367	$114,500

[1]$1.50 \times 198,450$
[2]$0.50 \times 198,450$
[3]$0.14 \times 198,450$

FIGURE 10.13

Michael's analysis will begin by looking at the flexible budget variance and the sales-volume variance.

Merv's Telemarketing Services Performance Report For the Six Months Ending June 30, 2011					
	Actual	Flexible Budget Variance	Flexible Budget	Sales-Volume Variance	Static Budget
Revenue	$257,985	$39,690 U	$297,675	$27,675 F	$270,000
Variable Costs					
Direct Labor	100,265	1,040 U	99,225	9,225 U	90,000
Variable Overhead	23,247	4,536 F	27,783	2,583 U	25,200
Total Variable Costs	123,512	3,496 F	127,008	11,808 U	115,200
Contribution Margin	134,473	36,194 U	170,667	15,867 F	154,800
Fixed Costs					
Rent	12,000	0	12,000	0	12,000
Insurance	900	0	900	0	900
Hydro	2,400	0	2,400	0	2,400
Manager's Salary	25,000	0	25,000	0	25,000
Total Fixed Costs	40,300	0	40,300	0	40,300
Operating Income	$94,173	$36,194 U	$130,367	$15,867 F	$114,500

FIGURE 10.14

The sales-volume variance in figure 10.14 measures changes in volume and shows a favorable variance of $15,867. If Merv's Telemarketing had been able to keep the budgeted sales price and costs, the increase in hours worked and the increase in calls per hour would have created a favorable variance.

The flexible budget variance measures operating performance and shows an unfavorable variance of $36,194. This is due to variances in selling price, direct labor cost and variable overhead cost. Since there is no change in fixed costs, there is no fixed overhead costs variance.

The overall static budget can be calculated as follows:

$$\text{Static Budget Variance} = \text{Flexible Budget Variance} + \text{Sales-Volume Variance}$$
$$= \$36,194\ U + \$15,867\ F$$
$$= \$20,327\ U$$

Michael now prepares a detailed flexible budget to measure the selling price variance and the price and efficiency variances of direct labor and variable overhead. In Michael's case, the flexible budget variances can be a result of:

- Selling price is not $1.50 per call
- Employees not getting paid $10 per direct labor hour
- Employees not working the expected 9,000 hours for the six months
- Variable overhead not being charged at $2.80 per direct labor hour

The selling price variance will measure the variance between the budgeted selling price and the actual selling price. Since actual sales were $257,985 and sales volume was 198,450 calls, the actual selling price was actually $1.30 per call ($257,985 ÷ 198,450 calls).

$$\text{Selling Price Variance} = \text{(Actual Selling Price per Call - Budgeted Selling Price per Call)} \times \text{Actual Amount of Calls}$$
$$= (\$1.30 - \$1.50) \times 198,450 \text{ calls}$$
$$= \$39,690\ U$$

Since the actual selling price of $1.30 was lower than the budgeted price of $1.50, this causes an unfavorable variance of $39,690. This figure also shows up as the variance in revenue in the flexible budget column of figure 10.14. Michael realizes that the decrease in selling price was necessary to keep their existing clients and remain competitive in the marketplace. The price change occurred at the beginning of the year, so Michael was expecting an unfavorable variance.

For direct labor, Michael paid his employees $100,265 for 9,450 direct labor hours. As a result, employees were being paid $10.61 per hour ($100,265 ÷ 9,450). The formula to determine the direct labor price variance is given below.

$$\text{Direct Labor Price Variance} = \text{(Actual Labor Rate - Standard Labor Rate)} \times \text{Actual Labor Hours Used}$$

$$= (\$10.61 - \$10.00) \times 9,450 \text{ hours}$$

$$= \$5,765 \text{ U}$$

Since the actual hourly rate of $10.61 per hour was higher than the standard of $10 per hour, this causes an unfavorable price variance of $5,765 U. After contemplating reasons for the price variance, Michael realizes that two employees had quit during the last six months and Michael had to hire temporary workers through an agency which cost him more than $10 per hour. This explains the unfavorable price variance.

The next step is to identify the direct labor efficiency variance. The efficiency variance reveals the dollar effect of working too many or too few hours, and whether the change in hours was efficient.

$$\text{Direct Labor Efficiency Variance} = \text{(Actual DLH - Standard DLH for Actual Output)} \times \text{Standard Rate}$$

$$= [9,450 \text{ hours} - (0.05 \text{ DLH} \times 198,450 \text{ calls})] \times \$10 \text{ per hour}$$

$$= \$4,725 \text{ F}$$

Michael's employees were supposed to work for 9,000 hours, but during the last six months they worked for 9,450 hours. Michael realized when the budget was created, he did not consider the overtime needed to meet the demands of several picky clients. Although the increase in hours would have translated into an unfavorable variance, the employees were more efficient than what was budgeted for. They made an average of 21 calls per hour instead of only 20. This ends up providing a favorable efficiency variance of $4,725.

Therefore, the total direct labor flexible budget variance can be calculated.

$$\text{Direct Labor Flexible Budget Variance} = \text{Direct Labor Price Variance} + \text{Direct Labor Efficiency Variance}$$

$$= \$5,765 \text{ U} + \$4,725 \text{ F}$$

$$= \$1,040 \text{ U}$$

Notice that the direct labor flexible budget variance is the same variance in direct labor in the flexible budget variance column in figure 10.14.

Michael now turns his attention to the variable overhead spending variance.

$$\text{Variable Overhead Spending Variance} = \text{(Actual Rate - Standard Rate)} \times \text{Actual Quantity}$$

$$= [(\$23,247 \div 9,450 \text{ hours}) - \$2.80] \times 9,450 \text{ hours}$$

$$= \$3,213 \text{ F}$$

Michael investigates the variable overhead and discovers that the phone company dropped the rates charged to Merv's Telemarketing with a special package for long-distance calls. This decrease in the phone bill has contributed to the favorable spending variance of $3,213.

The other portion of variable overhead is the efficiency variance.

Variable Overhead   =   (Actual Quantity - Standard Quantity for Actual Output) ×
Efficiency Variance   Standard Rate

                      =   [(9,450 hours - (0.05 DLH × 198,450 calls)] × $2.80 per DLH

                      = $1,323 F

Merv's Telemarketing had a new phone system installed at the beginning of the year. This new phone system was more robust than their old one and required less maintenance and repair. This newer phone system decreased down-time and increased the efficiency of the employees, thus helping to explain the favorable efficiency variance.

Therefore, the total variable overhead flexible budget can be calculated.

Variable Overhead Flexible   =   Variable Overhead Spending Variance +
Budget Variance   Variable Overhead Efficiency Variance

                               = $3,213 F + $1,323 F

                               = $4,536 F

Notice that the variable overhead flexible budget variance is the same variance in variable overhead in the flexible budget variance column in figure 10.14.

Recall that Michael's flexible budget is actually made up of three detailed budgets: selling price variance, direct labor flexible budget variance and variable overhead flexible budget variance. To prove this, Michael adds all three variance together.

Flexible Budget Variance   =   Selling Price Variance + Direct Labor Flexible Budget
                                   Variance + Variable Overhead Flexible Budget Variance

                             = $39,690 U + $1,040 U + $4,536 F

                             = $36,194 U

Notice that the flexible budget variance is the same figure that is the variance in operating income in the flexible budget variance column in figure 10.14. A summary of how the flexible budgets relate to each other is shown in figure 10.15.

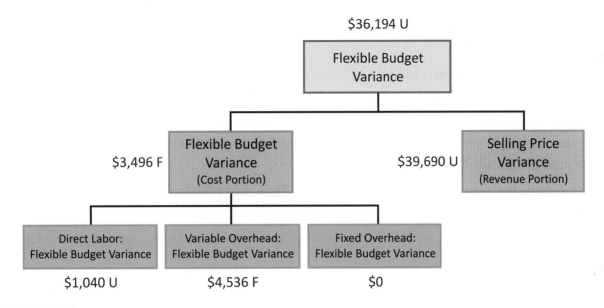

FIGURE 10.15

As you can see, the variance calculations for both manufacturing and service industries are very similar. Also, regardless of the industry, managers are encouraged to not only compare their expectations with the actual performance, but understand the root cause of these differences.

Ethical Considerations

It is unethical for managers to compromise the quality and safety of a product to make a particular variance more favorable. For instance, consider Marcy Skin Care Company (MSC). One of the products manufactured by MSC is a 2-in-1 shampoo/conditioner. There is no price difference for one of the chemicals used in the shampoo/conditioner (i.e. the actual price of input equals the standard price of input). However, the manager of the product line wants to impress his boss by creating a favorable price variance.

To create the favorable price variance, the manager will discontinue the use of the current chemical and buy a similar chemical from another supplier at a much lower price. However, the manager understands the new chemical poses a slight health risk. It can cause skin rashes if it is used in an extremely high water temperature.

The manager decides to use the new chemical in the product and convinces himself that since no one takes showers in such high temperatures, there is no true health risk. Even though the material price variance is considered "favorable", the manager's decision was unethical since the health of consumers is now put at risk. A high internal standard on the safety of materials should be in place, in order to ensure that this type of unethical behavior is not practiced.

In Summary

↪ **Management control** is the process by which managers set targets for performance, measure actual performance and address differences between actual and budgeted performance.

↪ At different points throughout the fiscal period, managers compare budgets with actual results. This process of analyzing *variances* that occur between budgeted amounts and actual amounts is called **management by exception**.

↪ A **static budget** is prepared using budgeted selling prices, budgeted costs and *budgeted* sales volume.

↪ A **flexible budget** is prepared using budgeted selling prices, budgeted costs and *actual* sales volume.

↪ The difference between the flexible budget and static budget is called the **sales-volume variance**.

↪ The difference between the flexible budget and actual result is called the **flexible budget variance**.

↪ **Selling-price variance** is another way of analyzing the revenue variance between the flexible budget and actual results.

↪ Many companies set **standards** in order to prepare their budgets and investigate variances. **Price standard** refers to an ideal cost for an operating activity, and **quantity standard** refers to an ideal quantity of input that should be used in production.

↪ Flexible budget variance can be broken down into direct materials, direct labor, variable overhead, and fixed overhead variances.

↪ Direct material and direct labor flexible budget variances can be broken down into price and efficiency variances. **Price variance** relates to the difference between actual price and standard costs. **Efficiency variance** relates to the difference between actual quantity and standard quantities for actual output.

↪ Variable overhead flexible budget variance can be broken down into spending and efficiency variance. **Spending variance** holds actual activity constant to find the variance caused by differences in overhead rates. **Efficiency variance** holds the standard rate constant to find the variance caused by differences in consumption of units in the base.

Review Exercise

Gerald Smith is the owner of GS Company. The company manufactures winter tuques and sells them to various department stores. Based on GS's 2010 static budget, it expected to produce and sell 160,000 tuques, use 440,000 ounces of direct materials, use 8,000 direct labor hours (DLH), spend $250,000 on variable manufacturing overhead and spend $400,000 on fixed manufacturing overhead. Variable manufacturing overhead costs are calculated based on number of direct labor hours. Each tuque is expected to sell for $15.65. The following information shows standard quantities, standard prices and standard unit costs for direct materials, direct manufacturing labor and manufacturing overhead.

	Direct Materials	Direct Labor	Manufacturing Overhead
Standard Quantity	2.75 ounce	0.05 DLH	0.05 DLH
Standard Price	$0.55 per ounce	$25.00 per DLH	$31.25 per DLH

To prepare the static and flexible budgets, GS used the standard amounts to determine variable costs. By the end of the year, the company actually produced and sold 159,000 units for $16.25 each. GS purchased and used 450,000 ounces of direct materials, at a cost of $0.50 per ounce. Direct labor hours used to produce the 159,000 tuques were 9,000. Direct labor cost was applied at the rate of $30.00 per DLH. Total actual variable manufacturing overhead amounted to $245,000 and total actual fixed manufacturing overhead amounted to $400,000.

Required:

Determine the following variances:

1. Static Budget Variance
2. Flexible Budget Variance (Assume Fixed Manufacturing Flexible Budget Overhead is $400,000)
3. Sales Volume Variance
4. Selling-Price Variance
5. Direct Material Price Variance
6. Direct Material Efficiency Variance
7. Direct Material Variance
8. Direct Labor Price Variance
9. Direct Labor Efficiency Variance
10. Direct Labor Variance
11. Variable Manufacturing Overhead Spending Variance
12. Variable Manufacturing Overhead Efficiency Variance
13. Variable Manufacturing Overhead Variance

Review Exercise – Answer

Part 1

Actual

= Sales Budget – [Direct Materials Budget + Direct Labor Budget + Variable Manufacturing Overhead Budget + Fixed Manufacturing Overhead Budget]

= ($159,000 × $16.25) – [($0.50 × 450,000) + ($30 × 9,000) + $245,000 + $400,000]

= $2,583,750 – [$225,000 + $270,000 + $245,000 + $400,000]

= $1,443,750

Static Budget

= Sales Budget – [Direct Materials Budget + Direct Labor Budget + Variable Manufacturing Overhead Budget + Fixed Manufacturing Overhead Budget]

= (160,000 × $15.65) – [($0.55 × 440,000) + ($25 × 8,000) + $250,000 + $400,000]

= $2,504,000 - [$242,000 + $200,000 + $250,000 + $400,000]

= $1,412,000

Static Budget Variance

= Actual – Static Budget = $1,443,750 - $1,412,200 = $31,750 F

Part 2

Flexible Budget

= (159,000 × $15.65) – [($0.55 × 2.75 ounces) × 159,000] – [($25 × 0.05 DLH) × 159,000] – [($31.25 × 0.05 DLH) × 159,000] - $400,000

= $1,400,675

Flexible Budget Variance

= Actual – Flexible Budget

= $1,443,750 - $1,400,675

= $43,075 F

Part 3

Sales Volume Variance

= Static Budget Variance – Flexible Budget Variance

= $31,750 F - $43,075 F

= $11,325 U

Part 4

Selling – Price Variance

= (Actual Selling Price per Unit – Budgeted Selling Price per Unit) × Actual Units Sold

= ($16.25 - $15.65) × 159,000

= $95,400 F

Part 5

Direct Material Price Variance

= (Actual Price of Input – Standard Price of Input) × Actual Quantity of Input

= ($0.50 – $0.55) × 450,000

= $22,500 F

Part 6

Direct Material Efficiency Variance

= (Actual Quantity of Input – Standard Quantity for Actual Output) × Standard Price

= [450,000 – (2.75 × 159,000)] × $0.55

= [450,000 – 437,250] × $0.55

= $7,012.50 U

Part 7

Direct Material Variance

= Price Variance + Efficiency Variance

= $22,500 F + $7,012.50 U

=$15,487.50 F

Part 8

Direct Labor Price Variance

= (Actual Labor Rate – Standard Labor Rate) × Actual DLH Used

= ($30.00 – $25.00) × 450,000

= $45,000 U

Part 9

Direct Labor Efficiency Variance

$$= (\text{Actual DLH} - \text{Standard DLH for Actual Input}) \times \text{Standard Labor Rate}$$
$$= [9,000 - (0.05 \times 159,000)] \times \$25$$
$$= [9,000 - 7,950] \times \$25$$
$$= \$26,250 \text{ U}$$

Part 10

Direct Labor Variance

$$= \text{DL Price Variance} + \text{DL Efficiency Variance}$$
$$= \$45,000 \text{ U} + \$26,250 \text{ U}$$
$$= \$71,250 \text{ U}$$

Part 11

Variable Manufacturing Overhead Spending Variance

$$= (\text{Actual Rate} - \text{Standard Rate}) \times \text{Actual Quantity}$$
$$= [(\$245,000 \div 9,000) - \$31.25] \times 9,000 \text{ DLH}$$
$$= \$36,250 \text{ F}$$

Part 12

Variable Manufacturing Overhead Efficiency Variance

$$= (\text{Actual Quantity} - \text{Standard Quantity for Actual Input}) \times \text{Standard Rate}$$
$$= [9,000 - (0.05 \times 159,000)] \times \$31.25$$
$$= [9,000 - 7,950] \times \$31.25$$
$$= \$32,812.50 \text{ U}$$

Part 13

Variable Manufacturing Overhead Variance

$$= \text{DL Price Variance} + \text{DL Efficiency Variance}$$
$$= \$36,250 \text{ F} + \$32,812.50 \text{ U}$$
$$= \$3,437.50 \text{ F}$$

Chapter 11

RELEVANT COST AND DECISION MAKING

LEARNING OUTCOMES:

❶ Distinguish between relevant and irrelevant costs

❷ Define sunk costs

❸ Describe differential and opportunity costs

❹ Show how a manager can decide whether to keep or drop a product or service

❺ Identify the costs that will affect a make or buy decision

❻ Discuss the various costs that manager should consider when accepting a special order

❼ Demonstrate how scarce resources can be allocated

Relevant and Irrelevant Costs: A Personal Example

Before addressing the topic of relevant costs in the world of business, it is useful to understand the meaning of certain key concepts from a personal point of view.

Assume you currently own a 2001 Honda Civic and are offered a great deal on the 2007 model that has additional features. While owning a new car sounds attractive, you need to consider the financial implications of buying the car.

The initial financial decision involves separating all the costs relating to the purchasing decision. The following is a list of costs that are related to the decision to purchase the car:

2007 Honda Civic Purchase Price	$10,000
Parking at Apartment (annual)	600
Insurance (annual)	1,800
Certification for Old Car	100
Advertising to Sell Old Car	200
Gas Consumption (annual)	5,000
Licensing (annual)	100

FIGURE 11.1

Let us now discuss whether these costs can impact your decision making.

You have identified that the new model will use the same engine as your current car, which means there will be no change in gas consumption. Next, you have contacted your auto insurance company, and they have confirmed that the annual car insurance will remain the same. You also note that regardless the vehicle you are driving, the annual licensing fee stays at $100 and you will pay $600 for parking at your apartment. Due to the fact that your decision to purchase a new car will not impact these costs, they are referred to as **irrelevant costs** and can be ignored in the decision. Irrelevant costs are costs that will not change regardless of which decision is made.

After some research, you have noted that you can sell your old car for $4,000. This $4,000 can be viewed as **relevant revenue**, because you would only receive this amount if you decide to replace your old vehicle. Net relevant revenue is defined as revenue that differs between alternatives in a specific decision. If you do not purchase the new car, then you would not sell your old car and your revenue would be $0. If you do purchase the new car, then you would sell your old car and your revenue would be $4,000. The net relevant revenue in this case would be $4,000 ($4,000 - $0). The net relevant revenue, or the difference in revenue, can be referred to as **differential revenue**.

At the same time, the purchasing decision requires you to spend $200 to advertise the old car for sale, spend $100 for certification and pay $10,000 for the 2007 Honda Civic. Since these are the only additional costs that you will incur if you were to buy the new car, they are the only ones that are relevant to your decision. In other words, **relevant costs** are costs that differ between the alternatives in a specific decision. In this case, total relevant costs amount to $10,300 ($10,000 + $100 + $200). The net relevant cost, or the difference in cost, can be referred to as **differential cost.**

Figure 11.2 summarizes the irrelevant and relevant items for the purchasing decision:

	Irrelevant Costs	Relevant Costs	Relevant Revenue
Selling Old Car – 2001 Honda Civic			$4,000
2007 Honda Civic Purchase Price		$10,000	
Parking (annual)	$600		
Insurance (annual)	1,800		
Certification		100	
Advertising to sell old car		200	
Gas (annual)	5,000		
Licensing (annual)	100		

FIGURE 11.2

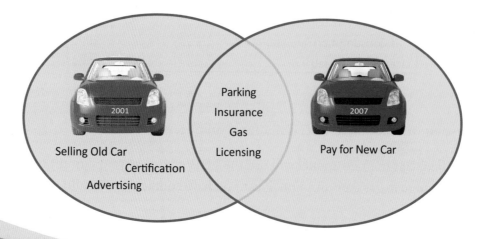

There is also the **opportunity cost** to consider. Opportunity cost is the value of the next best alternative that you have foregone in order to accept a particular alternative. Therefore, if you do not buy the car, you can use the money you would have spent elsewhere. Some options can include investing, traveling or obtaining further education. As a result, your opportunity cost can either be the return from investing, the experience from traveling or the knowledge obtained from school. Note that opportunity cost is only the one best alternative, and these costs sometimes cannot easily be quantified.

Ultimately, the decision to purchase the 2007 Honda Civic and sell the old 2001 Honda Civic will cost you $6,300 ($4,000 - $10,630), plus whatever value can be attributed to the opportunity costs. The purpose of the car example is to demonstrate the importance of identifying the difference between irrelevant and relevant costs to your decision.

Sunk Costs

Sunk costs are costs that have already been incurred and can never be recovered. Sunk costs are therefore irrelevant to a decision. For example, consider a meal you ordered in a restaurant but found that you did not care for the taste of it. It would not be fair to send it back since the meal was prepared to standard. You can try to eat the meal despite the taste, give it to someone else at the table that may enjoy it or order another meal. Whatever your decision, the cost of the meal is a sunk cost and cannot be recovered.

Sunk costs are those costs that are totally irretrievable and, therefore, should be considered irrelevant to future decision making. This term emanates from the oil industry. The decision to abandon or operate an oil well is made based on the amount of oil expected from the well and the profits derived from the oil, rather than how much money was spent in drilling it. Sunk cost is also sometimes referred to as embedded cost, prior year cost, stranded cost or sunk capital.

Businesses will often have sunk costs. For example, you pay for the services of a consultant whose advice was not as useful as you expected. You can either continue using his advice because you feel that it would be wrong to waste it, or regard the cost as a bad experience and consider it as a sunk cost. Whatever your decision, the cost is sunk. The money is not recoverable and should have no bearing on how you move forward.

It can be difficult to ignore sunk costs, especially when large figures are involved. Consider the following scenario. A company has an old piece of machinery that was purchased 12 years ago for $2 million. It has been breaking down lately, so the company spends $500,000 repairing the machine. The total of $2.5 million is a sunk cost. Towards the end of the repair job, it is discovered that a major component is nearly worn out and will need to be replaced. Replacing this major component will cost $1.2 million, but will return the machine to proper working order and it will work like new. If the component is not replaced, the machine would be worthless. Management has found that a brand new machine costs $3 million and would work just as well as the old machine, once the old one is repaired. Should the company repair the old machine or purchase the new machine?

Using the idea that sunk costs are irrelevant, the company will only consider future costs and compare the two options. Repairing the old machine will only cost $1.2 million, while the new machine will cost $3 million. Since repair is $1.8 million cheaper, this is the option the company chooses. If you take all the cost relating to the old machine into account, the company has spent a total of $3.7 million ($2.5 million + $1.2 million).

Although this sounds like a lot of money, consider the alternative if sunk costs are considered in the decision making process. If sunk costs are considered, the company would compare total costs of the old machine of $3.7 million with the cost of the new machine, which is $3 million. Based on this comparison, the company will purchase the new machine because it is cheaper. Unfortunately the $2.5 million in sunk costs cannot be recovered, so the company spends a total of $5.5 million on the machines ($2.5 million + $3 million).

Comparing the two results, an overall expenditure of $3.7 million on the machine is more desirable than an overall expenditure of $5.5 million. Note that the difference between the two overall expenditures is equal to $1.8 million. That is also the difference between the options when sunk costs are ignored. As a result, the easiest and correct way is to compare the cost of the major component with the cost of the new machine.

IN THE REAL WORLD

When one makes an investment with no hope of success, it is common to want to continue with the project even when it does not make economic sense. One can rationalize the continuance of the project for all sorts of reasons such as: "I can't stop now; otherwise what I've invested so far will be lost" or "My pride is at stake".

To continue to invest in a hopeless project is irrational. Of course, when a project has no hope of success, it is simply a fallacy to imagine that "one day it will come right so let's continue pursuing the idea". This type of fallacy is also sometimes referred to as the Concorde Fallacy. The term originated from the continuous funding in the supersonic transport jet, which was jointly created by the governments of France and Britain in the late 1960s and early 1970s. Although it was apparent that the aircraft would not be generating any profit, France and England continued to invest in the project. It was not until 2003 that the Concorde was retired. However, by then, they had already spent a large amount of money that they could not recover.

Relevant Costs and Decision Making in Business

The rest of this chapter will focus on relevant costs in the decision making process. When a manager is required to make a decision, it is important to compare the costs with the benefits of each decision. Suppose a company is considering purchasing a new piece of equipment. Management should consider the costs of getting this equipment and determine how the company can benefit from purchasing this asset. If the costs outweigh the benefits, then the company should reject the project.

Although this section will put more emphasis on the financial effects of these decisions, managers must also take into account the qualitative considerations. For example:

- A firm producing websites may find that it is more cost effective to outsource their programming to India. However, despite the fact that it is more expensive to use local labor, they may make a strategic decision to forfeit the labor cost in favor of quick service and higher quality.
- After conducting a sound relevant cost analysis, a factory may choose to continue making an unprofitable product in order to capture the marketing benefits of maintaining a full product line.

Most business managers face decisions that are based on the relevant cost principles. Some of these decisions include:

1. Keep or drop a product or service
2. Make or buy a product
3. Accept or reject a special order
4. How to allocate a scarce resource – the product mix decision

We will address each of these concepts separately.

Keep or Drop a Product or Service

Organizations are often faced with decisions relating to whether to keep or abandon products whose profitability is declining. These types of decisions involve considering strategic, cost cutting and human resource objectives in an organization. As mentioned earlier, our focus is only on the financial aspects of the relevant cost examples that we consider. Therefore, the decision to keep or drop a product or service will depend mainly on the impact on operating income.

Keep or Drop: A Service Business Example

Paula's Beauty Spa offers three types of services to its customers: hair dressing, massages and facial treatments.

Until three years ago, her salon was very profitable while offering hair dressing services. However, once she expanded the store space and offered massages and facial treatment, she noticed that her profits were eroding. She was confused by this, especially since her gross revenues had increased substantially. She had her accountants complete an analysis on her behalf. In order to properly evaluate the performance of each service, the accountants prepared a segmented contribution margin statement (figure 11.3). Note that each service segment incurs its own fixed costs.

Paula's Beauty Spa Segmented Contribution Income Statement For the Year Ending December 31, 2010				
	Hair Dressing	Massage	Facial Treatment	Total
Revenue*	$250,000	$130,000	$100,000	$480,000
Less: Variable Costs*	140,000	100,000	50,000	290,000
Contribution Margin	110,000	30,000	50,000	190,000
Less: Fixed Costs	90,000	20,000	60,000	170,000
Operating Income	$20,000	$10,000	($10,000)	$20,000

*Based on number of customers

FIGURE 11.3

As Paula examines the information, she immediately notices that the facial treatment service is providing a contribution margin of $50,000 but an operating loss of $10,000. Thus, dropping the service will mean Paula will lose the contribution margin and save the $60,000 in fixed costs.

However, it is also important to consider the complementary effects of dropping the facial treatment service. Since past performances indicate that facial treatment customers often get hair treatment or a massage during the same visit, Paula predicts that dropping this service will reduce sales volume for the hair dressing and massage segments by 5% and 10% respectively. This decrease in sales volume will reduce the amount of revenue, variable costs and contribution margin for the remaining services. For example, the revenue for the hair dressing segment will now become $237,500 ($250,000 × [1 - 0.05]). Figure 11.4 shows the updated segmented contribution income statement if the company decides to stop offering the facial treatments.

Paula's Beauty Spa Segmented Contribution Income Statement For the Year Ending December 31, 2010			
	Hair Dressing	Massage	Total
Revenue	$237,500	$117,000	$354,500
Less: Variable Costs	133,000	90,000	223,000
Contribution Margin	104,500	27,000	131,500
Less: Fixed Costs	90,000	20,000	110,000
Operating Income	$14,500	$7,000	$21,500

FIGURE 11.4

Since the decision to keep or drop a service will depend mainly on the impact of the operating income, figure 11.5 compares the contribution margins for the two decisions. The table shows that Paula should drop the facial treatment service because overall operating income will increase by $1,500 ($21,500 - $20,000).

Paula's Beauty Spa **Contribution Income Statement** **For the Year Ending December 31, 2010**		
	Keep **Facial Treatment**	**Drop** **Facial Treatment**
Revenue	$480,000	$354,500
Less: Variable Costs	290,000	223,000
Contribution Margin	190,000	131,500
Less: Fixed Costs	170,000	110,000
Operating Income	$20,000	$21,500

FIGURE 11.5

$1,500
Increase in Operating Income

The above analysis is presented in comparative form in order to develop the analysis clearly for instructional purposes. Another form which focuses directly on the incremental effects can be used to develop and communicate the keep or drop analysis more quickly and conveniently. Figure 11.6 shows the incremental analysis approach to the above problem.

Lost Contribution Margin - Facial Treatment	($50,000)
Cost Savings - Facial Treatment's Fixed Costs	60,000
Decrease in Sales Volume:	
Hair Dressing: $110,000 × 5%	(5,500)
Massage: $30,000 × 10%	(3,000)
Incremental Effect	$1,500

FIGURE 11.6

It should be noted that in this particular example of the keep or drop decision, each service segment incurs its own fixed costs. However, in reality, the fixed cost for each segment may be comprised of two components: fixed costs that can be eliminated if each segment is closed (segment fixed costs) and ongoing fixed costs that can only be eliminated if the entire company is shut down (company-wide fixed costs). In such a case, when dropping a segment, the segment fixed costs are eliminated (relevant) and the company-wide fixed costs remain with the company and are allocated among the remaining segments of the company (irrelevant).

The Make or Buy Decision

In a **make or buy decision**, also known as the **outsourcing** decision, an organization considers whether to make a good or purchase it from an outside supplier. Outsourcing refers to buying goods and services from outside vendors. For instance, Kodak prefers to produce its own film, but it outsources its data processing to IBM. Many automobile manufacturers like Toyota rely on outside vendors to supply some auto parts, but choose to manufacture other parts internally. A company often chooses to make a product or provide a service if they feel its core activities add significant value to it. If a product or service is less essential, then the company will strongly consider outsourcing the product or service to an outside vendor.

IN THE REAL WORLD

Many companies have outsourced a number of job functions to India, China and other countries in efforts to cut costs and increase profits. Back in 2003, AT&T Wireless began outsourcing IT support and customer support to India. Bell Canada also began outsourcing customer support to India in 2006. However, both AT&T and Bell Canada later began cutting back the amount of work being sent overseas and starting using local labor for IT support and customer service. Why?

The decision to outsource must be made with financial costs and benefits in mind, as well as the qualitative considerations. Both telecommunication companies found that there were some problems with the level of customer service from the outsourced labor. Although companies may outsource to cut costs, the quality of work must still meet the company's standards.

The following example will illustrate the role of analyzing relevant costs in a make or buy decision.

Make or Buy Decision: A Manufacturing Business Example

Assume New Tech Audio Company (New Tech), a manufacturer of audio systems, currently produces a three-in-one stereo consisting of a CD player, an MP3 dock and a digital radio. The company's accounting department has reported the following annual costs of producing the stereo system internally as shown in figure 11.7.

New Tech Audio Company Annual Production Costs for Three-in-One Stereo		
	Per Unit	**15,000 Units**
Direct Materials	$15	$225,000
Direct Labor	12	180,000
Variable Overhead	7	105,000
Supervisor's Salary	3	45,000
Depreciation of Special Equipment	6	90,000
Allocated General Overhead	4	60,000
Total Costs	$47	$705,000

FIGURE 11.7

In addition to the financial information presented, the following points are also important to keep in mind while making decisions:

- The supervisor will take over duties in another department if the stereos are purchased from the outside supplier. His salary will remain the same.
- The special equipment has no other use aside from producing the three-in-one stereos. Also, it has no salvage value and will not be sold.
- The general overhead costs allocated to the stereos are common to all items manufactured in the factory.

An external supplier has offered to provide New Tech 15,000 units of the same stereo per year at a price of $32 each. Should the company stop manufacturing the stereos internally and begin purchasing them from the external supplier? New Tech now faces a make or buy decision.

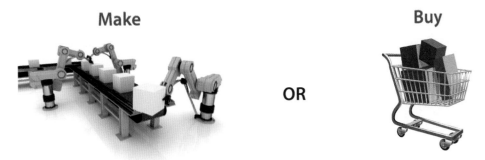

Make   OR   **Buy**

From a financial perspective, the manager should only focus on the relevant costs to make this decision. In other words, the sunk costs and the costs that will remain the same in the future regardless of the make or buy decision should be eliminated. The company should buy the stereos from the outside supplier only if the purchase price is less than the total costs to produce the stereos internally.

Looking at the information provided, it should be noted that whatever price was paid for the special equipment is a sunk cost. If the special equipment could be sold, then its salvage value would be a relevant cost. However, there is no salvage value in this particular case, it would be irrelevant to the make or buy decision. The depreciation of the machine will remain constant regardless of which decision is made.

The general overhead costs allocated to the stereos are common to all items produced in the factory. Assuming that they would remain the same, even if the stereos are purchased from the outside supplier, means this cost is irrelevant. Also, the supervisor's salary will remain the same regardless of the make or buy decision. Therefore, in our New Tech example, these costs are irrelevant costs and should be eliminated from the make or buy analysis.

The variable costs of manufacturing the stereos internally can be avoided by purchasing the stereos from the external supplier. Therefore, direct materials, direct labor and variable overhead are relevant costs and should be considered in the make or buy analysis. The full make or buy analysis is shown in figure 11.8. New Tech finds that they can make the three-in-one stereo for $34 or they can buy it premade for $32. It would make financial sense to purchase the stereo from the outside supplier. If they buy 15,000 units, they would save $30,000.

New Tech Audio Company Make or Buy Analysis					
	Production Cost Per Unit	Per Unit Differential Costs		Total Differential Costs (15,000 Units)	
		Make	**Buy**	**Make**	**Buy**
Direct Materials	$15	$15		$225,000	
Direct Labor	12	12		180,000	
Variable Overhead	7	7		105,000	
Supervisor's Salary	3				
Depreciation of Special Equipment	6				
Allocated General Overhead	4				
Direct Materials			32		480,000
Total Cost	$47	$34	$32	$510,000	$480,000
Difference in favor of buy			$2		$30,000

FIGURE 11.8

Accept or Reject a Special Order

Management often has to decide whether a special order should be accepted. A **special order** is a one-time purchase order received by the company, which is not considered part of the company's normal operations. If the order is accepted, management must also decide a price to charge for the order. The goal in setting the price is to attain a positive incremental operating income (i.e. increase overall operating income).

Suppose that New Tech Audio Company has just received a request from a customer to produce 200 units of a modified CD stereo system that New Tech does not produce in its normal ongoing business. These stereos enable a higher audio volume and have a more vibrant exterior design. The normal selling price of the regular CD stereo is $50 and its unit product cost is $34. The unit product cost is shown in figure 11.9.

Special Order: 200 Modified CD Stereo Systems

Direct materials	$11
Direct labor	8
Variable manufacturing overhead	10
Allocated fixed manufacturing overhead	5
Unit product cost	**$34**

FIGURE 11.9

New Tech would charge $48 per stereo for the special order as negotiated with the customer. This is less than the selling price of its regular CD stereo. The special order would not affect the company's total fixed manufacturing costs and will not impact other sales or production processes. The extra costs pertaining to the higher audio volume levels and more vibrant exterior design are as follows:

- Special unit for louder sound costs $5 per unit
- Paying design studio to create stencils for the exterior costs $1,000
- Extra paint required for vibrant design costs $2 per unit

In order for New Tech to make a final decision on accepting or rejecting the special order, New Tech must know what the effect on operating income will be if the company accepts the order. In this analysis, only the incremental benefits and costs are relevant, so irrelevant costs must be eliminated. Since it was mentioned that the total fixed manufacturing overhead costs would remain the same even if the special order was accepted, it is not relevant in our analysis. Figure 11.10 shows the effect on operating income if New Tech accepts the special order for 200 units.

	Per Unit	Total (200 Stereos)
Incremental revenue	$48	$9,600
Incremental costs:		
Variable costs:		
Direct materials	11	2,200
Direct labor	8	1,600
Variable manufacturing overhead	10	2,000
Special modification - volume	5	1,000
Special modification - paint	2	400
Total variable cost	$36	7,200
Fixed cost:		
Outsourced design and stencil purchases		1,000
Total incremental cost		8,200
Incremental operating income		$1,400

FIGURE 11.10

The order would result in positive incremental operating income even though the price for the special order is below the normal unit price and the special order requires incurring additional costs. Therefore, in the above case, New Tech should accept the special order.

One of the assumptions made for the initial analysis was that New Tech's other sales and production processes would not be affected. In the real world, filling a special order often cuts into normal sales or there may not even be enough idle capacity to produce the special order units. If New Tech must temporarily stop or slow down production on regular CD stereos to produce the special order, this will impact the sales for this product. As a result, the lost sales are the opportunity cost.

Suppose New Tech is operating at full capacity prior to receiving the special order. In this case, production and sales of regular CD stereos must be given up to fulfill the special order. Therefore, for every special order unit produced and sold, the contribution margin on the sale of a regular CD stereo would be foregone, or considered an opportunity cost. Since the regular CD stereo sells for $50 and has the unit costs shown in figure 11.9, New Tech can determine what the minimum acceptable price should be on the special order. Keep in mind that the fixed manufacturing overhead is irrelevant to the decision, since the amount of fixed manufacturing overhead will stay the same regardless of the decision. Thus, the analysis shown in figure 11.11 shows what the relevant costs are for this decision.

Opportunity costs per regular CD stereo:	
Regular selling price	$50
Variable costs:	
Direct materials	11
Direct labor	8
Variable overhead	10
Total variable costs	29
Foregone contribution margin	**$21**
Total relevant costs per special order:	
Incremental costs:	
Variable	$36
Fixed ($1,000 ÷ 200 units)	5
Foregone contribution margin	21
Total relevant costs	**$62**

FIGURE 11.11

The top portion of figure 11.11 calculates the opportunity cost of each regular CD stereo that is not sold. Since New Tech will not be producing and selling regular CD stereos when they are working on the special order, they will be giving up $21 of contribution margin. The relevant costs for each unit of the special order now include the $36 variable costs and $5 fixed costs from figure 11.11 and the opportunity cost of $21.

The total relevant cost of $62 is greater than the special offer price of $48. Therefore, New Tech should decline the offer. The minimum acceptable price for the special order is $62 per stereo. If the price is set at $62 per unit, management would be indifferent between selling the regular CD stereos to other customers and filling the special order from a financial perspective. If the price exceeds $62, then from a financial perspective, it would be beneficial for management to accept the special order.

Note that the above scenario assumes switching back to producing their regular CD players will not incur additional costs. If, however, a business incurs a setup cost when there is a change in production, this setup cost should also be considered in the analysis.

Product Mix Decision

There has been increasing pressure on companies to use resources more efficiently and effectively. This has led to an increased interest from managers in finding tools and methods to help with resource allocation decisions. An analysis of relevant cost can be used to gain insight into optimal resource allocation decisions. The idea is to use the concept of relevant cost and opportunity cost to compare the incremental benefits of allocating a scarce resource amongst its alternative uses. Managers would desire the allocation that provides the highest incremental benefit. The process used to decide on this particular allocation of a scarce resource is known as the **product mix decision**.

Product Mix Decision: A Manufacturing Business Example

VJ Music Corporation (VJ Music) manufactures three standard types of instruments: drums, guitars, and trumpets. Data on the price and costs for the units are shown in figure 11.12.

	Trumpet	Drum	Guitar
Price	$60	$100	$70
Direct Materials	20	50	25
Direct Labor	15	30	30
Manufacturing Overhead	10	6	5
Profit per Unit	$15	$14	$10

FIGURE 11.12

An investigation by the general manager reveals that while all direct materials and labor costs are variable, all manufacturing overhead is fixed. Manufacturing overhead is allocated to the three products using a rate of $50 per machine hour consumed by the product. The company is under contract to produce various amounts of the three products. However, there are 500 uncommitted hours of machine time that can be used to manufacture more products. If VJ Music can sell any additional product within capacity, what is the best way to allocate the extra 500 machine hours? In other words, which product(s) should be produced using the available machine hours?

Identifying the relevant costs for each alternative use of the scarce resource would be useful. Figure 11.13 identifies the contribution margin for each product. Since all manufacturing overhead is fixed, it is ignored when determining contribution margin.

	Trumpet	Drum	Guitar
Price	$60	$100	$70
Variable Cost	35	80	55
Contribution Margin per Unit	$25	$20	$15

FIGURE 11.13

Recall that there are only 500 machine hours available for use. Therefore, the objective is to use this production constraint in the most profitable way.

The first step in this process is to identify the amount of machine time a unit of each product requires. As stated earlier, VJ Music knows that the fixed manufacturing overhead allocation rate is $50 per machine hour. Therefore, they can divide the manufacturing overhead allocation in figure 11.12 by $50 to identify the number of machine hours each product consumes.

Machine hours used per:

Trumpet	$10 ÷ $50 per hour	= 0.20 hours
Drum	$6 ÷ $50 per hour	= 0.12 hours
Guitar	$5 ÷ $50 per hour	= 0.10 hours

Now VJ Music can compile a table to determine each product's relevant contribution margin per unit of the scarce resource. In this case, it is contribution margin per machine hour.

	Trumpet	Drum	Guitar
Price	$60	$100	$70
Variable Cost	35	80	55
Contribution Margin per Unit	$25	$20	$15
Machine Hours	÷ 0.20	÷ 0.12	÷ 0.10
CM per Machine Hour	$125	$167	$150

FIGURE 11.14

From figure 11.14, it is determined that the drum provides the greatest contribution margin per machine hour of all three products. Therefore, the product mix decision that should be made is to use all 500 available machine hours to produce 4,167 (500 ÷ 0.12) drums.

Opportunity cost should also be considered to complete the relevant cost analysis as shown in figure 11.15. Recall that opportunity cost is the value of the next best alternative given up. For example, if a machine hour is used to produce trumpets, VJ Music gives up the best alternative, which is producing drums. By producing trumpets to earn $125 of contribution margin per hour, VJ Music gives up earning $167 of contribution margin per hour from the drums. Thus, it does not make financial sense to produce trumpets. The same logic can be applied to the production of guitars.

If VJ Music decides to produce drums to earn $167 of contribution margin per hour, they would give up earning $150 of contribution margin per hour from the guitars. The choice to allocate all of the available machine hours to the drum has the lowest opportunity cost. Therefore, it is the most beneficial product mix decision for VJ Music.

	Trumpet	Drum	Guitar
Price	$60	$100	$70
Variable Cost	35	80	55
Contribution Margin per Unit	$25	$20	$15
Machine Hours	0.2	0.12	0.1
CM per Machine Hour	$125	$167	$150
Opportunity Cost	$167	$150	$167

FIGURE 11.15

Using the concept of relevant cost gives managers an effective approach to making critical operational decisions. Only the future benefits and costs that differ between the alternatives should be considered. Irrelevant costs such as sunk or common costs should be ignored. Opportunity cost should be included as a relevant cost. The difficulty in the relevant cost decision making approach is to identify all future consequences.

Ethical Considerations

When a business is in the process of considering dropping a segment of their operations, they likely need the assistance of a managerial accountant to provide accurate figures about the segment in question. The accountant must ensure that all internal discussions and documents about dropping the segment are kept confidential. This is in line with the confidentiality standard under the *Statement of Ethical Professional Practice* (see chapter 1).

Suppose the accountant is related to the manager of an external company. Over the years, this company has been competing with this particular segment. The manager has repeatedly stated that he would be greatly benefited if he knew more about that segment. The accountant would be tempted to provide confidential information to his relative concerning the possible discontinuance of the segment. However, the accountant must realize that doing this would violate the *Statement of Ethical Professional Practice*, as well as provide the relative with an unfair advantage over the other companies that also compete with the segment.

In Summary

⇨ **Irrelevant costs** are costs that will not change regardless of what decision is made.

⇨ **Relevant revenue** are revenue that will change depending on the decision that is made.

⇨ **Differential revenues** or net relevant revenues are the total revenues that differ between alternatives in a specific decision.

⇨ **Relevant costs** are costs that will change depending on the decision that is made.

⇨ **Differential costs** or net relevant costs are the total costs that differ between alternatives in a specific decision.

⇨ An **opportunity cost** is the value of the next highest valued alternative that is foregone.

⇨ A **sunk cost** is a cost that cannot be recovered. Since sunk costs cannot be recovered, they are irrelevant costs.

⇨ **Keep or drop** decisions involve analyzing relevant costs to decide whether to continue to provide a product or shut production down.

⇨ Segment fixed costs can be eliminated if a segment of a company is shut down.

⇨ Company-wide fixed costs are allocated among the segments of the business. If a segment is shut down, company-wide fixed costs will be allocated among the remaining segments.

⇨ The **make or buy** decision is whether a company should make a product or purchase it from an outside vendor. This can also be called the **outsourcing decision.**

⇨ A **special order** is a one-time purchase order received by a company that is outside their normal operations.

⇨ Analyzing the relevant costs involved with a special order will allow management to set a price on the product to achieve positive incremental operating income.

⇨ If a special order would require production of another item to be temporarily suspended, opportunity costs must also be accounted for.

⇨ The **product mix** decision allows for the best allocation of resources.

⇨ Relevant costs and opportunity costs must be considered when deciding upon the most profitable product mix.

Review Exercise 1

Mike's BBQ is a fast food restaurant that specializes in grilled items such as hamburgers and chicken burgers. Mike's BBQ offers traditional sides such as French fries and onion rings, and also sells ice cream and milkshakes. Mike's accountant has prepared a segmented contribution margin statement because Mike feels that the ice cream and milkshake portion of his business is not doing so well. Therefore, it may be shut down. The accountant has segmented the business into grilled items, sides and ice cream. The fixed cost for each segment is the rental price of the specialized equipment needed for food preparation. If a segment is shut down, the equipment will no longer be needed.

Mike's BBQ Segmented Contribution Margin Statement For the Year Ending November 30, 2011	Grill	Sides	Ice Cream	Total
Revenue	$60,000	$50,000	$35,000	$145,000
Less: Variable Costs	39,000	35,000	26,250	100,250
Contribution Margin	21,000	15,000	8,750	44,750
Less: Fixed Costs	8,000	8,500	10,000	26,500
Operating Income	$13,000	$6,500	($1,250)	$18,250

Mike knows that some people come to the restaurant just for milkshakes or ice cream, while others prefer to have milkshakes with their burgers and sides. Mike feels that sales of grilled items and sides will both decrease by 5% if the ice cream segment is shut down.

Required:

Determine whether Mike should shut down the ice cream segment.

Review Exercise 1 – Answer

If Mike shuts down the ice cream segment, he loses the contribution margin, but will save the fixed costs. He would also lose some sales and contribution margin from the other two segments. An incremental analysis shows that overall operating income for Mike's BBQ would decrease by $550, if the ice cream segment is shut down.

Lost Contribution Margin - Ice Cream	($8,750)
Cost Savings - Ice Cream Fixed Costs	10,000
Decrease in Sales Volume:	
Grill: $21,000 × 5%	(1,050)
Sides: $15,000 × 5%	(750)
Incremental Effect	($550)

Therefore, Mike should not shut down the ice cream segment of the restaurant.

Review Exercise 2

Honba Motors manufactures cars and makes most of the components that are used in assembling the vehicle. An outside supplier has approached Honba and offered to supply bumpers at a cost of $71 each. Honba requires 120,000 bumpers per year and the supplier will be able to supply that quantity. Honba's cost per bumper is presented below.

Honba Motors Annual Production Costs for Bumpers		
	Per Unit	120,000 Units
Direct Materials	$24	$2,880,000
Direct Labor	36	4,320,000
Variable Overhead	8	960,000
Supervisor's Salary	1	120,000
Depreciation of Equipment	2	240,000
Allocated General Overhead	5	600,000
Total Costs	$76	$9,120,000

If Honba stops making the bumpers, the supervisor will have to be laid off since there is no other position available. The equipment can only make bumpers and has no other use. There is no salvage value for the equipment. The allocated overhead is common to all items manufactured at the factory.

Required:

Should Honba make or buy the bumpers?

Review Exercise 2 – Answer

The depreciation and the overhead are irrelevant to the decision and can be ignored. The direct materials, direct labor, variable overhead and supervisor's salary can all be eliminated if Honba buys the bumpers.

Honba Motors Make or Buy Analysis					
	Production Cost Per Unit	Per Unit Differential Costs		Total Differential Costs (120,000 Units)	
		Make	Buy	Make	Buy
Direct Materials	$24	$24		$2,880,000	
Direct Labor	36	36		4,320,000	
Variable Overhead	8	8		960,000	
Supervisor's Salary	1	1		120,000	
Depreciation of Equipment	2				
Allocated General Overhead	5				
Purchase Price (from Supplier)			71		$8,520,000
Total Cost	$76	$69	$71	$8,280,000	$8,520,000
Difference in favor of make		$2		$240,000	

It is cheaper for Honba to continue to make the bumpers. If they buy the bumpers, it would cost them an additional $240,000 per year.

Review Exercise 3

Top Hats Inc. manufactures a variety of dress hats with various designs. They are currently working at full capacity. They have recently received an order from a customer requiring 2,000 fedora hats with a special design embroidered on it. Manufacturing costs of the regular fedora produced by Top Hats in their normal operations are presented below:

Direct Materials	$9
Direct Labor	7
Variable Manufacturing Overhead	5
Allocated Fixed Manufacturing Overhead	2
Unit Product Cost	**$23**

Fixed manufacturing overhead will remain the same, whether Top Hats decides to accept the special order. The usual selling price of the regular fedora is $45. However, Top Hats has negotiated a selling price of $59 with the customer for the special fedoras. If Top Hats accepts the order, they would have to get special thread for the embroidered design which would cost $1 per hat. They would also need a template created for the design which would cost $4,000.

Required:

Should Top Hats accept or reject the special order?

Review Exercise 3 – Answer

Since Top Hats is currently working at full capacity, the opportunity cost of the basic fedora must be considered. This is because the basic fedora must stop production temporarily while the special order is fulfilled.

Opportunity costs of basic fedora	
Regular selling price	$45
Variable Costs	
Direct Materials	9
Direct Labor	7
Variable Overhead	5
Total Variable Costs	21
Foregone Contribution Margin	**$24**

The incremental costs of making the special order fedora must also be considered.

	Per Unit	Total (2,000 fedoras)
Variable Costs:		
Direct Materials	$9	$18,000
Direct Labor	7	14,000
Variable Manufacturing Overhead	5	10,000
Special Modification - Thread	1	2,000
Total Variable Costs	$22	$44,000
Fixed Costs:		
Embroidered Template	2	4,000
Total Incremental Costs	**$24**	**$48,000**

Combining the two costs, incremental operating income is shown below.

	Per Unit	Total (2,000 fedoras)
Incremental Revenue	$59	$118,000
Incremental Costs:		
Variable	22	44,000
Fixed ($4,000 ÷ 2,000 units)	2	4,000
Foregone Contribution Margin	33	66,000
Total Incremental Costs	$57	$114,000
Incremental Operating Income	**$2**	**$4,000**

Since incremental operating income is positive, Top Hats Inc. should accept the special order.

Review Exercise 4

Bored Games Inc. manufactures board games for a number of toy store chains. While analyzing the production schedule, it was found that there are 300 machine hours that are not being used and can be devoted to manufacturing more games. Bored Games is able to sell all additional games they make. Manufacturing overhead is fixed and is allocated at a rate of $50 per machine hour. Information on the products is shown below.

	Duopoly	Scribble	Risky
Price	$18	$20	$24
Direct Materials	3	4	8
Direct Labor	3	5	4
Manufacturing Overhead	8	5	6
Profit per Unit	$4	$6	$6

Required:

Which product should Bored Games make with the extra 300 machine hours? How many additional units of the selected product will be produced as a result?

Review Exercise 4 – Answer

Calculate how many machine hours are used by each product.

Duopoly	$8 ÷ $50 per hour =	0.16 hours
Scribble	$5 ÷ $50 per hour =	0.10 hours
Risky	$6 ÷ $50 per hour =	0.12 hours

Then, calculate the contribution margin per machine hour for each product.

	Duopoly	Scribble	Risky
Price	$18	$20	$24
Variable Cost	6	9	12
Contribution Margin per Unit	12	11	12
Machine Hours	÷0.16	÷0.10	÷0.12
CM per Machine Hour	$75	$110	$100

Since Scribble provides the highest contribution margin per machine hour, Bored Games should devote the 300 machine hours in making 3,000 (see below) Scribble games.

Number of products	300 hours available ÷ 0.1 hours/unit =	3,000 units

Notes

Chapter 12
CAPITAL BUDGETING

LEARNING OUTCOMES:

❶ Describe and calculate return on investment (ROI)

❷ Describe the concept of cost of capital

❸ Recognize the different types of investment decisions

❹ Evaluate investments using the accounting rate of return (ARR) method

❺ Evaluate investments using the payback technique

❻ Explain and understand the importance of time value of money

❼ Evaluate investments using net present value (NPV)

❽ Evaluate investments using internal rate of return (IRR)

Capital Budgeting: An Introduction

Suppose you win a $50,000 lottery today. You can either spend the $50,000 instantly or invest the excess cash. If you spend it now, you would lose the opportunity of earning more than the initial $50,000. Assume that you want to increase the value of your winnings and currently have no interest in making large purchases.

Suppose your personal bank account is earning a 2% interest rate on the daily balance. If you prefer taking less risks, you may choose to deposit a portion of your winnings into your bank account and transfer the remaining into a long-term deposit that earns a set rate of 3%. However, if you have a higher risk tolerance, there are other choices available to you with a greater return on your money. For example, you can invest in the stock of a publicly traded company. By investing in a stock, you can receive dividends and obtain an attractive increase in the value of your stock when you sell it. If your stock performs well, it can provide you with a higher rate of return than the interest rate on your savings account. On the other hand, there is also the risk that the stock price will fall and you could lose a good portion of your money. Therefore, your investment decision depends on both the rate of return and the level of risk you are willing to tolerate.

Consider a manufacturing firm that is investing in new machinery to reduce the costs of production. If they can successfully decrease their costs, their overall profitability will increase. One way to determine whether it is worth purchasing the new machinery is to use the return on investment (ROI) concept.

Return on Investment (ROI)

Before discussing the ROI concept, let us begin with an example:

Theo See works as a salesperson for an electronics store. He saved some money and invested it in a technology company on the stock market. A year later, he sold his stock for a profit and made $500. Theo's girlfriend, Leanne Fernandopulle, also invested in the stock market at the same time Theo did. However, she invested in a mining company instead. A year later, she sold her stock for a profit of $200. At first glance you might think that Theo made a better investment because he made a greater profit than Leanne made. However, if we provide you with some more details regarding their situations, you may be convinced otherwise. When Theo invested, he purchased $5,000 worth of stock of the technology company. When Leanne invested, she purchased only $1,000 worth of stock of the mining company. Let's look at the return on each of their investments.

$$\text{Return on Investment (ROI)} = \frac{\text{Profit from Investment}}{\text{Investment Amount}}$$

Using the above formula, Theo's return on investment is 10% ($500 ÷ $5,000) since it cost him $5,000 to earn a profit of $500. Over the course of a year, he would earn 10 cents of profit for every dollar he invested. Leanne invested $1,000 and earned $200 so her ROI is 20% ($200 ÷ $1,000). With a higher ROI, she can risk less money and earn a greater amount of profit. For every dollar invested over the course of a year, Leanne would make 20 cents of profit. Therefore, since Leanne's return is higher than Theo's (by 10 percentage points), she made the better investment. Imagine if Theo had invested $5,000 in Leanne's mining stock, instead of investing in the technology stock. He would have made a profit of $1,000 (20% × $5,000) instead of the $500 he made on the technology stock. Therefore, had he known better, Theo would have invested in the stock that would yield the higher return. As figure 12.1 shows, Leanne made a more profitable investment since her ROI is double that of Theo's.

$$ROI = \$500 \div \$5,000 = 10\%$$

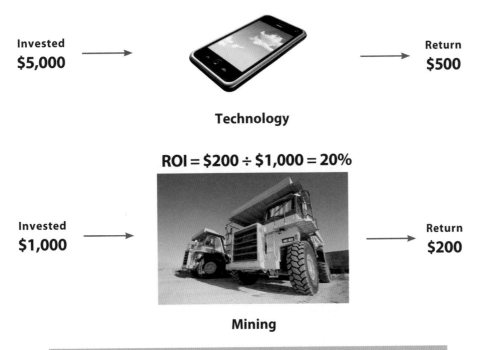

Invested		Return
$5,000		$500

Technology

$$ROI = \$200 \div \$1,000 = 20\%$$

Invested		Return
$1,000		$200

Mining

Although Theo earned a higher *dollar* return, he had a lower rate of return on investment than Leanne.

FIGURE 12.1

IN THE REAL WORLD

Return on investment is an investment criterion that appears to have been developed and implemented in the period 1910 – 1920 by Donaldson Brown who was a Treasurer at DuPont Company. Recall the return is computed by dividing net income (profit) by investment. This basic ratio can be expanded as follows:

Return on investment = profit ÷ investment = (profit ÷ sales) × (sales ÷ investment)

The profit to sales ratio is a measure of organizational efficiency, since it computes the fraction of each sales dollar that goes toward providing a return to shareholders after all costs have been considered. The ratio of sales to investment is a measure of productivity (the output is sales and the input is investment). This ratio shows how well the organization has used its investment to generate sales. Therefore, the return on investment is a product of organization efficiency and productivity which are two very important managerial considerations.

Just like return on investment is an important consideration in personal financial planning, it is also a useful tool for managers in organizations. Companies need to invest their cash in some form to make a profit and realize a certain rate of return. Unlike personal finance, organizations can not only invest in stock or park their money in the bank, but can also re-invest the cash back into the business. This is done through capital expenditures. **Capital expenditures** are investments in capital assets that change or improve an organization's current operations. Some examples of capital expenditures are new machinery and new factories that are used to expand current production facilities.

Cost of Capital

From the discussions so far, it is evident that the return on investment is a great way to evaluate an investment and make comparisons. The issue now becomes what is considered as a "good" rate of return. As a result, many companies use the **cost of capital** to help them determine whether or not to make a capital investment. The cost of capital is referred to as the minimum rate of return that owners or investors expect from a capital expenditure. Let us use a simple example to illustrate this concept.

Suppose Alvin Tsu would like to invest $10,000 in a friend's business. Alvin's friend is a dependable hard-working individual with a good track record for running profitable businesses. It is almost certain that Alvin will earn a 12% return if he invests in his friend's business. However, Alvin does not have $10,000 cash to invest, so he considers taking out a bank loan. The bank manager agrees to offer Alvin the cash but only at an interest rate of 14%. This is because Alvin has declared bankruptcy in the past and, thus, the bank considers him a high risk borrower. In this case, Alvin's cost of capital is 14% since it costs him that much to borrow from the bank. He will require a rate of return that is greater than 14% in order to earn a profit from his investment. Since the investment in his friend's business will only yield a return of 12%, it does not make financial sense to borrow money at 14%.

Similarly, businesses have to consider potential investments in relation to their cost of capital. They should only invest in projects or expenditures with the potential to yield a higher return than their cost of capital. In practice, the cost of capital is calculated using relatively complex financial tools which incorporate a company's cost of debt (rate paid to lenders) and the cost of equity (rate paid to stockholders). This topic is outside the scope of this course. For now, just note that companies use the cost of capital as a benchmark to assess the attractiveness of capital investments. For example, suppose a manufacturing company has a cost of capital of 7% and it has determined that an investment in factory equipment will yield a return of 10%. All things being equal, it should consider investing in the equipment because the return is higher than the cost of capital.

This chapter will address the various considerations before making investment decisions. The discussion will demonstrate how companies assess each investment and decide whether or not it is worthwhile. This process of analyzing and evaluating investment criteria for capital expenditures is known as **capital budgeting.**

Types of Investment Decisions

Often, businesses make a variety of investment decisions which include expansion, equipment replacement, equipment selection, cost reduction and lease-buy. The following example defines these different investment decisions and illustrates how they can be applied in a small business scenario. Consider each investment decision independently.

Val and Keerie's Variety Store (VKVS) is a small convenience store that sells magazines, newspapers, calling cards and lottery tickets in a suburb near a major city.

1. Expansion Decision

Recently, Val has noticed that many customers ask whether the store offers a photocopying service. Val is considering whether the store should invest in a photocopier to add another revenue stream for the business. Since Val is thinking about expanding the business, this type of decision is a called an **expansion** decision. Factors that will influence Val's investment in a photocopier include the price

of a copier, maintenance costs, resale value, and the potential revenue that can be generated.

2. Equipment Replacement Decision

Now, assume VKVS already has a photocopier. However, the copier is old and often breaks down. In fact, it seems that every couple of weeks VKVS has to pay a maintenance worker from the copier company to repair the machine. Val and Keerie are seriously contemplating purchasing a new copier to replace the old one. This type of decision is called an **equipment replacement** decision. Factors that will influence the decision include how much they can sell the old copier for, how much a new copier will cost, future maintenance costs and the resale value of the new copier in the future.

3. Equipment Selection Decision

Val and Keerie have decided to purchase a photocopier but are deciding between two models. One model has a higher purchase price but will have lower maintenance costs than the other. Val and Keerie will have to weigh the costs and benefits of each alternative before choosing which model to purchase. This type of decision is called an **equipment selection** decision.

4. Cost-Reduction Decision

Assume Val and Keerie already have a photocopier that is in relatively good working condition. However, a new and better model has recently been released. Val and Keerie have had a few discussions on whether they should upgrade to the newest model. The latest model has a new feature that will allow the store to reduce its costs. In addition to being able to make photocopies, the newer machine also has the ability to scan documents on to a computer hard drive. Val and Keerie would like to start scanning all their business documents to store them electronically. This will reduce the amount of paper that they have in storage, which will save on storage costs. This type of decision is called a **cost-reduction** decision. Val and Keerie will have to consider the cost of the new photocopier, the trade-in value of the old photocopier and the value of the related cost reductions.

5. Lease-Buy Decision

Suppose Val and Keerie have decided on a photocopier. The copier company has now presented them with a choice. They can either purchase the photocopier or lease it. This type of decision is called a **lease-buy** decision. Some of the factors that Val and Keerie will have to consider when making this decision are the initial purchase price of the copier, the dollar value of lease payments, the number of lease payments that have to be made, the interest rate within the lease agreement and the economic life of the photocopier.

The five scenarios above are just simple examples of the common decisions that most managers face when running their company or division. Although there are many factors to take into consideration before investing in capital assets, managers need to ensure that these costs are actually *relevant* in making the investment decisions. Identifying the **relevant costs/revenue** is important because it removes unnecessary costs and concerns that can complicate the decision-making process.

Once managers have determined the relevant costs and revenue, they use capital budgeting to help them make investment decisions. **Capital budgeting** provides the tools to help them analyze whether an investment in a capital expenditure is worth pursuing (i.e. does it have a reasonable rate of return?). This chapter will discuss the two major categories of capital budgeting methods: non-discounted and discounted techniques.

Non-Discounted Capital Budgeting Approach

The **non-discounted capital budgeting approach** assesses the attractiveness of an investment without considering the time value of money. Note that the time value of money will be discussed in the discounted capital budgeting approach section. This section will discuss two capital budgeting methods that follow the non-discounted approach: the accounting rate of return and payback methods.

Accounting Rate of Return Method

The **accounting rate of return** (ARR) method is a capital budgeting method that uses the non-discounted approach. Similar to ROI, the ARR also evaluates the return of an investment. The only difference is that the ARR looks at the return in terms of accounting operating income. The following shows the formula to calculate the ARR:

$$ARR = \frac{\text{Average Annual Increase in Operating Income}}{\text{Initial Investment*}}$$

*Subtract salvage value of equipment being replaced, if applicable.

Unlike most capital budgeting methods (which will be discussed later), ARR is based on accrual accounting. As a result, the numerator of the ARR formula takes the average operating income from the budgeted income statement. Let us illustrate the ARR calculation by using a simple scenario:

Suppose Anthony Sung is considering a project that costs $92,000. The project will last five years and produce the incremental (additional) operating income shown in figure 12.2. Anthony has a required rate of return of 12%.

Year	Incremental Operating Income
1	$25,000
2	32,000
3	25,000
4	18,000
5	15,000

FIGURE 12.2

To calculate the ARR of the project, the ARR formula will be used.

$$\text{Average Annual Increase in Operating Income} = \frac{(\$25,000 + \$32,000 + \$25,000 + \$18,000 + \$15,000)}{5 \text{ years}}$$

$$= \$23,000$$

$$\text{Accounting Rate of Return} = \frac{\text{Average Annual Increase in Operating Income}}{\text{Initial Investment}}$$

$$= \frac{\$23,000}{\$92,000}$$

$$= 25\%$$

With an average incremental operating income of $23,000 and initial investment of $92,000, the accounting rate of return for the project is 25%. Therefore, for every dollar invested the project will generate an operating income of $0.25. Since the return of 25% is greater than Anthony's required rate of return, he should proceed with the project.

Advantages and Disadvantages

As illustrated in the above example, the main purpose and advantage of using ARR is that it shows managers how investment decisions can affect the amount of operating income reported in their income statements. On the other hand, some may not prefer using ARR to make investment decisions. Unlike most capital budgeting methods (that will be discussed later in this chapter), ARR uses operating income rather than cash flow. Also, similar to any non-discounted capital budgeting methods, it does not take time value of money into consideration.

Payback Method

Another non-discounted capital budgeting method is to determine the payback period of the investment. This is known as the **payback method**. The payback period is the length of time it takes a business to recover the initial investment from cash generated by the investment. In other words, the payback method allows managers to answer the question, "How long does it take to get my money back?"

The payback method follows a general rule, which states that the shorter the payback period, the better. This is because a shorter payback period suggests the investor will get his/her money back sooner. It is important to note that not all businesses use the same strategy to set their payback periods. Some businesses specifically state the number of years while others simply require the payback period to be less than the asset's useful life.

One of two methods can be used to calculate the payback period: the formula method or the cumulative method.

The **formula method** can only be used if the project generates *uniform* cash flows. Uniform cash flows mean that the net cash flows of a project are expected to be the same for every period. The following is the formula to calculate the payback period:

$$\text{Cash Payback Period} = \frac{\text{Initial Investment}}{\text{Annual Net Cash Flow}}$$

We will demonstrate the calculation by using a simple scenario:

Steve Harris wants to purchase a new machine that will pay him back in four years or less. Currently, he is considering whether he should purchase a machine from W&T Company for $100,000. He expects the machine will generate a uniform net cash flow of $25,000 per year.

Let us use the cash payback period formula to determine how long it takes for Steve to recover his initial investment.

$$\text{Cash Payback Period} = \frac{\text{Initial Investment}}{\text{Annual Net Cash Flow}}$$

$$= \frac{\$100,000}{\$25,000}$$

$$= \ 4 \text{ years}$$

From the calculation, it will take four years to recoup the cost of the machine. Since the machine's payback period is within the time frame required, Steve should invest in the machine.

However, it may not be realistic to simply assume the cash flows are equal for every period. If the cash flows of the investment are *not uniform*, the payback period formula cannot be used. This is because the denominator (annual net cash flow) varies depending on the period. As a result, the cash payback period will be calculated by taking the sum of the cash flows until the amount of the initial investment has been recovered. This way of calculating the payback period is known as the **cumulative method**.

Let us return to Steve Harris' scenario. This time Steve expects the cash flow for the $100,000 machine to be inconsistent. For the first six years, he expects the machine to generate net cash flows of $10,000, $15,000, $25,000, $30,000, $40,000 and $50,000 respectively.

Due to the fact that the Steve now expects the machine to generate different cash flows for each year, the payback calculation will require adding the cash flows until Steve recovers his original investment. Figure 12.3 shows the payback period calculation for the machine.

Year	Expected Net Cash Flow	Cumulative Net Cash Flows
0	($100,000)	($100,000)
1	10,000	(90,000)
2	15,000	(75,000)
3	25,000	(50,000)
4	30,000	(20,000)
5	40,000	20,000
6	50,000	70,000

FIGURE 12.3

The above table outlines the expected and cumulative net cash flows for the machine. The first column lists the years. Year 0 represents the point in time the initial investment of $100,000 to purchase the machine was made. Year 1 refers to the point in time that is exactly one year after the machine was purchased. The second column, Expected Net Cash Flow, outlines the expected net cash flow for each year. This includes the outflow of cash from the initial investment. In Year 0, the expected net cash flow is -$100,000. This is because to purchase the machine, Steve needs to spend $100,000 cash. Outflows are presented in brackets. For years one to six, the expected net cash flow is positive. The third column, Cumulative Net Cash Flows, outlines the cumulative net cash flows for each year in the forecast. For example, the cumulative net cash flow for Year 1 is -$90,000 (-$100,000 + $10,000) and for Year 2 is -$75,000 (-$90,000 + $15,000).

From the table, the cumulative net cash flows switch from negative to positive between years 4 and 5. Therefore, it will take Steve five years (highlighted in gray) to recover the cost of purchasing the machine.

Based on the payback period calculations, the machine did not meet his requirement (i.e. have a payback period of four years or less). Since the machine does not meet Steve's requirements, he should not purchase the machine.

Advantages and Disadvantages

As the above simple scenario has illustrated, the payback method is relatively simple and easy to understand. Another advantage is that it highlights how a capital investment can affect a company's liquidity. Projects with longer payback periods can hinder other investments, since the funds for other projects are not readily available. On the other hand, the payback method neglects the time value of money and does not consider the cash flows after the original investment has been recovered. For example, a project with a payback period of four years can produce a steady cash flow initially but show a decrease in cash flow after four years. A project that has a four year payback period may appear to be an attractive investment. However, relying only on the payback method may cause the investor to simply accepting the project without considering the subsequent decrease in cash flow.

Both the ARR and the payback methods follow the non-discounted capital budgeting approach. In both of the capital budgeting methods, they highlighted how investments decisions can be made easily without considering the time value of money.

The following section will now discuss the discounted capital budgeting approach, the time value of money and other capital budgeting methods.

IN THE REAL WORLD

Even though business schools have promoted using net present value for capital budgeting purposes, payback continues to be the most widely used capital budgeting tool. The reason for the continuing popularity of the payback method is that many managers consider the payback period to be a good proxy for risk (i.e. the longer the payback period the higher the project risk). Although the payback period requirement varies across firms and across projects, surveys of practice suggest that organizations often require a payback period of two to three years or less.

Discounted Capital Budgeting Approach

The **discounted capital budgeting approach** assesses the attractiveness of an investment while considering the time value of money. Before discussing the effectiveness of the discounted capital budgeting approach, let us first discuss the concept of the time value of money.

Time Value of Money

Money has a price. If it is lent, it gets repaid with interest. A deposit in a bank account is essentially a loan to a bank—with interest. Of course, a loan from a bank also comes with a price tag (in the form of interest).

The world of finance often refers to this phenomenon as the **time value of money**. It is important for managers to be familiar with the time value of money because it is a basic principle of economics and finance. The concept of the time value of money can be applied to a variety of situations in both financial and managerial accounting.

In the context of our current discussion of investments, the time value of money matters because it affects the attractiveness of each capital expenditure. Since money has time value, people prefer to receive cash flows sooner rather than later. Businesses prefer that capital expenditures generate cash flow soon after the initial investment. To find the value of this cash over time, calculations are made concerning the value of money at different points in time. The interest rate will ultimately determine the value of money. There are two ways to calculate how interest is earned, using simple interest or compound interest

Simple Interest

Simple interest is interest calculated on the initial investment. Assuming the investment and interest rates remain the same, the same amount of interest will be earned every year. For example, if you have invested $100 for one year at 10% you will have made $10 ($100 × 10%) in interest by the end of the year. Using simple interest means that every year you keep this $100 invested you will earn $10 interest. Figure 12.4 illustrates how the investment will increase in value over a period of 10 years.

Year	Opening Balance	Interest at 10%	Closing Balance
1	$100.00	$10.00	$110.00
2	110.00	10.00	120.00
3	120.00	10.00	130.00
4	130.00	10.00	140.00
5	140.00	10.00	150.00
6	150.00	10.00	160.00
7	160.00	10.00	170.00
8	170.00	10.00	180.00
9	180.00	10.00	190.00
10	190.00	10.00	200.00

FIGURE 12.4

After 10 years, the investment value has doubled to the closing balance of $200. The amount of interest earned each year remained constant. Application of the simple interest rate is limited. Most applications use compounding interest.

Compound Interest

Compound interest refers to the piling on effect of applying the same interest rate on an account over a period of time. Essentially, the interest rate is applied to the initial investment plus any interest that has been earned.

Using the same example as shown for simple interest, if you have $100 and you invest it for one year at an annual interest rate of 10%, you will have made $10 ($100 × 10%) in interest. By the end of the year, you would have a total of $110 in the investment account. After the first year, compound interest will behave differently from simple interest.

At the beginning of the second year, you start with $110. The interest for the year will amount to $11 ($110 × 10%) and produce a year-end balance of $121 ($100 + $100 × 10% + $110 × 10%).

Year	Opening Balance	Interest at 10%	Closing Balance
1	$100.00	$10.00	$110.00
2	110.00	11.00	121.00
3	121.00	12.10	133.10
4	133.10	13.31	146.41
5	146.41	14.64	161.05
6	161.05	16.11	177.16
7	177.16	17.72	194.88
8	194.88	19.49	214.37
9	214.37	21.44	235.81
10	235.81	23.58	259.39

FIGURE 12.5

You should see a pattern developing. The more money that is left in an interest-bearing account, the more the interest grows each year. In the first year, interest was $10. In the second year, it was $11. The chart in figure 12.5 represents the interest that would accumulate in the account over a period of 10 years.

As you can see, the amount of interest earned in year 10 is over $23, more than double the amount of interest earned in year 1. Also, the original investment value has more than doubled to the closing balance of over $250.

The amount in the bottom right-hand corner of our chart ($259.39) will be the value of the money in the account after year 10. It can also be referred to as the **future value (FV)**.

Following this basic logic, the future value of the $100 after the second year is $121.00. After the fifth year, it is $161.05, and so on. Of course, calculating the value of money can work in reverse, too. In other words, an accountant can try to calculate what amount needs to be invested today to produce a certain amount in the future. This is known as the **present value (PV)**.

The difference between simple interest and compound interest is evident when we examine the value of a $100 investment after 10 years using both methods. Figure 12.6 shows the comparative value to the investments over time. Compound interest provides for greater increases over time, thus illustrating the time value of money.

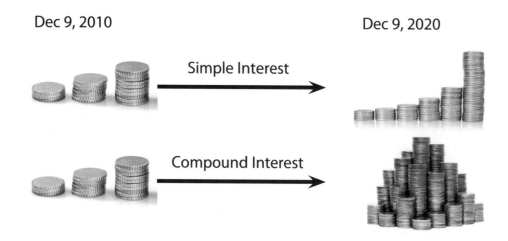

FIGURE 12.6

The formulas used to calculate present value are beyond the scope of this textbook. They are not used often by accountants since most spreadsheet programs and calculators come with functions to calculate both present value and future value. Alternatively, a present value table can be used. This table can be found in the Appendix II at the end of the book and it is labeled as *Present Value Factors for a Single Value*. A portion is also recreated in figure 12.7.

Present Value Factors for a Single Value

Period	1%	2%	3%	4%	5%	6%	7%	8%	9%	Interest 10%
1	0.9901	0.9804	0.9709	0.9615	0.9524	0.9434	0.9346	0.9259	0.9174	0.9091
2	0.9803	0.9612	0.9426	0.9246	0.9070	0.8900	0.8734	0.8573	0.8417	0.8264
3	0.9706	0.9423	0.9151	0.8890	0.8638	0.8396	0.8163	0.7938	0.7722	0.7513
4	0.9610	0.9238	0.8885	0.8548	0.8227	0.7921	0.7629	0.7350	0.7084	0.6830
5	0.9515	0.9057	0.8626	0.8219	0.7835	0.7473	0.7130	0.6806	0.6499	0.6209
6	0.9420	0.8880	0.8375	0.7903	0.7462	0.7050	0.6663	0.6302	0.5963	0.5645
7	0.9327	0.8706	0.8131	0.7599	0.7107	0.6651	0.6227	0.5835	0.5470	0.5132
8	0.9235	0.8535	0.7894	0.7307	0.6768	0.6274	0.5820	0.5403	0.5019	0.4665
9	0.9143	0.8368	0.7664	0.7026	0.6446	0.5919	0.5439	0.5002	0.4604	0.4241
10	0.9053	0.8203	0.7441	0.6756	0.6139	0.5584	0.5083	0.4632	0.4224	0.3855
11	0.8963	0.8043	0.7224	0.6496	0.5847	0.5268	0.4751	0.4289	0.3875	0.3505

FIGURE 12.7

The rows of the Present Value Factors for a Single Value table represents the specific periods, while the different interest rates (or discount rates) are found at the top of the columns. The point where a particular period intersects a particular interest rate is the present value factor for a single value. Then, *present value* of a future amount can easily calculated by multiplying the factor by the future amount.

In order to further discuss the compound interest and present value concepts, the 10% interest rate column of Present Value Factors for a Single Value table will be used. According to the table, an investor requiring $1.00 after one year would have to invest about 91 cents right now (as indicated on the first line).

For example, if Serena Harvey, an investor, requires $100 at the end of the year 1, she will need to invest $91 (100 × 0.91) today. If instead, she wants $100 after 10 years, she would only need to invest approximately $39 right now (as shown in the tenth row of figure 12.7). Indeed, the difference between the amounts is a testament to the power of compound interest. *Note that, the greater the interest rate and the longer the interest rate is applied, the more compound interest is earned.*

Instead of simply requiring $100 next year, assume Serena now wants $100 annually for three consecutive years. This example is a representation of an **annuity.** Annuity refers to a stream of fixed amounts that are received or made at regular intervals during a given period of time. Similar to the present value table used to determine the factors a single value, an annuity has its own table as well. This table can be found in the Appendix III at the end of the book, and it is labeled as *Present Value Factors for an Annuity*. A portion of the table is also recreated in figure 12.8.

There are two ways to determine the amount of the initial investment. The first method will require adding all the factors in the 10% interest column of the Present Value Factors for a Single Value table for the first three years. This will approximately result in an investment amount of $248.68 [$100 × (0.9091 + 0.8264 + 0.7513)]. As you can see, this can get tedious and is prone to error. For example, assume the investor now wants $250 per year (starting one year from now) and the specified period is twelve years. In order to calculate the amount of investment required today, the investor will need to multiply $250 by each factor for twelve years. It is much easier to use the Present Value Factors for an Annuity table.

Present Value Factors for an Annuity

Period	1%	2%	3%	4%	5%	6%	7%	8%	9%	Interest 10%
1	0.9901	0.9804	0.9709	0.9615	0.9524	0.9434	0.9346	0.9259	0.9174	0.9091
2	1.9704	1.9416	1.9135	1.8861	1.8594	1.8334	1.8080	1.7833	1.7591	1.7355
3	2.9410	2.8839	2.8286	2.7751	2.7232	2.6730	2.6243	2.5771	2.5313	2.4869
4	3.9020	3.8077	3.7171	3.6299	3.5460	3.4651	3.3872	3.3121	3.2397	3.1699
5	4.8534	4.7135	4.5797	4.4518	4.3295	4.2124	4.1002	3.9927	3.8897	3.7908

FIGURE 12.8

The first column of the Present Value Factors for an Annuity table refers to the number of periods, while the different interest rates (or discount rates) are found at the top of the columns. The point where a particular interest rate intersects a particular period is the annuity's present value factor. By multiplying this factor by the recurring payment amount, the result is the *present value of the annuity*.

Let us return back to Serena's situation. By understanding the concept of annuity, Serena can now easily determine the investment amount by looking in the 10% column of the Present Value Factors for an Annuity table. As shown in figure 12.8, the annuity present value factor for three years at 10% is 2.4869. This means in order to receive $100 per year for the next three years, Serena will need to currently invest $248.69.

Figure 12.9 compares the two methods (i.e. single present value factor and annuity present value factor). The small difference in the totals is due to rounding the factors and will not cause discrepancies that could lead to bad decision making.

Single Present Value Factors:

Present Value	Single Present Value Factors	Year 1	Year 2	Year 3
$90.91 ←	0.9091 ←	$100		
82.64 ←	0.8264 ←		$100	
<u>75.13</u> ←	0.8264 ←			$100
$248.68				

Annuity Present Value Factor:

Present Value	Annuity Present Value Factor	Year 1	Year 2	Year 3
		$100	$100	$100
$248.69 ←	2.4869 ←			

FIGURE 12.9

Now that you know the impact of the time value of money, let us discuss capital budgeting methods that follow the discounted approach. These methods are the net present value (NPV) and internal rate of return (IRR).

Net Present Value Method

One of the discounted capital budgeting methods is to make a decision based on the **net present value** of an investment. The net present value compares the present value of the cash inflows of an investment with the present value of the cash outflows. The difference between the cash inflows and the cash outflows is known as the net present value (NPV). This tool will now be applied to evaluate capital investments. Let us demonstrate the NPV calculation with the following scenario:

Suppose you have the opportunity to invest in a new piece of equipment that costs you $1,250. You also know with great certainty, that for the next two years you will generate costs savings worth $870 per year. You require at least a 10% return on your money in order to begin considering an investment. Figure 12.10 below outlines the cash flows related to this scenario.

Year	Expected Net Cash Flow
0	($1,250)
1	870
2	870

FIGURE 12.10

In order to use the net present value method, let us first determine the present value of the net cash flows by using the annuity present value table in Appendix III. The annuity present value factor for two years at 10% is 1.7355; therefore, the present value of the cash inflow is $1,509.89 ($870 × 1.7355). Next, since the only cash outflow is an initial investment of $1,250, the present value of this outflow maintains at $1,250.

Given that the present value of future cost savings is $1,509.89 and the present value of the outflows is $1,250, the net present value for the equipment is $259.89 ($1,509.89 - $1,250). Note that the discount rate used in a NPV calculation is the minimum rate of return you require in order to consider the investment. Figure 12.11 summarizes the NPV calculation.

	Present Value	Annuity Present Value Factors	Year 1	Year 2
Initial Investment	($1,250)			
			$870	$870
Annual Cash Inflow	1,509.89	1.7355		
NPV	$259.89			

FIGURE 12.11

The general rule behind the NPV method is to accept projects with positive NPVs, and reject projects with negative NPVs. This is because a net present value greater than zero suggests that the present value of the future net cash flows are greater than the net initial investment. As a result, you should invest the required $1,250 in the equipment.

Advantages and Disadvantages

The main advantage of using the NPV method is that the calculation ends with a dollar figure, whereas other methods end their results in percentages (i.e. ARR and IRR methods) or number of periods (i.e. payback method). Like any other discounted capital budgeting method, NPV incorporates the time value of money in the calculation. However, compared to the non-discounted capital budgeting methods (ARR and payback methods), NPV can be difficult to understand.

Internal Rate of Return Technique

Similar to the NPV method, the internal rate of return (IRR) method considers time value of money when evaluating capital investments. In the IRR method, the expected net cash flows are discounted as well, but they are discounted by the rate that will result in an NPV of zero. The interest rate (or discount rate) at which the NPV is zero is called the **internal rate of return**. Once the IRR is determined, it is compared to the company's required rate of return. If the IRR is greater than the company's required rate, then the project or capital investment should be accepted. If the IRR is less than the company's required rate of return, then the project or capital investment should not be accepted.

Suppose you have found an investment which will require and yield the following cash flows as shown in figure 12.12. With an initial investment of $1,000, the investment will yield $592 after the first year and $591 after the second year. Assume that your required rate of return is 10%.

Year	Expected Net Cash Flow
0	($1,000)
1	592
2	591

FIGURE 12.12

One method of determining the IRR is through a trial and error process.

We will use an interest rate of 8%. Using the present value factors for a single value table in Appendix II, we find that the NPV of the investment is approximately $55 when using a discount rate of 8% (figure 12.13).

	Present Value	Single Present Value Factors (8%)	Year 1	Year 2
Initial Investment	($1,000)			
Year 1 Cash Flow	548.13 ⟵	0.9259 ⟵	$592	
Year 2 Cash Flow	506.66 ⟵	0.8573 ⟵		$591
NPV	$54.79			

FIGURE 12.13

Since discounting at 8% did not yield an NPV of zero, let us try another discount rate. In our next trial, the discount rate should be greater than 8%. *Note that the higher the discount rate, the lower the NPV.* If using a discount rate of 8% had instead yielded a negative NPV, it would suggest that the next trial should involve using a discount rate less than 8%.

We will try discounting using a rate of 14%. The results are prepared in figure 12.14.

	Present Value	Single Present Value Factors (14%)	Year 1	Year 2
Initial Investment	($1,000)			
Year 1 Cash Flow	519.30 ⟵	0.8772 ⟵	$592	
Year 2 Cash Flow	454.77 ⟵	0.7695 ⟵		$591
NPV	($25.93)			

FIGURE 12.14

From figure 12.14, you can see that a discount rate of 14% results a NPV of approximately -$26. Therefore, the discount rate was too high. Let us try again and this time, use a 12% discount rate.

Figure 12.15 outlines the NPV results when using a discount rate of 12%. At a discount rate of 12%, NPV is approximately $0 ($0.25).

	Present Value	Single Present Value Factors (12%)	Year 1	Year 2
Initial Investment	($1,000)			
Year 1 Cash Flow	528.60 ←	0.8929 ←	$592	
Year 2 Cash Flow	471.15 ←	0.7972 ←		$591
NPV	($0.25)			

FIGURE 12.15

This means that the IRR for this investment is 12%. By comparing the IRR with the required rate of return of 10%, the IRR method suggests that the investment should be accepted because the IRR is higher than the required rate of return.

Since a trial and error method is used to determine the IRR, it may take you a couple more tries to calculate the IRR. Note that if your discount rate yields a very small NPV such as -$3 or $2, it is close enough to $0 that you can be assured that you have approximated the IRR.

As you can see, this process of trial and error can be extremely time consuming. In addition, the example we have used is unrealistic because it only contains two years' worth of cash flows whose amounts are essentially identical. In the real world, cash flows can extend well beyond two years and will rarely be identical. While this may seem overwhelming, there is nothing to fear. Nowadays, managers and finance professionals can easily use computer programs (such as Excel) to determine the exact IRR of capital investments.

Advantages and Disadvantages

Similar to any discounted capital budgeting methods, IRR incorporates the time value of money in the calculation. Also, in comparison to the NPV method, managers often find the IRR method easier to understand. At the same time, IRR has its own limitations. In fact, this method cannot be used if the required rate of return varies over the life of the asset, because there is no single required rate of return figure to compare to the IRR. However, the NPV method can still evaluate projects by using different discount rates to calculate the net present value. Moreover, the IRR method makes the assumption that cash flows are reinvested at the IRR, which might not be realistic. As a result, the NPV method is more robust than the IRR method because it assumes funds are reinvested at the company's required rate of return.

Under the discounted capital budgeting approach, the NPV and the IRR methods were discussed. Both methods have shown how time value of money is incorporated when evaluating capital investments. We will now use a business case to compare the various capital budgeting methods and show how salvage values can impact the calculations.

Business Case: Opening a Restaurant at a Golf Club

Brahm, the golf course manager at Pine Golf Club (PGC), is presented with an investment opportunity. The club has deposited $200,000 in bonds that are earning 3% interest and are about to mature. In response to a survey asking members how they can improve the club, various suggestions were made. In the end, all the members agreed to consider investing the cash towards opening up a small restaurant in one of the unused buildings on the grounds. The building is 1,000 square feet in size and is currently being used for storage. Knowing that he would have to spend $200,000 on capital asset additions such as equipment, cookware, decorations and furniture for the restaurant, Brahm developed the following budgeted income statement for the restaurant for the upcoming year (see figure 12.16). Assume the amounts stated on the budgeted income statement (except for depreciation) are all cash items.

Pine Golf Club - Restaurant Budgeted Income Statement For the Year Ending December 31, 2010	
Revenue	$300,000
COGS	110,000
Gross Profit	190,000
Operating Expenses	
Kitchen Staff	75,000
Waiter	30,000
Insurance	2,000
Electricity	1,000
Other	12,000
Total Expenses	120,000
Income before Depreciation	70,000
Depreciation	36,000
Operating Income	$34,000

FIGURE 12.16

Brahm has forecasted that the restaurant will generate $300,000 in revenues, which will result in an operating income of $34,000. Note that although the effect of taxes will not be taken into account, this will not affect the concepts discussed in this chapter. The income before depreciation is budgeted to be $70,000. Brahm expects to consistently generate this income for each of the next five years (2010 to 2014). Also, if he decides to shut down the restaurant at the end of the fifth year, he would be able to sell the equipment for $20,000. Since figure 12.16 assumes all revenues are collected in cash and all expenses other than depreciation are paid with cash, the net cash earnings per year are $70,000.

Let us now use the ARR, payback, NPV and IRR methods to evaluate the restaurant project.

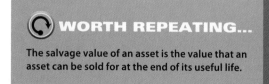

WORTH REPEATING...

The salvage value of an asset is the value that an asset can be sold for at the end of its useful life.

Accounting Rate of Return (ARR) Method

To calculate the ARR method, Brahm can use the information in the forecasted budgeted income statement. Recall that the ARR method is based on accrual accounting, which means the operating income will be used in the calculation. The average annual increase in the company's income will be $34,000 and it costs the company $200,000 for this project.

$$\text{Accounting Rate of Return (ARR)} = \frac{\text{Average Annual Increase in Operating Income}}{\text{Initial Investment*}}$$

*Subtract salvage value of equipment being replaced, if applicable.

$$= \frac{\$34,000}{\$200,000}$$

$$= 17\%$$

As you can see, the ARR method does not account for the residual value of the investment from the sale in year 5. The ARR method simply looks the impact on the operating income portion of the income statement and any gain or loss from selling the equipment is not part of operating income. From the above calculation, it means that for every dollar Brahm invested in the project, 17 cents will be contributed to operating income. Assume Brahm requires an ARR of 10% for the restaurant project. Under the ARR method, Brahm should accept the project since it produces a higher ARR than required (17% versus 10%).

Payback Method

Since the project has a salvage value, the annual cash flows will not be uniform. Recall that inconsistent cash flows require using the cumulative method to calculate the payback period. In year 0, the expected net cash flow is -$200,000, since Brahm needs to spend that amount of cash to start up the restaurant. From year 1 to 5, Brahm is expecting a positive cash flow of $70,000. There are two points to be made about this amount. First, the $70,000 represents the net cash flow from the business. With cash earnings of $300,000 (see figure 12.16) and cash expenses, including COGS, totaling $230,000 ($110,000 + $120,000), the net cash flow into the company is $70,000. Second, since depreciation is not a cash expense, Brahm considered the income *before* depreciation. In year 5, there is an additional $20,000 cash flow representing the salvage value of the equipment. By selling the equipment, it will increase the company's cash flow by $20,000 in year 5.

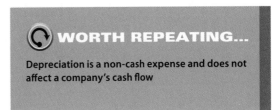

WORTH REPEATING...

Depreciation is a non-cash expense and does not affect a company's cash flow

Figure 12.17 outlines the expected and cumulative net cash flows for Brahm's restaurant.

Year	Expected Net Cash Flow	Cumulative Net Cash Flows
0	($200,000)	($200,000)
1	70,000	(130,000)
2	70,000	(60,000)
3	70,000	10,000
4	70,000	80,000
5	90,000	170,000

FIGURE 12.17

From figure 12.17, the cumulative net cash flows switch from negative to positive from year 2 to year 3. After three years of operations, Brahm will be able to fully recover the initial cost of $200,000 through the restaurant's cash earnings.

Assume the company has a policy to accept projects that take less than five years to recover initial costs. Brahm should definitely invest in the restaurant since its payback period is less than the maximum acceptable payback period indicated in the policy.

Net Present Value (NPV) Method

Figure 12.18 summarizes the expected net cash flows for the Golf Club's restaurant. Recall that there is an initial investment of $200,000 followed by five years of net cash flows of $70,000. In year 5, it is assumed that the restaurant will shut down and the equipment, furniture, and cookware will be sold for $20,000. Hence, the cash flow in year 5 is $90,000 ($70,000 + $20,000). In order to calculate the project's NPV, assume Brahm requires the restaurant to provide a 10% rate of return.

Year	Expected Net Cash Flow
0	($200,000)
1	70,000
2	70,000
3	70,000
4	70,000
5	90,000

FIGURE 12.18

Since there are annual net cash flows and salvage value at the end of the fifth year, it will require calculating the present value of the recurring $70,000 annual net cash flows and the present value of the salvage value separately. As a result, both the present value factors for a single value and for an annuity will be used. The single present value factor for five years at 10% is 0.6209, and the annuity present value factor for five years at 10% is 3.7908. The present value of the annual net cash flows is $265,356 ($70,000 × 3.7908) and the present value of the salvage is 12,418 (0.6209 × $20,000). Therefore, the net present value for the restaurant is $77,774 (-$200,000 + 265,356 + 12,418). According to the NPV method, Brahm should accept the project because the project's NPV is greater than zero. Figure 12.19 summarizes the net present value calculations.

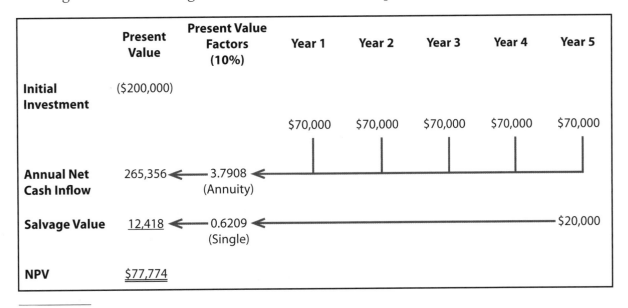

	Present Value	Present Value Factors (10%)	Year 1	Year 2	Year 3	Year 4	Year 5
Initial Investment	($200,000)						
			$70,000	$70,000	$70,000	$70,000	$70,000
Annual Net Cash Inflow	265,356 ←	3.7908 ← (Annuity)					
Salvage Value	12,418 ←	0.6209 ← (Single)					$20,000
NPV	$77,774						

FIGURE 12.19

Internal Rate of Return (IRR) Method

IRR can be easily calculated by using the IRR function in Microsoft Excel. In Excel, input the initial investment and the individual cash flows for each year in cells A1 to A6 (-$200,000, $70,000, $70,000, $70,000, $70,000 and $90,000). In cell A7, type "=IRR(A1:A6)". Note that the exercises in this book will not require spreadsheet programs. Using Excel, the IRR for the restaurant investment is approximately 23.77%. This means that if the above cash flows are discounted at 23.77%, the NPV will be $0. Since the IRR (23.77%) is greater than the required rate of return (10%), the capital investment, based solely on this financial assessment, should be accepted by the golf club.

Overall, the results from each of the four capital budgeting methods suggest that Brahm should invest in the restaurant.

Summary of Capital Budgeting Methods

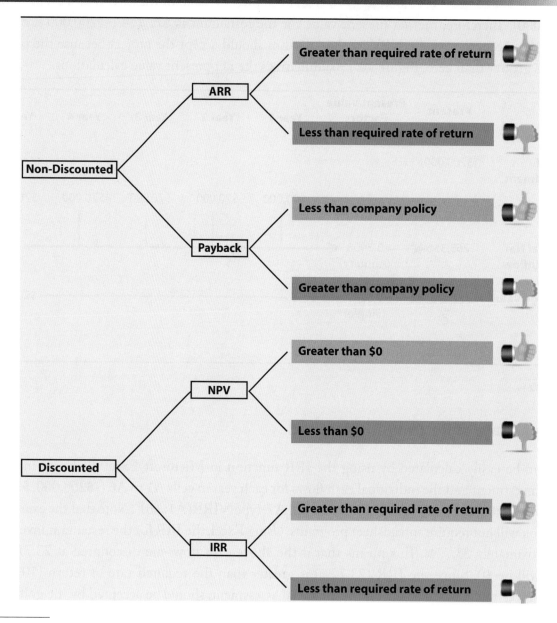

FIGURE 12.20

Figure 12.20 provides a summary of the four different capital budgeting techniques. Let us now use a case and refer to decision rules in figure 12.20 to illustrate how decisions would vary based on different capital budgeting methods.

The following case of Delish Hot Dog Stand will be used to demonstrate an equipment selection decision. Many companies, particularly those that rely on machinery and equipment have to regularly make decisions on whether or not to replace their current machinery for newer machinery. This is because the current machinery may be aging, not as efficient, outdated in terms of functionality, or causing high maintenance costs. This is an example of an equipment selection decision and will be covered next.

Business Case: Delish Hot Dog Stand

You are the owner of Delish Hot Dog Stand and have been in business for a number of years. Your current equipment is becoming worn out, resulting in various issues including wasted product due to burning, gas inefficiencies and high maintenance costs. You can either keep the current equipment or invest $18,000 in a new unit. In figure 12.21, you will find a comparative contribution margin statement. A comparative contribution margin simply compares the two options line-by-line. It compares the current performance of the old hot dog unit with the budgeted performance of a new hot dog unit. Assume that all amounts in figure 12.21 are cash items.

Delish Hot Dog Stand Contribution Margin Statement For the Year Ending December 31, 2010			
	Old Unit	**New Unit**	**Difference**
Sales	$150,000	$150,000	
Variable Costs			
Hot dog (sausage)	48,000	48,000	
Buns	6,000	6,000	
Condiments	6,000	6,000	
Wasted food due to burning	1,000	500	-$500
Contribution Margin	**89,000**	**89,500**	**500**
Fixed Costs			
Part time helper	20,000	20,000	
Gas for BBQ	6,000	5,000	-1,000
BBQ maintenance	4,000	1,000	-3,000
Operating licence	2,000	2,000	
Truck lease	6,000	6,000	
Operating costs for truck	7,000	7,000	
Owner salary	40,000	40,000	
Insurance	2,000	2,000	
Total Fixed Costs	**87,000**	**83,000**	**-4,000**
Operating income	**$2,000**	**$6,500**	**$4,500**

FIGURE 12.21

As you can see, the purchase of the new hot dog stand will reduce the costs related to wasted food, gas and BBQ maintenance by a total of $4,500 ($500 + $1,000 + $3,000). In this case, you are comparing two courses of action. You can either purchase the new hot dog unit or stick with the old one.

If you purchase the new unit, you will save $4,500 in cash each year. Therefore, the incremental increase in cash flow is $4,500. This is what you should consider when preparing the cash flows to evaluate this capital investment. You will have to consider two more factors that will affect the cash flow. If you purchase the new stand, you can sell the old one immediately for $500 (the old hot dog stand has a salvage value of $500). In addition, assume that you plan to shut down your hot dog stand in four years. At the end of the four years, you can sell the new hot dog unit for $2,000 (the new hot dog stand has a salvage value of $2,000). Therefore, in this example, you are taking into account both the salvage value of the old unit to be sold now and the salvage value of the new unit to be sold in four years. These amounts are included in the cash flow table in figure 12.22.

Year	Expected Net Cash Flow
0	($17,500)
1	4,500
2	4,500
3	4,500
4	6,500

FIGURE 12.22

Note that the initial investment amounts to $17,500 in year 0. This is because there is an initial outflow of $18,000 to purchase the new stand. However, there is also a cash inflow from the sale of the old unit for $500. Therefore, the net cash flow at the starting point is -$17,500. It is assumed that the net cash flow due to operations ($4,500) will occur consistently for the next four years. In the fourth and final year, you also take into account the salvage value of the new machine. Therefore, the cash inflow for year 4 is $6,500 ($4,500 + $2,000). Let us now start our evaluation using the payback technique.

Payback Technique

In figure 12.23, the cumulative net cash flow for the potential equipment replacement is calculated.

Year	Expected Net Cash Flow	Cumulative Net Cash Flows
0	($17,500)	($17,500)
1	4,500	(13,000)
2	4,500	(8,500)
3	4,500	(4,000)
4	6,500	2,500

FIGURE 12.23

According to the above table, the payback period is four years because the cumulative net cash flows switch from negative to positive from year 3 to year 4. Whether or not this amount is reasonable depends on what you consider to be a reasonable payback period. Assume Delish Hot Dog Stand will only accept a project if the payback period is less than the asset life. Since the asset life of the equipment is four years and the payback period is between three and four years, Delish Hot Dog Stand should replace the old equipment.

Accounting Rate of Return Method

To calculate the ARR for Delish Hot Dog Stand, use the information shown in figure 12.24 and assume that the required rate of return is 10%.

Year	Incremental Operating Income
1	$4,500
2	4,500
3	4,500
4	4,500

FIGURE 12.24

Recall that the ARR formula is:

$$ARR = \frac{\text{Average Annual Increase in Operating Income}}{\text{Initial Investment*}}$$

*Subtract salvage value of equipment being replaced, if applicable.

$$ARR = \frac{\$4,500}{\$18,000 - \$500}$$

$$= 25.7\%$$

By comparing the ARR with the required rate of return, it is readily apparent that the ARR of 25.7% is much greater than the required rate of return of 10%. Since the ARR is greater, Delish Hot Dog Stand should replace the old equipment.

Let us now use the NPV and IRR methods to evaluate the project, again assuming that the required rate of return is 10%.

Net Present Value Method

The NPV is calculated for this particular investment in figure 12.25 below.

	Present Value	Annuity Present Value Factors (10%)	Year 1	Year 2	Year 3	Year 4
Initial Investment	($17,500)					
			$4,500	$4,500	$4,500	$4,500
Annual Net Cash Inflow	14,264.55 ←	3.1699 ←				
Salvage Value	1,366.00 ←	0.6830 ←				$2,000
NPV	($1,869.45)					

FIGURE 12.25

Similar to the calculations done in the previous business case (Golf Club), the present value calculation is separated into initial investment, annual net cash flows and salvage value. As a result, figure 12.25

shows that the NPV for this investment is approximately -$1,870. Since the NPV is negative, this investment is unattractive and should not be considered because it does not recover its cost of capital. For the investment to become attractive, any or all of the following needs to happen:

- Purchase price of the new hot dog stand decreases
- The operating cash flows for the four years increase
- Salvage value of the new hot dog stand increases
- Salvage value of the old hot dog stand increases
- You decide upon a lower required rate of return

Internal Rate of Return Method

As shown earlier, Excel can easily calculate IRR for an investment. From cells A1 to A5, the cash flows are entered (-$17,500, $4,500, $4,500, $4,500 and $6,500). In cell A6, enter the formula =IRR(A1:A5). The result is an IRR of 5.24%. Since the calculated IRR of 5.24% is less than the required rate of return of 10%, this investment should not be considered. It does not provide you with the 10% return that you require.

The hot dog case is an example of an equipment replacement decision. In this example, we have accounted for the incremental changes in costs and revenues and the salvage value of both the old machine (to be sold now) and the new machine (to be sold in the future). This example demonstrates that Delish Hot Dog Stand's investment decision will vary depending on the capital budgeting technique. Both NPV and IRR have concluded that this project should not be accepted, while the payback and ARR techniques suggests that you should purchase the new equipment.

Tax Implications

In the previous examples, tax has been ignored. However, in reality, most tax authorities require businesses to pay taxes on income. Therefore, taxes must be considered when a decision maker is considering a capital project.

In an example where sales and operating expenses are assumed to all be cash, tax would be calculated on the net cash flows. The depreciation on a capital investment will protect some of the cash flow from taxation. Thus, in a taxation environment, depreciation is referred to as a tax shield. Cash flow from investing in equipment or selling equipment for the salvage value is not taxable and therefore does not require a tax shield. Thus, any cash flow resulting in the purchase or sale of equipment must be treated separately from cash flow resulting from operations. All cash flows are then discounted using the company's required rate of return.

> **⟳ WORTH REPEATING...**
>
> Remember that depreciation is not a cash expense and would normally not impact net cash flows.

An example will help illustrate how tax can complicate the cash flow calculations. Suppose a project has a life of five years and requires an initial investment of $250,000 in equipment. The equipment has a salvage value of $50,000 and will be sold for that amount at the end of the project life. The project produces the incremental operating cash flow shown in figure 12.26 and the organization requires a rate of return of 10%. The $100,000 in year 5 includes $50,000 of operating cash flow plus the $50,000 salvage value of the equipment.

Year	Expected Net Cash Flow
0	($250,000)
1	$75,000
2	150,000
3	175,000
4	100,000
5	100,000

FIGURE 12.26

The organization is allowed to deduct depreciation on the equipment from the operating cash flows each year to calculate taxable income. If straight line depreciation is used, depreciation will be $40,000 per year [($250,000 - $50,000) ÷ 5 years]. Subtracting the allowed depreciation from the operating cash flows provides the amount of the cash flow that will be taxed. In this example, assume that the tax rate is 30%. This rate will be applied to the taxable cash flow. The after tax cash flow is calculated by subtracting the income tax amount from the operating cash flow. Figure 12.27 summarizes the after tax cash flow calculation. Note that for year 5, only the $50,000 in operating cash flow is used. The other $50,000 cash flow is from selling the equipment and will be dealt with later.

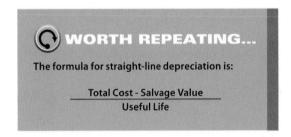

WORTH REPEATING...

The formula for straight-line depreciation is:

$$\frac{\text{Total Cost - Salvage Value}}{\text{Useful Life}}$$

Year	Operating Cash Flow	Tax Shield from Depreciation	Taxable Cash Flow	Taxes at 30%	After Tax Cash Flow
	a	b	c = a - b	d = c × 0.3	a - d
1	$75,000	$40,000	$35,000	$10,500	$64,500
2	150,000	40,000	110,000	33,000	117,000
3	175,000	40,000	135,000	40,500	134,500
4	100,000	40,000	60,000	18,000	82,000
5	50,000	40,000	10,000	3,000	47,000

FIGURE 12.27

The last step is to calculate the net present value of all the cash flows. In figure 12.28, the initial cash investment is shown in year 0. The after tax cash flow from our calculations in figure 12.27 are shown for year 1 to 5, along with the present value factor for a single value at the required rate of return of 10%. The last row in the table represents the cash received from selling the equipment for $50,000.

Year	After Tax Incremental Cash Flow	Single Present Value Factor (10%)	Present Value
0			($250,000)
1	$64,500	0.9091	58,637
2	117,000	0.8264	96,689
3	134,500	0.7513	101,050
4	82,000	0.6830	56,006
5	47,000	0.6209	29,182
5	50,000	0.6209	31,045
NPV			$122,609

FIGURE 12.28

After adding together the present value of all the cash flows, the NPV is over $122,000. As a result, the project should be accepted since the NPV is a positive value.

Other Considerations

Since future cash flows and financial performance are uncertain, managers may find it useful to perform sensitivity analysis. In the case of Delish Hot Dog Stand, the following questions could be considered in the calculations:

- What happens if the discount rate changes from 10% to 8% or 12%?
- What happens if you are unable to resell the new equipment?
- What happens if the net cash flows increase or decrease by 10%?

The situations presented in this chapter are only some of many capital expenditure decisions that a company may encounter. There are also several qualitative factors to take into consideration. For example, how does the new equipment fit into the company's business model? Although cost is important, the quality of the products produced may equally impact the decision. Over time, the quality of the products will likely impact the company financially, but the effect is difficult to quantify.

In this text, we have used the capital budgeting tools to decide whether or not a project should be invested in. In practice, managers also have to evaluate the *rankings* of the different projects. Which projects are preferred? This decision involves the qualitative factors which include evaluating risk, alignment to business strategy, and more. As you can see, capital budgeting decisions require a thorough process of evaluating options, ranking preferences and making assumptions for future performance. Managerial accounting provides the tools to aid managers in this decision-making process.

IN THE REAL WORLD

Research In Motion Ltd. (RIM) is known as the manufacturer and provider of BlackBerry® wireless devices and e-mail services. The company's award-winning BlackBerry® Smartphone is currently being used by millions of individuals around the world. RIM created solutions to the communication market by allowing users to have access to their e-mail, applications and many more. Of course, there is a cost involved in their success. Over the years, RIM has spent a significant amount on their research and development. In fact, R&D expense in fiscal 2010 amounted to $964.8 million, compared to $684.7 million in fiscal 2009.

Without a doubt, spending almost one billion dollars, representing almost 50% of RIM's profit, on researching new technology is a significant amount of money. However, this type of capital commitment is essential for innovative businesses that participate in high growth markets, such as telecommunications. At the same time, the R&D managers at RIM are required to prepare budgets for the current and upcoming developments, and also utilize capital budgeting to justify the ROI of their investments. As suggested in the company's financial statements, developing these capital budgets is definitely not an easy task:

"It is difficult to estimate the level of economic activity for the economy as a whole. It is even more difficult to estimate growth in various parts of the economy, including the markets in which the Company participates. Because all components of the Company's budgeting and forecasting are dependent upon estimates of economic activity in the markets that the Company serves and demand for its products and services, economic uncertainties make it difficult to estimate future income and expenditures."

Ethical Considerations

There are ethical implications in many of the investment decisions. For example, assume that a company is faced with an equipment selection decision. Assume that the two pieces of equipment being considered, machine A and machine B, have the same purchase price and the same maintenance costs. However, machine A is a newly developed product, and thus its useful life cannot be estimated. Machine B has been used in practice for several years and its useful life is known.

A managerial accountant is responsible for performing an analysis on both machines and providing a recommendation on which one should be purchased. The supplier of machine A is owned by a good friend of the accountant, so the accountant would likely recommend machine A to give more business to her friend. Therefore, the accountant clearly discloses all the information to the company's CEO, except she states that machine A has a longer useful life than machine B in hopes that the CEO selects machine A. Since the accountant knew very well that the useful life for machine A could not be estimated, she violated the standard of credibility in the *Statement of Ethical Professional Practice* which states that each member must disclose delays or deficiencies in information.

In Summary

- ⤷ **Return on investment (ROI)** is a way to determine whether the investment in a capital asset is worth the increase in profits.
  - ✧ ROI can be calculated by dividing the profit from investment by the cost of investment.
- ⤷ **Capital expenditures** are investments in capital assets that change or improve an organization's current operations.
- ⤷ **Capital budgeting** refers to the process of analyzing and evaluating investment criteria for capital expenditures.
- ⤷ The five common investment decisions are expansion, equipment replacement, equipment selection, cost-reduction and lease-buy.
- ⤷ There are two capital budgeting approaches: non-discounted and discounted approach.
  - ✧ Under the non-discounted approach, there are the accounting rate of return and the payback methods.
  - ✧ Under the discounted approach there are the net present value (NPV) and internal rate of return (IRR) methods.
- ⤷ The **accounting rate of return (ARR)** is based on accrual accounting and uses operating income to calculate the return.
  - ✧ Managers should accept a project if the ARR is greater than the required rate of return.
- ⤷ **Payback** technique measures the length of time it takes a business to recover the initial investment from cash generated by the investment.
  - ✧ An advantage of using payback technique is that it is easy to use.
  - ✧ The disadvantage of using the payback technique is that it does not account for time value of money.
  - ✧ Under the payback method, a project should be accepted if the payback period is less than the period indicated in the company's policy.
- ⤷ **Time value of money** recognizes the change in the value of money over time.
- ⤷ **Compound interest** is the piling on effect of applying the same interest rate on an account over a period of time.
- ⤷ **Future value** refers to how much a sum of money is worth in the future, given a specified time period and interest rate.
- ⤷ **Present value** refers to the current worth of a future sum of money, given a specified time period and interest rate.
- ⤷ **Annuity** refers to a stream of fixed payments that are received or made at regular intervals during a given period of time.
- ⤷ **Salvage value** of an asset is the value that an asset can be sold for at the end of its useful life.

- ⇨ **Net present value (NPV)** technique compares the present value of the cash inflows of an investment with the present value of the cash outflows.

  - ✧ Under the NPV method, as long as NPV is positive, managers should accept the project.

- ⇨ **Internal rate of return (IRR)** is the discount rate where NPV is equal to zero.

  - ✧ Under the IRR method, companies should accept the project if IRR is greater than the required rate of return.

- ⇨ Both NPV and IRR methods are powerful tools in evaluating the attractiveness of an investment, because they incorporate the time value of money in a way that caters to the individual needs of a corporation.

- ⇨ NPV method assumes cash flows are reinvested into the company at the required rate of return, while IRR method assumes cash flows are reinvested at the IRR.

—————————————— **Review Exercise 1** ——————————————

Karem Enterprises requires a new machine for use in their manufacturing process. They can lease the machine and pay $16,000 at the end of each year for five years. At the end of the five year lease, Karem would return the machine to the lessor. All major repairs and overhauls are covered by the lease contract; however Karem would still have to spend about $2,000 per year on regular maintenance.

The other option is to buy the machine for $65,000 cash. Karem would spend $2,000 per year on regular maintenance. A major overhaul is expected in year three, which would cost $12,000. Karem required rate of return is 8%.

Required:

Perform an analysis using NPV to determine if Karem Enterprises should lease or buy this machine.

Review Exercise 1 – Answer

The $2,000 regular maintenance each year is common to both scenarios, so it can be considered an irrelevant cost and ignored.

NPV for the lease option is
-$16,000 × 3.9927 (PV for an annuity at 8% for 5 years) = -$63,883.20

NPV for the buy option includes the initial payment, less the NPV of the overhaul in year three.

Initial Investment (Year 0)	-$65,000	
Repairs (Year 3)	-9,526	[-$12,000 × 0.7938 (PV annuity, 8%, 3 years)]
NPV	-$74,526	

Since the NPV for the lease is greater than the NPV for the buy option, Karem Enterprises should lease the machine.

—————————————— **Review Exercise 2** ——————————————

Parthenon Design Inc. is deciding between two models of plotters, each capable of printing on 60 inch wide paper. Model A costs $15,090.40 and Model B costs $20,415.30. Model A would increase sales by $52,000. Model B is more robust and would increase sales by $60,000. Both models will last three years , at which point they have to be replaced. Assume that at the end of three years, the plotters will have no value. Parthenon's required rate of return is 10% and requires investments to have a payback period of less than the asset's life.

The additional operating income generated by each model is shown in the projected income statements for each model are presented below. Parthenon assumes that all items on the income statements, except depreciation, are cash.

Parthenon Design Inc. Budgeted Income Statement - Model A For the Year Ending December 31, 2012	
Revenue	$52,000
Operating Expenses	
Utilities	9,500
Ink	17,500
Maintenance	8,500
Other	10,000
Total Expenses	45,500
Income Before Depreciation	6,500
Depreciation	5,030
Operating Income	$1,470

Parthenon Design Inc. Budgeted Income Statement - Model B For the Year Ending December 31, 2012	
Revenue	$60,000
Operating Expenses	
Utilities	9,500
Ink	19,000
Maintenance	10,500
Other	12,500
Total Expenses	51,500
Income Before Depreciation	8,500
Depreciation	6,805
Operating Income	$1,695

Required:

1. Based on the ARR method, which model should Parthenon Design Inc. purchase?
2. Based on the payback method, which model should Parthenon Design Inc. purchase?
3. Based on the NPV method, which model should Parthenon Design Inc. purchase?
4. Calculate the IRR for each model. Are Model A and Model B worth considering?

Review Exercise 2 – Answer

Part 1

$$ARR = \frac{\text{Average Annual Increase in Operating Income}}{\text{Initial Investment}}$$

$$\text{ARR (Model A)} = \frac{\$1,470}{\$15,090.40} = 9.74\% \qquad \text{ARR (Model B)} = \frac{\$1,695}{\$20,415.30} = 8.30\%$$

Model A has a higher ARR, therefore the company should purchase Model A.

Part 2

Since cash flow is identical for all three years, use the formula method for the payback period.

$$\text{Cash Payback Period} = \frac{\text{Initial Investment}}{\text{Annual Net Cash Flow}}$$

$$\text{Payback (Model A)} = \frac{\$15,090.40}{\$6,500} = 2.32 \text{ years} \qquad \text{Payback (Model B)} = \frac{\$20,415.30}{\$8,500} = 2.40 \text{ years}$$

Model A has a lower payback period, therefore the company should purchase Model A.

Part 3

Since cash flow is identical for all three years, use an annuity PV for three years.

Investment (Model A)	($15,090.40)	
Cash Flow	16,164.85	$6,500 × 2.4869 (PV annuity, 10%, 3 years)
NPV	$1,074.45	

Investment (Model B)	($20,415.30)	
Cash Flow	21,138.65	$8,500 × 2.4869 (PV annuity, 10%, 3 years)
NPV	$723.35	

Model A has a higher net present value than Model B, therefore the company should purchase Model A.

Part 4

Investment (Model A)	($15,090.40)	
Cash Flow	15,090.40	$6,500 × 2.3216 (PV annuity, 14%, 3 years)
NPV	$0	

Model A: Since the IRR of 14% is greater than the required rate of return of 10%, the company should consider purchasing Model A.

Investment (Model B)	($20,415.30)	
Cash Flow	20,415.30	$8,500 × 2.4018 (PV annuity, 12%, 3 years)
NPV	$0	

Model B: Since the IRR of 12% is greater than the required rate of return of 10%, the company should consider purchasing Model B.

Chapter 13
BALANCED SCORECARD

LEARNING OUTCOMES:

❶ Discuss the importance of a vision and a mission statement

❷ Define and identify the possible strategies of a company

❸ Understand the use of the balanced scorecard

❹ Understand the use of key performance indicators (KPI)

❺ Understand the steps in creating a balanced scorecard

Vision and Mission Statement

Every business owner has a vision for their company. For example, an individual running a dog grooming service may have a vision to run the best dog grooming service in the country. As another example, the owner of a business that provides health care services to the community may have a vision to be the health service provider of choice for customers. As you can see, a vision is a clear, definite picture of the organization's direction. A vision might seem like a simple ambition but it is not easy to achieve. Successful businesses are ones that have been able to convert their vision into a profitable business.

A company's **mission statement** outlines its purpose and over-arching goals and acts as the starting point for decision-making within the organization. It is a constant reminder to its employees of why the company exists and concisely conveys the direction of the organization. By crafting a clear mission statement, you can powerfully communicate your intentions and motivate your organization to realize an inspiring common vision of the future. Here are some examples of mission statements:

Dell Inc.:

"Dell's mission is to be the most successful computer company in the world at delivering the best customer experience in markets we serve. In doing so, Dell will meet customer expectations of highest quality, leading technology, competitive pricing, individual and company accountability, best-in-class service and support, flexible customization capability, superior corporate citizenship and financial stability"

Dell sells custom built computers directly to consumers. In 2010, Dell had revenues of $52 billion and a team of 96,000 employees.

Pilgrim's Pride Corporation:

"Our Job Is Outstanding Customer Satisfaction . . . Every Day".

Pilgrim's Pride Corporation is one of the largest chicken producers in the United States and Mexico with net sales in fiscal 2009 totalling $7.1 billion. Pilgrim's Pride is currently ranked No. 317 on the Fortune 500 list of largest U.S. corporations. As shown in their mission statement, Pilgrim's places a high value on customer satisfaction.

Hard Rock Café:

"To spread the spirit of Rock 'n Roll by delivering an exceptional entertainment and dining experience. We are committed to being an important, contributing member of our community and offering the Hard Rock family a fun, healthy, and nurturing work environment while ensuring our long-term success."

Hard Rock Café is a chain of themed restaurants, with more than 125 locations in 45 countries. From its mission statement, it is evident that there is heavy emphasis on employee satisfaction. They aim to create a family environment that employees will enjoy. If employees are comfortable and having fun, this will create a dining experience that is entertaining and friendly for the customer. Ultimately, this will mean greater customer satisfaction and long-term success.

Strategy

Mission statements can vary greatly from one organization to the next. The important point is that the mission statement should set the general direction for the organization. It sets the basis from which business strategies are developed and represents the organization's corporate culture. A **strategy** refers to a plan of action designed to achieve a particular goal. For businesses, strategies are formulated to help achieve the direction outlined in the mission statement.

However, a good strategy is difficult to implement unless the objectives are clearly defined and can easily be measured. In other words, strategies should be SMART. The SMART concept relates to developing effective strategies that are **S**pecific, **M**easurable, **A**chievable, **R**ealistic and **T**imely.

For example, imagine that you work as a sales clerk and your boss requests that you "improve your performance by selling more products". It would be tough to meet this objective since he did not specify how much more product you should sell and by when this should be achieved. In this case, the instructions were neither specific nor measurable. Let us examine another scenario.

Suppose that your manager asked you to increase sales by 400% in one month. This statement is specific because it tells you exactly what you need to do – increase sales by 400%. It is also measurable because your manager keeps track of how much product you sell. However, this statement is not achievable, realistic, or timely. It is very unlikely that sales can quadruple in one month. For objectives to be successful, it should comply with the SMART principle.

In general, organizations adopt strategies that resemble either a *differentiation* strategy or a *cost leadership* strategy. A **differentiation strategy** involves producing goods or services that customers perceive as better or unique from other products in the market. If successfully implemented, this will allow the organization to charge a premium price for its goods or services. A **cost leadership** strategy involves producing goods or services at the lowest possible price by reducing inefficiencies and waste in the value chain.

Once a company's strategy has been developed, the company can now implement the necessary processes to achieve their strategy. The question of how to implement a sound strategy and measure progress is not an easy one to answer. However, there are tools in the business world that are useful in accomplishing such tasks. One of these tools is the balanced scorecard, which will be covered in the next section.

Balanced Scorecard

The **balanced scorecard (BSC)** is a strategic performance management framework that allows organizations to manage and measure the delivery of their strategy. The concept was first introduced by Robert S. Kaplan and David P. Norton in The Balanced Scorecard, a *Harvard Business Review* article, in 1992. It has since been voted as one of the most influential business ideas for the past 75 years.

The concept of the balanced scorecard is very simple. Kaplan and Norton state, "Every measure of a balanced scorecard should be an element of a chain of cause-and-effect relationships that communicates the meaning of the business unit's strategy to the organization." Cause-and-effect relationships can be expressed through a sequence of *if-then* statements. An example from a personal perspective is, "*If* you study, *then* you will likely improve your grades." A business example for an auto repair shop is, "*If* we train our mechanics to be more honest when repairing vehicles, *then* customers will likely be more loyal to us. *If* they trust us, *then* they will likely pay a premium for our services. *If* they pay a premium for our services, *then* we will likely make more profit."

Creating a Balanced Scorecard

After analyzing the cause-and-effect relationships, you will gain a better understanding of what measures affect the company's strategy. This understanding can then be used to create the balanced scorecard. To that end, Kaplan and Norton developed a framework that connects four primary perspectives of the scorecard, as illustrated below in figure 13.1. Note that all four perspectives are interconnected and impacted by the company's vision and strategy.

Balanced Scorecard Perspectives

Source: Adapted from Balanced Scorecard, Robert S. Kaplan and David Norton

FIGURE 13.1

1. The **Financial Perspective** covers the financial measures of an organization and allows managers to track financial success and stockholder value. Managers determine what financial results are needed to instill stockholder confidence.

2. The **Customer Perspective** covers customer measures such as customer satisfaction, market share goals, as well as product and service attributes. Managers determine what goals should be in place to achieve customer satisfaction.

3. The **Internal Business Process Perspective** covers internal operational goals and outlines the key processes necessary to deliver the customer objectives. Managers determine what operational benchmarks should be set to satisfy stakeholders and customers.

4. The **Learning and Growth Perspective** covers the intangible drivers of future success. Some examples are human capital, organizational capital and information capital. These types of capital include skills, training, organizational culture, leadership, systems and databases. Managers determine what goals should be set to encourage innovation, change and leadership within the organization.

Each of the four perspectives is inter-dependent and ultimately impacts the financial results of the business. For example:

Suppose a business develops new and innovative products that can be delivered in an efficient and reliable manner (internal business process). With the appropriate training, employees can learn to sell the unique innovative services to customers (learning and growth perspective). Customers will be happier (customer perspective), resulting in a more profitable business (financial perspective). Notice that the arrows in the framework illustrated above are directed in both directions. This means that there is no particular sequence in the manner in which the various perspectives impact one another.

Balanced Scorecard Components

For each of the four perspectives of the balanced scorecard, the following components should be considered:

1. Objectives – strategic goals to be achieved
2. Key Performance Indicators (KPIs) – measures how successful the company is in meeting their strategic objectives
3. Targets – specific values for KPIs
4. Initiatives– action plans to meet the targets

Let us discuss the second component in more detail. **Key performance indicators** measures the company's ability to meet their strategic objectives. The development of KPIs requires managers to carefully research their processes and identify the cause-and-effect relationships within their company. KPIs focus the attention of employees on those tasks and processes which top management considers the most important to succeed in a particular business area. This requires creativity, judgment and practice. It is imperative that the KPIs chosen for the balanced scorecard are aligned with the company's objectives.

For example, a manufacturing company whose strategy focuses on manufacturing high quality products will likely have an indicator to measure the number of defective returns. The lower the number of defective returns, the higher the likelihood that the product is of high quality. Indicators should reflect the strategy and goals of the company. If they do not, employees will not be motivated since significant effort will give no measurable results. Hence, it is extremely important to correctly identify the cause-and-effect relationships in the business.

A list of KPIs that can be used in developing a balanced scorecard is presented below. In this case, a manufacturing corporation is used as an example. More examples can be found at www.kpilibrary.com which is a free listing of more than 5,500 KPIs for different industries. Note that the KPIs that an actual manufacturing corporation uses will differ from the list below since each business' KPIs should be unique to that business' goals and strategic objectives.

Key Performance Indicators (KPIs):

- Return on capital
- Accounts receivable days
- Inventory levels
- Return on investment
- Cash flow
- Downtime due to process bottlenecks
- Percentage of process automation
- Number of processes per function
- Time taken to settle a customer inquiry or complaint

- Employee turnover rate
- Job satisfaction
- Training/Learning opportunities
- Average order size
- Quality performance for customer
- Customer satisfaction rate
- Percentage of customers returning

You will notice that the balanced scorecard includes financial measures of performance such as "return on capital", "accounts receivable days" and "return on investment". In addition, the balanced scorecard also includes measures of *non-financial* performance such as "down time due to process bottlenecks", "customer satisfaction rate" and "time to settle a customer inquiry or complaint".

Balanced scorecards include both financial and non-financial measures because financial measures alone do not provide a complete picture of how the company is performing. In fact, many financial measures are considered as **lag indicators** because they indicate the results of *past* actions. For example, poor customer service will not have an immediate effect on net income. However, over time, profitability will decrease as more and more customers are left dissatisfied. As a result, tracking non-financial measures becomes beneficial since they can serve as **leading indicators** of future financial performance. Using a similar example, if the organization measures process error rates and finds that they are increasing, the effects of this will not be immediately reflected in the financial measures. Therefore, non-financial measures provide the company information on the financial returns in the long-run.

Tracking non-financial aspects of an organization are also important for not-for-profit businesses. Consider the mission statement of the famous Johns Hopkins Hospital in Maryland.

"The mission of The Johns Hopkins Hospital is to improve the health of the community and the world by setting the standard of excellence in patient care. Diverse and inclusive, The Johns Hopkins Hospital in collaboration with the faculty of The Johns Hopkins University supports medical education and research, and provides innovative patient-centered care to prevent, diagnose and treat human illness"

Therefore, non-financial measures of patient care such as "patient recovery rate", "number of incorrect prescription orders" and "number of doctors on duty per in-patient" can be used to help measure the performance and progress of health care at Johns Hopkins Hospital.

Balanced Scorecard Case: Interactive Websites Inc.

A detailed level of understanding and application of the balanced scorecard is out of the scope of this course, but given its importance and practical application in the "real world", the topic will be addressed from a high level of understanding. This next section illustrates a typical step-by-step scenario where a balanced scorecard might be adopted. This will provide you with an excellent foundation of the concept.

Let us use an example of a small website production company, Interactive Websites Inc. (IWI). IWI has been operating for a few years and has ambitious goals for the future. It has been very successful for the past five years but the owners are concerned that many customers are migrating to their competitors. IWI has received complaints regarding their service quality. Current staff turnover is high and profits have been suffering. IWI received services from Oscar, a consultant to help them identify the root causes of the problems and to provide a solution. The sequence in which this case is being diagnosed is for illustrative purposes. There is no predefined formula that dictates the manner in which a consultant should go about this process. For example, a mission statement may not yet exist and the consultants' role may be to help establish one.

Step 1: Extract information from IWI's mission statement.

IWI's mission statement is:

"We will provide the highest quality websites using leading technology, world class customer care and service, while creating a satisfied employee culture and sustainable stockholder value"

From the above statement, Oscar can determine the company's ultimate goal and how the company will achieve this objective. IWI has implemented a differentiation competitive strategy, and they will differentiate by providing the highest quality websites and outstanding customer service. In addition, the company will be using leading technology, creating satisfied employee culture and delivering sustainable stockholder value.

Step 2: Identify challenges that affect the organization's ability to deliver the promises made in the mission statement.

Oscar interviewed the employees, customers and the financial controller to understand the issues that are currently impacting the integrity of the mission statement. Following is a summary of his findings:

Employees:

   a. They were spending a significant amount of time fixing quality issues from previous jobs.
   b. Most of the quality problems are due to inexperienced new hires (due to high staff turnover).
   c. They were promised performance bonuses, but due to poor operating results, the financial results were poor and the bonuses never materialized.
   d. They have little control over processes.
   e. Production was compromised because their technology was no longer leading edge. The owners said that they did not have the financial means to reinvest into the business.

Customers:

   a. The sales representatives made promises relating to quality and delivery that were seldom met.
   b. There were many defects in the websites resulting in expensive delivery delays.

   c. Returning customers had noticed a significant decrease in the level of service by both the sales support and technical staff. They were very slow to respond to inquiries.

   d. Potential customers chose other vendors during the bidding process because they had heard about the issues when calling references. Rather than take a chance with IWI, they chose to use other website designers with a better reputation.

Financial Controller:

   a. Revenues and profits decreased to the extent that the company is now suffering losses.

   b. Cash flow was suffering because of the losses. This required more borrowing, which increased debt.

   c. Stockholders were worried about the future viability of the business.

Step 3: Create a cause-and-effect map to identify actions that will help address the issues in IWI's mission statement.

1. If the sales team were better trained, then they would not make promises that the support team could not keep. By delivering on promises, IWI can improve customer service (addresses *"world class customer care and service"*).

2. If promises could be kept, then customers would be happier and be willing to pay a premium for services. This would increase profits while retaining customer loyalty for the long term (addresses *"creating sustainable stockholder value"*).

3. If new technology were used, then defects would be found prior to delivering services (addresses *"using leading technology"*).

4. If managers encouraged more input from employees regarding processes and performance evaluation measurements, then employees would become more motivated at work. This would lead to higher job satisfaction and lower turnover (addresses *"satisfied employee culture"*).

5. In conclusion, employees should have the technology to perform more efficiently, the mandate to make decisions, the training to improve customer service and be accountable for their actions. Over time, these factors would result in improvements in profits and cash flow (addresses *"creating sustainable stockholder value"*).

Step 4: Develop objectives for each perspective.

The cause-and-effect relationships identified in step 3 impacts the different perspectives of the balanced scorecard. For example, developing "world class customer care and service" relates to the customer group on the balanced scorecard. "Creating sustainable stockholder value" relates to the financial group on the balanced scorecard. As a result, Oscar, along with IWI management, used the cause-and-effect relationships to develop the following objectives for each perspective of the balanced scorecard (figure 13.2).

Perspective	Objective
Financial Perspective:	• Increase stockholder's value
Customer Perspective:	• Increase customer satisfaction
Internal Process Perspective:	• Reduce error and defects • Improve post sales service • Use of leading technology
Learning and Growth Perspective:	• Enhance employee skills • Empower workforce

FIGURE 13.2

Step 5: Create key performance indicators.

Oscar recommended that the organization keep the KPI simple. This means that KPIs should be easy to understand, measurable and controllable. After considerable consultation with the owners and many of the employees, he recommended the following list of simple and effective KPIs for each objective (figure 13.3):

Objectives	KPIs
Increase stockholder's value	• Net profit margin • Return on equity • Current ratio
Increase customer satisfaction	• Customer satisfaction ratings • Number of complaints received per month
Reduce errors and defects	• Defects per job
Reduce delivery time	• Time between order and delivery
Increase efficiency	• Time to build a website
Enhance employee skills	• Employee satisfaction rating • Number of professional development hours
Empower workforce	• Percentage of employees empowered to manage processes

FIGURE 13.3

To assess whether there is an increase in stockholder's value, Oscar and IWI management chose three financial ratios. They chose net profit margin because it represents the profitability and efficiency of the company. The second financial ratio is return on equity. This is an important ratio to stockholders because it assesses the risk and reward of investing in IWI. Lastly, the current ratio is used as a KPI for this objective because it measures IWI's ability to pay short-term obligations.

Step 6: Discuss target performance for each KPI.

Oscar has discussed the KPIs with employees of IWI to ensure the targeted measures are realistic and achievable. Oscar provides the following target performance for each KPI:

- **Net profit margin, return on equity and current ratio.** Oscar discussed with top management and looked at past financial performance. Target performance for net profit margin and return on equity are 25% and 10% respectively. IWI aimed to achieve a 2:1 current ratio.

- **Customer satisfaction ratings and number of complaints.** For the past 12 months, more than 300 customer complaints had been logged, averaging 25 per month. These stemmed from a lack of proper customer and technical service. While a zero complaint objective should be considered in the long term, it is unlikely to have zero complaints at this time. The team therefore agreed that there should be no more than five complaints per month for the next 12 months. Based on Oscar's interview with IWI's clients and upper management, they have agreed IWI will regularly ask their clients to fill out customer feedback surveys. They agreed that IWI should aim for a score of 75%.

- **Defects per job.** The current average number of defects per job is eight. After consultation, all the technical personnel agreed that according to industry standards, it was unlikely that a technical website could be delivered without any bugs. Therefore, they settled for five defects per job as a reasonable objective.

- **Time between order and delivery, and the time to build a website.** Based on industry standards and the interview with the development team, they established that on average, the time to build a website and time between the order and delivery should be five and seven weeks respectively.

- **Number of professional development hours.** To address the issue of hiring inexperienced employees at IWI, the company has agreed to increase training hours and development programs. IWI decided to provide each employee with at least ten professional development hours per month.

- **Employee satisfaction ratings.** Oscar conducted an interview with all the employees. Based on a scale of 1-10, with 1 being the lowest satisfaction level and 10 being the highest satisfaction level, they scored a low 4. They all agreed that while 10 would be ideal, it probably was not realistic at this time. A new target for the next year was set at 7. This number would be examined again next year.

- **Percentage of employees empowered to manage processes.** IWI is looking towards increasing the amount of autonomy within the organization. Top management plans to target 85% of junior web developers to manage processes.

Step 7: Create a balanced scorecard.

Oscar used the information provided from steps 4 to 6 and created the following balanced scorecard for IWI (figure 13.4).

		Target Performance
Financial Perspective		
Increase stockholder's value	Net profit margin	25%
	Return on equity	10%
	Current ratio	2:1
Customer Perspective		
Increase in customer satisfaction	Customer satisfaction ratings	75%
	Number of complaints received per month	5
Internal Processes Perspective		
Reduce error and defects	Defects per job	5
Reduce delivery time	Time between order and delivery	5 weeks
Increase efficiency	Time required to build a website	7 weeks
Learning and Growth Perspective		
Enhance employee skills	Number of professional development hours	10
Empower workforce	Employee satisfaction rating	7
	Percentage of employees empowered to manage processes	85%

FIGURE 13.4

IWI's management team reviewed and approved all of Oscar's recommendations. Once the balanced scorecard is implemented, actual performance will be compared with the target performance. It was agreed that if the target performances above are satisfied, the company would be well-positioned to meet the promises made in the mission statement.

This business case illustrates how a cause-and-effect thought process can help design a sound balanced scorecard environment. The level of detail of the balanced scorecard initiative will largely depend on the size of the business, the number of departments, and the number of KPIs required. In the above case, Oscar and the managers could have developed many more KPIs to monitor. However, this would make the process complicated and time-consuming. Employees should only focus on indicators that they can control and are most critical to the organization's strategy.

Other Considerations

The balanced scorecard involves isolating critical KPIs and measuring them over time. It is extremely important for management to constantly evaluate the cause-and-effect relationships between the attainment of KPI objectives and financial results. For example, in the above case, it was hypothesized that if the number of complaints received per month dropped, this would result in greater customer satisfaction and would increase profitability. However, if there is no strong correlation between reduced complaints and profitability, then over time management will have to revise their cause-and-effect relationships. In this way, it is highly advisable that management consistently review their results in relation to the KPIs they are measuring.

The level of success will largely depend on the level of commitment by employees and the accuracy of the data that is being tracked. If there is not enough commitment from management, lower level employees will not take the requirements seriously and the true benefits of the process will not be realized. Hence, the tone set by upper management is crucial for the success of the balanced scorecard. Similarly, the scorecard also relies heavily on tracking accurate and reliable data. As a result, part of the development of the balanced scorecard will involve some investment in reporting systems and internal controls to ensure that indicators are being measured correctly.

In a sense, this chapter highlights the importance of what you have learned in your financial and managerial accounting courses. It could be said that "this is what it's all about". No matter what your role may be when you reach the professional world, your job will ultimately impact an item on a financial statement. Being well-informed, educated, ethical and responsible will make employees ultimately more successful in their careers. This chapter demonstrated the importance of accurate financial statements and information, and how they are used by managers in every type of business. Therefore, it is evident that financial literacy is important for all employees throughout all levels of an organization.

Ethical Considerations

It is common to pay employees a performance bonus based on various indicators, both financial and non-financial. Here is an example of a non-financial measurement which could be abused. Susanna is a service manager whose performance and bonus is based on customer satisfaction ratings. To help increase her number of positive performance reviews, she created personal relationships with some of her customers by buying them lunches and gifts in hopes of persuading them to give her an excellent review. This type of conduct is highly unethical. Many businesses and government organizations have policies in place that do not allow their employees to accept gifts worth more than a small nominal amount, if at all.

In Summary

- A **vision** is a clear, definite picture of an organization's direction.

- A **mission statement** outlines the purpose and over-arching goals and acts as the starting point for decision-making within the organization.

- A clear mission statement can communicate a leader's intentions and motivate the employees to realize a common vision.

- A **strategy** refers to a plan of action designed to achieve a particular goal.

- Strategies should be SMART. In other words, they should be **S**pecific, **M**easurable, **A**chievable, **R**ealistic and **T**imely.

- Organizations adopt strategies that resemble either a *differentiation* strategy or a *cost leadership* strategy.

  - A **differentiation strategy** involves producing goods or services that customers perceive as better or unique from other products in the market.

  - A **cost leadership** strategy involves producing goods or services at the lowest possible price by reducing inefficiencies and waste in the value chain.

- The **Balanced Scorecard (BSC)** is a strategic performance management framework that allows organizations to manage and measure the delivery of their strategy.

- Each relationship on the balanced scorecard is based on a causal relationship between two events.

- Cause-and-effect relationships can be expressed in a sequence of *if-then* statements.

- There are four primary perspectives to the balanced scorecard (financial, customer, internal business process, and learning and growth).

  - The **Financial Perspective** covers the financial measures of an organization and allows managers to track financial success and stockholder value.

  - The **Customer Perspective** covers customer measures such as customer satisfaction, market share goals, as well as product and service attributes.

  - The **Internal Business Process Perspective** covers internal operational goals and outlines the key processes necessary to deliver the customer objectives.

  - The **Learning and Growth Perspective** covers the intangible drivers of future success. Some examples are human capital, organizational capital and information capital.

- In each perspective, managers should consider their objectives, KPIs, targets and initiatives.

- KPIs are used to measure how successful a company is in meeting its strategic objectives.

- Some measures are considered **lag indicators** because they indicate the results of *past* actions.

- **Leading indicators** provide an indication of future performance.

⇨ It is extremely important for management to constantly evaluate the cause-and-effect relationships between the attainment of KPI objectives and financial results because these relationships may change over time.

⇨ The level of success of the use of the balanced scorecard will largely depend on the level of commitment by management, employees and the accuracy of the data that is being tracked.

⇨ No matter what your role may be when you reach the professional world, your job will ultimately impact an item on a financial statement.

Chapter 14
JUST-IN-TIME AND QUALITY MANAGEMENT

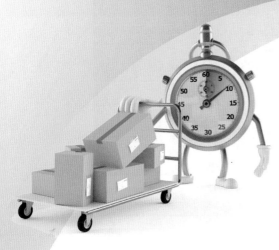

LEARNING OUTCOMES:

❶ Explain how inventory affects cash and profitability

❷ Describe the just-in-time (JIT) inventory system

❸ Identify the differences between the push and pull strategies

❹ Explain the advantages and disadvantages of JIT

❺ Identify the seven areas of waste according to lean manufacturing

❻ Describe the four costs of producing quality products

❼ Explain total quality management (TQM)

❽ Explain the theory of constraints

Inventory and Cash Flow Management

This textbook has discussed materials related to categorizing costs, accumulating costs, providing future predictions, assessing investment decisions and discovering inefficiencies within an organization. All these theories and calculations provide valuable information for managers. Recall from the first chapter that managerial accounting provides information to make informed business decisions. With an increasingly competitive business environment, managers constantly seek ways to improve quality and efficiency. This chapter is dedicated to examine decisions surrounding the efficiency of production and the quality of products or services.

There are two key elements required for business sustainability: cash flow and profitability. This section addresses how a business can maximize profits while conserving cash through better inventory management. Inventory is closely tied to cash, since cash ultimately must be used to purchase inventory. Figure 14.1 demonstrates how cash decreases when inventory is purchased.

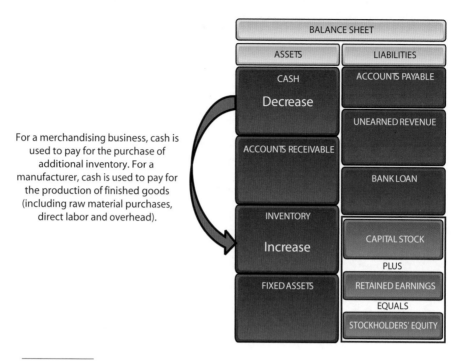

For a merchandising business, cash is used to pay for the purchase of additional inventory. For a manufacturer, cash is used to pay for the production of finished goods (including raw material purchases, direct labor and overhead).

FIGURE 14.1

Inventory is closely tied to profitability. When inventory is sold, the value of that inventory increases cost of goods sold and decreases operating income. Cost of goods sold will also be affected by inventory shrinkage. **Inventory shrinkage** is the reduction of the level of inventory due to a variety of factors other than making sales. Some common causes are employee theft, spoilage and misplacement. Figure 14.2 shows the effect of $1,000 in inventory shrinkage on the income statement. Inventory shrinkage increases the cost of goods sold and therefore decreases operating income.

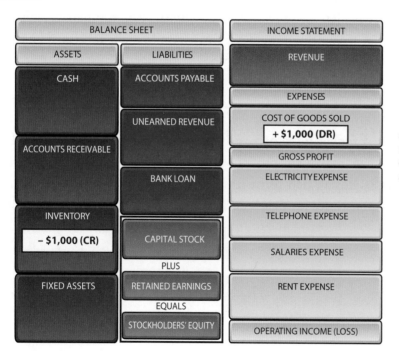

A decrease in inventory is recorded as cost of goods sold and decreases operating income and stockholders' equity.

FIGURE 14.2

In a perfect world, the ideal business model would require that a business purchases or manufactures inventory only when it has already been ordered by a customer. The following are some advantages of using this ideal business model:

- No additional cash is required to finance inventory
- The business takes no risk of losing inventory due to shrinkage
- The business will not be subjected to storage-related costs such as rent, insurance, handling etc.

In practice, most merchandising and manufacturing businesses are required to hold a certain amount of inventory with which to service customers. The challenge with holding high levels of inventory is incurring the holding expense and having cash tied up in inventory. The challenge with maintaining low levels of inventory is still being able to supply customers in a timely fashion without compromising serviceability. Having too little inventory can be expensive since businesses may lose customers if they cannot fulfill their orders in time. The art is to maintain inventory at the lowest possible levels to improve cash flow, reduce the risk of shrinkage and reduce holding costs while still having sufficient inventory to service customers.

There are multiple techniques applied by management in order to improve the efficiency of business operations. One technique is an inventory management system called **just-in-time (JIT).** A just-in-time inventory management system is a system where a minimal amount of goods are kept in stock from the point the goods are manufactured or purchased to the point of sale. Items are planned to arrive precisely at the time they are required for use or shipping.

Just-In-Time System

Just-in-time, or JIT, describes a manufacturing process developed in Japan by Toyota during the 1950s. However, the credit for the initial concept should go to Henry Ford of Ford Motor Company. Although this particular manufacturing process was not referred to as JIT, it was first used by Henry Ford. Ford only bought materials for his immediate needs in the manufacturing process. He planned transportation of materials so the flow of his product would be smooth. This gave him a rapid turnover and decreased the amount of money tied up in raw materials. Ford stated:

"We have found in buying materials that it is not worthwhile to buy for other than immediate needs. We buy only enough to fit into the plan of production, taking into consideration the state of transportation at the time. If transportation were perfect and an even flow of materials could be assured, it would not be necessary to carry any stock whatsoever. The carloads of raw materials would arrive on schedule and in the planned order and amounts, and go from the railway cars into production. That would save a great deal of money, for it would give a very rapid turnover and thus decrease the amount of money tied up in materials." (My Life and Work, 1922)

The Use of JIT in Different Industries

Some industries are forced to use a JIT system just by the very nature of their business. A good example is a bakery that makes specialty cakes and other sweets. The shelf life of both the ingredients and the baked goods are extremely short.

There are two key parts to managing inventory in a bakery: the amount of inventory (ingredients and baked goods) in stock and the cost of baking (processing) the goods.

Suppose a specialty bakery constantly ends the day with a large amount of unsold cakes and other sweets. These unsold products may not last until the following day and are a waste of material and labor to the company. This waste of material and labor decreases the amount of profit that the company can generate. Why would this bakery make products that cannot be sold?

The answer lies in the bakery's nature of business and how management decides on the production schedule of making cakes and sweets. If the bakery waits until customers place an order, then it will only bake what is required and not have any unsold items at the end of the day. On the other hand, if management dictates what to make without paying attention to customer orders, there will likely be unsold items at the end of the day.

Other industries may not fully implement the JIT system. These industries may find that the benefits of JIT do not outweigh the costs of implementation. For example, a coffee shop that is focused on quick customer service will brew pots of coffee before customers order it so the coffee is ready to serve. If any coffee is not sold after a short period of time, the coffee is disposed of and a new pot is brewed. The wasted coffee is an acceptable trade-off to ensure quick customer service. Here are a few industries where JIT can be applied.

JIT in the Retail Industry

Walmart, the largest retailer in the world, is among the many successful retailers that use the JIT system. Being such a powerful and voluminous buyer, it is in the fortunate position to request that its suppliers hold sufficient inventory to supply them on demand when they need it. While this practice increases the inventory for the vendors, it reduces the inventory and holding costs for Walmart. Essentially, Walmart is transferring the burden and costs of holding inventory in storage to its suppliers. Other retailers, such as the Home Depot, also use JIT.

JIT in the Manufacturing Industry

Inventory management in the manufacturing industry is more complex than retail or distribution because there are more factors to consider such as:

- How much raw material should be held in stock?
- How much raw material should be processed (i.e. work in process)?
- How many units of finished goods (ready for sale) should be held in inventory?

As mentioned earlier, the higher the value of inventory, the higher the demand on cash flow. The JIT system reduces the amount of raw material held in stock, only produces what is needed to fulfill customer orders and holds the minimum amount of finished goods necessary to supply these customers.

The traditional inventory system purchases or manufactures a product before it is required for sale and holds the product until it can be sold. This approach does have its benefits, especially where every production run or purchase has expensive setup or one-time costs. JIT takes a different approach in attempt to reduce costs.

JIT: A Manufacturing Business Case

The following case will illustrate the benefits of inventory management using the JIT system in a manufacturing business.

Andrew and Jim joined an intramural sports league at their school. After registering for a team, the boys heard that the league was looking for a vendor to supply league jerseys. The business-savvy boys decided to start their own company, AJ Sport Jerseys which made jerseys for the league. By the time the boys reached senior year, they were supplying jerseys for all the leagues at the school. When planning for the upcoming season, the boys realized they had 30 unused jerseys from the prior year that were outdated and could not be sold.

Determined to eliminate waste and increase their profits, the boys decided to use a JIT system to manage their jersey production. They identified the three main processes required to manufacture the jerseys: dying, printing and order fulfillment.

To get the jerseys, the boys set up a contract with a local business that sells plain white jerseys and can quickly deliver them when AJ Sport Jerseys places an order. These plain white jerseys represent the material used in the first step of production, dying. From the dying department, the jerseys are processed by the printing department and then by the order fulfillment department.

The final department to process the product initiates the flow of goods. This means that the order fulfillment department would tell the printing department how many completed (printed and dyed) jerseys are required for the customer. The printing department would request the appropriate amount of dyed jerseys from the dying department. Finally, the dying department would request an order of plain, unprocessed jerseys from the supplier. In this situation, since inventory is only processed based on demand, inventory should not be sitting idle between stages of processing.

As shown in figure 14.3, the customer initiates communication by placing an order. The customer is the driver behind production, pulling the item from the last department of the production line. Each department must then pull the item from the previous department or supplier. The entire manufacturing process only makes what the customer demands, and there will not be any unsold goods accumulating in inventory or discarded.

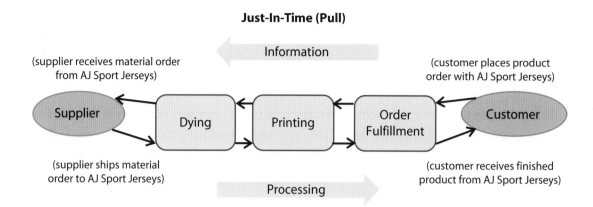

FIGURE 14.3

Once the plain jerseys reach AJ Sport Jerseys, the dying department will process the jerseys and pass them on to the next department. Each department in turn will process the jerseys and pass them on until the customer finally receives the finished product.

By pulling the jerseys through the process, AJ Sport Jerseys should not have any unusable jerseys in ending inventory when they begin taking orders for the next season. The benefits include reduced waste and costs, as well as more cash on hand that is not tied up in inventory.

Differentiating Push and Pull Strategies

Marketing people often classify their promotion strategies into two basics categories: push or pull. Thus, they can try to "push" products through the distribution channel to the customers, or just "pull" it through. More specifically, a business that adopts a pull strategy will buy or produce products as the customer requires it. In other words, the customer "pulls" the product from the supplier. For example, Orange County Choppers custom makes motorcycles that are produced upon demand by the customer. That is, the market "pulls" the product from Orange County Choppers who will only produce custom-made motorcycles upon request. In the example above, AJ Sport Jerseys uses a JIT pull strategy where the customer orders the product before any manufacturing begins. Refer to figure 14.3 above for an illustrative example of the JIT pull strategy.

A customized training program can also use the pull strategy. If a company provides custom training packages for its customers, these packages would only be designed when a customer orders them.

Conversely, a bakery in a supermarket will first decide how much product is likely to be sold by making an accurate forecast. Based on the forecast, the bakery purchases ingredients in order to prepare for the baking process. After a set of final products are made, they are stocked in the store and each product is "pushed" to the customer when an order is made. This is a typical push strategy and is demonstrated in figure 14.4 below.

Referring to the training example, if the company designs generic training packages then it must push these packages to the customer. It would be up to the marketing department to find customers to make the sale.

Forecast Production (Push)

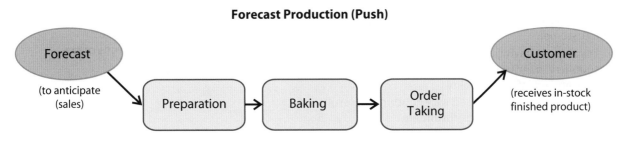

FIGURE 14.4

It is quite common to use a combination of both strategies. Let us return to the Orange County Choppers example. Suppose the company forecasts the amount of bikes they will sell in a given period of time, and purchase standard materials, which include tubing for frames, sheet metal for producing gas tanks, welding rods and nuts and bolts that can be used on most models. The purchasing of these components is based on a push strategy because the amount of materials required is based on the sales forecast. The custom-made bikes, however, rely on the pull strategy which is market driven through advertising, word of mouth, dealers and trade shows.

In order to properly implement JIT, an organization must invest time and money to get it set up, get employees to buy in to the process and create long-term relationships with reliable suppliers. Since this can be a timely and costly process, some companies are unable to implement JIT fully. They instead rely on forecasting to drive production. The following table shows the advantages and disadvantages of the pull and push strategies.

Just-in-Time (Pull)	
Advantages	**Disadvantages**
• Minimizes inventory and raw material on hand, thus reducing the amount of cash tied up in inventory. • Increases quality of product, since material and manufacturing must be of high quality to reduce re-work. • Less inventory and raw materials on hand means less warehouse space is required for storage. • Reduces or eliminates overproduction, since products are manufactured only when required by a customer. • Encourages having better relationships with suppliers to ensure raw materials are delivered on time and are of good quality. • Saved costs due to reduced warehousing can result in a lower selling price for customers.	• May incur an expensive one-time cost to make the environment appropriate for JIT. • Business is at risk of a temporary shutdown if suppliers are unable to deliver raw materials on time. • Problems in one department of the manufacturing process will cause delays in all subsequent departments because there is no reserve stock. • May have difficulty responding to sudden spikes in demand for the product. • Exposed to volatile price fluctuations of raw materials.

Forecast Production (Push)	
Advantages	**Disadvantages**
• Business is still able to operate if suppliers are unable to deliver raw materials on time. • By stockpiling raw materials and partially completed inventory, problems in one department may not immediately affect subsequent department. • Stockpiled inventory allows the business to respond quickly to sudden spikes in demand. • Stockpiling raw materials allows the business to take advantage of lower priced material and avoid being exposed to volatile price fluctuations.	• Cash is tied up in inventory and raw materials. • Problems in the manufacturing process may not be identified, resulting in a lower quality product being made. • Higher expenses due to warehousing and having to rework the product. • Risk of manufacturing too much of a product that becomes obsolete. • Possibility of poor quality raw materials not being detected immediately if they are stockpiled in a warehouse.

FIGURE 14.5

IN THE REAL WORLD

JIT has been adopted by a lot of corporations since its inception. Dell is well-known for nearly eliminating finished goods inventory by cutting out resellers and selling directly to customers. Dell carries inventory for an average of two hours in its factories, and finished goods inventory throughout the entire organization lasts three days at most. To keep everything running smoothly, demand and supply are monitored on a real-time basis.

Dell's production starts after it receives payment from customers. It then pulls the parts directly from its suppliers then builds and ships the product within three to four days. Dell does not pay its suppliers for about one month. So Dell has achieved a cash-conversion cycle of negative one month. That means it operates with negative working capital because it is paid by customers before they have to pay suppliers.

Dell's suppliers are close to its assembly plant. The suppliers are required to hold more than a week's worth of stock. This is important because Dell does not pull the part until it has a customer order. The advantage? Dell does not have to hold any inventory in warehouses, but can get the inventory delivered to the assembly plant in about an hour. **In summary, a significant part of Dell's success is from its superior ability to manage inventory using JIT.**

Lean Manufacturing

Lean manufacturing, which is also known as the Toyota Production System, is the systematic elimination of waste. In Japan, this is referred to as *muda* which is the Japanese word for waste and is often combined with *kaizen*, which refers to continuous improvement. The more formal definition of lean manufacturing is: a manufacturing strategy that seeks a high level of production with a minimal inventory balance while reducing costs that do not produce value. This concept can also be applied to the service industry to help reduce costs and deliver a high level of output.

The lean manufacturing system identifies seven areas of waste:

1. Transportation
2. Inventory
3. Motion
4. Waiting
5. Overproduction
6. Over-processing
7. Defects

An easy way to remember these seven areas is to use the acronym TIM WOOD.

While the seven waste areas of lean manufacturing initially grew out of the Toyota Production System, lean manufacturing has also successfully been applied to supply chain management, administrative tasks and service elements in both the private and government sectors.

The identification and elimination of waste is at the heart of the lean process. Just as mass production is recognized as the production system of the 20th century, lean manufacturing is viewed as the production system of the 21st century.

Lean manufacturing is a philosophy of thinking that includes JIT as part of an entire business culture (refer to waste area 2 above). It is a production practice that regards any expense that does not create value for the consumer to be wasteful, and thus a target for elimination.

For example, the training of employees to better serve customers should not be removed. Conversely, spending a significant amount of money on fancy cars for corporate managers should be eliminated because they do not create value for customers.

The Seven Areas of Waste

Let us describe each of the seven areas of waste separately.

Waste Area 1: Transportation

Most businesses will have some sort of transport expense. This is especially relevant in the manufacturing and merchandising industries, which require goods to be shipped to and from a place of business (i.e. freight). Trimming unnecessary transportation costs can save a considerable amount of expenses and increase profits.

Waste Area 2: Inventory

Excess inventory is one of the more obvious waste areas because one can see it piling up in a warehouse. Refer to JIT in the previous section for a discussion of excess inventory.

Waste Area 3: Motion

If an employee must walk halfway across a large production floor to pick up a part or a tool then this is a clear sign of unnecessary motion. However, what you might not immediately notice is the time it takes them to hunt for the appropriate part or for clerical staff to rifle through a poorly arranged filing cabinet. Proper physical layout and planning will reduce the amount of motion required to process work.

Waste Area 4: Waiting

Every minute that goods spend either not moving or waiting to be processed is time wasted. This is also true when employees are waiting for an individual or a process to be completed before they can begin their work. It is not uncommon for more than 20% of labor dollars spent in a business to be wasted due to avoidable unproductive time.

Waste Area 5: Overproduction

Overproduction is the opposite of just-in-time processing. It is making excess product that is not immediately sold. In other words, the volume of goods produced is higher than the current demand. This will cause a build up of inventory, which leads to waste area 2.

Waste Area 6: Over-Processing

While the cost of a process may be obvious, it is often a "hidden cost" that many people fail to identify. For example, the cost of manufacturing a chair in a production line might be quite obvious. However, the cost of inputting a customer order or the cost of calling a supplier due to a late shipment may not be obvious but can still be very costly to a business. Identifying the cost of processing is very important to make a business more efficient and eliminate unnecessary labor costs. If a business employs a clerk to process credit notes due to customer returns, it makes more sense to focus on eliminating returns by improving quality rather than focusing on a quicker way to process credit notes.

Waste Area 7: Defects

Defects which lead to rework or scrap are perhaps the most obvious waste. Not only do they have a direct impact on profitability, they also lead to additional waste through unnecessary processes, transportation, waiting time and motion. Defects can also apply to the retail industry. Have you ever purchased a product that you had to return due to a defect? The cost of processing the return is very expensive. The clerk needs to refund the customer, the product then has to be returned to the supplier who then has to refund the retailer. Sometimes there is a dispute which requires more paperwork. The more there is to process, the higher the cost.

This concept of waste applies to any industry. For example, if a dentist fails to correctly perform a simple procedure like a filling, the patient will return for the filling to be redone. The cost is significant not only to the dentist, but also to the patient who may have to take off work or pay for transportation. There are other hidden costs relating to defects such as the patient not recommending the dentist to others or even bad mouthing the dentist for such a painful experience.

IN THE REAL WORLD

As discussed above, Toyota is a household brand that associates its cars with reliability. However, despite its strict quality controls that include lean manufacturing and Kaizen (Japanese for "improvement" or "change for the better"), its quality slipped resulting in massive recalls that cost the company billions of dollars.

Due to the safety problems in 2010, Toyota estimated its worldwide recall of 8.5 million cars will costs them approximately $2 billion. Analysts, however, believe that the total cost should be even higher. They expect Toyota will take a one-time hit of $5.5 billion for the recall-related costs and litigation settlements.

The Concept of Quality

Different people have different definitions of quality. You may consider the report you handed in to your business professor to be a quality paper because it was free of spelling errors and it used concepts from the textbook. Your professor may view the report as a quality paper because the concepts required by the assignment were included, and the paper demonstrated knowledge of the concepts by using real life examples. Businesses and their customers may also have different interpretations of quality. For example, product engineers may focus on the product and view quality as being free of defects and made in line with their design plans. Customers may focus on their wants and define quality, for example, as a product that just looks good.

Since companies are expected to provide customers with quality products and services, organizations have realized the importance of measuring quality. To measure quality, businesses must understand what the customer wants. For instance, a customer of an auto repair shop expects the mechanic to identify why the brakes are squealing on their car, fix the problem and finish the repairs quickly and conveniently. The auto repair shop can measure the cost of quality by adding together all the costs of providing quality services to the customer.

The following is a breakdown of the types of costs included in the total cost of quality:

1. **Prevention costs**: Prevention is a proactive approach. Actions are taken to ensure a quality product or service is provided before problems arise. Prevention costs can include process design, planning, scheduled maintenance, training employees and working with suppliers. For the auto repair shop, prevention costs might include training employees how to quickly diagnose car problems and developing standard procedures to repair common problems. Suppliers may also provide training or education on new car parts or technologies.

2. **Appraisal costs**: Appraisal costs would include all costs associated with the measurement, evaluation and audits of quality before the product is delivered to the customer. Appraisal costs include inspection, equipment testing and quality control audits. The auto repair shop may have appraisal costs that include test drives or a second mechanic inspecting the installation of parts.

3. **Internal failure**: Any problem discovered during the appraisal process that must be corrected is considered an internal failure. The term *internal* indicates that the product has not yet been delivered to the customer. Types of costs that are classified as internal failures include product disposal, rework, additional inspections or tests, or discounting products because of imperfections. For example, if a test drive by the mechanic indicates that the installation of the new brakes did not fix the squealing noise, the auto repair shop can fix the problem through re-diagnosis and rework.

4. **External failure**: Any problem that is discovered by the customer after the the product is received is considered an external failure. Some external failure costs can be measured and include items such as warranty claims, refunds, rework or product recalls. Other external failure costs are not as easily measured, such as lost customers. After the auto repair shop has returned the car to its customer, external failure costs can still impact the total cost of quality. If after a few days of driving, the customer returns to the auto repair shop because the squealing in the brakes has returned, the total cost of quality is going to include refunds or rework. The auto repair shop's cost of quality will not include implicit costs, such as the customer bringing their car to another mechanic the next time a problem occurs.

Once managers are aware of the costs being incurred and the total cost to the business, they can work towards decreasing the overall cost of quality. The first three categories of costs prevent quality issues from reaching the customer, while the last category is a quality issue that the customer is aware of. Generally, an increased focus on prevention will likely cost less than any type of failure. Following this logic, the auto repair shop will reduce its overall cost of quality by investing more to train mechanics how to diagnoses problems correctly, and by establishing processes to ensure that repairs are completed in a timely and effective manner. Additionally, ensuring suppliers provide good quality parts can decrease quality issues appearing in the appraisal and failure stages.

Total Quality Management

Dr. W. Edwards Deming is known as the father of the Japanese post-war industrial revival and was regarded by many as the leading quality guru in the United States. During World War II he assisted the United States to improve the quality of war materials.

Deming's business philosophy is summarized in his famous 14 Points. These 14 Points, which include topics relating to quality, have inspired significant changes among companies competing in the world's increasingly competitive environment. Some of the 14 Points which relate specifically to quality are: improve every process, permit pride of workmanship and implement training on the job. Deming is also considered the founder of Total Quality Management.

Total Quality Management (TQM) is a management concept that focuses on the goal of continuously reducing errors and satisfying customers. A company that works with this philosophy and establishes a TQM program will adjust processes in the organization to meet this goal. Striving towards process perfection has many positive results:

- Better customer satisfaction
- Reduced waste and cost
- Higher commitment from management and employees
- Improved culture within the organization

In an ideal world, most companies would want to continually improve the quality of their product or service. The disadvantage of TQM is that there are associated up-front costs such as starting the program and maintaining it, while visible benefits may take time to appear. It is also not realistic or feasible for a company to spend unlimited time or money on quality improvements.

Returning to the example of the report you handed in to your professor, suppose your professor expected certain concepts to be fully elaborated on. Since the report you handed in did not include certain concepts, it would not be considered a quality report by your professor. To avoid falling below expectations, TQM can be applied to your assignments. Firstly, identify the issue. In this case, it is a gap between what the professor expected and what you submitted. Secondly, identify the measurement of quality the professor expects. To improve the quality of future submissions, it is necessary to identify the problems with your current report. Analyze and understand why not all of the requirements were included, and how to improve your submissions. For the next report, use the ideas you generated to improve the content and structure of your response. If this submission meets your professions expectations, continue to apply the changes you made for the remainder of your course.

Theory of Constraints

Theory of Constraints (TOC) is a management philosophy introduced by Dr. Eliyahu M. Goldratt in his book titled *The Goal*. The purpose of this philosophy is to help organizations continually achieve their objectives.

Essentially TOC focuses on constraints or **bottlenecks**. A bottleneck is resource or activity that holds up progress. Imagine driving along a three-lane highway when the traffic suddenly slows due to an accident. Since one of the lanes is now blocked, the traffic moves forward at a snail's pace. The point at which all the cars from the three lanes are trying to squeeze through the two free lanes is called a bottleneck or constraint. It does not matter how fast the vehicles can move when using three lanes. What matters is how fast traffic will move through two lanes instead of three.

In the book *"The Goal"*, the concept of the constraint is explained nicely with a Boy Scout story.

The main character, Alex, takes his son and a group of Boy Scouts out on a hiking expedition. All the boys must stay in view of Alex along the trail. Alex faces a constraint in the form of the slowest boy, Herbie, who is in the middle of the group. When a boy in the front tries to go faster, Herbie holds the group back. The same problem arises when someone behind Herbie tries to go faster. In other words, the speed at which the group can move forward is defined by the speed at which Herbie can walk. Herbie is the constraint.

The same concept applies in business. Process (output) is defined by the slowest resource which can be a technical constraint or even an attitude.

A constraint is anything that prevents the system from achieving its goal. There are many ways that constraints can occur, but a core principle within TOC is that there is usually at least one and at most, a few in any given system. Constraints can be internal or external to the system. An internal constraint is evident when the system cannot meet market demand. For example, if customers order 100,000 units when the business can only supply 80,000 units in a given timeframe, then the business has an internal constraint because it cannot produce what is required. If this is the case, then the focus of the organization should be on discovering the constraint that is preventing the business from providing the balance of 20,000 units required by its customers. The following are examples of internal constraints:

- **Equipment**: The way equipment is currently used limits the ability of the system to produce more salable goods/services.
- **People**: Lack of skilled people limits the system. Sometimes people's attitudes can cause behavior that becomes a constraint.
- **Policy**: A written or unwritten policy prevents the system from producing more.

An external constraint exists when the system can produce more than the market will bear. If this is the case, then the organization should focus on mechanisms to create more demand for its products or services. For example, if a business is able to produce 120,000 units but only has orders for 100,000 units, then the business must focus on how to increase sales.

The TOC process identifies the constraint and restructures the rest of the organization around it, through the use of the five focusing steps shown below.

1. Identify the constraint (i.e. what is the Herbie that prevents the organization from reaching its goal?)

2. Decide how to exploit the constraint (i.e. maximize the productivity of the Herbie)

3. Subordinate all other processes to the above decision (i.e. all other processes must work with the Herbie and not impact the productivity of the Herbie)

4.   Elevate the constraint (i.e. get rid of Herbie)

5.   If, as a result of these steps, the constraint has moved, return to step 1 (i.e. if there is a new constraint preventing the organization from reaching its goal, return to step 1 and go through the process again).

Theory of Constraints Example: AJ Sport Jerseys

Referring to our previous example of AJ Sport Jerseys, suppose the market requires 10,000 jerseys. In a perfect world, AJ Sport Jerseys will be able to supply exactly what the market requires. Thus, they will be able to buy the right amount of jerseys from their supplier, the dye house will be able to process all the jerseys, the printers will have no problem printing them and the customer will get them on time. In other words, there are no constraints.

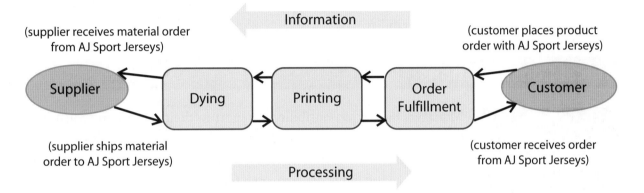

FIGURE 14.6

However, assume that the sales people are now able to sell 20,000 jerseys. The supplier is able to provide the white jerseys but the dye house does not have enough capacity to process that quantity. It does not matter that 20,000 jerseys can be printed or that order fulfillment can pack them all, the Herbie is the dye house. This is an internal constraint because the business cannot supply what the external market needs. The challenge for AJ Sports Jerseys is finding a way to overcome the constraint. Let us examine this problem using the five focusing steps.

1.   Identify the constraint (i.e. what is the Herbie that stops the organization from reaching its goal?). *Answer: The dye house*

2.   Decide how to exploit the constraint (i.e maximize the productivity of the Herbie). *Answer: Some possibilities include persuading the dye house to delay another customer who may not be in a hurry, or finding another dye house.*

3.   Subordinate all other processes to the above decision (i.e. all other processes must work with the Herbie and not impact the productivity of the Herbie). *Answer: Salespeople might have to accept the fact that production is limited to 10,000 units.*

4. Elevate the constraint (i.e. get rid of the Herbie). *Answer: Maybe the salespeople cannot accept lost sales. Perhaps they should consider not dying the jerseys and buy another type of jersey that the customer will accept with the same dye and print already on it.*

5. If, as a result of these steps, the constraint has moved, return to step 1 (i.e. if there is a new constraint preventing the organization from reaching its goal, return to step 1 and go through the process again). *Answer: The customer accepts the deal for the new type of jerseys but since it took a some time to find the new jerseys, the printing department cannot print all the jerseys in the time given. AJ Sport Jerseys will now have to go back to step 1 and proceed through the five focusing steps to resolve the printing constraint.*

There are many tools available to managers to monitor costs and improve profitability. Whether or not a business is able to implement JIT, producing high quality products and minimizing waste is something every business should strive for. Ultimately, better quality products and reducing waste will reduce costs and improve profitability.

Ethical Considerations

Managers have a responsibility to report to their seniors any constraints that are impeding the financial progress of the company. For example, Jim, a department manager, assisted in the hiring of his sister-in-law, Melissa, to work in his department a few months ago. Jim initially helped hire Melissa mainly as a favor for his wife. However, Melissa's level of productivity within the company is extremely low, and well below the acceptable production standards.

Because of Melissa's lack of competence and skills, the entire department is struggling to meet deadlines and produce an acceptable quality of output. However, Jim has not reported Melissa as a constraint to his manager, because if Melissa were to be terminated as a result, Jim fears the news would not go well with his wife. Not only is Jim's protection of Melissa detrimental to the department's overall performance, but it is also unethical.

In Summary

⇨ **Inventory shrinkage** is the reduction of inventory through causes such as theft, spoilage or misplacement and reduces profits.

⇨ **Just-in-time (JIT)** is an inventory management system which minimized the amount of inventory kept in stock.

⇨ JIT can be used by merchandising and manufacturing businesses.

⇨ Businesses can use a **push** or a **pull strategy.**

 ⬥ A push strategy is based on forecast sales, where management will decide how much will be purchased or manufactured and the product is pushed to the customer.

 ⬥ A pull strategy bases purchases or manufacturing on customer demand, where the customer pulls the product from the supplier.

⇨ JIT uses the pull strategy to drive production.

⇨ Advantages of JIT are reduced inventory, lower overhead costs and increased cash flow.

⇨ Advantages of forecast production are the ability to respond quickly to increased customer demand and taking advantage of volatile price fluctuations.

⇨ **Lean manufacturing** identifies seven areas of waste: transportation, inventory, motion, waiting, overproduction, over-processing and defects.

⇨ A waste area is an activity that does not create value for the customer.

⇨ Quality has four costs associated with it: prevention, appraisal, internal failure and external failure.

 ⬥ **Prevention costs** are proactive and can reduce the cost of quality in the long-run.

 ⬥ **Appraisal costs** measure or evaluate the quality of a product.

 ⬥ **Internal failure costs** are quality problems discovered before the customer receives the product.

 ⬥ **External failure costs** are quality problems discovered by the customer after the customer receives the product.

⇨ **Total Quality Management (TQM)** is a management concept that focuses on continuously reducing errors and satisfying customers.

⇨ **Theory of Constraints (TOC)** focuses on removing constraints or bottlenecks in production or processes.

⇨ An internal constraint exists when the business process cannot meet market demand. The constraint can be in the form of equipment, people or company policy.

⇨ An external constraint exists when the business can produce more than the market demands.

Notes

Chapter 15
THE CASH FLOW STATEMENT

LEARNING OUTCOMES:

❶ Understand the importance of cash flow within a business

❷ Classify operating, investing and financing activities

❸ Prepare a cash flow statement using the indirect method

❹ Prepare a cash flow statement using the direct method

Beyond the Balance Sheet and Income Statement

Cash is important for operating a business. As shown earlier in the text, creating a cash budget is important to properly forecast cash requirements before running out of cash. At the end of the year when a company prepares its balance sheet and income statement, it is also important to prepare a summary of all the sources and uses of cash that occurred during the year.

There are two reasons why analyzing the state of a business requires more than just the balance sheet and income statement.

First, balance sheets and income statements are prepared on an accrual basis. In other words, the matching principle dictates that revenues and expenses be recorded for the period in which they are earned or incurred. However, these types of transactions do not always involve an actual exchange of cash. Conversely, other transactions such as borrowing or repaying loans do not affect net income.

Second, well-publicized accounting scandals have exposed some of the flaws of balance sheets and income statements. In other words, some businesses have become adept at manipulating them for their advantage. The financial statements are not necessarily flawed, but analysts have, to a certain extent, less confidence in them.

Cash flow statements essentially follow the cash within a business. They ignore accruals and other book transactions, and actual changes to a company's cash account are revealed and analyzed more closely. Cash flow statements involve a different way of looking at financial numbers. For this reason, preparing a statement of cash flow can take some time to get used to. In other words, it takes practice. This chapter provides the basis for enhancing your understanding of, and proficiency with, cash flow statements.

Cash Flow Statements: Follow the Money

Accountants are required to prepare balance sheets and income statements for the business. These important documents represent the state of company finances and adhere to the matching principle, accruals and so on. Balance sheets and income statements are filled with promises of an exchange of money that must be recorded in one period, but may take place in another period. Company bills may not get paid for several months. Prepaid expenses can be left unadjusted for a number of periods. A borrower may default on a loan. Depreciation is recorded in the books, not with an exchange of cash.

Because of the way these transactions are accounted for in balance sheets and income statements, it can be difficult to know where the cash is actually going within the business. As a result, the accounting profession has devised another form of financial statement whose purpose is to specifically indicate both the *sources* of cash and the *uses* of cash within an organization. This document is known as the ***statement of cash flow*** and is the focus of this chapter.

The statement of cash flow shows how net income is converted to cash. Remember, net income does not necessarily translate into cash in the bank. The way a business is structured – in terms of financing, dividend schedules, debt collection, etc. – can have a significant impact on the way net income is turned into cash. It is this aspect of a business that a statement of cash flow reveals to readers, who may include management, accountants, potential lenders and investment analysts.

Note too that though cash flow statements can be of significant help to these financial players, they also constitute a requirement under GAAP. In other words, cash flow statements are not only useful but necessary. Knowing what they are, understanding what they can do and becoming familiar with preparing them, are essential tasks for an accountant. In this chapter, we explain how to perform these tasks.

Three Ways of Generating Cash Flow

A business generates and consumes cash in one of the following three ways:

- Operations
- Investments
- Financing

In fact, all cash flow statements are structured in this manner.

Cash flow from operations

This component of the cash flow statement tracks the movement of cash within a business on the basis of day-to-day activities. All items listed in this section affect the value of owner's equity. It is the most important section of the cash flow statement because the future of a business largely depends on the activities reported in this section.

Cash flow from investments

This component of the cash flow statement tracks the movement of cash in a business on the basis of the purchases and sales of long-term assets. For example, if a truck was sold during the year, cash flow would have increased. Alternatively, if the business purchased land, cash flow would have decreased, since the business had to use cash to buy the land.

Cash flow from financing

This component of the cash flow statement tracks the movement of cash within a business, on the basis of the way a company receives money from those providing financing and pays it back. These providers of finance could be banks or bondholders. These financiers could also be stockholders, who are paid with dividend payments. All these exchanges of cash need to be accounted for in this section of the cash flow statement.

Preparing a Statement of Cash Flow

Two methods are used to prepare a statement of cash flow: the **indirect method**, which is the most common method used, and the **direct method**.

Examine the Balance Sheet and the Income Statement

The first document we need is the balance sheet (or a comparative balance sheet for two periods) that tells us how much is in the cash account. We will refer to column and row numbers in figure 15.1. For example, accounts receivable of $1,065,812 in period 1 is referenced as C2. We will use this specific balance sheet for the remainder of the chapter, and keep referring to it as we move along.

When you examine the balance sheet, you will see that column D calculates the difference between period 1 and period 2. This difference will be used when calculating the cash flow statement. As you can see from line 1 of the balance sheet, the cash account decreased from $72,642 in period 1 to $13,265 in period 2. This represents a decrease of $59,377.

	A	B	C	D
	Balance Sheet	**Period 2**	**Period 1**	**Changes**
	Assets			
	Current Assets			
1	Cash	$13,265	$72,642	–$59,377
2	Accounts receivable	1,286,138	1,065,812	220,326
3	Prepaid expenses	48,612	42,625	5,987
4	Inventory	1,683,560	840,091	843,469
5	**Total Current Assets**	3,031,575	2,021,170	
6	**Long-Term Assets**			
7	Plant & equipment	322,518	170,000	152,518
8	Less accumulated depreciation	(89,262)	(46,000)	–43,262
9	**Total Long-Term Assets**	233,256	124,000	
10	**Total Assets**	**$3,264,831**	**$2,145,170**	
11	**Liabilities**			
12	**Current Liabilities**			
13	Accounts payable & accrued liabilities	783,602	475,645	307,957
14	Current portion of bank loan	380,000	240,000	140,000
15	Stockholders' loans	170,000	200,000	–30,000
16	**Total Current Liabilities**	1,333,602	915,645	
17	Long-term debt	420,000	356,000	64,000
18	**Total Liabilities**	1,753,602	1,271,645	
19	**Stockholders' Equity**			
20	Contributed Capital	10,000	10,000	
21	Plus Retained earnings	1,501,229	913,525	
22	Less Dividend		(50,000)	
23	**Stockholders' Equity**	1,511,229	873,525	
24	**Liabilities + Equity**	**$3,264,831**	**$2,145,170**	

FIGURE 15.1

We now need to examine the income statement.

	A	B	C
	Income Statement	Period 2	Period 1
1	Sales	$8,685,025	$6,482,000
2	Cost of goods sold	5,998,612	4,397,200
3	Gross Profit	2,686,413	2,084,800
4	Operating Expenses		
5	Administration charges	8,652	6,861
6	Advertising & marketing	42,645	32,975
7	Depreciation of long-term assets	43,262	15,862
8	Bonuses	65,000	62,432
9	Commission	420,250	325,210
10	Interest	51,875	31,253
11	Insurance	16,000	12,000
12	Sales and admin salaries and benefits	610,325	435,951
13	Management salaries	320,560	226,548
14	Occupancy (rent, cleaning, etc.)	52,000	48,000
15	Other operating expenses	61,200	48,672
16	Consulting	22,500	21,356
17	Repairs and maintenance	36,860	26,845
18	Professional fees	11,560	8,642
19	Total Expenses	1,762,689	1,302,607
20	Operating Income Before Tax	923,724	782,193
21	Tax	286,020	223,652
22	Net Income added to Retained Earnings	$637,704	$558,541

FIGURE 15.2

As has been highlighted, the company's net income is $637,704 for period 2. We will be using this income statement for the remainder of the chapter, so keep it handy as we assemble our cash flow statements.

You may have asked yourself an obvious question after noticing a change in balance in the cash account (which reflects a decrease of $59,377) and a net income of $637,704. What happened to all the cash? This type of question can be answered by the cash flow statement. Let us start getting some answers.

Indirect Method

The figure we start with is the balance in cash, which is $72,642 at the start of period 1 in our balance sheet.

Balance Sheet	Period 2	Period 1
Assets		
Current Assets		
Cash	13,265	72,642

FIGURE 15.3

Cash Flow from Operations

The following illustrations will help you understand the change in cash through day-to-day operations.

As the value of various current assets and liabilities change from one period to another, cash flow is affected. The next four figures illustrate this principle.

If accounts receivable decreases, it means that the cash has been collected, resulting in an increase to cash (as shown in figure 15.4).

If inventory increases, it means that the cash has been used to pay for it, resulting in a decrease in cash (as shown in figure 15.5).

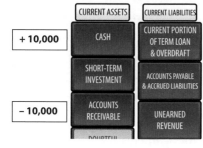

FIGURE 15.4

If accounts payable decreases, it means that cash has been used to pay for it, resulting in a decrease in cash (as shown in figure 15.6).

If prepaid expenses increases, this means that cash has been used to pay for it, resulting in a decrease in cash (as shown in figure 15.7).

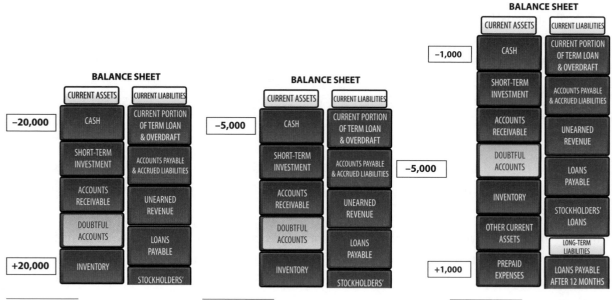

FIGURE 15.5   FIGURE 15.6   FIGURE 15.7

Now let us start preparing our cash flow from operations. Remember that cash flow from operations is essentially the company's net income (or net loss). In our current example, the company's net income is $637,704 (reference B22 of our income statement). Net income can also be calculated by subtracting retained earnings of period 2 from that of period 1, after deducting the dividend in period 1.

Net income is added to (or net loss is deducted from) our opening cash account balance. Since we are focusing on cash flow instead of accruals, we need only account for the money that actually changes hands during a period. Since depreciation is simply the decrease in the value of an asset, without any change to cash, depreciation deductions are taken out of any equations involving cash flow.

Therefore, the next step in assembling cash flow from operations is to add back any depreciation that was originally deducted. This figure can be obtained from one of two places. We can get it directly from the income statement, which in this case is located in cell B7 of our income statement and is the amount of $43,262. Alternatively, we can get the depreciation expense from cell D8 of our comparative balance sheet, which shows the difference in accumulated depreciation between periods 1 and 2.

Here is how our opening cash balance changes: As you can see in figure 15.8, we take our opening cash balance, add the net income (or deduct the net loss), and add back the depreciation. This gives us a new cash balance of $753,608.

> This column is used to calculate the updated cash balance to help you understand the process.
>
> **You will not see this theoretical column illustrated in a regular cash flow statement.**

Add or subtract the increases or decreases from the balance sheet accounts

Cash Flow Statement	Cash Flow	Updated Cash Balance
Opening Cash Balance		**$72,642**
Cash flow from Operations		
Add Net Income	$637,704	710,346
Add Depreciation	43,262	753,608
Record the change in balance for the remainder:		
Change in Assets and Liabilities		
Accounts Receivable	(220,326)	
Prepaid Expenses	(5,987)	
Inventory	(843,469)	
Accounts Payable	307,957	
Net cash flow from operating activities		

FIGURE 15.8

This is the first part of our cash flow from operations. We start with cash, then add net income or deduct losses and then add depreciation. The second part involves referring back to our comparative balance sheet and going down the list of current assets and liabilities. Loans will be dealt with in the cash flow from financing section, below.

Add or subtract the increases or decreases from the balance sheet accounts

Cash Flow Statement	Cash Flow	Updated Cash Balance
Opening Cash Balance		$72,642
Cash Flow from Operations		
Add Net Income	$637,704	710,346
Add Depreciation	43,262	753,608
Record the change in balance for the remainder:		
Change in current assets & liabilities (excluding loans)		
Accounts Receivable	(220,326)	533,282
Prepaid Expenses	(5,987)	527,295
Inventory	(843,469)	(316,174)
Accounts Payable	307,957	(8,217)
Net Cash Outflow from Operating Activities	(80,859)	

FIGURE 15.9

Our first listed current asset in our comparative balance sheet (after cash) is accounts receivable. As reference D2 indicates from the balance sheet, this account increased by $220,326 from period 1 to period 2. (Remember that since accounts receivable increased, it will decrease cash because it is yet to be collected.) We therefore deduct this amount from the cash balance of $753,608. As indicated above, the new cash balance is $533,282.

Prepaid expenses increased by $5,987 resulting in a decrease in cash because the prepaid expenses must have been paid with cash, resulting in a new cash balance of $527,295.

Inventory increased by $843,469, resulting once again in a decrease in cash because cash must be used to pay for the additional inventory resulting in a negative cash balance of $316,174.

Accounts payable increased by $307,957. This will result in more cash in the bank, causing the new cash balance to increase and ending up with an outflow of cash from operations of $80,859, as highlighted.

Cash Flow from Investments

Changes in the value of long-term assets affect cash flow. An increase in long-term assets will result in a decrease in cash and vice versa.

The next section of the cash flow statement deals with the way cash flow changes through investing in or selling capital assets. In our current example, putting together the cash flow from investments is relatively simple. All we need to do is go back to our balance sheet and look at the change in our long-term assets from period to period. Remember that we do not take depreciation into account when examining this element of the cash flow statement since it has already been addressed in the operations section of the analysis.

This means that we only have to look at line 7 of our comparative balance sheet, *Plant & Equipment*. As cell D7 indicates, this account increased in value from period to period by an amount of $152,518. Since assets increased, cash decreased by $152,518.

Cash Flow Statement	Cash Flow	Updated Cash Balance
Opening Cash Balance		**$72,642**
Cash Flow from Operations		
Add Net Income	$637,704	710,346
Add Depreciation	43,262	753,608
Record the change in balance for the remainder:		
Change in current assets & liabilities (excluding loans)		
Accounts Receivable	(220,326)	533,282
Prepaid Expenses	(5,987)	527,295
Inventory	(843,469)	(316,174)
Accounts Payable	307,957	(8,217)
Net Cash Outflow from Operating Activities	**(80,859)**	
Cash Flow from Investment		
Long-term Assets	(152,518)	(160,735)
Net Cash Outflow from Investing Activities	**(152,518)**	

FIGURE 15.10

This is our change in cash due to investments, and essentially constitutes that entire section of the cash flow statement.

Cash Flow from Financing

Cash flow from financing is the last section of the cash flow statement that we need to prepare. As loans or contributed capital increase or decrease, cash flow is correspondingly affected.

If loans or contributed capital increases, this means that cash has been received, resulting in an increase in cash; if, on the other hand, loans or contributed capital decreases, this would lead to a decrease in cash.

Remember that this section accounts for cash resulting from any financing activities during the year. It includes borrowing money or receiving cash as a result of a stock issue. In addition, this section also includes any payments involved with financing, such as dividend payments or loan repayments.

Cash flow from the financing section is somewhat different from the other cash flow sections in that it involves changes to more than one section of the statement. For example, in the operations section of the cash flow statement, accounts receivable is one account, inventory is another, and so on.

Cash flow from financing is divided into two areas in our balance sheet: long term and short term. In addition, payments in the form of dividends also affect the cash position directly from year to year. That is why it is especially important to keep track of money as it changes hands while the cash flow statement, particularly the financing section, is being assembled.

First, we need to take a look at our balance sheet again and check all aspects pertaining to financing. The three parts that are affected are stockholder loans, bank loans and dividends.

Let us look at stockholder loans in the current liabilities section of the balance sheet. This is relatively simple since there is only one account here. And since stockholder loans decreased by $30,000, the cash balance also decreased by $30,000 from period 1 to period 2. That figure is shown in cell D15 of our balance sheet.

Now look at bank loans. An extra step is involved because bank loans are divided into two areas on our balance sheet: short term (current) and long term. We must extract from the balance sheet the changes from period to period that occurred for both.

The current portion of the bank loan is found on line 14 of the balance sheet. The change from period to period is in cell D14, in the amount of $140,000 (see figure 15.1, our original balance sheet, for specific cell references).

For the rest of the bank loan, which is found under long-term debt on line 17 of the balance sheet, the change from period to period is $64,000.

Liabilities			
Current Liabilities			
Accounts Payable & Accrued Liabilities	783,602	475,645	307,957
14 → Current Portion of Bank Loan	380,000	240,000	140,000
Stockholder's Loans	170,000	200,000	–30,000
Total Current Liabilities	1,333,602	915,645	
17 → Long-term debt	420,000	356,000	64,000
Total Liabilities	1,753,602	1,271,645	

FIGURE 15.11

Adding up the changes in both short-term and long-term loans, we get a total increase of $204,000 ($140,000 + 64,000, see D14 and D17). This is the figure that we enter into the appropriate section of the cash flow statement.

Finally, we need to look at dividends. As line 22 of the balance sheet indicates, no dividends were paid in period 2. This means that there was no change in the company's cash position as a result. So a zero is entered into this section of the cash flow statement. Figure 15.12 shows the entire section with our numbers for stockholder loans, bank loans and dividends inserted.

As should now be clear, changes in cash due to financing account for an increase to our cash account of $174,000 ($204,000 - $30,000).

Cash Flow Statement	Cash Flow	Updated Cash Balance
Opening Cash Balance		$72,642
Cash Flow from Operations		
Add Net Income	$637,704	710,346
Add Depreciation	43,262	753,608
Record the change in balance for the remainder:		
Change in current assets & liabilities (excluding loans)		
Accounts Receivable	(220,326)	533,282
Prepaid Expenses	(5,987)	527,295
Inventory	(843,469)	(316,174)
Accounts Payable	307,957	(8,217)
Net Cash Outflow from Operating Activities	(80,859)	
Cash Flow from Investment		
Long-term Assets	(152,518)	(160,735)
Net Cash Outflow from Investing Activities	(152,518)	
Cash Flow from Financing		
Stockholders' Loans	(30,000)	(190,735)
Dividends	0	(190,735)
Bank Loans	204,000	13,265
Net Cash Inflow from Financing Activities	174,000	

FIGURE 15.12

Summary of the Indirect Method

We have now completed the three sections of our cash flow statement: cash flow from operations, investments and financing. It is now just a matter of putting them all together to form one complete cash flow statement for the period. Figure 15.13 shows the information in a formal cash flow statement format.

Collin Company
Cash Flow Statement
For the Year Ending on December 31, 2010

Cash Flow from Operations		
Net Income	$637,704	
Add Depreciation	43,262	
Change In Current Assets & Liabilities		
Accounts Receivable	(220,326)	
Prepaid Expenses	(5,987)	
Inventory	(843,469)	
Accounts Payable	307,957	
Net Cash Outflow from Operating Activities		$(80,859)
Cash Flow from Investment		
Long-term Assets	(152,518)	
Net Cash Outflow from Investing Activities		(152,518)
Cash Flow from Financing		
Stockholders' Loans	(30,000)	
Bank Loans	204,000	
Net Cash Inflow from Financing Activities		174,000
Net Decrease in Cash		(59,377)
Opening Cash Balance		72,642
Closing Cash Balance		$13,265

FIGURE 15.13

Direct Method

We have assembled a cash flow statement using the *indirect method*. The term indirect refers to tracking the changes to cash without direct reference to cash receipts or payments. In other words, this method analyzes cash flow indirectly by starting with accrual-based net income and making related adjustments for changes on the balance sheet and income statement.

We will now turn our attention to the **direct method**, which is another way of tracing the changes to cash from one period to the next. Like the indirect method, the **direct method** breaks down the three ways of generating and using cash into: operating, investing and financing activities. In this section, we will illustrate how the direct method accomplishes this by looking at, specifically, *cash receipts* and **payments**. The direct method is not often used because it can be burdensome to execute.

Here is a simple example to illustrate the fundamental difference between the indirect method and the direct method presented in this chapter. Jane is a student who currently pays her tuition in cash and gets paid in cash for her part-time job. In an attempt to control her spending, she has opted to use her debit card for all purchases and never pay by credit card. Suppose that, at the end of the year, Jane wants to determine by how much her cash situation changed in the year. There are two ways she can go about doing this:

1. She can review her bank statements and calculate the difference between the December (end of year) bank balance and January (beginning of year) bank balance. Since all her transactions are made with cash, she can simply subtract the beginning of year balance from the end of year balance and determine how her cash situation changed during the year. Or,

2. Jane can calculate her cash flow for the year by adding together all the individual purchase receipts and pay stubs she received throughout the year.

Both methods will add to the same value, assuming all receipts and stubs are accounted for and there are no errors.

Method 1 is, essentially, the indirect method. This is because Jane indirectly determined her cash flow situation by reading off the balances on her bank statements. Method 2, on the other hand, demonstrates the direct cash flow method because Jane directly summed up all her collections and disbursements for the year using source documents. Notice that the direct method can be a lot more time-consuming and prone to error since Jane would have to search for all her documents (she may have accidentally thrown out some receipts). Similarly to Jane, most companies opt to use the indirect method for simplicity purposes.

Following we will walk through an example and determine the cash flow of a company using the direct method.

Suppose ArmorVilla Corporation had the following transactions for the year ending on July 31, 2011.

a)	Amortization expense	$22,000
b)	Cash sales	284,000
c)	Loan to another company	75,000
d)	Credit sales	966,000
e)	Cash received from issuing short-term debt	26,000
f)	Dividends received in cash on investments in stock	9,000
g)	Payments of salaries	180,000
h)	Accrued salary expense	105,000
i)	Collection of interest on notes receivable	32,000
j)	Cash received from issuing common stock	81,000
k)	Purchase of inventory on credit	605,000
l)	Declaration and payment of cash dividends	144,000
m)	Collections from credit customers	638,000
n)	Payments to suppliers	313,000
o)	Payment of long-term debt	175,000
p)	Cash received from selling equipment	30,000
q)	Interest expenses and payments	21,000
r)	Cash payments to acquire capital assets	204,000
s)	Cash balance: August 1, 2010	$178,000
	July 31, 2011	$166,000

FIGURE 15.14

Since we are using the direct method, we are interested, primarily, in *cash receipts* and *payments*. Therefore, let's identify only those items that affect cash flow:

b)	Cash sales	$284,000
c)	Loan to another company	75,000
e)	Cash received from issuing short-term debt	26,000
f)	Dividends received in cash on investments in stock	9,000
g)	Payments of salaries	180,000
i)	Collection of interest on notes receivable	32,000
j)	Cash received from issuing common stock	81,000
l)	Declaration and payment of cash dividends	144,000
m)	Collections from credit customers	638,000
n)	Payments to suppliers	313,000
o)	Payment of long-term debt	175,000
p)	Cash received from selling equipment	30,000
q)	Interest expenses and payments	21,000
r)	Cash payments to acquire capital assets	204,000

FIGURE 15.15

Now let's categorize each cash item into the appropriate category to create our statement of cash flow. First, we will consider cash receipts/disbursements that relate to regular business operations.

Cash Flow from Operations		
Cash Sales	$284,000	
Collections from Credit Customers	638,000	
Dividends Received on Investments in Stock	9,000	
Collection of Interest on Notes Receivable	32,000	
Total Cash Receipts		$963,000
Payment of Salaries	180,000	
Payments to Suppliers	313,000	
Interest Expenses and Payments	21,000	
Total Cash Payments		514,000
Net Cash Inflow from Operating Activities		$449,000

FIGURE 15.16

Notice that to perform a cash flow calculation using the direct method, a company has to be able to track information regarding cash inflows and outflows. This makes it more difficult to use the direct method.

Note that the cash flow calculations for investing and financing activities using the direct method are very similar to the indirect method.

Cash Flow from Investing		
Loan to Another Company	$(75,000)	
Sale of Equipment	30,000	
Capital Asset Acquisition	(204,000)	
Net Cash Outflow from Investing Activities		$(249,000)
Cash Flow from Financing		
Issuance of Short-Term Debt	26,000	
Issuance of Common Stock	81,000	
Declaration And Payment of Dividends (Cash)	(144,000)	
Payment of Long-Term Debt	(175,000)	
Net Cash Outflow from Financing Activities		$(212,000)

FIGURE 15.17

Summary of the Direct Method

In summary, the cash flow statement of ArmorVilla Corporation prepared by using the direct method is shown in figure 15.18.

ArmorVilla Corporation Cash Flow Statement For the Year Ending on July 31, 2011		
Cash Flow from Operations		
Cash Sales	$284,000	
Collections from Credit Customers	638,000	
Dividends Received on Investments in Stock	9,000	
Collection of Interest on Notes Receivable	32,000	
Total Cash Receipts		$963,000
Payment of Salaries	180,000	
Payments to Suppliers	313,000	
Interest Expenses and Payments	21,000	
Total Cash Payments		514,000
Net Cash Inflow from Operating Activities		449,000
Cash Flow from Investing		
Loan to Another Company	(75,000)	
Sale of Equipment	30,000	
Capital Asset Acquisition	(204,000)	
Net Cash Outflow from Investing Activities		(249,000)
Cash Flow from Financing		
Issuance of Short-Term Debt	26,000	
Issuance of Common Stock	81,000	
Declaration and Payment of Dividends	(144,000)	
Payment of Long-Term Debt	(175,000)	
Net Cash Outflow from Financing Activities		(212,000)
Net Decrease in Cash		(12,000)
Opening Cash Balance, August 1, 2010		178,000
Ending Cash Balance, July 31, 2011		$166,000

FIGURE 15.18

Although the direct and indirect method use different approaches to determine the cash flow, both approaches still provide the same end result and allow for an assessment of a company's cash management effectiveness.

IN THE REAL WORLD

The accounting scandals that began in 2001 served as a warning to much of the financial community that income statements and balance sheets can be manipulated to present a false financial picture of a business. As a result, an increasing number of people started using the statement of cash flow as a more revealing snapshot of a company's financial well-being.

Indeed, the motivation behind relying more on cash flow statements to analyze company performance is understandable. Cash flow statements are supposed to show where the money is coming from and where it is going. However, no financial statement is immune from flaws, and this is certainly the case with cash flow statements.

The following three situations should be viewed with caution when the cash flow statement of a business is analyzed:

- *Some companies may stretch out their payables.* One way of artificially enhancing a company's cash position from operations is to deliberately delay paying bills. In fact, some companies will even go so far as to institute such a policy and label it as a form of shrewd cash flow decision making. Of course, the company has not improved its underlying cash flow, but has simply manipulated it.

- *Some companies may finance their payables.* Some companies try to manipulate their statement of cash flow by having a third party pay their payables for them – although regulators have tried to crack down on this practice. This means that the company itself shows no payments in its cash flow and, instead, pays a fee to the third party at a later date. Picking and choosing the periods in which this is done artificially manipulates the statement of cash flow — almost at will.

- *Cash flow categories can be artificial.* Although businesses may handle their finances differently, including receiving and paying out cash, cash flow statements should exhibit the same categories listed under the same headings for every business. In essence, information can be lost in translation, and analysts can become too dependent on numbers that are made to fit into the cash flow statement.

 ## In Summary

- ⮕ Balance sheets and income statements are prepared on an accrual basis, which involves recording transactions that do not necessarily involve any exchange of money. Cash flow statements differ in that they reveal both the sources and uses of cash within a business.

- ⮕ The three ways of generating cash flow, which form the basis of the way cash flow statements are structured, are operations, investments and financing.

- ⮕ There exist two generally accepted methods of preparing a cash flow statement for a business: the direct method and the indirect method.

- ⮕ Both methods of preparing cash flow statements involve starting with the beginning balance in cash, then moving on to the balance sheet and income statement to track specific changes in the cash account. Both methods should produce the same results.

- ⮕ The indirect method of preparing cash flow statements starts with net income and then tracks changes in balances.

- ⮕ The direct method of preparing cash flow statements breaks down cash flows based on actual receipts and payments associated with major sales and expense items.

- ⮕ Both methods of preparing a cash flow statement contain three sections that should produce the same changes in cash amounts: cash flow from operations, cash flow from investments and cash flow from financing.

- ⮕ The indirect method tends to be universally used in preparing cash flow statements, since the direct method takes a more burdensome approach to tracking cash receipts and payments.

Review Exercise

Shown below is the balance sheet for MLF. Net income for 2010 was $207,144.

Required: Prepare the statement of cash flow for 2010. Use the indirect method.

MLF Balance Sheet As at December 31, 2010		
	2010	**2009**
Assets		
Current Assets		
Cash	$28,222	$64,494
Other Current Assets	605,379	902,417
Total Current Assets	633,601	966,911
Long-Term Assets		
Property, Plant and Equipment	3,490,970	3,389,108
Less: Accumulated Depreciation	(1,126,727)	(1,080,293)
Total Long-Term Assets	2,364,243	2,308,815
Total Assets	$2,997,844	$3,275,726
Liabilities		
Current Liabilities	$591,199	$778,299
Long-Term Liabilities	1,245,218	1,502,985
Total Liabilities	1,836,417	2,281,284
Stockholders' Equity		
Contributed Capital	790,027	790,027
Opening Retained Earnings	204,415	231,907
Net Income for the Year	207,144	4,525
Dividends Paid	(40,159)	(32,017)
Closing Retained Earnings	371,400	204,415
Total Stockholders' Equity	1,161,427	994,442
Total Liabilities and Stockholders' Equity	$2,997,844	$3,275,726

Assume current liabilities include only items from operations (e.g., accounts payable, tax payable). Long-term liabilities include items from financing (e.g. bonds and other long-term assets)

MLF Balance Sheet Cash Flow Statement For the Year ended December 31, 2010	Change	New Cash Balance
Opening Cash		$64,494
Cash Flows from Operations		
Net Income	$207,144	271,638
Add: Depreciation	46,434	318,072
Decrease in Other Current Assets	297,038	615,110
Decrease in Current Liabilities	(187,100)	428,010
Total Increase in Cash from Operations	363,516	
Cash Flows from Investment		
Purchase of Property, Plant and Equipment	(101,862)	326,148
Total Decrease in Cash from Investing	101,862	
Cash Flows from Financing		
Paid Long-Term Liabilities	(257,767)	68,381
Dividends Paid	(40,159)	28,222
Total Decrease in Cash from Financing	(297,926)	
Total Decrease in Cash from All Sources	(36,272)	
Closing Cash		$28,222

Notes

Chapter 16

FINANCIAL STATEMENT ANALYSIS

The Importance of Financial Statement Analysis

A complete set of financial statements for a public corporation includes comparative balance sheets, income statements, a cash flow statements and notes. All of this is to provide information about the company. However, these statements do not provide all the answers needed to form conclusions on where the business is heading. But these answers are needed by the organization's accountants, its management team, potential lenders and investors, or others with an interest in the state of the business.

In order to start getting answers, and to draw conclusions on the financial state of the business, accountants and other interested parties perform what is known as a **financial analysis** of the financial statements. **Financial ratios** are used to perform this kind of analysis.

Some financial ratios provide answers relative to profitability, while others address inventory, accounts receivable or other aspects of the business. No financial ratio, on its own, can form the basis of the financial analysis of a business. Instead, a combination of ratios must be used to draw a complete picture of the state of an organization's finances. In a sense, financial analysis is much like peeling an orange. An orange with its peel on can give you a sense of how ripe it is. Peel away the skin, and you get a closer picture. Does it have bruises? Is it firm or soft? To truly know how good the orange is, it is then necessary to take a bite. Finally, more bites are taken and a conclusion is formed as to the taste and quality of the orange.

Our approach to financial analysis follows a similar logic. Here is the progression that we take:

Revenues are Vanity

Much like an orange with its peel on, glancing at business revenues does not necessarily give us an accurate picture. In other words, sales do not guarantee profits. We demonstrated this phenomenon in chapter 15 when discussing cash flow statements. We will do the same in the current chapter.

Profits are Sanity

Some serious weaknesses can exist within a business if profits are not quickly transformed into cash. In other words, a business should have a good degree of liquidity. Just as taking off the orange peel provides a better look at the fruit, but not necessarily an accurate judgment as to its quality, a company's profit figures may not provide all the information we need.

Cash Flow is Reality

Getting more information about the well-being of a business comes from looking at its cash flow. It gives us the most accurate picture of the true state of the financial affairs of a business. Accountants and analysts can only give a business a clean bill of health if they are satisfied that profits result in enough cash flow for the business.

Management Ensures Stability

You will not get a sense of what the orange tastes like unless you put it in your mouth and start savoring its flavor. Similarly, you will not get a sense of how the company's cash flow is managed unless you take a look at some management ratios.

The rest of this chapter is dedicated to performing a financial analysis based on this precise sequence.

Revenues are Vanity

The first part of our approach is to consider changes in revenues. Using the same financial statements that we used in chapter 15, our current income statement will look like this:

	Income Statement	Period 2	Period 1
1	**Income Statement**	**Period 2**	**Period 1**
2	**Revenue**	$8,685,025 ⬅	$6,482,000
3	Cost of Goods Sold	5,998,612	4,397,200
4	**Gross Profit**	2,686,413	2,084,800

FIGURE 16.1

So, let's take a look at the revenue figures provided. As you can see in line 2 of the income statement, revenue jumped from $6,482,000 in the previous period to $8,685,025 in the current one. This constitutes an increase of $2,203,025 (or 34%).

Revenues only form the first superficial glance at the numbers for the business. In this case, growing revenues, numbering in the millions of dollars, might look great. However, we need more analysis and ratios to determine if they are in fact great figures, or merely superficial indicators of business health. For example, if revenues increased by $2.2 million but costs increased by $4 million then just looking at changes in revenues alone will not give us a true understanding of how the company has performed in the past year.

Profits are Sanity

The next step in our approach to financial analysis is to look at profits. Remember, profits are sanity. In other words, profits can serve as a deeper indicator of financial stability, beyond revenues. In this case the gross profit figure (revenues minus cost of goods sold), can be found on line four of the income statement. This figure has increased by an amount of $601,613, (given that gross profits were at $2,084,800 in the previous period, and $2,686,413 in the current period).

However, just as with revenues, gross profit figures can only tell us so much. In this case, they indicate the business is turning revenues into profit. But we need more information — which means that we need to introduce some ratios into the mix. Let's start with gross profit margin.

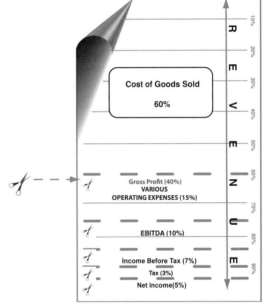

Our approach to analyzing the entire income statement is rather simple, and is depicted in this diagram of a piece of paper. The entire paper represents business revenues. As our analysis proceeds, a certain chunk - or percentage - is taken from revenues, which leaves something behind for us to analyze. By the end of the income statement, we're left with the smallest chunk, which is net income. By then it will be time to move on to the balance sheet.

FIGURE 16.2

Gross Profit Margin

We use the gross profit margin to demonstrate the impact of cost of goods sold on the financial statements. In other words, gross profit margin subtracts cost of goods sold from sales revenue, the result of which is divided by sales revenue. Here is the formula:

$$\text{Gross Profit Margin} = \frac{\text{Gross Profit*}}{\text{Sales Revenue}}$$

* Gross profit = Revenue − Cost of Goods Sold

Gross profit margin tells us how much money is left to pay expenses, other than those directly involved in producing the goods or services of the business. That is, how much profitability remains after deducting the cost of goods sold.

The following chart calculates the gross profit margin using figures from the income statement:

	Period 2	Period 1
Revenue	$8,685,025	$6,482,000
Cost of goods sold	5,998,612	4,397,200
Gross Profit	2,686,413	2,084,800
Gross Profit Margin	30.93%	32.16%

FIGURE 16.3

As you can see, gross profit margin has decreased by more than one percentage point over the course of the period. There are various reasons why this might occur, ranging from discount prices and changes in product mix, to inventory shrinkage and under-valuation.

EBITDA

It might be tempting to believe that the next step in our analysis is to start peeling away all costs after gross profit has been calculated. This part of our income statement has been highlighted in yellow as shown in figure 16.4.

	Income Statement	Period 2	Period 1
1	**Income Statement**	**Period 2**	**Period 1**
2	**Revenue**	$8,685,025	$6,482,000
3	Cost of Goods Sold	5,998,612	4,397,200
4	**Gross Profit**	2,686,413	2,084,800
5	**Operating Expenses**		
6	Administration Charges	8,652	6,861
7	Advertising & Marketing	42,645	32,975
8	Depreciation of Long-Term Assets	43,262	15,862
9	Bonuses	65,000	62,432
10	Commission	420,250	325,210
11	Interest	51,875	31,253
12	Insurance	16,000	12,000
13	Sales and Admin Salaries and Benefits	610,325	435,951
14	Management Salaries	320,560	226,548
15	Occupancy (Rent, Cleaning, etc.)	52,000	48,000
16	Other Operating Expenses	61,200	48,672
17	Consulting	22,500	21,356
18	Repairs and Maintenance	36,860	26,845
19	Professional Fees	11,560 ⬅	8,642
20	**Total Expenses**	1,762,689	1,302,607
21	**Operating Income Before Tax**	923,724	782,193
22	Tax	286,020	223,652
23	**Net Income added to Retained Earnings**	$637,704	$558,541

In fact, removing operating expenses and taxes from gross profit gives us our net income figure, located at the bottom of the income statement

FIGURE 16.4

As enticing as it might be to jump from gross profit to net income, there is a step in between that many accountants and analysts take to get an even clearer picture of business performance. Specifically, certain costs (that are considered largely under the control of management) are added back after net income is calculated. These costs generally include interest, tax, depreciation and amortization. Together, they are referred to as EBITDA or earnings before interest, tax, depreciation and amortization.

Adding these costs back after net income is calculated essentially levels the playing field when analyzing the performance of one business compared to another. In other words, items such as depreciation and taxes are not the result of day-to-day managerial decision-making. Instead, these types of costs can vary from jurisdiction to jurisdiction or from one business to another. Net income, therefore, does not reflect the direct performance that the business controls.

The following income statement has been adjusted to indicate what expenses are added back to calculate EBITDA (EBITDA for Period 1 is $829,308, and for Period 2 is $1,018,861):

	Income Statement	Period 2	Period 1	
1	**Income Statement**	**Period 2**	**Period 1**	
2	**Revenue**	$8,685,025	$6,482,000	
3	Cost of Goods Sold	5,998,612	4,397,200	
4	**Gross Profit**	2,686,413	2,084,800	
5	**Operating Expenses**			
6	Administration Charges	8,652	6,861	
7	Advertising & Marketing	42,645	32,975	
8	Depreciation of Long-Term Assets	43,262	15,862	**Add back**
9	Bonuses	65,000	62,432	
10	Commission	420,250	325,210	
11	Interest	51,875	31,253	**Add back**
12	Insurance	16,000	12,000	
13	Sales and Admin Salaries and Benefits	610,325	435,951	
14	Management Salaries	320,560	226,548	
15	Occupancy (Rent, Cleaning, etc.)	52,000	48,000	
16	Other Operating Expenses	61,200	48,672	
17	Consulting	22,500	21,356	
18	Repairs and Maintenance	36,860	26,845	
19	Professional Fees	11,560	8,642	
20	**Total Expenses**	1,762,689	1,302,607	
21	**Operating Income Before**	923,724	782,193	
22	Tax	286,020	223,652	**Add back**
23	**Net Income added to Retained Earnings**	$637,704	$558,541	

FIGURE 16.5

EBITDA Percentage to Sales

Given that we now have a better understanding of what EBITDA is, and why associated expenses are added back to net income; it is time to start formulating some ratios as a result. You may have noticed a trend in the ratios we have used so far. Specifically, we have taken that part of the pie remaining after certain expenses are deducted — such as COGS, operating expenses, and so on — and divided it by revenues. In other words, we have been deducting slices of expenses from revenue and then dividing the remainder by revenue itself. This gives us a corresponding percentage relative to revenue, which, in essence, tells us how much money we are working with on a percentage basis. The exact same thing is done with EBITDA.

In other words, we want to take our EBITDA number and divide it by revenue, to obtain yet another percentage figure to work with in our analysis.

$$\text{EBITDA Percentage to Sales} = \frac{\text{EBITDA}}{\text{Sales Revenue}}$$

This ratio has been calculated for us in the following chart:

	Period 2	Period 1
Revenue	$8,685,025	$6,482,000
Net Income		
Add back	637,704	558,541
Interest	51,875	31,253
Tax	286,020	223,652
Depreciation	43,262	15,862
EBITDA	$1,018,861	$829,308 ↑
EBITDA Percentage to Sales	11.73%	12.79% ↓

FIGURE 16.6

As you can see, although EBITDA has increased in absolute dollars from period 1 to period 2, the percentage has, in fact, decreased. This probably means that the business has become less efficient during the period and further analysis needs to be done to find out which expenses are contributing to the decline.

Interest Coverage Ratio

You may have noticed that financial ratios are often nothing more than a comparison of numbers involving one figure divided by another. In fact, most of the ratios analyzed so far in this chapter involve dividing a number by revenues, which provides us with a percentage relative to revenues.

The second ratio we will look at with respect to EBITDA is the **interest coverage ratio** which is very similar to the EBITDA to sales ratio. The only difference is that instead of dividing EBITDA by revenues, it is interest that serves as the denominator in the ratio. In other words, the interest coverage ratio measures the extent to which earnings before interest, taxes, depreciation and amortization covers the interest payments that are to be made by the business. That is, to what extent does EBITDA cover the ability to pay lenders cash in the form of regular interest payments that are due within the period?

For example, an interest coverage ratio of 1:1 would mean that the business has just enough earnings (before EBITDA expenses are deducted) to cover the amount of interest paid during the year. Ideally, a business should have an interest coverage ratio of at least 2, which means that it has twice as much EBITDA to cover any interest payments to be made in the year.

Here is how the interest coverage ratio is calculated:

$$\text{Interest Coverage Ratio} = \frac{\text{EBITDA}}{\text{Interest}}$$

The interest number that we need is found on line 11 of the income statement:

9	Bonuses	$65,000	$62,432
10	Commission	420,250	325,210
11	Interest	51,875	31,253
12	Insurance	16,000	12,000

FIGURE 16.7

The corresponding numbers related to interest coverage are provided in the following chart:

EBITDA	$1,018,861	$829,308
Interest	51,875	31,253
Interest Coverage Ratio	19.64 :1	26.54 :1

FIGURE 16.8

As you can see, total interest has increased at a rate greater than that for EBITDA. Although the interest coverage ratios for both periods are well above 2:1 (which is desirable), if this downward trend continues, it may mean that the business will have an increasingly difficult time covering its interest payments with EBITDA.

There is one last thing about EBITDA. As useful a tool as it can be when analyzing financial statements, it is not sanctioned by GAAP. This means that businesses may exercise some flexibility when it comes to what is included in EBITDA calculations. This should be kept in mind when reading published financial reports released by an organization.

Net Profit Margin

Now that we have taken EBITDA into account, we can finally move on to net income. Specifically, we can use **net profit margin** to assess profitability after all expenses have been deducted.

$$\text{Net Profit Margin} = \frac{\text{Net Income}}{\text{Sales Revenue}}$$

Here are the net profit (i.e. net income) numbers from the income statement we have been using:

	Period 2	Period 1
Revenue	$8,685,025	$6,482,000
Net Income	637,704	558,541
Net Profit Margin	7.34%	8.62%

FIGURE 16.9

Although the absolute revenue and net income dollar figures have risen over the course of the period, the net profit margin has decreased. In order to perform a complete analysis of net profit margin, comparisons should be made on a monthly and yearly basis to historical company performance, industry averages and direct competitors. Only then will these net income figures be placed in context so that assessments can be made and conclusions drawn.

As was alluded to earlier in this chapter, you should notice another trend in the ratios we have been calculating so far, especially those done with respect to revenues — where revenues serve as the denominator in the corresponding ratio.

Specifically, these percentages, or margins, are getting smaller as we go along. That is because as expenses get deducted from revenues, the remaining figure gets increasingly smaller. Therefore, gross profit margin will be larger than EBITDA percentage to sales, which will be larger than net profit margin. In other words, the more we break down the income statement, the less pie we have left to analyze.

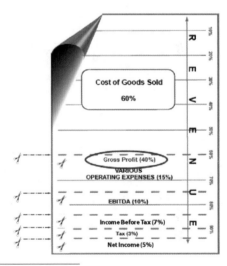

FIGURE 16.10

Linking the Income Statement to the Balance Sheet

The next part of our approach to analyzing financial statements takes us from the income statement to the balance sheet. Just as we went back to chapter 15 to take another look at the income statement, we will use the balance sheet for the same company's financial statements:

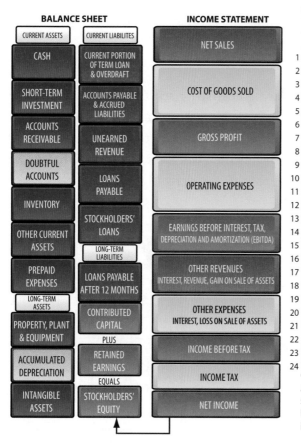

Balance Sheet	Period 2	Period 1
Assets		
Current Assets		
1 Cash	$13,265	$72,642
2 Accounts Receivable	1,286,138	1,065,812
3 Prepaid Expenses	48,612	42,625
4 Inventory	1,683,560	840,091
5 **Total Current Assets**	3,031,575	2,021,170
6 **Long-Term Assets**		
7 Plant & Equipment	322,518	170,000
8 Less Accumulated Depreciation	(89,262)	(46,000)
9 **Total Long-Term Assets**	233,256	124,000
10 **Total Assets**	$3,264,831	$2,145,170
11 **Liabilities**		
12 **Current Liabilities**		
13 Accounts Payable & Accrued Liabilities	$783,602	$475,645
14 Current Portion of Bank Loan	380,000	240,000
15 Stockholders' Loans	170,000	200,000
16 **Total Current**	1,333,602	915,645
17 Long-Term Debt	420,000	356,000
18 **Total Liabilities**	1,753,602	1,271,645
19 **Stockholders' Equity**		
20 Contributed Stock	10,000	10,000
21 Plus Retained Earnings	1,501,229	913,525
22 Less Dividend		(50,000)
23 **Stockholders' Equity**	1,511,229	873,525
24 **Liabilities + Equity**	$3,264,831	$2,145,170

As the diagram shows, the next step in our analysis of financial statements is to essentially link the income statement to the balance sheet. We do this by moving from net income on the income statement to stockholders' equity on the balance sheet.

FIGURE 16.11

Return on Equity (ROE)

We went from gross profit margin, to EBITDA, to net profit margins. Each step of the way told us something more about how well the company was using the revenues it earned. It is now time to move onto the balance sheet of the business, which essentially tells us how strong a position the organization is in with respect to what it owns versus what it owes. We proceed with our analysis of financial statements by assessing owners' equity, stockholders' equity, capital accounts, and other accounts that describe the net worth of the business.

IN THE REAL WORLD

One of the most important assessments that owners of a business can make is to know if they are getting a decent return on their investment. How is this done and how do they know if they are getting their money's worth out of the business?

Any determination of return on investment revolves around stockholders' equity. In other words, how much cash would the owners have left if they sold all the assets of the business and paid off all their debt? Given that this is a hypothetical question, and that the owners don't have to sell everything to assess the return on investment, there are other ways of assessing the value of the investment in the business.

For example, the owners could ask themselves another theoretical question: should we keep our money in the business, or put it elsewhere? Safe investments such as fixed deposit accounts come with relatively lower returns on investment. Investing in a friend's new business comes with a potentially much larger return on investment — but also with greater risk.

In fact, a general rule of thumb can be applied to assessing return on investment associated with certain levels of risk. Generally speaking, investments in publicly traded companies come with the expectation of a return ranging from 15%- 25%. Alternatively, the rate of return associated with private companies is expected to be much higher. In fact, it is not unusual to expect a rate of return of 100% or more for an investment in a small private company.

As with most things in life, everything comes at a price. With return on investment, the price can be a matter of risk. If owners want a better return, they must have a greater tolerance for risk.

The first basic analysis to be performed on the balance sheet involves assessing **return on equity (ROE)**. ROE is a measure of what the owners are getting out of the business relative to the amount they invested.

Although there are various ways to calculate ROE, we will examine the most common method:

$$\text{Return on Equity} = \frac{\text{Net Income}}{\text{Average Stockholders' Equity}}$$

First, we calculate average stockholders' equity by adding opening stockholders' equity and closing stockholders' equity and then dividing the result by two. Second, net income is the numerator for the ratio, which means that the last figure on the income statement serves as the basis from which we start measuring balance sheet performance. That is, net income serves as our link to the balance sheet at this stage of our financial analysis. Third, the above formula assumes there is no preferred stock equity included in stockholders' equity. Where such equity exists, the formula would be as follows:

$$\text{Return on Equity} = \frac{\text{Net Income} - \text{Preferred Dividends}}{\text{Average Common Equity}}$$

The following chart provides a breakdown of the ROE calculation for our ongoing example. Two assumptions are made. One, assume that the beginning stockholders' equity balance related to period 1 is $726,475. Two, assume that the sample company has no outstanding preferred stock.

	Period 2	Period 1
Net Income	$637,704	$558,541
Stockholder's Equity	1,511,229	873,525
Average Stockholder's Equity	1,192,377	800,000
Return on Equity	53.48%	69.82%

FIGURE 16.12

Although net income and average stockholders' equity values have increased, the return on equity has decreased fairly significantly from period 1 to period 2. The reasons for this change will be discussed later in the chapter (see section on the DuPont framework).

Return on Assets (ROA)

During the income statement portion of our financial analysis, we peeled away certain layers by starting with revenues and then working our way down to net income. We do much the same thing during the balance sheet portion of our financial analysis. Specifically, we start with net income from the income statement, jump over to the stockholders' equity account on the balance sheet, and are now ready for the next step. That is, we are ready to take liabilities out of the equation and focus specifically on assets. We do this by using the **return on assets (ROA)** ratio, which is calculated as follows:

$$\text{Return on Assets} = \frac{\text{Net Income}}{\text{Average Total Assets}}$$

ROA essentially provides an assessment of what the company does with what it's got; it measures every dollar earned against each dollar's worth of assets. A business invests in assets for the purpose of generating sales and making a profit. This is what ROA tries to measure. Although assessing ROA depends on the type of business being analyzed, a higher ROA number is generally considered better than a lower one. A higher ratio means that the business is earning more money on its investment in assets.

Let us, now, calculate ROA using our sample company. We have already used the net income numbers needed from the income statement. The total asset figures are to be found on the balance sheet. Assume that total assets prior to period 1 were $1,854,830.

Balance Sheet	Period 2	Period 1
Assets		
Current Assets		
1 Cash	$13,265	$72,642
2 Accounts Receivable	1,286,138	1,065,812
3 Prepaid Expenses	48,612	42,625
4 Inventory	1,683,560	840,091
5 **Total Current Assets**	3,031,575	2,021,170
6 **Long-Term Assets**		
7 Plant & Equipment	322,518	170,000
8 Less Accumulated Depreciation	(89,262)	(46,000)
9 **Total Long-Term Assets**	233,256	124,000
10 **Total Assets**	$3,264,831	$2,145,170

FIGURE 16.13

The following chart provides the necessary ROA calculations:

	Period 2	Period 1
Net Income	$637,704	$558,541
Assets	3,264,831	2,145,170
Average Total Assets	2,705,001	2,000,000
Return on Assets	23.58%	27.93%

FIGURE 16.14

As you can see, although both net income and asset values have increased for the period, the rate of return has decreased. This discrepancy between absolute figures and percentages is precisely why we use the latter. It also reveals a trend in the business. Specifically, although revenue, income, and asset values keep increasing, they can also go down in relative terms.

Regarding our ROA calculations, the ratio for the current year is 23.58%. This essentially means that the business earned almost 24¢ for each dollar invested in assets. This is a decrease from 28¢ in the previous period. Various factors might explain the decrease ranging from an increase in the cost of fixed assets, to an increase in production costs that affect the cost of goods sold directly.

In fact, the list of factors contributing to a change in ROA can be almost endless. Some of the most important business decisions by managers pertain to how well resources are allocated. Efficient use of assets should increase ROA. A less productive use of assets can ultimately lead to a decrease in ROA. In essence, ROA measures how efficiently business assets are used relative to profits generated.

As a general rule, an ROA of below 5% is considered capital-intensive or asset-heavy. This means that the business is investing a considerable amount in assets relative to profits. Industries that tend to display low ROA figures include manufacturers and large transportation companies such as railroads. Alternatively, an ROA of over 20% is considered much less capital-intensive or asset-heavy. In other words, such businesses tend to get more 'bang for the buck' when it comes to investing in assets. Examples include professional practices, software companies and retailers.

Asset Turnover

Another way to assess how well business assets are being utilized is to test how much revenue is generated for every dollar of assets. This is calculated by dividing (the amount of) revenue in dollars by average total assets.

Asset turnover measures the ability of a company to generate sales revenue from asset investments - the higher the number the better.

Example:

$$\text{Asset turnover} = \frac{\text{Revenue}}{\text{Average Total Assets}}$$

Using our sample statements, let's compare the results from periods 1 and 2.

	Period 2	Period 1
Net Income	$8,685,025	$6,482,000
Assets	3,264,831	2,145,170
Average Total Assets	2,705,001	2,000,000
Asset Turnover	3.21:1	3.24:1

FIGURE 16.15

In period 1, the business generated $3.24 of revenue for every dollar tied up in assets. In period 2 however, the return dropped to $3.21 in revenue for every dollar tied up in assets. What does this tell us? If the business invested less cash in assets but generated more revenue this would mean that the business is "selling more with less". The higher the revenue per dollar tied up in assets the more efficiently the assets are being utilized.

The DuPont Framework

Return on equity is one of the most important profitability ratios frequently reviewed by investors. In this chapter, we have learnt that the ratio is calculated using the following equation:

$$\text{ROE} = \frac{\text{Net Income}}{\text{Average Stockholder's Equity}}$$

Return on equity measures the amount of return earned in comparison to the resources the owners provide. In general, the higher the ROE, the more efficient a company is in using its owners' resources.

Suppose that you are examining the return on equity ratio for a company in two consecutive years. If the ratio remains the same from the first to second year, it me be easy to conclude that the company performed equally well in both years. However, the manner in which the company generated the ROE can be drastically different and would be of interest to stockholders.

Looking back to the concepts taught in this course, stockholders' equity is equal to assets minus liabilities (denominator of ROE). Based on the ROE equation, this indicates that an increase in ROE can be caused by an increase in net income, a decrease in assets, or an increase in liabilities. If a company's ROE increases or decreases, examining ROE in its simplest form does not provide information on what caused ROE to change.

The **DuPont Framework** resolves this problem by breaking the ROE equation into three components to provide more information on where the changes in ROE are coming from. The ROE equation can be expanded and rearranged to formulate the DuPont formula as shown below:

$$\text{ROE} = \frac{\text{Net Income}}{\text{Revenue}} \times \frac{\text{Revenue}}{\text{Average Total Assets}} \times \frac{\text{Average Total Assets}}{\text{Average Stockholder's Equity}}$$

The formulation of this equation from ROE is mainly mathematical and easy to understand. It starts with the basic ROE equation:

$$\text{ROE} = \frac{\text{Net Income}}{\text{Average Stockholder's Equity}}$$

Then apply two common multipliers (revenue and average total assets) to both numerator and denominator.

Apply the first common multiplier:

$$ROE = \frac{Net\ Income}{Average\ Stockholders'\ Equity} \times \frac{Revenue}{Revenue}$$

$$= \frac{Net\ Income}{Revenue} \times \frac{Revenue}{Average\ Stockholders'\ Equity}$$

Apply the second common multiplier:

$$ROE = \frac{Net\ Income}{Revenue} \times \frac{Revenue}{Average\ Stockholders'\ Equity} \times \frac{Average\ Total\ Assets}{Average\ Total\ Assets}$$

Finally, the equation can be rearranged to formulate the DuPont framework:

$$ROE = \frac{Net\ Income}{Revenue} \times \frac{Revenue}{Average\ Total\ Assets} \times \frac{Average\ Total\ Assets}{Average\ Stockholders'\ Equity}$$

The DuPont framework provides important insight to ROE by connecting the following three measurements together:

1. Net Profit Margin (Net Income ÷ Revenue): This measures operating efficiency
2. Asset Turnover Ratio (Revenue ÷ Average Total Assets): This measures asset usage efficiency
3. Total assets as a percentage of stockholders equity (Average Total Assets ÷ Average Stockholders' Equity): This measures how much a company relies on the use of equity vs. debt. In financial accounting, this ratio is called *an equity multiplier.*

Substituting the above three measurements, ROE can be represented as:

ROE = Net Profit Margin × Asset Turnover Ratio × Equity Multiplier

Based on this DuPont framework, an increase in ROE can be caused by an increase in one of the three components or a combination of all components. Recall from the previous sections that an increase in net profit margin and total assets turnover is generally a positive sign for a company. However, an increase in equity multiplier could mean that a company is using more debt (i.e. hence lower stockholders' equity) to finance its business. While this could represent an efficient usage of debt to generate returns, it also makes the business riskier.

Let us now return to our sample financial statements. Recall that ROE decreased from 69.82% in period 1 to 53.48% in period 2. Using the values calculated earlier in the chapter, we can calculate the components of ROE for period 1 and period 2 as follows:

	Period 2	Period 1
Net Profit Margin	7.34%	8.62%
Asset Turnover	3.21	3.24
Equity Multiplier	2.27	2.50

FIGURE 16.16

The net profit margins and asset turnover ratios were taken from figure 16.9 and figure 16.15 respectively. The equity multiplier was calculated using average total assets (from figure 16.14) divided by average stockholders' equity (from figure 16.12).

For our sample company, the net profit margin and the equity multiplier had significant decreases from period 1 to period 2. The asset turnover ratio was approximately the same in period 1 and period 2, which means asset usage efficiency was approximately constant for both periods. Therefore, the asset turnover ratio can be factored out of the analysis on the change in ROE. Therefore, the company's reduction in ROE can be explained by a combination of a decrease in net profit margin and a decrease in the equity multiplier. The decline in net profit margin suggests that the company's ability to control expenses decreased from period 1 to period 2. The decrease in the equity multiplier suggests that the company was relying on less debt and more equity (as a percentage) in period 2 than in period 1 to finance its assets. A combination of the discussed effects results in a decreased ROE from period 1 to period 2.

The DuPont framework demonstrates that examining ROE as a single number is not enough to make sound business decisions. Even if a company's ROE stays the same from year to year, applying the DuPont framework can provide useful insights. If a company's net profit margin and total assets turnover have increased from year 1 to year 2 but equity multiplier has decreased, this is generally a good indicator although the overall ROE may remain the same. On the other hand, if the company's net profit margin and totals assets turnover have decreased from year 1 to year 2 but equity multiplier has increased significantly, this most likely is not a favorable sign.

Cash Flow Is Reality

Our analysis of the balance sheet so far has been related to net income. It is now time to leave the income statement altogether. We will focus on the balance sheet exclusively to look at cash flow and related financial ratios.

If you recall from our discussion of cash flow statements in chapter 15, an analysis of business cash flow determines the extent to which profits are transformed into actual cash in the bank. In other words, cash flow analysis is an attempt to assess the liquidity of the business. Will the business have enough cash on hand when needed? Does it have the ability to get cash when necessary? Can this cash cover debts and more? We will provide the answers to these questions as we look at liquidity ratios.

Current Ratio

The **current ratio** assesses the ability of the business to pay its current debt. The formula for the ratio is:

$$\text{Current Ratio} = \frac{\text{Current Assets}}{\text{Current Liabilities}}$$

The "current" label on the balance sheet almost always refers to a period of 12 months or less. Therefore, current assets and current liabilities both have terms of less than a year.

Balance Sheet	Period 2	Period 1
Assets		
Current Assets		
Cash	$13,265	$72,642
Accounts Receivable	1,286,138	1,065,812
Prepaid Expenses	48,612	42,625
Inventory	1,683,560	840,091
Total Current Assets	3,031,575	2,021,170
Long-Term Assets		
Plant & Equipment	322,518	170,000
Less Accumulated Depreciation	(89,262)	(46,000)
Total Long-Term Assets	233,256	124,000
Total Assets	$3,264,831	$2,145,170
Liabilities		
Current Liabilities		
Accounts Payable & Accrued Liabilities	$783,602	$475,645
Current Portion of Bank Loan	380,000	240,000
Stockholders' Loans	170,000	200,000
Total Current Liabilities	1,333,602	915,645
Long-Term Debt	420,000	356,000
Total Liabilities	1,753,602	1,271,645

FIGURE 16.17

The current ratio assesses business liquidity by determining the extent to which current assets can cover current debts. No business wants to find itself in a position of having to sell fixed assets to pay current bills. It should therefore strive for a current ratio of at least 2:1, which means that it has twice as much invested in current assets as it does in current liabilities.

Depending on the industry in question, a current ratio of 2:1 or above usually ensures that the business has enough of a cushion that it can afford to have some cash tied up in current assets, such as inventory and accounts receivable. Once these assets are cashed, so to speak, they can be used to pay for current liabilities such as current portions of bank loans or bills to suppliers.

It may seem counter intuitive to say that a business that is too liquid is using its capital inefficiently. For example, if the current ratio of a business is 5:1, it has $5.00 in current assets for every dollar that it owes in the next 12 months. This would indicate that the business does not need so much cash. Money in a bank account earning 3% is not an efficient use of assets, especially if the business is earning a return on investment of 20%. Cash should either be invested in new fixed assets or perhaps invested in the short-term until a better use for the cash can be established.

The following chart calculates the current ratio using the numbers provided in our sample financial statements:

	Period 2	Period 1
Current Assets	$3,031,575	$2,021,170
Current Liabilities	1,333,602	915,645
Ratio	2.27:1	2.21 :1

FIGURE 16.18

In this case, our ratio indicates a healthy state of affairs. Not only is the ratio above 2:1 for both periods, but it has increased from one period to the next.

Investing too much money in fixed assets that are not liquid enough could compromise a healthy current ratio. As will be examined further in a moment, long-term or fixed assets should be financed with long-term liabilities such as term loans. Current liabilities should not be used for this purpose.

Quick Ratio

The other liquidity ratio that is relevant to our current analysis of business cash flow, is the **quick ratio** (also known as the acid test).

Here is the calculation for this ratio:

$$\text{Quick Ratio} = \frac{\text{Cash} + \text{Short Term Investments} + \text{Net Accounts Receivable}}{\text{Current Liabilities}}$$

The quick ratio is much like the current ratio; the only difference is that the quick ratio excludes some current assets which are to be liquidated after three months (such as inventory and prepaid expenses).

In essence, the quick ratio assesses the ability of the business to meet its most immediate debt obligations without relying on the liquidation of inventory (which may take some time to sell). A ratio of at least 1:1 is generally seen as the minimum requirement. Anything below one might mean the business has too much of its money tied up in inventory and may be unable to pay its short-term bills.

Quick ratios have been calculated using the numbers in our sample financial statements:

	Period 2	Period 1
Cash + Short Term Investments + Net Accounts Receivables	$1,299,403	$1,138,454
Current Liabilities	1,333,602	915,645
Ratio	0.97:1	1.24:1

FIGURE 16.19

With a quick glance, you will notice that the quick ratio has decreased from period 1 (1.24) to period 2 (0.97). This means that the business has gone from a sound short-term liquidity position to a potentially dangerous one.

To address any potential problems here, and since the balance sheet provides only a snapshot of business finances, further analyses should be performed over the course of the next three months on the specific assets and liabilities of the business. This is to ensure that bills can in fact be paid on time.

The situation could have developed due to too much money being invested in inventory or fixed assets. A review should be performed to address the situation and rectify any problems found.

Debt-to-Equity Ratio

The **debt-to-equity ratio** is used to assess how much of a company is being financed by lenders, and how much is being financed by the owners or stockholders. In other words, this ratio assesses the extent to which a business is indebted to lenders and whether it can afford to borrow more cash if necessary.

Here is the how the debt-to-equity ratio is calculated:

$$\text{Debt-to-Equity Ratio} = \frac{\text{Total Liabilities}}{\text{Total Stockholders' Equity}}$$

It is simply not healthy for a business to borrow too much relative to what it is worth. Ideally, a business should have a debt-to-equity ratio of about 0.5:1. In other words, for every $0.50 of debt it has, it should have $1.00 in stockholders' equity.

WORTH REPEATING...
Acquiring loans or paying back loan principals has no effect on equity.

Look at the debt-to-equity numbers from our sample balance sheet:

Liabilities		
Current Liabilities		
Accounts Payable & Accrued Liabilities	$783,602	$475,645
Current Portion of Bank Loan	380,000	240,000
Stockholders' Loans	170,000	200,000
Total Current Liabilities	1,333,602	915,645
Long-Term Debt	420,000	356,000
Total Liabilities	1,753,602	1,271,645 ⬅
Stockholders' Equity		
Contributed Capital	10,000	10,000
Plus Retained Earnings	1,501,229	913,525
Less Dividend		(50,000)
Stockholders' Equity	1,511,229	873,525 ⬅
Liabilities + Equity	$3,264,831	$2,145,170

FIGURE 16.20

Entering these numbers into the debt-to-equity formula, we get the following:

	Period 2	Period 1
Total Liabilities	$1,753,602	$1,271,645
Equity	1,511,229	873,525
Ratio	1.16:1	1.46:1

FIGURE 16.21

As you can see, although the debt-to-equity ratio has improved from period 1 to period 2, it is still above the level of 1:1. This means that the business owes more to its creditors than to its owners.

There are a few ways a business can improve the debt-to-equity ratio. First, simply making more profit might do the trick, since it directly results in an increase to stockholders' equity. Second, the business might think about issuing equity (possibly in the form of stocks), in exchange for cash.

Management Ensures Stability

We have reached the last part of our approach to analyzing the financial statements of a business. We started with revenues on the income statement, worked our way down to net income, jumped over to stockholders' equity on the balance sheet, and looked at various relationships between assets and liabilities on that balance sheet. Now it is time to assess some of the decision-making aspects of running a business. We need to take a look at what management is doing.

Using financial ratios, we can assess managerial performance by looking at two components of the business: accounts receivable and inventory. Ratios related to each of these components provide us with some sense of what people are doing with the business. It's not just about the bottom line. The further we get into our analysis, the more we try to go beyond the bottom line. That is why we look at managerial performance indicators.

Accounts Receivable Ratios

One key to business success is the ability to collect on its bills. In other words, sales have to result in cash. If customers are buying a product or service on credit, they have to pay within a reasonable amount of time to ensure cash flow and financial health. That is what the **day-sales-outstanding** (DSO) and **accounts receivable turnover** are all about.

Days-Sales-Outstanding (DSO):

The formula to calculate the day sales outstanding (DSO) is:

$$\text{Day Sales Outstanding} = \left(\frac{\text{Average Net Accounts Receivable}}{\text{Net Credit Sales}} \right) \times 365$$

From here on in, we will assume that all revenues are credit sales for the DSO calculation. The DSO provides an indication of how many days it takes for customers to pay their bills. This number is important because late payments can cost a business lost interest from cash, or additional administration costs required to collect payments from customers.

We will take a look at DSO as they relate to our ongoing example. Assume accounts receivable prior to period 1 was $934,188.

	Period 2	Period 1
Accounts Receivable	$1,286,138	1,065,812
Average Accounts Receivable	1,175,975	1,000,000
Revenue	8,685,025	6,482,000
Days Sales Outstanding	49.42 Days	56.31 Days

FIGURE 16.22

As you can see, the business is improving its ability to collect from customers. The DSO decreased from over 56 days in period 1, to below 50 days in period 2. That is the kind of performance that owners, investors and analysts want to see from an organization.

However, there are some cautionary notes to keep in mind related to the DSO. First, the revenue figure used in the ratio should exclude all cash sales, since it is only sales on account (credit sales) that are of concern, relative to collecting customer payments. Second, sales to a major customer should be kept out of the total revenue figure used to calculate DSO, because they can skew the ratio.

Accounts Receivable Turnover

The accounts receivable turnover ratio (ART) is similar to DSO. It involves dividing a company's net credit sales by the average amount of net accounts receivable.

Accounts Receivable Turnover (ART) = Net Credit Sales ÷ Average Net Accounts Receivable

A higher ratio indicates a greater ability to convert accounts receivable into cash. If a business turns its receivables over 12 times per year, it would mean that it is collecting the average balance of receivables every month.

Inventory Ratios

The second component of a business that we look at to assess managerial performance is inventory. We will use two ratios to measure how successful a business is at moving inventory out the door: **inventory days on hand** (also known as day-sales-on-hand) and **inventory turnover**.

Inventory Days on Hand

There are various ways of calculating some of these ratios. For our present purpose, we'll calculate inventory days on hand this way:

$$\text{Inventory Days on Hand} = \left(\frac{\text{Average Inventory}}{\text{Cost of Goods Sold}} \right) \times 365$$

In other words, the inventory days on hand ratio calculates approximately how many days inventory stays on the premises before being moved out.

Inventory Turnover

The inventory turnover ratio is calculated as follows:

$$\text{Inventory Turnover} = \frac{\text{Cost of Goods Sold}}{\text{Average Inventory}}$$

In other words, inventory turnover takes the basic fraction used for the inventory days on hand calculation, flips it, and leaves out the factor of 365 days. The result essentially tells us how many times inventory is "turned over" within a year. For example: if the value of the inventory on hand is equivalent to 100% of how much was used (Cost of Goods Sold) for one year, then it was turned only once. If however, the value of the inventory on hand is equivalent to 50% of how much was used then it was turned twice. Here is an example: If the cost of goods sold for the year is $120,000 and the value of inventory at the end of the year was $40,000 then the inventory was turned three times ($120,000 ÷ 40,000).

Now, we apply these two inventory ratios to the same set of financial numbers that we have been using so far.

Balance Sheet	Period 2
Assets	
Current Assets	
Cash	$13, 265
Accounts Receivable	1,286,138
Prepaid Expenses	48,612
Inventory	1,683,560
Total Current Assets	3,031,575

Income Statement	Period 2
Sales	$8,685,025
Cost of Goods Sold	5,998,612
Gross Profit	2,686,413

FIGURE 16.23

Assume that the inventory balance prior to period 1 was $359,909. Applying our inventory days on hand formula to these numbers gives us the following:

	Period 2	Period 1
Inventory	$1,683,560	$840,091
Average Inventory	1,261,826	600,000
COGS	5,998,612	4,397,200
Inventory Days on Hand	76.78 : Days	49.80 Days

FIGURE 16.24

As you can see, the average number of days that inventory was on the premises rose dramatically, from 50 to 77 days in one period. Unless something unusual occurred during the year that can account for such an increase, the business might be in jeopardy of having too much inventory on hand. This freezes capital that could be used in other parts of the organization.

Now let's apply the inventory turnover ratio to the same inventory and cost of goods sold figures:

	Period 2	Period 1
COGS	$5,998,612	$4,397,200
Inventory	1,683,560	840,091
Average Inventory	1,261,826	600,000
Inventory Turnover Ratio	4.75 : 1	7.33 : 1

FIGURE 16.25

In essence, inventory turnover tells us the same thing, but in a different way. It tells us that in period 2; inventory was turned over only slightly more than 4.7 times. This is a sharp decrease from 7.3 times in the previous period and indicates that inventory is staying too long in the organization's warehouse.

On a broader scale, inventory performance should be assessed relative to the industry involved. For example, winter skis will be turned over less frequently (and on a seasonal basis), as compared to loaves of bread in a bakery. It might take months for a sporting goods store to sell a pair of skis it has stored in the back room, and probably much longer in the summer. Conversely, a loaf of bread normally stays on the shelf no longer than a couple of days — regardless of the time of year.

Horizontal And Vertical Financial Statement Analysis

Now that we have a better understanding of the various ratios at our disposal, we need to look at a few methods of comparing the results from the above calculations.

Management and other readers of financial statements use **horizontal analysis** to quickly compare the changes, both in dollars and percentages, in a given financial statement from one period to the next. Using the balance sheet accounts from the above examples, we can now calculate the dollar and percentage changes.

Balance Sheet	Period 2	Period 1	$ Change	% Change
Assets				
Current Assets				
Cash	$13,265	$72,642	($59,377)	-81.74%
Accounts Receivable	1,286,138	1,065,812	220,326	20.67%
Prepaid Expenses	48,612	42,625	5,987	14.05%
Inventory	1,683,560	840,091	843,469	100.40%
Total Current Assets	3,031,575	2,021,170	1,010,405	49.99%
Long-Term Assets				
Plant & Equipment	322,518	170,000	152,518	89.72%
Less: Accumulated Depreciation	-89,262	-46,000	(43,262)	94.05%
Total Long-Term Assets	233,256	124,000	109,256	88.11%
Total Assets	$3,264,831	$2,145,170	1,119,661	52.19%
Liabilities				
Current Liabilities				
Accounts Payable & Accrued Liabilities	$783,602	$475,645	$307,957	64.75%
Current Portion of Bank Loan	380,000	240,000	140,000	58.33%
Stockholders' Loans	170,000	200,000	(30,000)	-15.00%
Total Current Liabilities	1,333,602	915,645	417,957	45.65%
Long-Term Debt	420,000	356,000	64,000	17.98%
Total Liabilities	1,753,602	1,271,645	481,957	37.90%
Stockholders' Equity	1,511,229	873,525	637,704	73.00%
Liabilities & Equity	$3,264,831	$2,145,170	1,119,661	52.19%

FIGURE 16.26

To calculate the dollar increase (or decrease), we simply take the current year amount for one line and deduct the amount reported for the previous year. For example, we see that cash decreased by $59,377, a decrease of 81.74%, calculated as follows:

$$(\$59,377) \div \$72,642 = (81.74\%)$$

This appears to be a significant decrease and may prompt readers to inquire about the reason for such a large decrease in cash.

Horizontal analysis is most effective when comparing a number of years, say, three to five. Comparative statements for these years are presented and, using horizontal analysis techniques, we can determine possible trends in the results.

Let us look at some key elements of a published income statement for American Eagle Outfitters, a U.S. retail chain.

American Eagle Outfitters In Millions of USD				
	2009	**2008**	**2007**	**2006**
Revenue	$2,988.87	$3,055.42	$2,794.41	$2,321.96
Operating Income	279.25	598.75	586.79	458.69
Net income	179.06	400.02	387.36	294.15

FIGURE 16.27

We must first select a base year. In this case we will pick 2006 as the year against which we will compare all other years.

Here are the results:

	2009	**2008**	**2007**	**2006**
Revenue	$2,988.87 ÷ $2,321.96	$3,055.42 ÷ $2321.96	$2,794.41 ÷ $2,321.96	$2,321.96 ÷ $2,321.96
% of Base Year	128.72%	131.59%	120.35%	100.00%

FIGURE 16.28

The horizontal analysis reveals that sales in all three years were higher than in the base year, and 2008 was the highest of the four years.

However, when we do a horizontal analysis of net income, we get a different picture of the company. Using the data from the above table, we calculate the following:

	2009	**2008**	**2007**	**2006**
Net Income	$179.06 ÷ $294.15	$400.02 ÷ $294.15	$387.36 ÷ $294.15	$294.15 ÷ $294.15
% of Base Year	60.87%	135.99%	131.69%	100%

FIGURE 16.29

What happened during 2009 to cause net income to be so much less than in the other years, even the base year? The answer to this question will require further financial analysis, perhaps using some of the ratios discussed above.

Vertical analysis is another common type of financial statement analysis. This method expresses individual accounts in the same period as a percentage of another account. For example, vertical analysis of the balance sheet indicates each account as a percentage of total assets. Vertical analysis of the income statement indicates each account as a percentage of net sales. Once again, we will use the financial statement data provided earlier in the chapter. Using the income statement data, the following table reports each line of this statement as a percentage of net sales:

Income Statement	Period 2	% of Net Sales	Period 1	% of Net Sales
Revenue (Net Sales)	$8,685,025	100.00%	$6,482,000	100.00%
Cost of Goods Sold	5,998,612	69.07%	4,397,200	67.84%
Gross Profit	2,686,413	30.93%	2,084,800	32.16%
Operating Expenses				
Administration Charges	8,652	0.10%	6,861	0.11%
Advertising & Marketing	42,645	0.49%	32,975	0.51%
Depreciation of Long-Term Assets	43,262	0.50%	15,862	0.24%
Bonuses	65,000	0.75%	62,432	0.96%
Commission	420,250	4.84%	325,210	5.02%
Interest	51,875	0.60%	31,253	0.48%
Insurance	16,000	0.18%	12,000	0.19%
Sales and Admin Salaries and Benefits	610,325	7.03%	435,951	6.73%
Management Salaries	320,560	3.69%	226,548	3.50%
Occupancy (Rent, Cleaning, etc.)	52,000	0.60%	48,000	0.74%
Other Operating Expenses	61,200	0.70%	48,672	0.75%
Consulting	22,500	0.26%	21,356	0.33%
Repairs and Maintenance	36,860	0.42%	26,845	0.41%
Professional Fees	11,560	0.13%	8,642	0.13%
Total Expenses	1,762,689	20.30%	1,302,607	20.10%
Operating Income Before Tax	923,724	10.64%	782,193	12.07%
Tax	286,020	3.29%	223,652	3.45%
Net Income (Loss) Added to Retained Earnings	$637,704	7.34%	$558,541	8.62%

FIGURE 16.30

For example, COGS is calculated as 69.07% by dividing $5,998,612 by net sales of $8,685,025. Finding out each item's percentage of net sales, using the vertical analysis, helps management and other company stakeholders to compare the financial results of the current and other years presented. For example, the income statement above clearly shows that gross profit as a percentage of net sales has decreased by approximately 3% from period 1 to period 2. This could indicate a serious problem such as theft of inventory or errors in recording transactions, and should be investigated.

Other methods of analyzing the financial statements exist, such as preparing **common-size statements** and benchmarking. Preparing common-size statements simply involves stating all dollar amounts on the statements as percentages. All items on the balance sheet are reported as a percentage of total assets and all items on the income statement are reported as a percentage of net sales. The above data have been used to prepare the common-size income statement below.

Common-size Income Statement	Period 2	Period 1
Revenue (Net Sales)	100.00%	100.00%
Cost of Goods Sold	69.07%	67.84%
Gross Profit	30.93%	32.16%
Operating Expenses		
Administration Charges	0.10%	0.11%
Advertising & Marketing	0.49%	0.51%
Depreciation of Long-Term Assets	0.50%	0.24%
Bonuses	0.75%	0.96%
Commission	4.84%	5.02%
Interest	0.60%	0.48%
Insurance	0.18%	0.19%
Sales and Admin Salaries and Benefits	7.03%	6.73%
Management Salaries	3.69%	3.50%
Occupancy (Rent, Cleaning, etc.)	0.60%	0.74%
Other Operating Expenses	0.70%	0.75%
Consulting	0.26%	0.33%
Repairs and Maintenance	0.42%	0.41%
Professional Fees	0.13%	0.13%
Total Expenses	20.30%	20.10%
Operating Income Before Tax	10.64%	12.07%
Tax	3.29%	3.45%
Net Income (Loss) Added to Retained Earnings	7.34%	8.62%

FIGURE 16.31

The purpose of preparing common-size statements is to make the statements as easy to read as possible without overwhelming the reader with details and large numbers. Because dollar amounts are not used, these statements are quite often used to compare and analyze the results of different companies within the same industry. For example, suppose Company A had a net income of $100,000 and Company B had a net income of $200,000. If the statements were only reported in dollars, we might conclude that Company B had a more profitable year than Company A; however, after converting the dollar amounts into percentages, we see that Company A's net income represented

20% of net sales whereas Company B's represented only 5%. A common-size statement would have revealed this difference immediately.

Another term often used in conjunction with common-size statements is **benchmarking**, whereby the financial statements are compared against averages in the relevant industry, not just with the financial statements of another company. Using the data for the above company, we will now benchmark the company's performance against the following industry averages:

Common-Size Income Statement for Comparison with Industry Average		
Period 1	Company	Industry
Revenue (Net sales)	100.00%	100.00%
Cost of Goods Sold	69.07%	68.50%
Gross Profit	30.93%	31.00%
Operating Expenses	20.30%	25.00%
Income Taxes	3.29%	3.00%
Net Income	7.34%	3.00%

FIGURE 16.32

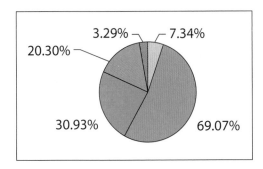

FIGURE 16.33

Pie charts and other graphics are often used to report differences between the company and others in the industry when benchmarking tools are applied. The above reveals that our company is more effective at generating net income from its sales (7.34% vs. 3.0%) than players in the same industry.

In Summary

⇨ Performing a comprehensive financial analysis on a business is important because it gleans important information from the financial statements.

⇨ The financial ratio is the primary tool used to analyze financial statements. The well-being of a business can be assessed by using a combination of these financial ratios.

⇨ Our approach to analyzing financial statements can be summarized in four phrases: "revenues are vanity", "profits are sanity", "cash flow is reality", and "management ensures stability".

⇨ The income statement is broken down by expense category. This produces a percentage relative to revenues along the way. We start with gross profit, and then consider EBITDA (earnings before interest, taxes, depreciation and amortization). Finally, we move onto net income.

⇨ The jump over to the balance sheet portion of our analysis is made through net income and stops first at stockholders' equity. The analysis then breaks down the balance sheet just as it did the income statement.

⇨ Cash flow analysis tends to focus almost exclusively on the balance sheet and assesses the extent to which the company has satisfactory liquidity.

⇨ The performance of management can be assessed by using financial ratios that measure accounts receivable and inventory. It is these components of a business that are a result of decisions made by real people in the business.

⇨ Other methods and tools used in financial statement analysis include horizontal and vertical analysis of the balance sheet and income statements as well as preparation of common-sized statements used in benchmarking.

Review Exercise

Use the financial statements below to calculate the ratios indicated for 2009.

Balance Sheet		
	2009	**2008**
Assets		
Current Assets		
Cash	$1,605	$987
Accounts Receivable	1,175	573
Inventory	396	256
Other Current Assets	301	103
Total Current Assets	3,477	1,919
Long-Term Assets	2,034	1,170
Total Assets	$5,511	$3,089
Liabilities		
Current Liabilities	$1,474	$547
Long-Term Liabilities	104	58
Total Liabilites	1,578	605
Stockholders' Equity	3,933	2,484
Total Liabilities & Stockholders' Equity	$5,511	$3,089

Income Statement		
	2009	**2008**
Revenue	$6,009	$3,037
Cost of Goods Sold	2,928	1,379
Gross Profit	3,081	1,658
Operating Expenses		
Interest	518	413
Depreciation	108	77
Other Operating Expenses	723	361
Total Operating Expenses	1,349	851
Income from Operations	1,732	807
Investment Income	79	52
Income before Income Taxes	1,811	859
Income Taxes	516	227
Net Income	$1,295	$632

Review Exercise – Answer

Name	Ratio (2009)	Calculation
Gross Profit Margin	51.3%	$\dfrac{3{,}081}{6{,}009}$
Net Profit Margin	21.6%	$\dfrac{1{,}295}{6{,}009}$
EBITDA	2,437	$1{,}295 + 518 + 516 + 108$
EBITDA Percentage to Sales	40.6%	$\dfrac{2{,}437}{6{,}009}$
Interest Coverage Ratio	4.7 : 1	$\dfrac{2{,}437}{518}$
Return on Equity	40.4%	$1{,}295 \div \dfrac{3{,}933 + 2{,}484}{2}$
Current Ratio	2.36 : 1	$\dfrac{3{,}477}{1{,}474}$
Quick Ratio	1.89 : 1	$\dfrac{1{,}605 + 1{,}175}{1{,}474}$
Debt to Equity Ratio	0.4 : 1	$\dfrac{1{,}578}{3{,}933}$
Day Sales Outstanding	53.09 days	$\dfrac{(1{,}175 + 573) \div 2}{6{,}009} \times 365$
Inventory Days on Hand	40.64 days	$\dfrac{(396 + 256) \div 2}{2{,}928} \times 365$

Notes

The following is a summary of formulas used in the text. It is important to understand how these formulas are used and when they are applicable.

An Overview of Costing Methods

Cost of Goods Sold (COGS) – Merchandising

Beginning Inventory + Purchases + Freight-in - Ending Inventory	Calculate the cost of goods sold in a merchandising environment

Cost of Goods Sold (COGS) – Manufacturing

Beginning Direct Material Inventory + Direct Material Purchases - Direct Material Ending Inventory + Direct Labor Costs + Manufacturing Overhead Costs + Beginning WIP Inventory - Ending WIP Inventory	Calculate the cost of goods sold in a manufacturing environment.

Cost of Goods Manufactured (COGM)

Beginning Inventory + Cost of Goods Manufactured - Ending Inventory	Calculate how much it costs to manufacture the goods.

Job-Order Costing

Predetermined Manufacturing Overhead Rate

$$\frac{\text{Total Estimated Manufacturing Overhead Costs}}{\text{Total Estimated Cost Allocation Base}}$$	Used to allocate manufacturing overhead costs to different jobs.

Process Costing

Total Costs Added

Cost of Direct Materials + Conversion Costs	Calculate the total costs added to a department during a period.

Physical Flow of Units

Beginning Inventory **+ Number of Units Started During the Period** **= Number of Units Completed + Number of** ** Units in Ending Inventory**	Determine the physical flow of units.

Equivalent Units of Production

Number of Units x % of Completion in Current Period	Approximation of number of whole units that have been produced during a period in process costing.

Cost per Equivalent Unit

$$\frac{\textbf{Costs}}{\textbf{Number of Equivalent Units}}$$	To calculate the cost per EQU. Cost can be direct materials or conversion costs.

Cost of Units

Cost per Equivalent Unit x Number of Equivalent Units	Calculate to the total costs of EQU.

Cost-Volume-Profit Analysis

Variable Cost per Unit

$$\frac{\textbf{Change in Cost}}{\textbf{Change in Production}}$$	Used to calculate the variable cost portion of a mixed cost.

Fixed Cost

High Production Cost - (Variable Cost per Unit x High Production Units)	Used to calculate the fixed cost portion of a mixed cost.

Or

Low Production Cost - (Variable Cost per Unit x Low Production Units)	Used to calculate the fixed cost portion of a mixed cost.

Contribution Margin

Revenue – Variable Costs	Represents the excess of sales over total variable costs.

Operating Income

Sales - Variable Costs - Fixed Costs	Calculate operating income using the contribution margin method.

Break-Even Number of Units

$$\frac{\text{Fixed Costs}}{\text{Contribution Margin per Unit}}$$	Calculate number of units needed to break-even.

Target Operating Income (Number of Units)

$$\frac{\text{Fixed Costs + Target Operating Income}}{\text{Contribution Margin per Unit}}$$	Calculate how many units must be sold to reach a target operating income.

Contribution Margin (CM) Ratio

$$\frac{\text{Contribution Margin}}{\text{Revenue}}$$	Contribution margin achieved per dollar of sales.

Target Operating Income (Revenue)

$$\frac{\text{Fixed Costs + Target Operating Income}}{\text{Contribution Margin Ratio}}$$	Calculate how much revenue is needed to reach a target operating income.

Margin of Safety (in dollars)

Current Sales - Break-Even Sales	The excess of sales over break-even revenue.

Margin of Safety (in units)

Current Output- Break-Even Output	The excess actual sales over break-even sales.

Margin of Safety Percentage

$$\frac{\text{Margin of Safety (in dollars)}}{\text{Current Sales}}$$	Percentage of which sales exceed the break-even point.

Weighted-Average Contribution Margin

(CM for Product A x Sales Mix for Product A) + (CM for Product B x Sales Mix for Product B) + ...	Calculate contribution margin if a business produces and sells multiple types of products.

Degree of Operating Leverage

$$\frac{\text{Contribution Margin}}{\text{Operating Income}}$$	Used to calculate how operating income changes in relation to changes in volume.

Master Budget

Budgeted Production Units

Budgeted Sales + Budgeted Ending Inventory - Beginning Inventory	Used to forecast how many units need to be produced.

Purchases of Direct Materials

Direct Materials to be Used + Budgeted Ending Direct Materials - Beginning Direct Materials	Used to prepare a purchasing budget.

Cost of Goods Sold (COGS) : Manufacturing Business

Beginning Finished Goods Inventory + Cost of Direct Material Used + Direct Labor Cost + Manufacturing Overhead Cost - Ending Finished Goods Inventory	To calculate the cost of goods sold for a manufacturer.

Capital Budgeting

Return on Investment (ROI)

$$\frac{\text{Profit from Investment}}{\text{Investment Amount}}$$	Evaluate the efficiency of an investment (i.e. the amount of profit from investment for every dollar invested).

Accounting Rate of Return (ARR)

$$\frac{\text{Average Annual Increase in Operating Income}}{\text{Initial Investment}}$$	Capital budgeting method to calculate the return based on operating income.

Cash Payback Period

$$\frac{\text{Initial Investment}}{\text{Annual Net Cash Flow}}$$	The amount of time it takes to recover the initial investment. Can only be used if cash flow is uniform.

Variance Analysis and Standard Costing

Selling-Price Variance

(Actual Selling Price per Unit – Budgeted Selling Price per Unit) x Actual Units Sold	Analyze the revenue variance between the flexible budget and actual results.

Static Budget Variance

Actual Result – Static Budget	Analyze the difference between the actual results and static budget.

Flexible Budget Variance

Actual Result – Flexible Budget	Analyze the difference between the actual results and flexible budget.

Sales-Volume Variance

Flexible Budget – Static Budget	Analyze the difference between the budgeted quantity of unitssold and the actual quantity of units sold.

Price Variance (Direct Materials)

(Actual Price of Input – Standard Price of Input) x Actual Quantity of Input Purchased	Analyze the difference between the actual price and standard price of input. A positive price variance is considered unfavorable

Efficiency Variance (Direct Materials)

(Actual Quantity of Input Used – Standard Quantity of Actual Output) x Standard Price	Analyze the difference between the actual quantity and the standard quantities for actual output. A positive efficiency variance is considered unfavorable.

Price Variance (Direct Labor)

(Actual Labor Rate – Standard Labor Rate) x Actual Direct Labor Hours Used	Analyze the difference between the actual price and standard price of direct labor. A positive price variance is considered unfavorable.

Efficiency Variance (Direct Labor)

(Actual Direct Labor Hours – Standard Direct Labor Hours) x Standard Labor Rate	Analyze the difference between the actual and standard labor hours for actual output. A positive efficiency variance is considered unfavorable.

Variable Overhead Spending Variance

(Actual Rate – Standard Rate) x Actual Quantity	Analyze the difference in overhead rates. A positive spending variance is considered unfavorable.

Variable Overhead Efficiency Variance

(Actual Quantity – Standard Quantity) x Standard Rate	Analyze the consumption of variable manufacturing overhead. A positive variable overhead efficiency variance is considered unfavorable.

Activity-Based Costing

Predetermined Overhead Rate

$$\frac{\text{Total Budgeted Overhead Costs}}{\text{Total Budgeted Cost Allocation Base}}$$

Used to allocate overhead costs to different products.

Costing and Pricing Strategies

Cost-Plus Pricing

Selling Price x (1 + Markup Percentage)

Calculate selling price using the cost-plus pricing method

Markup Percentage

$$\frac{\text{(Required Rate of Return x Investment) + G\&A Expenses}}{\text{Sales Volume in Units x Unit Product Cost}}$$

Calculate markup percentage

Target Cost

Predetermined Selling Price – Desired Profit

Calculate the maximum allowable cost (or target cost).

Segment Reporting and Transfer Pricing

Segment Margin Percentage

$$\frac{\text{Segment Margin}}{\text{Segment Sales}} \times 100\%$$

Segment margin percentage determines how much out of each dollar of segment sales that a segment keeps in earnings.

Appendix II: Present Value Factors for a Single Value

Interest Rate

Period	1%	2%	3%	4%	5%	6%	7%	8%	9%	10%	11%	12%	13%	14%	15%	16%	17%	18%	19%	20%
1	0.9901	0.9804	0.9709	0.9615	0.9524	0.9434	0.9346	0.9259	0.9174	0.9091	0.9009	0.8929	0.8850	0.8772	0.8696	0.8621	0.8547	0.8475	0.8403	0.8333
2	0.9803	0.9612	0.9426	0.9246	0.9070	0.8900	0.8734	0.8573	0.8417	0.8264	0.8116	0.7972	0.7831	0.7695	0.7561	0.7432	0.7305	0.7182	0.7062	0.6944
3	0.9706	0.9423	0.9151	0.8890	0.8638	0.8396	0.8163	0.7938	0.7722	0.7513	0.7312	0.7118	0.6931	0.6750	0.6575	0.6407	0.6244	0.6086	0.5934	0.5787
4	0.9610	0.9238	0.8885	0.8548	0.8227	0.7921	0.7629	0.7350	0.7084	0.6830	0.6587	0.6355	0.6133	0.5921	0.5718	0.5523	0.5337	0.5158	0.4987	0.4823
5	0.9515	0.9057	0.8626	0.8219	0.7835	0.7473	0.7130	0.6806	0.6499	0.6209	0.5935	0.5674	0.5428	0.5194	0.4972	0.4761	0.4561	0.4371	0.4190	0.4019
6	0.9420	0.8880	0.8375	0.7903	0.7462	0.7050	0.6663	0.6302	0.5963	0.5645	0.5346	0.5066	0.4803	0.4556	0.4323	0.4104	0.3898	0.3704	0.3521	0.3349
7	0.9327	0.8706	0.8131	0.7599	0.7107	0.6651	0.6227	0.5835	0.5470	0.5132	0.4817	0.4523	0.4251	0.3996	0.3759	0.3538	0.3332	0.3139	0.2959	0.2791
8	0.9235	0.8535	0.7894	0.7307	0.6768	0.6274	0.5820	0.5403	0.5019	0.4665	0.4339	0.4039	0.3762	0.3506	0.3269	0.3050	0.2848	0.2660	0.2487	0.2326
9	0.9143	0.8368	0.7664	0.7026	0.6446	0.5919	0.5439	0.5002	0.4604	0.4241	0.3909	0.3606	0.3329	0.3075	0.2843	0.2630	0.2434	0.2255	0.2090	0.1938
10	0.9053	0.8203	0.7441	0.6756	0.6139	0.5584	0.5083	0.4632	0.4224	0.3855	0.3522	0.3220	0.2946	0.2697	0.2472	0.2267	0.2080	0.1911	0.1756	0.1615
11	0.8963	0.8043	0.7224	0.6496	0.5847	0.5268	0.4751	0.4289	0.3875	0.3505	0.3173	0.2875	0.2607	0.2366	0.2149	0.1954	0.1778	0.1619	0.1476	0.1346
12	0.8874	0.7885	0.7014	0.6246	0.5568	0.4970	0.4440	0.3971	0.3555	0.3186	0.2858	0.2567	0.2307	0.2076	0.1869	0.1685	0.1520	0.1372	0.1240	0.1122
13	0.8787	0.7730	0.6810	0.6006	0.5303	0.4688	0.4150	0.3677	0.3262	0.2897	0.2575	0.2292	0.2042	0.1821	0.1625	0.1452	0.1299	0.1163	0.1042	0.0935
14	0.8700	0.7579	0.6611	0.5775	0.5051	0.4423	0.3878	0.3405	0.2992	0.2633	0.2320	0.2046	0.1807	0.1597	0.1413	0.1252	0.1110	0.0985	0.0876	0.0779
15	0.8613	0.7430	0.6419	0.5553	0.4810	0.4173	0.3624	0.3152	0.2745	0.2394	0.2090	0.1827	0.1599	0.1401	0.1229	0.1079	0.0949	0.0835	0.0736	0.0649
16	0.8528	0.7284	0.6232	0.5339	0.4581	0.3936	0.3387	0.2919	0.2519	0.2176	0.1883	0.1631	0.1415	0.1229	0.1069	0.0930	0.0811	0.0708	0.0618	0.0541
17	0.8444	0.7142	0.6050	0.5134	0.4363	0.3714	0.3166	0.2703	0.2311	0.1978	0.1696	0.1456	0.1252	0.1078	0.0929	0.0802	0.0693	0.0600	0.0520	0.0451
18	0.8360	0.7002	0.5874	0.4936	0.4155	0.3503	0.2959	0.2502	0.2120	0.1799	0.1528	0.1300	0.1108	0.0946	0.0808	0.0691	0.0592	0.0508	0.0437	0.0376
19	0.8277	0.6864	0.5703	0.4746	0.3957	0.3305	0.2765	0.2317	0.1945	0.1635	0.1377	0.1161	0.0981	0.0829	0.0703	0.0596	0.0506	0.0431	0.0367	0.0313
20	0.8195	0.6730	0.5537	0.4564	0.3769	0.3118	0.2584	0.2145	0.1784	0.1486	0.1240	0.1037	0.0868	0.0728	0.0611	0.0514	0.0433	0.0365	0.0308	0.0261
21	0.8114	0.6598	0.5375	0.4388	0.3589	0.2942	0.2415	0.1987	0.1637	0.1351	0.1117	0.0926	0.0768	0.0638	0.0531	0.0443	0.0370	0.0309	0.0259	0.0217
22	0.8034	0.6468	0.5219	0.4220	0.3418	0.2775	0.2257	0.1839	0.1502	0.1228	0.1007	0.0826	0.0680	0.0560	0.0462	0.0382	0.0316	0.0262	0.0218	0.0181
23	0.7954	0.6342	0.5067	0.4057	0.3256	0.2618	0.2109	0.1703	0.1378	0.1117	0.0907	0.0738	0.0601	0.0491	0.0402	0.0329	0.0270	0.0222	0.0183	0.0151
24	0.7876	0.6217	0.4919	0.3901	0.3101	0.2470	0.1971	0.1577	0.1264	0.1015	0.0817	0.0659	0.0532	0.0431	0.0349	0.0284	0.0231	0.0188	0.0154	0.0126
25	0.7798	0.6095	0.4776	0.3751	0.2953	0.2330	0.1842	0.1460	0.1160	0.0923	0.0736	0.0588	0.0471	0.0378	0.0304	0.0245	0.0197	0.0160	0.0129	0.0105
30	0.7419	0.5521	0.4120	0.3083	0.2314	0.1741	0.1314	0.0994	0.0754	0.0573	0.0437	0.0334	0.0256	0.0196	0.0151	0.0116	0.0090	0.0070	0.0054	0.0042
40	0.6717	0.4529	0.3066	0.2083	0.1420	0.0972	0.0668	0.0460	0.0318	0.0221	0.0154	0.0107	0.0075	0.0053	0.0037	0.0026	0.0019	0.0013	0.0010	0.0007
50	0.6080	0.3715	0.2281	0.1407	0.0872	0.0543	0.0339	0.0213	0.0134	0.0085	0.0054	0.0035	0.0022	0.0014	0.0009	0.0006	0.0004	0.0003	0.0002	0.0001

Appendix III: Present Value Factors for an Annuity

Period	Interest Rate																			
	1%	2%	3%	4%	5%	6%	7%	8%	9%	10%	11%	12%	13%	14%	15%	16%	17%	18%	19%	20%
1	0.9901	0.9804	0.9709	0.9615	0.9524	0.9434	0.9346	0.9259	0.9174	0.9091	0.9009	0.8929	0.8850	0.8772	0.8696	0.8621	0.8547	0.8475	0.8403	0.8333
2	1.9704	1.9416	1.9135	1.8861	1.8594	1.8334	1.8080	1.7833	1.7591	1.7355	1.7125	1.6901	1.6681	1.6467	1.6257	1.6052	1.5852	1.5656	1.5465	1.5278
3	2.9410	2.8839	2.8286	2.7751	2.7232	2.6730	2.6243	2.5771	2.5313	2.4869	2.4437	2.4018	2.3612	2.3216	2.2832	2.2459	2.2096	2.1743	2.1399	2.1065
4	3.9020	3.8077	3.7171	3.6299	3.5460	3.4651	3.3872	3.3121	3.2397	3.1699	3.1024	3.0373	2.9745	2.9137	2.8550	2.7982	2.7432	2.6901	2.6386	2.5887
5	4.8534	4.7135	4.5797	4.4518	4.3295	4.2124	4.1002	3.9927	3.8897	3.7908	3.6959	3.6048	3.5172	3.4331	3.3522	3.2743	3.1993	3.1272	3.0576	2.9906
6	5.7955	5.6014	5.4172	5.2421	5.0757	4.9173	4.7665	4.6229	4.4859	4.3553	4.2305	4.1114	3.9975	3.8887	3.7845	3.6847	3.5892	3.4976	3.4098	3.3255
7	6.7282	6.4720	6.2303	6.0021	5.7864	5.5824	5.3893	5.2064	5.0330	4.8684	4.7122	4.5638	4.4226	4.2883	4.1604	4.0386	3.9224	3.8115	3.7057	3.6046
8	7.6517	7.3255	7.0197	6.7327	6.4632	6.2098	5.9713	5.7466	5.5348	5.3349	5.1461	4.9676	4.7988	4.6389	4.4873	4.3436	4.2072	4.0776	3.9544	3.8372
9	8.5660	8.1622	7.7861	7.4353	7.1078	6.8017	6.5152	6.2469	5.9952	5.7590	5.5370	5.3282	5.1317	4.9464	4.7716	4.6065	4.4506	4.3030	4.1633	4.0310
10	9.4713	8.9826	8.5302	8.1109	7.7217	7.3601	7.0236	6.7101	6.4177	6.1446	5.8892	5.6502	5.4262	5.2161	5.0188	4.8332	4.6586	4.4941	4.3389	4.1925
11	10.3676	9.7868	9.2526	8.7605	8.3064	7.8869	7.4987	7.1390	6.8052	6.4951	6.2065	5.9377	5.6869	5.4527	5.2337	5.0286	4.8364	4.6560	4.4865	4.3271
12	11.2551	10.5753	9.9540	9.3851	8.8633	8.3838	7.9427	7.5361	7.1607	6.8137	6.4924	6.1944	5.9176	5.6603	5.4206	5.1971	4.9884	4.7932	4.6105	4.4392
13	12.1337	11.3484	10.6350	9.9856	9.3936	8.8527	8.3577	7.9038	7.4869	7.1034	6.7499	6.4235	6.1218	5.8424	5.5831	5.3423	5.1183	4.9095	4.7147	4.5327
14	13.0037	12.1062	11.2961	10.5631	9.8986	9.2950	8.7455	8.2442	7.7862	7.3667	6.9819	6.6282	6.3025	6.0021	5.7245	5.4675	5.2293	5.0081	4.8023	4.6106
15	13.8651	12.8493	11.9379	11.1184	10.3797	9.7122	9.1079	8.5595	8.0607	7.6061	7.1909	6.8109	6.4624	6.1422	5.8474	5.5755	5.3242	5.0916	4.8759	4.6755
16	14.7179	13.5777	12.5611	11.6523	10.8378	10.1059	9.4466	8.8514	8.3126	7.8237	7.3792	6.9740	6.6039	6.2651	5.9542	5.6685	5.4053	5.1624	4.9377	4.7296
17	15.5623	14.2919	13.1661	12.1657	11.2741	10.4773	9.7632	9.1216	8.5436	8.0216	7.5488	7.1196	6.7291	6.3729	6.0472	5.7487	5.4746	5.2223	4.9897	4.7746
18	16.3983	14.9920	13.7535	12.6593	11.6896	10.8276	10.0591	9.3719	8.7556	8.2014	7.7016	7.2497	6.8399	6.4674	6.1280	5.8178	5.5339	5.2732	5.0333	4.8122
19	17.2260	15.6785	14.3238	13.1339	12.0853	11.1581	10.3356	9.6036	8.9501	8.3649	7.8393	7.3658	6.9380	6.5504	6.1982	5.8775	5.5845	5.3162	5.0700	4.8435
20	18.0456	16.3514	14.8775	13.5903	12.4622	11.4699	10.5940	9.8181	9.1285	8.5136	7.9633	7.4694	7.0248	6.6231	6.2593	5.9288	5.6278	5.3527	5.1009	4.8696
21	18.8570	17.0112	15.4150	14.0292	12.8212	11.7641	10.8355	10.0168	9.2922	8.6487	8.0751	7.5620	7.1016	6.6870	6.3125	5.9731	5.6648	5.3837	5.1268	4.8913
22	19.6604	17.6580	15.9369	14.4511	13.1630	12.0416	11.0612	10.2007	9.4424	8.7715	8.1757	7.6446	7.1695	6.7429	6.3587	6.0113	5.6964	5.4099	5.1486	4.9094
23	20.4558	18.2922	16.4436	14.8568	13.4886	12.3034	11.2722	10.3711	9.5802	8.8832	8.2664	7.7184	7.2297	6.7921	6.3988	6.0442	5.7234	5.4321	5.1668	4.9245
24	21.2434	18.9139	16.9355	15.2470	13.7986	12.5504	11.4693	10.5288	9.7066	8.9847	8.3481	7.7843	7.2829	6.8351	6.4338	6.0726	5.7465	5.4509	5.1822	4.9371
25	22.0232	19.5235	17.4131	15.6221	14.0939	12.7834	11.6536	10.6748	9.8226	9.0770	8.4217	7.8431	7.3300	6.8729	6.4641	6.0971	5.7662	5.4669	5.1951	4.9476
30	25.8077	22.3965	19.6004	17.2920	15.3725	13.7648	12.4090	11.2578	10.2737	9.4269	8.6938	8.0552	7.4957	7.0027	6.5660	6.1772	5.8294	5.5168	5.2347	4.9789
40	32.8347	27.3555	23.1148	19.7928	17.1591	15.0463	13.3317	11.9246	10.7574	9.7791	8.9511	8.2438	7.6344	7.1050	6.6418	6.2335	5.8713	5.5482	5.2582	4.9966
50	39.1961	31.4236	25.7298	21.4822	18.2559	15.7619	13.8007	12.2335	10.9617	9.9148	9.0417	8.3045	7.6752	7.1327	6.6605	6.2463	5.8801	5.5541	5.2623	4.9995

GLOSSARY

A

Absorption Costing — Assigns direct materials, direct labor, variable overhead and fixed overhead costs to inventory.

Absorption Costing — (full cost) is the unit product cost determined using the absorption costing method.

Accounting Rate of Return — Evaluates the return of an investment by using operating income instead of cash flow.

Activity-Based Costing System — A costing system that determines the various activities and uses multiple cost allocation bases to assign overhead costs to products.

Activity-Based Management — Using ABC information to manage business operations more efficiently.

Activity Cost Pools — Activities in a business that are essential in providing goods or services to customers.

Annuity — A stream of fixed payments that are received or made in a given period of time.

Appraisal Costs — measure or evaluate the quality of a product.

Autonomy — is the right or power to govern oneself without external control and constraint.

B

Balanced Scorecard — A strategic performance management framework that allows organizations to manage and measure the delivery of their strategy.

Beginning Inventory — in WIP is a result of ending inventory carrying over from the end of the period.

Bottlenecks — Anything that holds up progress.

Bottom-Up Budgeting — A budgeting process where managers of all levels fully co-operate and contribute to budget creation.

Break-Even Point — The number of units that needs to be produced in order for total revenues to equal total expenses.

Budgetary Slack — The tendency of employees to intentionally underestimate revenues and overestimate expenses in the budgeting process.

Budgeted Balance Sheet — A concise summary of how expected operations in the upcoming year will affect the financial position of the company.

Budgets — Numerical tools that help managers reach those financial goals in their business plans.

C

Capacity — The amount of resource that can be utilized.

Capital Budget — A type of budget that involves changes in the company's financial resources.

Capital Budgeting — The process of analyzing and evaluating investments criteria for capital expenditures.

Capital Expenditures — Investments in capital assets that change or improve an organization's current operations.

Cash Budget — A type of budget that monitors cash flowing into and out of the bank account with no regards to profits.

Common Fixed Cost — is a fixed cost that supports more than one segment, but is not traceable in whole or in part to any one segment.

Compound Interest — The piling on effect of applying the same interest rate on an account over a period of time.

Compound Interest — Applying the same interest rate on an amount and on any interest that has been earned.

Contribution Margin — The excess sales over total variable costs.

Contribution Margin Per Unit — The difference between the sales price per unit and the variable costs per unit.

Contribution Margin Ratio (CM ratio) — can be determined by dividing the contribution margin by revenue.

Contribution Margin Statement — A managerial accounting report which outlines operational data for a specific time period by separating variable from fixed expenses and determining the contribution margin for the period.

Conversion Costs — Costs that are incurred while converting raw materials into finished goods.

Cost Accounting — A part of managerial accounting which tracks the costs incurred to produce a good or provide services.

Cost Allocation Base — Used to allocate overhead costs to products or services.

Cost-Based Approach — in setting transfer prices provides companies the option to either set the transfer price at the variable cost or full (absorption) cost.

Cost Behavior — Describes how costs change based on the level of business activity.

Cost Center — A department that only manages costs.

Cost Driver — Any activity in an organization that incurs cost.

Cost Leadership — Providing goods or services at the lowest possible price.

Cost Leadership Strategy — A type of strategy that involves producing goods or services at the lowest possible price by reducing inefficiencies and waste in the value chain.

Cost Object — Anything for which a separate cost measurement is desired.

Cost of Capital — The minimum rate of return that owners expect from a capital expenditure.

Cost of Goods Manufactured — The cost of new completed products ready for sale that is added to inventory.

Cost of Goods Sold Method — Writes off the difference between actual and estimated overhead costs to the cost of goods sold account.

Cost of Production Report — is prepared to summarize the activity of a processing department. It will report on all costs transferred in from earlier processing departments as well as all direct material, direct labor and manufacturing overhead costs that are added during the period.

Cost-Reduction Decision — An investment decision that involves decreasing costs.

Cost Structure — The portion of a company's costs that are fixed versus variable.

Cost-Volume-Profit (CVP) — Analyzes how production volume affects profits and costs.

Cost-Volume-Profit Graph — shows how costs, sales and operating profit (or loss) are related.

Cumulative Method — Summing the cash flows over a period of time until the amount of the initial investment has been recovered.

Customer Perspective — A Balance Scorecard perspective covers customer measures such as customer satisfaction, market share goals, as well as product and service attributes.

D

Decentralized Organization — is an organization in which decisions are not made exclusively by top managers, but are made by people with various decision-making roles at the lower levels.

Degree of Operating Leverage — refers to the effect fixed costs have on overall operating income as sales volume changes.

Differential Cost — or net relevant costs are the total costs that differ between alternatives in a specific decision.

Differential Revenues — or net relevant revenues are the total revenues that differ between alternatives in a specific decision.

Differentiation Strategy — A type of strategy that involves producing goods or services that customers perceive as better or unique from other products in the market.

Direct Costs — Costs that can be directly traced to the cost of the product or service provided.

Direct Labor — Employees who directly work on converting materials into products.

Direct Materials — Materials which are purchased for making a product and can be easily traceable as part of finished goods.

Discounted Capital Budgeting Approach — Assesses the attractiveness of an investment while considering the time value of money.

E

Efficiency Variance — The difference between actual quantity and standard quantities for actual output.

Ending Inventory — in WIP refers to units that are only partially complete by the end of the accounting period.

Equation Method Formula — formula for calculating number of units for BEP and targeted income is: the sum of fixed costs and operating income divided by contributed margin per unit.

Equipment Replacement Decision — An investment decision that involves determining whether a business should replace the old equipment.

Equipment Selection Decision — An investment decision that involves choosing a piece of equipment.

Equivalent Units of Production — Approximation of number of whole units that have been produced during a period in process costing.

Expansion Decision — An investment decision that involves determining whether to expand a business.

External Failure Costs — are quality problems discovered by the customer after the customer receives the product.

F

Financial Accounting — A branch of accounting that classifies, measures and records the transactions of a business to prepare formal financial statements.

Financial Perspective — A Balance Scorecard perspective that covers the financial measures of an organization and allows managers to track financial success and stockholder value.

Finished Goods — Products which have been completed but have not been sold or delivered.

First-In-First-Out (FIFO) Method — An inventory valuation method that assumes that inventory received first is the first inventory to be consumed.

Fixed Costs — Costs that do not change in relation to volume produced.

Flexible Budget — A budget that is prepared using budgeted selling prices, budgeted costs and actual sales volume.

Flexible Budget Variance — The difference between the flexible budget and actual result.

Future Value — Refers to how much a sum of money is worth in the future, given a specified time period and interest rate.

H

High-Low Method — uses the change in production and change in costs between the highest and the lowest level of production to factor fixed and variable costs from mixed costs.

I

Imposed Budgeting — A budgeting process where all the figures are determined by upper management and imposed throughout the organization.

Incremental Analysis — quickly determines the financial impact by examining only the items that have changed.

Incremental Budgeting — A budgeting process that involves creating a new budget which is based on gradual changes from the previous year's budget.

Indirect Costs — Costs that cannot, economically or practically, be tied directly to the product or service.

Indirect Labor — Wages paid to employees who do not directly work on the products.

Indirect Materials — Materials that cannot be easily traced to a product.

Intermediate Market — is an outside market in which the transferred product or service is sold in its present form.

Internal Business Process Perspective — A Balance Scorecard perspective covers internal operational goals and outlines the key processes necessary to deliver the customer objectives.

Internal Failure Costs — are quality problems discovered before the customer receives the product.

Internal Rate of Return (IRR) — The discount rate where NPV is equal to zero.

Inventory Shrinkage — Any reduction of inventory through theft, spoilage or misplacement.

Investment Center — A department that manages a company's excess capital.

Irrelevant Costs — Costs that do not change between two alternatives or have no impact on a decision and can be ignored.

J

Job-Order Costing — Costing method that involves calculating costs for a specific job.

Just-In-Time (JIT) — An inventory management system which minimizes the amount of inventory kept in stock.

K

Keep or Drop — decisions involve analyzing relevant costs to decide whether to continue to provide a product or shut production down.

Key Performance Indicator (KPI) — A measure that helps identify how successful a company is in meeting their strategic objectives.

L

Lag Indicator — A measure that indicates the results of past actions.

Leading Indicator — A measure that predicts the future.

Lean Manufacturing — The systematic elimination of waste by identifying seven areas of waste.

Learning and Growth Perspective — A Balance Scorecard perspective covers the intangible drivers of future success. Some examples are human capital, organizational capital, and information capital.

Lease-Buy Decision — An investment decision that determines to either lease or purchase a capital asset.

Least-Square Regression Method — uses statistical calculations to separate mixed costs. Spreadsheet software, such as Excel, can perform this calculation.

M

Make or Buy Decision — The decision to make a product or purchase it from a supplier.

Management by Exception — The process of analyzing variances that occur between budgeted amounts and actual amounts.

Management Control — The process by which managers set targets for performance, measure actual performance and resolve differences between actual and performance.

Managerial Accounting — Utilizes financial information produced by the financial reporting system to help predict future business operations through the use of various reports.

Manufacturing Overhead Account — A "temporary" account used to allocate estimated manufacturing overhead costs to inventory and to accumulate actual overhead costs incurred by the factory.

Manufacturing Overhead — Indirect factory-related costs that are incurred when a product is manufactured.

Margin of Safety — The excess of sales over break-even revenues.

Market-based Approach — sets transfer prices based on market price.

Market Price — is the price charged for a product or service on the outside market.

Markup — is the difference between a product's selling price and its cost.

Master Budget — A type of budget that encompasses all aspects of business operations, which include all organization's individual budgets.

Material Requisition Form — A form used to request raw materials from storage room.

Mission Statement — A statement that outlines an organization's purpose and over-arching goals and acts as the starting point for decision-making within the organization.

Mixed Costs — Costs that possess both variable and fixed characteristics.

N

Negotiated Transfer Price — is a transfer price agreed on between the buying and selling departments or divisions.

Net Present Value (NPV) Technique — An investment decision technique that technique compares the present value of the cash inflows of an investment with the present value of the cash outflows.

Non-Discounted Capital Budgeting Approach — Assesses the attractiveness of an investment without considering the time value of money.

O

Operating Budget — A budget that outlines budgeted changes to the income statement during the period.

Operating Expenses Budget — A type of budget that outlines the budgeted expenses not related to manufacturing activities.

Operating Leverage — The effect of fixed costs on overall net income as production volume changes.

Opportunity Cost — The value of the next best alternative that is foregone.

Outsourcing — Another name for the make or buy decision.

P

Participative Budgeting — A budgeting process where managers of all levels fully co-operate and contribute to budget creation.

Payback Method — Measures the length of time it takes a business to recover an initial investment.

Payback Technique — An investment decision technique that measures the length of time it takes a business to recover the initial investment from cash generated by the investment.

Period Costs — Costs which do not relate to the manufacturing phase of the product.

Periodic Inventory System — An inventory system that only updates the inventory account when a physical count takes place.

Perpetual Inventory System — An inventory system that updates the inventory account whenever a purchase or sale is made.

Practical Capacity — The reasonable level of activity that can actually be attained.

Predetermined Overhead Rate — The ratio of total budged overhead costs to the total budgeted cost allocation base.

Present Value — The current worth of a future sum of money, given a specified time period and interest rate.

Prevention Costs — are proactive and can reduce the cost of quality in the long-run.

Price Standard — An ideal cost for an operating activity.

Price Variance — The difference between actual price and standard costs.

Process Costing — Costing method applicable where goods or services result from a sequence of continuous or repetitive operations or processes.

Product Costs — Costs incurred during the manufacturing phase of the product.

Product Mix — decision allows for the best allocation of resources.

Production Budget — A type of budget that outlines how much product needs to be produced.

Profit Center — A department that manages both revenues and costs.

Profit-Volume Graph — determines operating profit (or loss) at various levels of production.

Proration Method — Applies a proportionate amount of the difference between the actual and estimated overhead costs to WIP, finished goods and cost of goods sold.

Purchases Budget — A type of budget that outlines how much material needs to be purchased.

Q

Quantity Standard — An ideal quantity of input that should be used in production.

R

Range of Acceptable Transfer Prices — is the range of prices for which the transfer will be profitable for both the selling and purchasing divisions.

Raw Materials — Materials that are used as building material to create a product.

Relevant Costs — Costs that differ between two alternatives.

Relevant Range — The range where certain cost behavior remains the same.

Relevant Revenue — Revenue that differs between two alternatives.

Responsibility Accounting — A process of collecting accounting data related to a responsibility center.

Responsibility Center — A subunit or department of an organization whose manager is responsible or held accountable for a particular set of activities.

Return on Investment (ROI) — A way to determine whether the investment in a capital asset is worth the increase in profits.

Revenue Center — is held accountable for the revenues only.

S

Sales Budget — A type of budget that outlines the budgeted quantity and selling price of products or services sold.

Sales Mix — The relative quantities of the types of products produced by a company.

Sales-Volume Variance — The difference between the flexible budget and static budget.

Salvage Value of an Asset — The value that an asset can be sold for at the end of its useful life.

Segment — is a part of a company for which the manager seeks to collect data on costs, revenue or profit.

Segment Reporting — is the process by which a company separates and reports financial information based on the business's segments.

Selling-Price Variance — A way of analyzing the revenue variance between the flexible budget and actual results.

Sensitivity Analysis — A type of analysis that helps managers answer "what if?" questions and helps them become more responsive to changes in operations.

Simple Interest — Interest that is calculated only on the initial investment.

Special Order — is a one-time order received by a company that is outside their normal operations.

Spending Variance — A variable overhead variance that analyzes the difference in overhead rates.

Static Budget — A budget that is prepared using budgeted selling prices, budgeted costs and budgeted sales volume.

Step Costs — Costs that increase or decrease in steps depending on the level of business activity.

Step Fixed Costs — Costs that will change once the volume of production exceeds the relevant range, or costs that change in increments.

Step Variable Costs — Variable costs that change as production volume exceeds the relevant range.

Strategy — Focuses on its resources and allows managers to create business plans which outline the business' financial and non-financial goals.

Strategy — Strategy refers to a plan of action designed to achieve a particular goal.

Sub-Ledger — Used to group information in the general ledger.

Sunk Costs — Costs that cannot be recovered and are irrelevant to a decision.

T

Target Analysis — is a form of CVP analysis where companies target an operating income greater than zero.

Target Costing — is the process of using the anticipated market price to calculate the maximum allowable cost for a product.

Theoretical Capacity — The level of activity that can be attained under ideal operating conditions.

Theory of Constraints — Focuses on removing constraints in production.

Time-Driven ABC — A type of activity-based costing system that uses time and practical capacity to assign overhead costs to different activities.

Time Value of Money — Recognizes the change in the value of money over time.

Top-Down Budgeting — A budgeting process where all the figures are determined by upper management and imposed throughout the organization.

Total Product Costs — include the costs of direct materials, direct labor and manufacturing overhead.

Total Quality Management (TQM) — A management concept that focuses on continually reducing errors and satisfying customers.

Traceable Fixed Costs — are those fixed expenses that can be directly linked to a segment of a business.

Transfer Price — is the price one department or division charges for a good sold or service rendered to another department or division within the same organization.

Transfer Pricing — is a method that focuses on the flow of goods and services between divisions of the same organization.

Transferred-In Costs — Costs that are transferred from one department to another.

Transferred-In Units — Units that are transferred from one department to another.

U

Unused Capacity — The difference between the current or budgeted operating level of activity and practical capacity.

V

Value Chain — All the steps that need to be completed in order to bring their products or services to market.

Variable Costing — Assigns only direct material, direct labor and variable overhead costs to the value of inventory.

Variable Costs — Costs that vary in relation to the change in volume produced.

Variable Overhead Efficiency Variance — A variable overhead variance that analyzes the consumption of variable manufacturing overhead.

Variance Report — A report that shows how actual amounts differ from budgeted amounts numerically.

Vision — The desired state of an organization in terms of its strategic direction.

W

Weighted-Average Contribution Margin — The contribution margin that takes into account the weighted average of the contribution margin of each product sold.

Weighted-Average Cost Method — An inventory valuation method that averages the cost of inventory throughout the entire period.

Work-In-Process — Includes unfinished items or services which are still in the production process.

Z

Zero-Based Budgeting — A budgeting process that requires managers to justify their budget requests in detail from scratch, regardless of the previous amounts spent.

INDEX

C